2500

Chinese Civilization

AMS PRESS

NEW YORK

PLATE I

NÜ-KUA AND FU-HSI

YU THE GREAT SETTING THE WORLD IN ORDER
(Bas-relief from Shan-tung. Rubbing by the Chavannes Expedition)

Chinese Civilization

By

MARCEL GRANET

Director of Studies at L'École des Hautes Études
Professor at L'École des Langues Orientales
Governor of L'Institut des Hautes
Études Chinoises de Paris

NEW YORK
ALFRED A. KNOPF
1930

Library of Congress Cataloging in Publication Data

Granet, Marcel, 1884-1940.
  Chinese civilization.

  Translation of La civilisation chinoise.
  Original ed. issued in series: The history of
civilization.
  Bibliography: p.
  1. China—Social life and customs. 2. China—
History—To 1643. I. Title.
DS721.G788   1974   915.1′03′1   74-38068
ISBN 0-404-56974-9

Reprinted from an original copy in the collections of
the Wilbur L. Cross Library, University of Connecticut

From the edition of 1930, New York
First AMS edition published in 1974
Manufactured in the United States of America

AMS PRESS INC.
NEW YORK, N.Y. 10003

CONTENTS

v

CONTENTS

SECOND PART—CHINESE SOCIETY

BOOK ONE

THE PEOPLE OF THE PLAINS

BOOK TWO

THE FOUNDATION OF THE CHIEFTAINSHIPS

BOOK THREE

THE SEIGNIORIAL TOWN

CONTENTS

LIST OF ILLUSTRATIONS

PREFACE

THE ORIGINALITY OF CHINA

Writers of world-history have only recently begun to give its due place to that considerable portion of humanity which lives in what we describe in relation to ourselves in the so-called West, as the Far East. The Far East came comparatively late into the great stream of this world-history ; but it was not a world entirely apart, cut off from communication and from the penetration of influences of any kind, even before the era when the two halves of the human race entered into closer relations. And if the separation had in fact been complete, in order to get outside the European standpoint and to include the whole evolution of humanity in its survey, it behoves us to show, before the close of the first section of our work, to what stage of social organization and of civilization this original section of the human race had attained, by the beginning of the Christian era.

The importance of the contribution which Marcel Granet brings to the " Evolution of Humanity " can scarcely be exaggerated, either with regard to the nature of the work, or with regard to the subject of his study.

Nothing is so little known as the ancient history of China. Granet has had not merely to gather together the results of previous achievements, and to set in order classical data—previous achievements are small. It is not that Chinese documents are wanting ; on the contrary, they abound. But the first task the scientific historian of China must set himself, is to be on his guard against historical tradition.

The history of China, as written by the Chinese historians, is, in fact, an edifice, a sort of postulate, *a* starting-point, *and not an attempt at objective reproduction.[1] It consists of the " fabrication of facts of history obtained by removing the*

---

[1] See pp. 16, 46-7, 49-50, 51, 55, 57, 58.

mythical element from an odd assortment of local legends, romances and heroic poetry." [1]

Generally speaking, modern criticism has been devoted, whether in China, " to the greater glorification of Reason," or in the West, to an absolute or a tentative scepticism.

No one, up to now, has, like Granet, understood and put into practice the necessary precautions, and been ready at the right moment with the appropriate interpretations, in order to rediscover in the Chinese texts certain facts which, no doubt, are landmarks, but above all—and we will press the point later— are subjective states of mind (the substrata of history), which the subjectivity of the texts themselves that have come down to us, puts at the disposal of the investigator.

To get to know China, Granet had to knock down a Chinese great wall—a great wall built up by " pious forgers."   In order to destroy it, he added to observations made during a long stay in the Far East the patient study of the festivals and songs, the dances and legends of ancient China.

We may apply to him, almost literally, the famous saying of Fustel de Coulanges, that to every day of synthesis must go years of analysis.   All the more in that, like Fustel and his disciples, from force of circumstances, he scarcely worked at all on any but original documents.   He himself, for the most part, elaborated the material of his work. [2]

Having its particular aim in view, this work owes its importance to the antiquity, to the stage of development, to the very special character of the civilization which it sets out to define.

We have spoken already of this " East and West " problem, which emerges more and more clearly in proportion as the two sections of the earth's population get to know each other better, and in proportion as they become more cognisant—above and beyond the superficial differences which travellers find entertaining—of fundamental differences which give psychologists and historians much cause for thought.

The exceptional character of Granet's attempt and the exceptional interest of this subject of study have brought us up sharply against a difficulty, which we have overcome in a

[1] See Granet, *Danses et légendes de la Chine ancienne*, p. 32.
[2] *Fêtes et chansons anciennes de la Chine*, 1919 ; *Danses et légendes de la Chine ancienne*, 1926.   Other exhaustive works already published or about to appear, form the basis of the present synthesis.

way that is equally exceptional. It was not possible for Marcel Granet to include all the matter which he had collected within the limits of one of our volumes ; he would have been obliged to mutilate his subject and could not have made sufficiently clear the ingenious sidelights which he has the merit of having thrown on Chinese mentality. How could we, when we conceived the plan, more than fifteen years ago, of our " Evolution of Humanity," possibly have allowed for the progress which would be made in the study of this little-known world, due above all to our collaborator ? We have now realized that the story of Chinese civilization had to go side by side with a definite and fundamental study of Chinese thought. This civilization is, less than others, made up of various elements, more or less contradictory and opposed to one another ; it is the emanation of a Weltanschauung, as the Germans say, of a particular conception of the world and of life ; and, after having given a picture of public and private life in China, a picture which revealed the underlying mentality—we came to the conclusion that this mentality and its manifestations required separate study.

As this conviction was borne in upon us at an opportune moment, and as it will be of use for certain complementary studies,[1] we decided to publish this volume in the " Library of Historical Synthesis," apart from the " Evolution of Humanity," and to make it Volume XXIV bis of the first section. We insist, nevertheless, on the fact that the history of China has the closest unity with world-history, and we put on record that we do not intend to create a precedent by this arrangement.

At first sight, the present volume exactly corresponds to our idea of permissible and scientific synthesis. We would compare a preceding volume with those " ancient tapestries, worn away by time, where the scenes which we behold are incomplete and the people mutilated."[2]

Granet uses all his gifts of style, not merely not to stop up the holes in the Chinese tapestries, but to call attention to them and to expose them. " I have," he says, " quite shamelessly left large gaps."[3] And he is absolutely right, for this is the very way to stimulate useful effort. If one day more light is thrown on China's past, this will only be by insisting on active measures

---

[1] For my forthcoming study of science in the ancient world.
[2] *La Mésopotamie*, Vol. VIII, p. vii.
[3] P. 5. Cf. *Danses*, p. 54.

of exploration and excavation.   Meanwhile, it is better to wait than to make rash assertions.

To the races which have peopled China, and to which he devotes only a few lines, some very cautious references are made by Pittard in our Fifth Volume.   Possibly reaction against the traditional assertions as to the vast antiquity of China has gone too far.   The earliest excavations reveal neolithic material ; but " as long as the human remains, which would enable us to define the somatological characteristics of populations at present known by some details of their technique, have not been carefully studied, it seems wise to refrain from all hypothesis, and not to transform a problem of technological into a problem of ethnographic history, and above all, not to intervene at too early a stage, with the question of migrations and conquests, in a problem of history proper." [1] *While Granet is looking forward to much excavation, well carried out, solely in the interests of science,* [2] *he urges us not to mix archæology and epigraphy ;   not to draw premature conclusions from linguistic data, not to extend undiscriminating analogies of language to the race or to the civilization.   " The problem of Chinese origins," he declares, " remains entirely unsolved."* [3] *His careful attitude and reserve prevents him from any categorical rejection of the orthodox conception of a Chinese civilization homogeneous and perfect from the beginning, thanks to the saintliness of its founders.   As a hypothesis, however, he puts forward tentatively the theory of two principal civilizations— without asserting they were original—that of the terraces and of millet, and that of rice and the plains.* [4] *Possibly the second of these may have been subjected to influences from a distance. In a general way, without giving any pronouncement as to active influences, he makes it clear that the tradition of China's splendid isolation is open to question.* [5]

Let us, however, search out and gather together the positive elements which, in spite of the extreme prudence of its author, this singularly rich book contains.

In his interpretation of the most ancient texts, Granet traces

---

[1] P. 64.

[2] Pp. 65, 68. Cf. J. de Morgan, Vol. II, pp. 126, 314.

[3] P. 68.   Chavannes has said truly that " The question of origins is . . . the goal of knowledge and should not be its starting-point. Premature attempts made to solve the problem are only a loss of time and effort. . . ."   *Rev. de Synthèse hist.*, Vol. I (1900), *Révue générale sur la Chine*, p. 274.

[4] P. 137.

[5] Cf. Chavannes, *art. cit.*, p. 277.

two simultaneous processes : the taming of nature, and the amalgamation of small primitive groups. The character of the country, the divisions of this vast region of Asia, separated by marshes, by forests inhabited by wild beasts, by precipitous mountains, brought about in the beginning the separate life of human groups, and necessitated on their part every strenuous effort, first to establish their centres of habitation and then to enlarge their sphere of activity. The districts most easy to cultivate were at the same time the most adapted to civilized life and the most exposed to the devastating incursions of the Barbarians.[1] But, amongst these small groups, shut away in a country difficult of access, those nearest to the Barbarians gain reserves of strength and make use of it to dominate the groups in the central regions. With much precaution Granet takes the reader with him through this agelong labour of " political concentration," through which an " archipelago of small feudal States " becomes unified.[2] He lays stress upon the moral tie which contributes, above all, to draw these peoples together : the Barbarians have " the nature of beasts, not of men " ; it is through civilization that communication is established in the world of men. " Whilst in the centre the Chinese nation was coming into being, on the outer borders States were forming which, aiming at annexing the centre of China, ended by themselves also becoming Chinese " (p. 84). Honan is the " central flower " ; but the provincial units share in the same civilization, oppose the Barbarians fiercely, organize to defend themselves against them, unite for the purpose, struggle to expand as their strength grows, and after a period of feudal rivalries, join together to form an Empire through the ability and energy of the kingdom of Ch'in. Rural communities, chiefdoms, feudal overlordships, States in embryo, Empire : here one can actually be present, as it were, at the formation of this original Chinese unity, among contingencies of which some can be precisely described,—and this is what Granet calls " political history." [3]

He throws into vigorous relief the remarkable personality of the first Emperor, Ch'in Shih Huang-ti. " An energetic and

---

[1] On the question of the Barbarians, little has been studied and little is known (they were certainly Huns for the most part) ; see Granet, *Danses*, Introduction, p.11.

[2] Pp. 75-83.

[3] It must be pointed out that this " political history " includes social history— social history meaning for us all that concerns the structure and functions of society, all that expresses the needs of society, considered as society.

*complete personality," he differed widely from the ordinary
Chinese. " His ruling qualities were, apparently, a reasoned
obstinacy, and a spirit of like stamp." He " saw clearly
and saw far." Ch'in Shih Huang-ti broke up feudalism, set up
a central administration, created a true nobility from the
body of officials, broke down the barriers between the different
parts of what was henceforth to be China, and made the Great
Wall by joining together the pieces of existing " long walls."
He worked to achieve moral at the same time as political unity.
Himself a materialist, he wished, nevertheless, to be accepted as
a " living divinity." He saw clearly that " for the newly founded
Empire a new religion was necessary, and that to an autocratic
power a worship of the imperial person ought to correspond." [1]
China, under his successors, except when it was a question of
fighting the Barbarians, remained a " collection of provinces."
The Emperor Wu alone, who reigned fifty-four years, endeavoured
to reduce the remainder of the feudal lords to impotence. He
developed the economic organization of the Empire, and, though
he lacked " the forceful and occult genius of the first Emperor "
(p. 123), he enlarged Chinese civilization, and left it much more
widespread. But he did not know how to create a solid state,
and over this he clearly lost an opportunity. " The Empire has
no other foundation than the Virtue peculiar to a dynasty.
Apart from the Emperor, the State is nothing." This is a
most important idea, and Granet constantly insists on it. The
principle of cohesion in this case, was not so much a water-
tight organization, in the manner of the West, as a cultural
tradition, a common ideal, a civilization.[2]*

*The essential chapters of this volume are those which reveal
Chinese " society," that is to say, the details of the institutions
of both public and private life.[3] In these pages of unique interest,
Granet, with rare penetration and a marvellously agile mind,
has accomplished the inverse of that effort to which the historians
and authorities on the laws of China have applied themselves.
Whilst these have projected into the past a state which was an
end in itself, Granet discovers the movement, retraces the evolution
which ends in immobility—in relative immobility. Under the
apparent rigidity he discovers actually live forces, a profound*

---

[1] Pp. 47, 104.   [2] See pp. 5, 6, 118, 125, 130.
[3] Cf. note 3 of the previous page.

plasticity—which the history of thought will cause to be better understood.[1] *And among all the documents, the " legends which have become history,"* [2] *he is a sort of explorer ; like the archæologist who, in his excavations, digs up the buried origins of the past, he delves in the texts of psychological excavation, and is able to bring to light instructive fragments of collective life and thought. In a realm where nearly everything had to be created, a subtle divination of the phenomena, at once naïve and complex, which took place in the souls of the people, reveals to him, if not the origins, at least the distant methods of social organization, in their relations with the experiences and beliefs of men. An evolution, moreover, " timeless " and " schematic," because, even if the data appear clearly, it is impossible to fix them in time and place.*

We see emerging first, in this astonishing reconstruction, the life of the country-side, in which the family group is a closed one, and relationship goes with the group, the members of one same generation forming a collective personality. Marriage implies a mixture of endogamy and exogamy. It takes place between two rival self-contained groups, which live on the soil of the same rural community. A certain opposition is thus reconciled with the mutual help necessary for the hard conquest of the earth— to which task, having early become settled in one spot, they apply themselves closely.

This earth—mountains, rivers, forests, plants—constitutes a " tutelary authority with indefinite powers," which is worshipped in a Sacred Place *where festivals are held. But the genius of the* Sacred Place *can become embodied in objects and in living beings. Society is not distinct from the universe.*[3] *Everything has its peculiar Virtue. Names themselves possess power and influence—they create the relationships, they " possess " the individuals much more than the individuals possess them* [4]

---

[1] See conclusion of this volume.

[2] *Danses*, p. 24. " Disintegrated, reduced to the condition of literary compilations, further degraded perhaps—history passed this stage—as a result of having served for various enterprises of learned reconstruction, there only remain of it unrecognisable shreds, confused, patched and mutilated—poor and precious documents ! I have played the gambler in making use of them." *Ibid.*, p. 1., cf. p. 597ı (" Badly understood, indeed, or intentionally misused, the stereotyped formulæ, rubrics or popular ballads, handed on from age to age, and imposing on all, dominate the scholar at the very moment when he is trying to substitute a reasonable history, worthy of reasonable people, for deceptive fables "), and all the conclusion, pp. 598 fol.

[3] See pp. 194, 219.

[4] See pp. 218, 248, 311-2.

b

Words, gestures, attitudes are endowed with efficacy [1]*—but above all things so endowed, are music and dancing ; these have as their function " to tame the world and to subdue nature for men's profit " (p. 195).*

Sexual life is specially closely bound up with the universal order. There is an analogy between the parts played by the maternal soil and the productive mother, and an identity of virtue. It is, in consequence the woman who, first among created beings, inspires reverence. From the beginning she exercises authority, by virtue of her title of mother. The sexes being, in principle, separated, " the peasant household was a feminine matter " (p. 154). Out of the close relationship which existed between rural life, the fundamental beliefs, and family organization, a régime was evolved which has some analogy to the matriarchate ; and ancestor worship, when it was combined with worship of the soil, was worship of the maternal ancestors.

It was only very slowly, by all sorts of indirect ways, that succession in the male line was able to establish itself. Gradually, as agriculture developed, the man, who cultivated the soil, took precedence over the woman, whose task was weaving ; but above all the rôle of the males as masters of fire, as potters and smiths, contributed to the growth of their reputation ; " within the masses of the labourers, there were formed brotherhoods of technicians, magicians, and masters of the secret of the supreme powers." These brotherhoods multiplied, rich with " new prestige," and their rivalries soon took on an importance above that of the village antagonisms which put the sexes into opposition.[2] *Here we come upon the birth of the authority of male chiefs, masters of the thunder, of the sun, workers in metal.*

This marks a great turning-point of Chinese life, which coincides, apparently, with a date in the history of technical progress : " the crystallising factor *seems to have been the emergence in China of work and trade in copper and bronze."* [3]

A new society is formed, politically and economically, in which further groupings,—relatively numerous and stable— give birth to the town, a fort and a market at the same time. There the leaders in war and in religious ceremonies, the nobles, rich in arms, in precious stones and metals, make the separation

---

[1] See pp. 261, 268-9, 278, 299. "To say, is to do," p. 295.
[2] See pp. 194, 203, 204.
[3] *Danses*, p. 53. Cf. Conclusion, p. 602.

of the sexes operate definitely to the detriment of the woman weaver. There social life, in more densely populous groups, favours the introduction of novelties like the authority or personal *dependence of the individual, as opposed to the categories of the rural community.*

Thus there is drawn for us a curious picture of feudal society, a society perpetually changing and varied, in which overlord and vassals form a sort of " sacramental unity," in a hierarchy of privilege. In this society the conquest of privilege is the aim of the noble, and it is based on virtue and honour ; but in many cases is achieved also by unmeasured violence and expenditure.[1] *In this society, battle is a test of purity, a trial by ordeal, until the day when the " morals of power" tend momentarily to replace those of honour and moderation (p. 282).*

Amongst the domains of the overlords, some tended, indeed, to develop into powerful states. Between the seventh and the third centuries B.C. *there was a period of tyrannies and moral crisis.*[2] *But in the small seigniorial courts was developed the type that was to impose itself on China. This type is that of the* civilized being, *the man who is truly a man, the* gentleman. *He is contrasted with the savage, the barbarian, whose spirit is uncontrolled, by mastery over himself, a sense of propriety, of decorous bearing, of correct intonation, right motions and modes of expression. Life at a court, being a " parade controlled by regulations," is a school of moral discipline.*[3] *Gradually the spoken word comes to play an increasing part, and the science of fine speech becomes the first of noble arts (p. 292). This preponderance of the spoken word, of " taking counsel," ends by pushing into the foreground the specialists, the technical experts, the lawyers.*[4] *The movement continues, in the populous and active towns, with new arrivals, industrialists or even merchants, whose merit is wealth, and who give a great impetus to luxury and to the arts. For a long time trade had been as much despised as agriculture was honoured, but—surprising phenomenon—there emerges from this " new setting," an " archaic morality ; " the ruin of the old nobility culminated in the spread of an ideal of life which was inspired by its traditions (p. 415). A return to simplicity was preached. Humanity,*

---

[1] Cf. the " Potlatch "—Davy, vol. vi, p. 106.   [2] See pp. 29-34.
[3] Pp. 289-90, 308.   [4] Pp. 300, 308.

justice, good form, were taught. The ancient rule of life, wisdom, *was preferred before the development of science, before wealth and luxury.*[1]

The same formalism which was elaborated in feudal society reigned in the family, when an organization based on succession in the male line had almost completely replaced the matriarchal organization of the clan. Nothing is more strange to the western mind, or more complicated, than the system of relationships so learnedly disentangled by Granet. They are not blood relationships but quite artificial bonds. The fact of paternity is of no value in itself ; the father is not a relative. Although his authority may continually increase, it is nevertheless not of the natural order, it is identical with seigniorial power ; in the sacramental unity of the family it proceeds from his quality as the family high-priest and possessor of the ancestral virtue. The son is not a son ; he is his father's man. *There is neither intimacy, nor familiarity, nor " tender privacies " between them. Their relations do not belong to the domain of affection, but to that of etiquette and honour.*[2] *Neither is there any greater intimacy between the husband and the wife,—the chief wife, for there was a combination of monogamy and polygamy. Their life is regulated by a protocol. " Mutual respect " forbids them to call each other by name.*[3] *As to the children, the chief wife considers as hers even those which she does not herself bear. The absolute indifference to " ties of blood " makes her feel only the added prestige of a multiple maternity. A son, in her case, is not a son, but an element in her prestige.*[4]

There is among the Chinese a lack of feeling, or rather a mastery of their sensibilities, that is simply extraordinary. Decorum, etiquette have repressed all spontaneous display and resulted in an at least apparent drying-up of feeling. The expression of the emotions—and notably of mourning—has an entirely conventional character.[5] *Thanks to this mastery which the Chinese exercises over himself,—perhaps thanks also to the nature of his nervous system—it seems as if he feels physical pain itself less acutely. Actions which, in Western eyes, appear cruel,*[6] *change their nature somewhat, if we take into account*

[1] Pp. 418, 423-4.   [2] See pp. 320, 343.
[3] See pp. 352, 356.   [4] Pp. 365-7.
[5] See Granet, " Le langage de la douleur d'après le rituel funéraire de la Chine l assique," in the *Journal de Psychologie*, Feb. 1922, pp. 97–118.
[6] See pp. 123, 216, 222, 230, 238, 269, 296, 321.

the scorn which the individual himself has for suffering and death.[1]

To sum up, a profound mysticism, but if one may so express it, of a positive kind, and with a tendency towards the practical, culminated, in China, in a reign of moral formalism. The absolute identification of nature and of society, after having endowed nature with something living, endowed society with that which is fixed and regular in nature.

From the rural community to the rule of chiefs, from feudal overlordship to kingdom, from kingdom to Empire, the whole history of China, as Granet reconstructs it, is a kidnapping of power, a utilizing of virtue, which is gradually individualized and concentrated. Continually enlarging the circle of his power,— which always is of the same character,—the Chieftain shares, or " duplicates," the sacred power of the Holy Place. From the Founder of the race he holds a store of Virtue.[2] *In consequence of this Virtue, he commands the seasons, regulates the sun's passage, orders the world ; in his domain he is the " unique inspirer ; " " he commands nature and men to be what they are ; " he is the main element in all success, the atoner for all adversity.*[3]

This conception of the Chief culminates, under the Empire, in the " Son of Heaven," who, by virtue of his office, " governs the course of Time," and is the great Man, the True Man, the Unique Man ; the one who maintains the order of the Universe by bringing in the reign of moral order ; who to play his part ought not to act and make rules and regulations, but to concentrate his power, to build up and to train ;[4] *for he does not impose order, he " secretes " it.*

Thus, through the worship of nature, combined with ancestorship, a sense of order is to be found at the base of all life, public or private, in what one must not designate the Chinese State. It was no " State," in spite of the efforts of lawyers to substitute law for custom, formal law for the living institution which manifests itself in the dances and the songs, authority for the task of instruction.[5]

---

[1] On suicide, see *l'Année Sociologique*, Vol. II, p. 423, ed. by Matignon, *le Suicide en Chine*.
[2] On the exhaustion of this Virtue, see pp. 15, 20, 43.
[3] Pp. 249 ff. Cf. 15, 217, 307.
[4] Pp. 12, 13, 38, 46, 381, 391, 392, 395, 396, 400-3.
[5] Pp. 248, 397.

Renouvier defined China as a " patriarchate." This profound philosopher of history, in his Introduction, *spoke very aptly of the Chinese mentality. " For the Chinese," he said, " all phenomena are connected, and . . . nothing can happen in the heavens, or in the air, or even on the back of the shell of a tortoise exposed to the fire, which is not a sign, a cause or effect bearing on human interests. . . . The harmony of nature or the disorder of the elements are consequences of the moral harmony of life or of the disorder of conduct. . . . Ethics were less a matter of legislation, than a rational conforming of life to the most inward,·and at the same time clearly manifest, laws of the universe and of society." [1]*

Granet defines this mentality, and furthermore explains by it the whole social system. He speculates amongst these relationships, these confusions, these substitutions, penetrates into this mysticism which underlies the whole of Chinese life, and which often recalls what has been named " primitive mentality."

Although the China which he shows us is strangely outside our normal classifications, our ways of living, feeling and thinking, we see clearly, thanks to him, that here, as everywhere, there develops early a " science," from the contact of the senses with reality, and under the stimulation of necessity. A certain positive power was thus able to grow, a material civilization to form itself—which knew very real refinements.[2] But various causes, connected with the genius peculiar to the race, and with the language which expresses this genius,[3] have had the result that, in its speculative and experimental form, the intellectual faculty which the western world calls reason, *and which in its fullness is the peculiar manifestation of the Greek genius, has not developed parallel with the practical faculty in the* homo faber. *This last faculty in the end was reduced to a kind of atrophy, when the stage was reached in which excessive moral preoccupation condemned " scientific instruction " (p. 424).[4]*

In contrast with primitive societies, a degree of national unification and of material progress was reached, which made of China a great Empire and a civilized country. But mystical knowledge and tradition replaced science ; *and the practice of*

[1] *Introd. à la Phil. Anal. de l'histoire*, pp. 255, 256, 265.
[2] See pp. 12, 117, 194, 204, 220, 285.
[3] See Vol. *bis.*
[4] On the other hand the leanings of the Chinese towards the concrete seem to have hindered the progress of means of exchange, of " finance," of forms which were symbols of property.

a codified wisdom, if it let the Chinese escape from " the uneasiness of mind which may result from an ill-regulated pursuit of the just and the true " (p. 309), prevented them from knowing anything of the noble unrest which accompanies intellectual and social progress.

We should estimate inadequately the value of this book if we did not emphasize its exceptional qualities of form.

Many times already we have declared that history is pure science ; but we have also frequently declared that being wholly a science, it attains to art by intensity of life. We have in Granet an artist, we might even say a poet ; for in his case, sympathetic imagination passes from the texts to the persons and the setting, and feels deeply the bonds that exist in simple people, in primitive crowds, between their soul and the soul of things.

He draws the most picturesque description of the life of the fields. He calls up before us the peasant, his clothing, his dwelling, his regular occupations, in the fruitful accord between the seasons and labour ; but above all he shows, with an incomparable felicity of expression, the effect on living beings of those two " marvellous moments," Spring and Autumn, when " nature, at one breath, begins or ceases to live." [1] He traces the effect also of the winter's retirement in the " house of men," when the stimulus of a dramatic liturgy corresponds with the work of germination in the soil which is preparing the earth for renewal. I do not think the attachments of humanity—and especially of Chinese humanity—to Mother Nature, have ever been better expressed ; these " sudden and collective emotions, in the highest degree contagious," [2] of the seasonal crowds, whose songs and dances are improvised to the rhythm of sentiments held in common; the joyous impulses, the outbursts of play, the overflow of energy,—above all in the magnificent hours of the collective celebrations of marriage.

He gives us pictures equally striking and precise of feudal life, the life of the Court, of the toilet of the overlord, his table, the events of family life—birth, marriage, death and burial.

This is not all. These songs, these formulæ, these sayings from the tangle of which Granet reconstructs ancient China, he quotes felicitously, and translates into appropriate rhythm— in such a way that the striking resurrection becomes when completed an impassioned anthology. **HENRI BERR.**

---

[1] P. 160 ; cf. pp. 147-8.   [2] P. 171 ; cf. p. 161.

THE CIVILIZATION OF CHINA

INTRODUCTION

THE civilization of China is deserving of more than an interested curiosity. It may appear strange, but it is a fact that in this civilization there is recorded a large proportion of the sum of human experience. No other has, for so many years, served as a bond between so many of the human race. No one who lays claim to the title of humanist dare be ignorant of a tradition of culture so rich in charm and of such permanent value.

This tradition was already fixed at about the time of the Christian era—towards the epoch when the country of China, at length united, forms a vast Empire. The civilization created in China soon spread its light throughout the whole of the Far East. Thanks to numerous contacts, it was itself enriched. The Chinese, however, endeavoured to realize a traditional ideal, which they defined with increasing strictness.

They are attached to this so passionately that they themselves represent it to be the finest heritage of their race. Several thousands of years before the Christian era, their ancestors (they did not doubt) were initiated by sages into that discipline of life which was their strength. The pure civilization of the earliest ages was the source of a perfect cohesion, and the greatest China dates from the most ancient times. Its unity is broken or is restored according to whether an order of civilization, in principle unchangeable, shines resplendent or more faint.

These systematic views have the value of dogma and correspond to an active belief. They have been the inspiration at the heart of all the attempts at historic synthesis; over long centuries they exercised a decisive influence on the

A 1

presentation, the transmission and the restoration of documents. We do not possess a single one that can be considered first hand and untampered with. Historians, archæologists, exegetes, remain impregnated with traditional piety, even when they pose simply as learned men, and even when a " fault-finding " spirit seems to animate them. They determine the facts or the dates, establish texts, lop off interpolations, classify works, not with objective detachment, but in the hope of rendering more acute and purer, in themselves and in their readers, the consciousness of an ideal that history cannot explain, for it precedes history.

Our inspiration will be drawn from a quite different source.

Formerly, Western historians told the history of China in the Chinese way (or something very near it) without even calling attention to its dogmatic character. Today they are endeavouring to disentangle the true in the traditions from the false. They make use of the works of indigenous criticism. They often forget to bring out the first principles, however, and they appear generally hardly aware of the insufficiencies of a purely literary exegesis. In spite of a critical attitude, they seldom make up their minds to admit that it is impossible to grasp the facts.

In order that the data in a document may be of use, is it sufficient merely to have dated it ? When we have decided, for example, on the date and month of the Chinese documents relating to the ancient forms of land-tenure, what reality have we got hold of, if we refrain from noting that, according to the documents, the portion of land assigned to one cultivator is five or six times as small as the field adjudged in our day as necessary to nourish a single man in the most fertile and best cultivated countries ? The literary history of the rituals is of great interest, but is it possible to write it if one has not taken care to observe : (i) That amongst the objects mentioned in the rituals there are hardly any that excavations have discovered ; (ii) That amongst the objects discovered by excavations [1] there are very few about which the rituals give any information ?

Possible fields for excavation are scarcely touched. Chinese archæology is inspired by a bookish spirit. It is necessary

---

[1] I agree on this point, and in the same terms, with M. Pelliot, so certain appears the conclusion. See **CXI**. Cf. Laufer, **LXXXVIII**.

at the beginning to utter a warning that the documents at our disposal bear a Utopian character. It remains to be seen whether, such as they are, they are without value.

It is not possible to discover from them the least detail of historical facts, nor is it possible to describe with any exactness the material aspects of Chinese civilization. We are ignorant equally of the details of the wars and political intrigues, the administrative customs, the economic practices, the manner of dress, etc. To make up for this lack we possess an abundance of precious testimony as to the various sentimental or theoretical attitudes which were adopted in different milieus in China on the subjects of costume, wealth, the administrative art, politics and war. We are specially well-informed about the attitude which orthodoxy supported in each case. But the Chinese do not like to lose anything of the past, even when they take care to present an ideal reconstruction ; they have allowed a mass of information to survive which contradicts the orthodox theories.

For the present (if we guard against illusory exactness), there is no means of writing a manual of Chinese antiquities. It is not, however, impossible to begin to know China, and even to make considerable progress in the knowledge, provided we limit our task to defining a combination of exterior manifestations characterizing the social system of the Chinese of antiquity.

The spirit in which I have conceived the present work is as follows. I have set myself to try to determine the social system of the Chinese ; to try to point out its distinctive features—in political life, in manners, in thought, and in the history of thought and of manners ; to try further to indicate what of wide human experience lies hidden within it, by making apparent the truth that, from one civilization to another, it is often only the outward symbols that differ ; to try, finally, to reveal this system of behaviour in the setting and movement which are natural to it. The same spirit has inspired my preparatory researches. I have published part of these,[1] taking care to point out their character of inductive studies, and at the same time progressively introducing a

---

[1] There remains for me to publish a work on the Chinese family and a work (*Le Roi boit*) in which I intend to make a study of the mystical elements of the Chinese idea of *Majesty*.

critical examination of the facts, ideas and documents. Today I have to present a consecutive narrative. It has been necessary to adopt a more dogmatic attitude. This has led me to dissociate the history of political and social facts from the history of thought. The latter will furnish material for a complementary volume, where it will be shown that Chinese thought (following upon a development which is in close connexion with the evolution of manners), seems to tend, *from the epoch of the Han*, towards a scholasticism which is a counterpart to the orthodox discipline of Chinese life. This thought, however, preserves with remarkable aptitude— concrete, poetic and plastic—a kind of free play which conceals itself, easily and as if under cover, under a veneer of conventional forms. These conclusions will strengthen, and will also complete, those to which the present volume will lead us. The evolution of manners bears witness to the successive pre-eminence of ideals peculiar to different settings. It seems to tend (as to a sort of dead centre) to the glorification of an extraordinarily rigid conformity. Thus the predominant part which the official class plays in the life of the nation, *beginning from the foundation of the Empire*, is very pronounced. This part is to all appearance sovereign, for the rôle of the State and that of the Administration is reduced (theoretically) to instruction concerning the moral and intellectual manifestations which characterize an honest man, and are the qualifications of an official. Chinese history is ill at ease in resigning itself to recording survivals, and more uneasy still over registering revivals. It is safe, however, to assume that under the veneer of an orthodoxy which claimed to reign uncontested, the moral life continued to develop freely. Valuable indications reveal the fact that it did not cease to draw inspiration from the ancient ideals, preserved without real impoverishment. It was also capable of renewing its ideals under the pressure of facts, for the *founding of the imperial unity* was accompanied by a quite new disposition of social activity.

The imperial era, in political history as in the history of society, seems to be a sort of dividing point. I have, therefore, brought this work on ancient China to a close at the epoch of the Han.

The first part is devoted to political history. It opens

with a chapter in which I analyse the traditional history, from its beginning up to the reign of the Emperor Wu of the Han dynasty (140–87 B.C.). The old traditions throw light, if not on the facts, at least on the ideas of the Chinese. From the point at which dated chronicles begin (eighth century B.C.), criticism seems to be prepared to establish some facts, but very few. These facts are, it must be emphasized, often schematic and very disconnected. A good deal of audacity is needed to embark on discovering even the main lines of political evolution which led to the creation of the Empire of China. In attempting to tell the story of this evolution, I have quite shamelessly left large gaps. I have refused to draw portraits of people concerning whom I had only proverbial data. I have not told tales of wars when my sole materials were recitals extracted from epics, romances or songs of heroic deeds. I have made no attempt to reconstruct the plans of strategists and the projects of politicians, where I barely succeeded in grasping the actual results. I have everywhere made use of examples and I have only laid stress on the decisive moments. The reigns of Ch'in Shih Huang-ti and of the Emperor Wu are only known through incomplete and unreliable documents, but events then loom so large that the critic has little fear of going astray. I have refrained from offering any hypothesis whatever on the usual questions, as for example on the population of China. The hypotheses which have been formed, based on preconceived linguistic theories, or on postulates of general history, have at least the inconvenience—a very serious one in my view—that they restrict the field of investigation in which prehistoric archæology ought to work. I have limited myself to the attempt to sketch the parallel progress of mastery over the soil and of political unification, and I have tried to throw some light upon one important fact—that is, that as soon as, absorbing the smaller chieftainships and flowing over the islets of barbarism, large overlordships which appeared to form provincial units had been set up, the senti-ment of a community of civilization decided the Chinese to defend themselves against the Barbarian confederations which were forming, and caused them to accept the unification of the country in the form of a great Empire. They thus reached the stage of forming what I will call a *grouping of civilization*, an active and powerful grouping, without however believing themselves under the obligation to give to the State and to the idea of the State that prestige and authority in which the Western mind very readily sees the indispensable protective armour of all national life.

Just as the political history of China can only be attempted under the condition of not introducing into it the western idea of the State, so, in approaching the history of society, which is the subject of our second part, it is necessary to free ourselves from the idea of Law which a narrow admiration of the Roman world has fastened on our minds. In the ancient Chinese world, social changes do not take place by the adoption of successive systems of laws and regulations. They take place by changes of orientation in the moral standpoint. These changes accompany the variations which occur in the general ordering of society, according to whether rural activity and village life—or rather the activity of the feudal establishments in the forts which expand practically into miniature capitals—predominate, or that of the wealthy traders for whom the big towns were built. On the outstanding facts connected with these displacements of the centre of the social life, the documents do not furnish any sort of chronological landmarks. Nothing certain is known of the foundation of the forts and of the seigniorial cities which brought about the replacement of peasant ideals of rhythmic equilibrium and measure by a morality of prestige. Suitable for the life of the camps, this changed, under the influence of the life of the court, into a cult of correct bearing and etiquette. Nothing exact is known of the development of industry, of wealth, of luxury, or of the extension of urban centres. It is by indirect means that we get glimpses of the acute crisis which was the result. It led to the acceptance, as principles of social discipline, of a formalism and a decorum, inspired by a traditional spirit and by an archaic symbolism. There is only one way of studying the history of this society ; that is to attempt a kind of stratigraphic reconstruction. It is clear why I have not proceeded by studying institutions, defined and grouped according to western methods—religion, law, habitation—but by studying the whole setting. Without even aiming at completeness, I have limited myself to presenting a choice of characteristic behaviours.

All that I have said in this work comes from direct analysis of the documents.[1] Once and for all, I give warning that it is only possible to find here the state of opinions to which my principles of research have led me. I have taken much trouble to shade the assertions, much pains to arrive at precise formulas, wherever I felt it possible. I have taken still more to eliminate merely ingenious hypotheses, and above all, misleading exactness. Given the state of the documents and the stage of investigation, it would be childish to pretend that the conclusions which can be reached are not subjective, incomplete, and to some extent superficial— and more childish still to make excuses about it. It is enough to express the hope that, taken for what they are worth, they will lead the reader to realize how necessary is a deep and thorough study of Chinese affairs. The study will afford an opportunity of comparing with the standards of value and experiences of a very great people, the classifications and judgments to which we are most firmly attached.

---

[1] I have, however, eliminated, as much as possible, from my notes, all the references which would have been of use only to specialists.

FIRST PART—POLITICAL HISTORY

BOOK ONE

TRADITIONAL HISTORY

Chapter I

THE FIVE SOVEREIGNS

TRADITIONAL History begins with the age of the Five Sovereigns (*Wu Ti*), who are sometimes preceded by the Three August Ones (*San Huang*).

The three first of the Five Sovereigns, Huang-ti, Chuan-hu and Kao-Sin, figure in the works connected with the Confucian tradition, but have a philosophic rather than a historical character.[1] The Book of History (*Shu-king*), attributed to Confucius, only mentions the two last, Yao and Shun. Ssu-ma Ch'ien, who, at the close of the second century B.C., made the first large compilation of general history, took as the subject of the first chapter of his " Historical Memoirs " the Five Sovereigns. Thus he made Chinese history begin with Huang-ti, who, as early as the epoch of the Han, was considered the great patron of the Taoist sects. Although Ssu-ma Ch'ien was accused of unorthodoxy on this account,[2] historical works continued to recount the reigns of the Five Sovereigns. An iconographic tradition, which goes back at least to the time of the second Han dynasty, relates that the Five Sovereigns were preceded by the Three August Ones (Fu-hsi, Nü-kua and Shên-nung, or alternatively, Fu-hsi and Nü-kua forming a couple, Chu-jung and Shên-nung).[3] The August Ones, as well as the three first Sovereigns, are named in the most ancient works, in both the orthodox and unorthodox traditions.

In making the history of the Sovereigns and of the Three August Ones precede that of the royal dynasties, the learned

---

[1] SMC, Introd., CXLIV. [2] SMC, Introd., XLIX. [3] **XVII**, 126 ff.

9

men of China set out to paint a picture of a halcyon age
when, with human characteristics, perfect virtue ruled. The
heroic figures of the early age in China preserve, however,
a number of mythical features. In Yao and Shun, the first
heroes of the *Shu-king*, the effacement of these features is
nearly complete. They mingle, however, in a dramatic history
of the Mighty Waters, in which the founder of the first royal
dynasty, Yü the Great, plays the principal part,—whilst other
tales bring on to the stage different August Ones (Nü-kua,
Chu-jung) or other heroes. The theme of the Mighty Waters
in flood is joined to a myth concerning the setting in order
of the world, and, on certain sides, appears connected with
various agrarian rites of a markedly shamanistic character ;
it is in tracing designs on the earth that waters are made to
burst from it, and their beds are marked out. But, in the
Shu-king, the development of this important theme changes
into a debate of a purely administrative interest : which is
to be preferred, the method of dikes or that of canals ? [1]
Again, when it is said of Yao that " he appeared like the
sun," it is to be understood that this expression is simply
metaphorical. There is nothing preserved by the historians
of the old myth in which Yao is presented as a subduer of
suns or as the sun itself.[2] If we discover, in the heroes not
mentioned by the *Shu-king*, more numerous and less distorted
mythical characteristics, we do so most often on the margin
of real history. Ssu-ma Ch'ien, for example, takes care to
relate that Huang-ti established his power by causing the
descent from heaven of the Drought, who was his own
daughter, and who remained a goddess.[3] In the same way
the historians refrain from telling how Shên-nung, the last
of the August Ones, had the head of an ox, and how Fu-hsi
and Nü-kua formed a pair by binding themselves together by
the tail.[4] Historical tradition will in general only have to
do with men.

Humanized long ago, Yao and Shun would without doubt
have remained the first sovereigns of China, if the theory
of the Five Elements had not played an important part in
the reconstruction of the national history. This theory, undoubtedly ancient, became, in the fourth and third centuries

---

[1] **LV,** 465 ff., and 530, n. 5.   Cf. for a different interpretation **XCV,** 47 ff.
[2] SMC, I, 42.   Cf. **LV,** 377.   [3] **LV,** 315.   [4] SMC, I, 9 and 12.

B.C., for political reasons, the subject of different schools of speculation. All held that the Order of the Universe and Time itself were ordained by the joint action of the Five Elementary Virtues. These were incarnated in Five Sovereigns successively. One of the ideas relating to the Five Elements involved the theory that they exercised their activity by triumphing one over the other. This idea led to the reconstruction under the form of historical facts, of the debris of old myths, in which the heroes were envisaged struggling against one another like demiurges. History annexed some of these heroes, in sufficient number to make the First Ages correspond to a perfect cycle of the Five Elementary Virtues.[1]

Each Sovereign has for an emblem a single Element. He possesses, however, a sort of complete " Virtue," and each one of them is, by himself, a creator of the national civilization. He is more than simply an inventor of scientific discoveries, or of institutions. This definition would be more applicable to the August Ones. Fu-hsi and Nü-kua, for example, together invented the rites of marriage and of the giving of presents, whilst Shên-nung, the sovereign with the head of an ox, made the plough and taught the laws of agriculture.[2] If Huang-ti, however, is sometimes given as the inventor of arms and as a metal-worker, it is more often to Ch'e-you, his minister, that we find attributed the discovery of smelting and the manufacture of the first weapons of war.[3] It is also told how Shun first made porcelain vases. The great inventions, however, which signalize his reign and that of Yao, are the achievement of the ministers who undertook to organize a department of the world. Hi-ho regulated the solar year ; K'i taught men to sow and to transplant ; Kao-yao fixed the penal law.[4] Above these heroes, thus reduced to " specialists," the Sovereigns, who are the most perfect realizations of a type, reign but do not invent. Invested with a more complete, and what seems in a sense a more abstract Virtue, they confine themselves to the task of civilizing by radiating a controlling power.

This authority spreads both in space and time When complete, it constitutes the unity of the Empire, identifying

---

[1] SMC, Introd., CXLIII ff. ; **LV**, 45 ; **XVII**, 128 and 129.
[2] SMC, I, 7.   [3] **LV**, 353, 271.
[4] SMC, I, 72. **LV**, 483 ; *Che pen*, 1 ; *Lu Che ch'un ch'iu*, 17, par. 2.

the frontiers of China with the limits of the Universe. This good result is secured when the Sovereign, moving his head-quarters about, himself carries his Virtue to the limits of the world. It is in this way that Huang-ti, visiting the four points of the compass, reached in the Extreme West the mountain K'ong-T'ong and Chuan-hü ; at the bound of the East, and to the tree P'an mu. But Yao is satisfied with sending delegates to the four Poles, and better still, a simple ceremony, carried out at the four gates of the capital, allows Shun to subject the Universe to the order he wishes to inaugurate.[1] The Sovereign rules over space because he is master of Time. Huang-ti " established everywhere the order for the sun, the moon and the stars." [2] " Kao-sin observed the Sun and the Moon in order to receive and to accompany them." [3] Yao charged Hi and Ho " to observe with attention the August Heavens and to apply the law of numbers to the Sun, the Moon and the Constellations." [4] The Sovereign " in acting according to the seasons, in order to conform to the Heavens, regulates the influences ($k'i$) in order to direct evolution." [5] He it is whose " universal liberality bestows favours on all Beings." He possesses a supreme gift, Efficacy ($ling$) which characterizes those whom we would call divine beings ($shen;$ $ling$ and $shen$ have the same value and are employed interchangeably ; one also says : $shen$-$ling$). " Huang-ti possessed Efficacy ($Shen$-$ling$) from his birth. Before the age of three months he could speak." [6] This Sovereign Virtue has as its immediate result, that " beings in movement and in repose, divine beings, great and small, all things on which the Sun and the Moon shine, become calm and docile." [7] This state of stability in which the earth and the waters, plants and beasts, gods and men prosper without encroaching on each others' domains, is called the Great Peace ($T'ai$-$p'ing$). A Sovereign has all the attributes with which a philosophy entirely in revolt against creationist conceptions, can endow a demiurge.

The Sovereigns whom traditional history has best succeeded in rendering real, are presented as sages rather than as heroes. Their primary function is to make order reign among men.

---

[1] SMC, I, 56, 79 ; **LV**, 249 ff.   [2] SMC, I, 33.   [3] SMC, I, 40.
[4] SMC, I, 43.   [5] SMC, I, 58 ff., and *ibid.*, 37 and 40.
[6] SMC, 26.   [7] SMC. 38.

Yao, who had the " intelligence of a divine being (*shen*) " inaugurated the reign of filial piety and civic virtues. He lived, as did Shun (and to a less degree Yü the Great, the founder of royalty), solely for the good of the people, and " without taking thought for himself." [1] Thus he did not dream of founding a dynasty. The Five Sovereigns are not fathers and sons in succession. Between the two sovereigns of the *Shu-king*, there is no relationship, for Shun can marry the daughters of Yao. He succeeded Yao, after Yao had put him to the proof as son-in-law and minister, and had recognized in him a Sage worthy of reigning. His merit, proclaimed by a predecessor who was a judge of wisdom, was recognized by the people. Yao banished Tan-chu, his own son, " in order not to show favouritism to one man only to the detriment of the Empire," and, on the death of Yao, allegiance passed not to Tan-chu, but to Shun. Poets and singers did not celebrate Tan-chu but Shun. Shun said : " Heaven wills it," and assumed power.[2]

He is a wise Sovereign who, possessing a " virtue " more human and at the same time more abstract than the " virtue " proper to heroes, civilizes the world by the direct effects of his efficacy and reigns, in harmony with the will of heaven, for the happiness of the people. He is, notably, the author of an exact and useful calendar. His ministers act, inspired by his Virtue. As for him, he reigns, without thinking of governing. He concerns himself with creating, or rather secreting, order. This order is, above all, moral, but it embraces all things. The epoch of the Sovereigns is the age of civic merit, the era of perfect humanity (*jen*).

---

[1] SMC, I, 40, 53 ff. ; **LV**, 27 ff.   [2] SMC, I, 40, 69.

Chapter II

THE THREE ROYAL DYNASTIES

THE history of the Three Dynasties is based on the *Shu-king* (completed by the *She-king*, the classic Book of Poetry) and on the *Annals written on Bamboo.*

To Shun, the last Sovereign, there succeeded Yü, founder of the dynasty of the Hsia. When the Hsia became perverted, the Yin (or Shang, or Yin-shang) destroyed them and took their place. The Chou at last drove out the Yin, when they had become evil-doers.

The power of every dynasty springs from a Virtue (*Tö*) or a Prestige (*Tö* or *Tö-yin*) which passes through a time of fullness (*cheng* or *sheng*), then declines (*ngai*) and after an ephemeral resurrection (*hing*), becomes exhausted and is extinguished (*mie*). The dynasty *ought* then to be extinguished (*mie*), suppressed (*tsüeh*, or *mie-tsüeh ;* exterminated), for *it no longer has heaven* on its side (*pu T'ien*). Heaven (*T'ien*) ceases to treat its kings like sons (*tsŭ*). A family can only provide China with Kings, sons of Heaven (*T'ien tsŭ*), during the period in which Heaven grants it investiture (*ming*). This investiture, this heavenly mandate, is always temporary. Heaven is changeable, and inexorable. Its favour is lost and wears away. The Great Happiness (*ta fu*) does not come twice.

Every dynasty which retains power when its time has passed, only possesses power *de facto*. *De jure*, it is a usurper. The founders of the dynasty whose hour has come, fulfil a heavenly mission by suppressing the dynasty that has become out-of-date and maleficent. They are the ministers of divine chastisement, and their victory is the proof that heaven has entrusted to them its mandate (*ming*).

The heavenly mandate, which authorizes a dynasty to reign, is the fruit of the merits (*kong*) of a great Ancestor. The great Ancestors of the Three Royal Dynasties (*San Wang*) were all ministers of Shun. It is under the last and wisest of the Sovereigns that, in making themselves famous for their rule over a province of the world, they acquire for their race a characteristic Virtue. Yü, who founded the power of the Hsia, was *Ssu-kong* (chief of public works); Sieh and K'i, ancestors of the Yin and of the Chou, were, one the controller of the people, the other in charge of agriculture. Furthermore, Yü, Sieh and K'i are the descendants to the fifth generation (founder included) of the first of the Sovereigns; Huang-ti. (In the fifth generation the collateral branches separate and form distinct lines.) Finally, the birth of each one of the three dynastic Ancestors was miraculous. They sprang from heavenly origins. All the dynasties of the Kings, Sons of Heaven, thus go back to a son of Heaven.[1]

From the beginning of the eighth century B.C., history attributes to the Chou a languishing existence, which only ends with the third century B.C. The Chou had then outlived their power. No demonstration is given of it after the historical period, characterized by a chronology, begins. The King P'ing, under whom chronology starts, had to abandon his capital, and referring to his father, King Yü, who perished in a disaster, it was declared that " the Chou were lost." Their Virtue was exhausted. The natural disasters which took place proved it. Like disorders appeared at the end of the Hsia dynasty as at the end of the Yin. The last sovereigns of a race are essentially tyrants and rebels. Blinded with pride, they act by themselves instead of conforming to Virtue which is identical with natural Order (*Tao*). They do not any longer carry out the heavenly mandate. Heaven abandons them, being no longer able to treat them as pious Sons.

The royal Virtue is obtained by obedience to the heavenly commands. It is ruined by the pride which is the attribute of tyrants. The history of the Three Dynasties is only a threefold illustration of this principle. It is told in the form of annals, which only contain fully developed stories for the periods of the foundation and the downfall. For all the intermediate periods (except for the moments in which a fleeting resurrection of the royal power appears) the annals are nothing more than a simple list of reigns. This history

---

[1] LIX, 17 ff.

sets out to show the principles underlying the greatness and the decadence of the royal houses. Its task is done when it has brought to light the glorious virtue of the royal Founders and the fatal character of the Kings of perdition.

I

The Hsia

Yü the Great, the founder of the Hsia dynasty, has all the characteristics of a Sovereign ; and indeed no Sovereign more resembles a demiurge than this creator of Royalty. In his honour, history incorporates the fragments of a poem in which he is seen taming the sacred Marshes, the venerable Mountains, and leading the Rivers to the sea " like lords who are going to a Court reception." The world, once in order, can be put into cultivation. The people can eat fresh meat, rice and millet. The earth was saved from the waters thanks to the labours of Yü. But these—no historian doubts—were purely human labours. They demanded only a special abundance of civic virtues. Yü " was active, obliging, capable, diligent, . . . he restricted his clothing and his food, while he displayed an extreme piety towards the divine powers ; he had only a humble dwelling, but he expended largely on ditches and canals." [1]

There was inherent in him a Virtue capable of unifying the Empire. " His voice was the standard of sounds, his body the standard of measures of length." He could thus determine the Numbers which serve to regulate Time and Space, as well as the Music which creates the universal harmony. He fixed the tributes payable, " put into perfect order the six domains of Nature," and planted Chinese and Barbarians at suitable places, so that the Empire enjoyed the " Great Peace." He travelled, as was fitting, to the Four Points of the Compass, in order to mark the boundaries of the World and of China. All these works he carried out as Minister of Shun. Then he was presented by Shun to Heaven. When he had succeeded Shun as Shun had succeeded Yao, Yü the Great had nothing to do except reign. His rôle then, as for every Sovereign, was to present a Minister to Heaven. He

[1] SMC, I, 101, 120, 154.

PLATE II

KIEH ON THE SHOULDERS OF HIS TWO FAVOURITES
(Bas-relief from Shan-tung taken from the Kın she suo)

presented Kao-yao, and, on his death, Yi (or Po-yi) who is sometimes described as a son of Kao-yao. Yü died, but the overlords, deserting Yi, came to render homage to K'i, saying : " Our Prince is (K'i), son of Yü the Sovereign." Thus the principle of dynastic heredity was established and the royal house of the Hsia founded.[1]

To Yü, a civilizing king, succeeded K'i, a warrior king. All that history knows of his reign, is one victory. Thanks to this victory, he consolidated the peaceful labours of his father. Until we come to Kieh, the last of the Hsia, the only fact that is registered at some length relates to a couple of dragons, whom Heaven sent down to the king K'ong-kia. The king ate the female. Some see in the heavenly gift of the dragons a confirmation of the royal Virtue, and they make of K'ong-kia a sage who conformed in every respect to the will of Heaven. Others, instead of placing in his reign a resurrection of the dynastic genius, see in him an amateur magician. This abetter of disorder " perverted the Virtue of the Hsia." [2]

Kieh succeeded in annihilating this Virtue. Kieh was not an incapable Sovereign ; he was a tyrant. He won excessive victories. " He terrorised the Hundred Families." He loved luxury. He gave himself up to debauch with the captives brought back from his expeditions. He slew the vassals who reprimanded him ; he freed himself of his principal wife, and imprisoned in a tower the most virtuous of his feudatories. Stars fell from Heaven, the earth trembled, the river Yi dried up. Two Suns, at last, appeared together. One, a setting sun, symbolized the decline of the kings of the Hsia dynasty. The other, a rising sun, symbolized T'ang, the feudatory, whom Kieh, after having imprisoned, had been obliged to set free. As soon as he was freed, T'ang received the overlords, who came to him with their homage, and the tyrant's vassals, who took refuge with him, among them the annalist of the Hsia. Then, T'ang (the rising sun) set his army in motion, taking care to have it march from East to West. Kieh, in his pride, had said : " On the day on which this sun dies you and I will both perish." He was beaten, and that was the end of the dynasty.[3]

---

[1] SMC, I, 99, 163 ; **LV**, 580.   [2] SMC, I, 164, 168 ; **LV**, 556.
[3] SMC, I, 169 ; **LV**, 394.

B

II

The Yin

T'ang the Victorious, founder of the Yin, was descended from the first of the Sovereigns, and also from Sieh, son of Heaven and of a Virgin Mother, who distinguished himself as a Minister of Shun. Among his ancestors was Ming (Hüan-ming) who regulated the course of the River and was drowned in its waters. "His Virtue extended even to birds and quadrupeds." Obedient to the desires of Heaven, he would only snare in his nets beasts " who had had enough of life." He gathered Sages round himself, and he secured a Minister, such as Yi Yin, who knew the proper nourishment for a sovereign and knew how to discourse on the royal Virtues. T'ang began by punishing the Count of K'o, " who offered no sacrifices," and then Kun-wu, who was an abetter of trouble. He took up arms against the Hsia, on the one pretext that they had not pity for their people. For himself, " fearing the Sovereign from on High, he did not dare not to correct Kieh . . . who, Heaven bade, should be put to death." His victory helped him to " pacify the Interior of the Seas." " He changed the initial month and the first day." He proclaimed his orders in spring in the regions of the East.[1] He reigned. He died.

The reign of T'ang is void of action. That of his immediate successors only has interest from the part played in the succession to the throne by Yi Yin, T'ang's minister. The succession was definitely established, from father to son. After that, the annals consist of no more than a list of reigns, in which are related, with several changes of capital, only a small number of notable events. Thus, under T'ai-mou, two marvellous mulberry-trees, and under Wu-ting a pheasant, appeared. These miracles were the cause of a reform in the conduct of the king and a renewal of Virtue for the dynasty. This nearly ended with Wu-yi, who drew his arrows on a leather bottle full of blood. He intended to aim at Heaven. A blow of thunder resounded, and Wu-yi, struck by fire from heaven, fell dead.[2]

The Yin perished with Shou-sin, of whom it is related

[1] SMC, I, 180, 185, 186 ; **LV**, 416 ff.   [2] SMC, I, 191 ff. ; **LV**, 537 ff., 422 ff.

also that he aimed his arrow at heaven [1] and that he was burnt with his treasures and his wives. Shou-sin was the most hateful of tyrants. He sinned from excess of ability and of ambition. " His strength was superhuman. With his hand he knocked down infuriated animals. His erudition enabled him to contradict those who remonstrated with him. . . . He intimidated his officers by his talents. He raised his renown high in the Empire, and he brought everything into subjection to himself." He gained fatal victories. He loved lascivious harmony and dances. He gave himself up to women, had a woman captive for his favourite, had those who blamed him executed, and killed his chief wife. He invented the punishment of the red-hot beam. He imprisoned in a tower the Chief of the West, the Prince of the Chou, who was the most virtuous of his vassals. The mountain Yao crumbled. A woman changed herself into a man. Two Suns appeared simultaneously. The Chief of the West, as soon as Shou-sin released him, received the homage of the nobles. The annalist of the Yin took refuge with him ; and the chief Preceptor and his assistant came also, bringing to the Chou the tyrant's musical instruments. The Chou at last gathered together their armies, and the rule of the Yin came to an end.[2]

III

THE CHOU

The Chou were descended both from Huang-ti and from K'i, son of Heaven and a Virgin Mother, who had acquired merit in the reign of Shun as Minister of Agriculture and Prince of the Harvests. The victory of the Chou was assured, in two periods, by the kings Wen and Wu. The first had a civilizing genius (*wen*) the second a warrior genius (*wu*). King Wen, who at first bore the title of Chief of the West, did not think of avenging himself on Shou-sin who had imprisoned him. On the contrary, he sacrificed part of his domains to obtain the suppression of the hideous punishment of the red-hot beam. " He did good in secret." In his domain, under the influence of his genius of moderation, all spirit of strife disappeared ; " The husbandmen gave way

---

[1] *Lun heng*, **XXXV**, vol. II, 172.   [2] SMC, I, 199 ff. ; **LV**, 394 ff.

to each other about the field boundaries, and all gave way to the aged." The nobles recognized in this the sign of a heavenly mandate. The Chief of the West drew Sages to himself. Once when he went hunting, it was not a beast that he took in his nets ; he brought back a Saint able to " assist a sovereign King." This Sage, by his conversation, taught him how " to draw his Virtue to him, and to overthrow the Yin." He only took up arms to punish the Barbarians or the guilty, such as the people of Mi-sü. At last, he decided to take the title of King. Then he " altered rules and measures and fixed the first day of the first month." [1]

His son, the warrior king, had only the task of securing a material victory. He only took up arms in order to " carry out with deference the heavenly chastisement," and because Shou-sin " practised his cruelty on the Hundred Families." As soon as he had conquered " he disbanded his troops and visited his fiefs." The reign of his successor, King Ch'êng, is chiefly interesting because of the part played in the transference of power by the Duke of Chou, who was his uncle and also his minister. Other uncles of the King revolted, helped by the last supporters of the Yin. They were conquered, and finally the dynasty was established with the principle of succession from father to son. Although we are now getting near to the period of dated annals, the reigns of Ch'êng's immediate successors are almost as empty as those of the Yin or Hsia Sovereigns. All that is known is that King Chao perished obscurely : " The royal virtue (*Wang tao*) had declined." [2]

It regained force with King Mu, Chao's son. King Mu, in fact, was of miraculous birth. He is a hero, sung by poets, like his ancestor King Wen. He is also the protagonist of an adventure romance and one of the favourite personages of the story-tellers of " inspired wanderings." He is celebrated above all for a great journey that he made to the Far West. This journey appears, in literary tradition, either as an " inspired wandering," or as a series of pilgrimages to different Holy Places. Historical tradition represents it as a military expedition, and condemns it under this head. It attributes

---

[1] **LV**, 406 ff., 394 ff. ; **LIX**, 17 ff. ; **LIV**, 95 ff. ; SMC, I, 219, 222, and 245 and IV, 94 ff.
[2] SMC, 231, 243, 250, and **LV**, 406 ff.

a long reprimand concerning it to a wise vassal. The subject of it is that it is not right to try to correct by arms the vassals or the Barbarians, who do not bring their tribute to the royal sacrifices. The only remedy in this case is, not to send the people (*i.e.* the army) to suffer in distant regions, but " to exercise his Virtue." King Mu, declares history as the moral of the story, had in fact no success, and only brought back from his expedition against the Jong of the West, four wolves and four white stags. From that time, the vassals of the desert regions ceased to appear at Court. To King Mu, again, is attributed the promulgation of a penal code. He found it necessary to issue it because, " amongst the nobles, there were some who did not keep the peace." [1]

Insufficient in King Mu, Virtue was still more lacking in his successors. Against them " the poets composed satires." Decadence increased in the time of King Li, who was stupid enough to hoard up his wealth though " a King ought to scatter his fortune and distribute it high and low, in such a way that among the gods, men, and all creatures, each one attains to the highest degree." He employed sorcerers to impose silence on criticism, though nothing is more fatal than to " close the people's mouths." He was obliged to resign from the throne. There was then an interregnum (841–828 B.C.) during which two ministers exercised power together (Kong-ho).[2] On the death of Li they handed over the power to the King Süan (828–782). History reproaches him with not having carried out the royal tillage and with having undertaken a census of the people, a forbidden act. It is known, further, that he loved pleasure too much, and that he had to be punished by a drought. But he corrected and confessed his faults and humiliated himself. This was, say some, the occasion of a renewal of the Virtue of the Chou. Others on the contrary insist on the tragic end of Süan, and relate how he was killed by an arrow shot by the ghost of one of his victims, after having suffered a defeat at the very spot where he had refused to till the ground. As for the impiety which was involved in the numbering of the people, the

---

[1] *Mu t'ien tsŭ chuan.* Cf. SMC, V, 481 ; *Tso chuan*, **C,** III, 208. **LV,** 587 ; **XCIII,** 581 ; SMC, I, 251 ; *Lieh-tsŭ*, 3 ; **CXLIII,** 105 ; **LV,** 562.

[2] These words are sometimes also taken to be the name of a person who held the regency alone ; Kong of Ho. *Kong* means " in common," and *ho*, " harmony." The expression *Kong-ho* has been chosen by the modern Chinese to signify democracy.

burden of that fell on his son, King Yü (781–771). He also was defeated and slain by the Barbarians. He had loved Pao-ssu, a beautiful and clever woman whose chattering tongue brought disaster and who, more ill-omened than an owl, destroyed the bulwarks of the State. Pao-ssu was born of the foam of a dragon which had fertilized a little girl seven years of age. The love which King Yü bore her caused trouble in Nature. The mountain K'i crumbled and three rivers dried up.[1] If the Chou, whose Virtue had worn away, were not therefore rooted out, it is because at that moment there did not appear any Sage in China, who had the beneficent genius of a founder of a dynasty.

[1] SMC, I, 269–78 ff.; **LV**, 538; **LIX**, 332 ff.; *Kuo yu*, 1.

Chapter III

THE EPOCH OF THE LEADERS AND OF THE "COMBATANT KINGDOMS"

The title of Son of Heaven was preserved in the royal house of the Chou almost up to the founding of the Empire. But between the eighth and the third centuries B.C. spreads a period characterized by struggles for prestige between some of the feudal states (*kuo*). The history of these times is based on seigniorial annals. The chief source from the eighth to the fifth century B.C. is the *Ch'un Ch'iu* (*Annals*) of the country of Lu, the fatherland of Confucius. The *Ch'un Ch'iu* furnishes only a dry list of facts. It is completed with the assistance of its three commentaries, the principal one of which, the *Tso Chuan* (which rests also, no doubt, on one or several local chronicles), contains anecdotes referring to the whole of Chinese territory ; and with the assistance also of *Kuo yu*, which is a collection of " contiones," of discourses (*yu*), classified according to countries (*kuo*). The following period is scarcely known except by a work resembling rather the *Kuo yu* than a book of annals :—the " Discourse on the Combatant Kingdoms." Ssu-ma Ch'ien writes the history of this age, in the form of monographs on the overlordships, adding them to the principal Annals, which he consecrates to the last Chou sovereigns. The historian does not introduce any division into this long period. An ancient custom tempts one to distinguish (according to the sources) the period *Ch'un Ch'iu* from that of the " Combatant Kingdoms." It should be written " Combatant Overlordships " but " Kingdoms " is used because at this time several leading nobles took the title of king. Some amongst them are qualified as Leaders. Tradition, however, ordinarily reserves this title for five persons who lived in the seventh century B.C. It sets the period of the Five Sovereigns and the Three Dynasties over against that of the Five Leaders. The first Leaders were princes ruling over wide lands who attempted to give China a new royal dynasty, and who played an important part in the epoch of the Combatant Kingdoms. These princes, their successors, and their imitators sought to take the place of the declining dynasty of the Chou, but history represents the first of them as half-respectful protectors of the royal house, and the rest as its declared rivals.[1]

I

THE LEADERS

" Leader " is used to translate two terms which the Chinese historians frequently use as interchangeable. The word *Pa* is used of a noble distinguished by great prestige and power of action. A Prince specially invested with the particular authority of the Son of Heaven is called *Po*. Tradition attributed to the King the right to promote or to degrade the nobles (*chu hou*). These possessed traditionally one of the titles, *Kong, Hou, Po, Tsŭ, Nan*—honorary titles which all suggest the ideal of virile or military power. All the nobles, in their own countries, were described by the word *Kong* (Duke), but it was admitted that there were hierarchic differences among them ; and it is customary to translate the terms of the hierarchy of nobles by the words : Duke, Marquis, Count, Viscount, Baron ; Dukes and Marquises formed the upper category, the rest the lower category. But the word *Po* (Count) was used also to designate the Chiefs (*fang-po*—" Leaders ") whose duty it was to secure order in a portion of the kingdom (*fang*). The same term (*po*), which describes the masculine divinities, is also a mark of primogeniture.[2] The King distinguished, among the nobles, those who had the same family name as himself, and those who bore a different name. He called the former *Fu* (paternal uncles—fathers) and the latter *Kiu* (maternal uncles—step-fathers). The investiture which conferred a special right of controlling a district (Leadership or Hegemony) was conferred on a *Po-fu* or a *Po-kiu*.

---

[1] LV, 63 ff.

[2] M. Maspero, **XCIII**, 98 ff., seems to admit that the hierarchy of titles had a definite meaning under the Chou and that this meaning can be discovered (p 99, note 2) ; **LV**, 75, note 1.

Ssu-ma Ch'ien, after having noted that King P'ing (770–720 B.C.), the son of King Yü, had to move his capital to the east to avoid the incursions of the Jong (Barbarians of the West) adds that, under his rule, " the royal house declined and grew feeble. The nobles used their strength to oppress the weak. Ch'i, Ch'ou, Ch'in and Chin began to increase in size ; power was exercised by whoever had hegemony in his region (*Fang-po*)." Ch'i, Ch'ou, Ch'in and Chin are (with Song) the countries from each one of which came one of the Five Leaders of tradition. Ssu-ma Ch'ien writes elsewhere : " At this period (under King Huei, 676–652) the House of the Chou was diminished in importance. Ch'i, Ch'ou, Ch'in and Chin alone were powerful. Chin (the Marquisate of Shan-si) had begun to take part in the gatherings of the nobles, but after the death of the Duke (Marquis) Hien, this State suffered from internal dissensions, the Duke (Viscount) Mu of Ch'in (Viscounty of Shen-si) was aloof and far-off. He did not take part in the gatherings and conventions of the Chinese Confederation (*Chong kuo*). The king (with a usurped title) Ch'êng of Ch'ou (Viscounty of Hu-pei) had begun to gather together the Man (Barbarians of the South) of the region of King and governed them. . . . There only remained Ch'i (Marquisate of Shantung) capable of organizing the gatherings and conventions of the overlordships of the Chinese Confederation. As the Duke (Marquis) Huan had given proof of " virtue," the nobles came as guests to the gatherings he held." [1]

Duke Huan of Ch'i (683–643 B.C.) is the first of the traditional Five Leaders. The most famous is Duke Wen of Chin (636–628). Huan of Ch'i could claim the title of *Po-kiu* (Leader-uncle on the maternal side). He was descended from T'ai-kong, the Sage, who was the Minister of the founders of the Chou dynasty and whose daughter had married King Wu. T'ai-kong had the repute of having received a special investiture : " Possess the right to punish the nobles of five degrees and the chiefs of the nine provinces in order to support and uphold the House of the Chou ! " Duke Wen of Chin bore the same family name as the Chou. History declares that he in fact received investiture with the title *Po-fu* (Leader-uncle on the paternal side). " Oh, my uncle !

[1] SMC, IV, 55, and I, 285.

Illustrious were the Kings Wen and Wu; they knew how to take care of their shining Virtue, which rose with splendour on High (towards Heaven) and whose renown spread wide on earth! That is why the Sovereign of On-High made the Mandate succeed in the case of the Kings Wen and Wu. Have pity on me! Cause me to continue (the line of my ancestors), me, the Unique Man, and cause (me and my line) to be perpetually on the throne!" No family tradition, no investiture justified the attribution of hegemony to the three other princes. Duke Siang of Song (Duchy of Ho-nan) (650–637 B.C.) was a scion of the Yin dynasty. He had a misplaced ambition, for "great Happiness does not come twice" to one family. Ssu-ma Ch'ien does not name Song amongst the countries which exercise Hegemony. History, however, reports the fact that Duke Siang presided over seigniorial gatherings. Neither Duke Mu of Ch'in (659–621 B.C.) nor King Chuang of Ch'ou (613–591 B.C.) presided at these. It is true that, later on, Ch'ou was just on the point of founding the Empire and that Ch'in founded it.[1]

The Leaders are princes who possessed imperfectly the genius of a founder King. The most celebrated of them, Wen of Chin, knew, before success came to him, all the trials of a wandering life. His Odyssey is full of epic traits.[2] A younger son, allotted an estate for his lifetime near the frontiers, he gained the affection of the inhabitants. But, less to escape from the assassins sent against him than to avoid revolting against his father, he fled and took refuge in the country of his mother, who was of Barbarian stock. Here he took a wife. His prestige was already such that the people of Chin, on his father's death, came to offer him the throne. He refused, not so much because his hour was not yet come, as because, not having been present at the mourning ceremonies in honour of his father, he did not feel qualified to succeed him. He undertook, however, to visit the most powerful of the overlordships. This journey added to his renown. He bore with patience the insults of those who rebuffed him. When on asking for food, he saw himself given a clod of earth, he succeeded in subduing his first feeling of wrath and took the clod as an emblem of investiture. To those, on the contrary, who—confident of his Virtue—hid

[1] SMC, IV, 40, 303; **LV,** 76 ff.
[2] SMC, IV, 283 ff., 304, 305.

a tablet of jade as a symbol of authority in a present of rice, he sent back the jade, but retained his gratitude. He was well received at Ch'i, and there he took a wife, and resolved to live and die with her. He refused to force Fate. It was his wife who, careful of his fame, forced him to depart. At Ch'u, although pressed by danger, he refused to engage the future of his country by making imprudent promises. The Prince of Ch'u, who saw in him a probable rival, could not make up his mind to have him killed. " He whom Heaven wishes to raise up, who can remove him ? To resist Heaven, is to draw upon oneself Misfortune by force ! " Everywhere people repeated, in speaking of Duke Wen : " Nothing can touch the man to whom Heaven has opened (the way) ! " Companions, who were Sages, followed him faithfully. One of them to nourish him in a day of misfortune, cut off a piece of his thigh. He never boasted of his deed, for he thought that the prince was indebted solely to Heaven who had shown him what to do. A father, threatened with death, refused to recall his son who was in the service of the future Leader. At last, Duke Wen went to Ch'in. There he took five wives. The armies of Ch'in conducted him victorious back to his own country. " He scattered his benefits to the Hundred Families." He rewarded " those who had helped him by their kindness and their justice, supplemented by their goodness and their beneficence," more than those who had given him only material aid. He sought the hegemony, but it was in order to honour the Chou. He brought King Siang (635 B.C.) back into his capital. When he had conquered Ch'u, who, moreover, hesitated to attack him (" Heaven has opened the way for him, I cannot oppose myself to him "), he celebrated a triumph (632 B.C.) only after having paid homage with his trophies to the King. He then received, together with the title of Leader, a rich present of precious objects. He did not grow proud with his success. He said, sighing like one afflicted : " I have learnt that a Sage alone can find calm in a victory achieved on the field of battle." Although he was fortunate in war he deserves to be called not (*Wu*) " the Warrior," but (*Wen*) " The Civilizer."

Heaven, however, did not endow him with the perfect Virtue of a Founder. Though he distinguished himself by numerous traits of humility, there was in him nevertheless that amount of arrogance which hinders all true elevation. He, a vassal, dared to request the King to be present at a gathering. " Once when Confucius was reading the ' Historical Memoirs,' on arriving at the history of Duke Wen, he said : ' Nobles have no right to give orders to the King.' "

It is in order to pass over (this fact) in silence that the *Ch'un Ch'iu* writes : " The King made an inspection at Ho-yang.[1] Worse usurpation still, Duke Wen had made, for his tomb, a subterranean passage, a royal privilege. The other leaders showed even more pride. Duke Huan of Ch'i, when he attacked Ch'u (656 B.C.) hit upon a lucky pretext, reproaching him for not having sent to the Chou the tribute of packets of couch-grass necessary for the royal sacrifices. As a matter of fact, Huan wished himself to sacrifice like a king on the chief mountain of the East, T'ai Shan. The Leader of Ch'u had the presumption to demand from the King (611 B.C.) the magic caldrons which the Chou had inherited from the Yin and the Hsia. The work of Yü the Great, the Founder of the Royal Line, these caldrons were the royal talismans, and were too heavy for those of insufficient Virtue. The Leader of Ch'in, intoxicated by a victory, intended to sacrifice a captive prince to the Sovereign on High, whom the King alone can honour with worship. Numerous human victims were to follow him to the tomb. The sages said : " Duke Mu of Ch'in has enlarged his territory and added to his estates ; . . . but he has not presided at the assembly of the nobles. That which has happened is good, because, at his death, he (causes) the sacrifice of (the best of) his people. . . . Thus one learns that Ch'in cannot govern in the East."

No king in the capital, no prince, in the large States, having a Virtue adequate to the heavenly Order, China, during the period *Ch'un Ch'iu*, could not enjoy true peace ; but in spite of violent annexations of small fiefs, in spite of wars between large States, in spite of constant hostility, opposing Chin to Ch'in and to Ch'i and above all to Ch'u, this period enjoyed an inferior kind of peace. This resulted from the custom of gatherings and treaties between the nobles. At these gatherings and at the making of these

---

[1] SMC, IV, 305, 53, 56, 351 ; *Tso chuan*, C, I, 370 ; **LV**, 94, note 1, 104, 489, 146, **221**.

treaties, Chin almost always presided, as being the country of the most celebrated Leader, whose princes bore the same family name as the Chou. The nobles aimed at securing a certain equilibrium, founded on respect for the royal rights, on the maintenance of positions already acquired, and on a certain obedience to the princes of Chin. The treaty of 562 B.C. is famous : " We all, who swear to this treaty together (*meng*), we will not gather up the harvests, we will not monopolise profits (*li*), we will not protect the guilty, we will not harbour trouble-mongers ; we will help those who are victims of calamity or of disaster, we will have compassion on those in misfortune or trouble. We will have the same friends and the same enemies. *We will help the royal house.* If anyone breaks this decree, may he be annihilated by the Protectors of Truth, the Protectors of Treaties, the ancient Mountains, the ancient Rivers, all the Gods (of mountains and of hills), all the gods of Houses (and of Towns) the deceased Kings, the deceased nobles, the Ancestors of the Seven Families and of the Twelve Overlordships — may he be annihilated by these glorious Gods ! May he be abandoned by his people ! May he lose the (heavenly) Mandate ! May his family perish ! May his overlordship be overthrown." [1]

A true peace, achieved by a wise prince, a disinterested tutor in the royal household—such is the ideal, which his biographers and tradition ascribe to Confucius (551–479 B.C.). The life of this saint ends the period *Ch'un Ch'iu.* Confucius felt himself charged with a mission. He could have accomplished it under the condition of becoming minister to a prince and inspiring his policy. He spent the greater part of his life in travelling from one overlordship to another, seeking for someone who would know how to employ his talent. He proposed to all, to " conform to the rules of the Three Dynasties and to set again in a place of honour the policy of Duke Chu," who had succeeded in consolidating the power of the dynasty of the Chou at its commencement, the Virtue of which he (Confucius) wished to restore. Confucius thought that if he found a prince " capable of making use of him, at the end of a cycle of *twelve* months some result, and at the end of *three* years *perfection*, would be achieved." The confidence of Confucius in his vocation was absolute. He was

---

[1] *Tso chuan*, **C**, II, 272.

surprised when hindrances met him. Even in his worst moments he could not make up his mind that his wisdom was insufficient. " When," he said, " one has fully achieved Wisdom, if one remains without employment, the shame is on the head of the nobles." [1] History deplores the lack of success of Confucius, but is not surprised at it. It is apparently admitted that at the opening of the fifth century B.C., confidence in the immediate efficacy of a Virtue, constituted by the observance of traditional rules, had become feeble.

II

THE TYRANTS

The fifth, fourth and third centuries B.C. are described as a period of anarchy and as a time of great moral crisis. The large States ended by absorbing the small overlordships almost entirely. The order of society ceases to be founded on tradition and on laws issued by protocol. Desire for power openly gets the upper hand over care for equilibrium ; the princes have only to do with a Virtue the prestige of which is held to be sufficient in itself. They seek, with the most varied prestige, material advantages and increase of power. They favour novelties, cease to justify themselves by precedents or by a sophistical theory of history. They are tyrants.

" The kings in ancient days had not identical customs . . . and what made the success of the Holy Men (of antiquity) is that they reigned without imitating each other. The merit that one acquires in conforming to established laws, does not suffice to raise a man above his epoch. The study which consists in taking antiquity as a model does not suffice for the regulation of modern times." " The Holy Man, if he can be effectively useful to his kingdom, will not maintain uniformity of customs. If he can thus accommodate himself to circumstances, he will not maintain uniformity of rites." Thus a prince expresses himself (307 B.C.) who wishes to adopt the style of dress and accoutrements of his Barbarian neighbours. Because he has desire for conquest and wishes " to accomplish great things, he does not consult the crowd."

[1] SMC, V, 347, 379.

" He is not concerned to be in agreement with the common herd," although he " aims at perfect Virtue." [1] The aim is always Virtue, but the idea now held concerning it fits in, we are told, with a revolutionary spirit.

At the moment when a horizon of larger ideas opened out, we are shown the increasing power of countries situated on the borders of the ancient Chinese Confederation. These countries received Barbarian influences and spread them in China. The most celebrated persons in this new period are two princes who lived at the very beginning of this epoch of barbarism. One is Ho-lu (514–496 B.C.), King of Wu (Wu-Ngan-huai is in theory a county), and the other Kou Chien (496–465 B.C.), King of Yue (Che-kiang). Both reigned over tattooed people with short hair. Sometimes they are classed as Leaders. They share with the classical Leaders the glory of having wise ministers. But their ministers are not vassals attached to their overlordship, neither are they, as their contemporary, Confucius, desired to be, counsellors permeated with traditional wisdom.

One, Wu Cheu-sü, is a fugitive, the other, Fan-Li, a mysterious man of unknown origin. Under the guise of ancient rhetoric, their advice is inspired by realist politics. Kou Chien, conqueror of Wu, who formerly having beaten him had shown him mercy, was disposed to clemency. " Once," Fan-Li told him, " Heaven made a gift to Wu of Yue. Wu did not take this gift. Now Heaven makes a gift of Wu to Yue. How can Yue oppose the will of Heaven (and not annex Wu) ? . . . When one does not take what Heaven gives, one exposes oneself to disaster." At the time of the first Leaders no one dared refuse grain to a rival suffering from famine. Kou Chien, it is told, received grain from his rival, but took advantage of this generosity as of a mad act, and profited by it to conquer him. History exalts his triumph and justifies his calculating act. In addition to borrowing grain a cunning politician knew eight ways of ruining an adversary. The first consisted in honouring the gods. All the others were of a realist and brutal nature.[2]

Kou Chien had a definite diplomacy. He had also an agrarian policy and a population policy, both ultimately

---

[1] SMC, V, 83, 93, 71, 73.
[2] LV, 79, note 1, 81 ff. ; SMC, V, 430, 432 ; *Yue tsüeh Shu*, 12.

military. In the same way, the State which made the greatest progress, from the fifth to the third century B.C., the State of Ch'in—regarded as half Barbarian during the preceding period—was the country of legislators and economists. In 361 " Duke Hiao (of Ch'in) showed himself a benefactor. He looked after orphans and lonely people ; he summoned warriors to his side ; outstanding merit was rewarded." [1] A fugitive, Wei-yang (Prince of Shang) attached himself to the fortunes of Ch'in. In 359 B.C. he caused " the laws to be modified, reformed punishments, encouraged tillage . . ., stimulated with rewards and punishments those who are ready to lose their lives in combat." In 350 B.C. a new capital was built at Hien-yang. " All the little towns and villages were gathered into great prefectures (to the number of 41) ; at the head of each was placed a prefect. . . . To make the fields (abandoning the traditional division of great squares of land into 9 equal squares), they opened up straight and cross-roads," and in 348 B.C., they replaced the tithe (which according to tradition was made up of the produce of the central squares ; the tithe of the ninth), by a system of taxes. All the traditions of the feudal régime were broken. War, ceasing to be thought of as a procedure destined to reveal and to carry out the judgment of Heaven, became an industry. It was no longer aimed at the correction of the guilty, but at the destruction of the enemy. It became slaughter. Ch'in is remarkable for having beheaded the prisoners taken and having made extermination his aim. In each battle, heads were cut off by tens of thousands. Ch'in was, says history, a country of ferocious beasts.

Formerly, it was the ideal for the noble to cultivate solely cucumbers and melons, which cannot be kept. He had to refrain from amassing grain. Now, on the contrary, the aim is to accumulate stocks and treasure. Luxury and extravagance take the place of moderation. It is the period of magnificent princes. They are endowed with all the characteristics which served to depict the kings of perdition in dying dynasties. They live surrounded with women, with musicians, with jesters, with gladiators, with sophists and with hired ruffians. Ambushes and assassinations become the heroic means of implementing policy. There is no longer any check

[1] SMC, II, 62, 64–68, 82 ff.

on cruelty or pride. Funeral ceremonies are the occasion of
horrible triumphs. Ho-lu of Wu (514–496 B.C.) buries
unheard-of riches with his daughter. Further, he sacrifices
to her, as well as dancers, a whole troop of boys and girls
of the common people. The prince, in his fury of ambition,
does not recoil from the most subversive apotheoses. Yen of
Song proclaims himself king under the name of K'ang in
318 B.C. He celebrates night-feasts and has great drinking
bouts where the " vivats " resound : " Ten thousand years !
Ten thousand years ! " He burns the tablets of his Gods of
the Soil, he beats the Earth, and finally (he was the descendant
of Wu-yi) he draws his arrows against Heaven. He wishes
thus to affirm his superiority over all the Gods.[1]

Certainly, as is proper, these orgies ended in disasters.
Anarchy grew, however, and the efforts of the Sages could
do nothing. They despaired. They had no other resource
than death. Thus is explained the fate of K'ü-yuan, prince
of the blood of Ch'u, sage and poet. King Huai (329–299 B.C.)
would not listen to his advice. K'ü-yuan had in vain called
to the aid of the Virtue, the power of poetry ; in vain, by
means of this vast allegory of his poem Li-sao,[2] he had recalled
to his master that the courtship of a holy adviser demands
as much as that of a perfect loved one. The conquest of
Virtue is the only goal for which a prince worthy of the name
should resolutely strive. K'ü-yuan, dismissed, banished,
and a wanderer, did not keep up hope like Confucius. He
ended by losing all confidence in Virtue. " What is lawful,
what is unlawful ? What should be avoided ? What should
be pursued ? This century is a slough of despond ! Nothing
is pure any longer ! . . . Informers are exalted ! And wise
men of gentle birth are without renown." Determined to
end his life, he pours out his bitterness of soul to an old
fisherman :—" This century is a slough of despond ! I alone
am pure ! . . . The entire crowd is intoxicated : I only
escape intoxication ! . . ."—" If the entire crowd is intoxicated, why not gorge oneself with food ? Why not drink to
repletion ? . . . When the waters of Ch'ang are clear, I use
them to wash my hair ! When the waters of Ch'ang are

---

[1] Li Ki, C, I, 597 ; LII, 188 ; XVII, 154 ff. ; LV, 221 ff. ; Wu Yue ch'un ch'iu,
4 ; LV, 540 ff. ; SMC, IV, 247 ; Lu She ch'un ch'iu, 23, § 4.
[2] Cf. Li sao, transl. by Hervey de St.-Denys and Legge in JRAS, 1895.

troubled I use them to wash my feet ! " [1] replied the man. Thus right and loyalty were condemned by the voice of a simple fisherman. K'ü-yuan drowned himself. Corruption was general. " The times of Wisdom and Honour seemed at an end."

[1] SMC, LXXXIV ; *Ch'u ts'ŭ*, 4.

Chapter IV

THE IMPERIAL ERA

The foundation of the Chinese Empire appears in history not as the close, but as the crowning-point of an era of anarchy and distraction. For the period which extends to the reigns in which the dynasty of the Han was solidly established, historical narratives are inspired by epic romances and embittered pamphlets which add a touch of pathos to the scanty annals.[1] They are, in what follows, made up with the aid of official documents, and aim first at relating the intrigues of the Court or, to use the words of Ssu-ma Ch'ien, " the affairs of the household." [2] Dynastic history attempts to judge the worth of the Emperors. If it sometimes admits that, under certain of them, China " enjoyed calm," it puts first evidence to prove that the sovereign Virtue was never restored in its native splendour.

I

The Ch'in

The Royal line came to an end in 256 B.C., when King Nan of the Chou dynasty died, in utter poverty, without descendants.[3] It was then that Ch'in carried off the dynastic caldrons.

In 221 B.C., China ceased to be a confederation of overlordships placed under the suzerainty of a King and became an Empire.[4] This new organization was destined to endure for long centuries. Nevertheless, the founder of the Empire is, by an almost unanimous verdict, regarded as the worst of tyrants.

In 325 B.C., the princes of Ch'in had taken the title of

---

[1] SMC, II, 225 and 231, pamphlets of Kia-Yi (198–105 B.C.). Chavannes compared, for their depth, the writings of Kia-Yi with those of Montesquieu. This judgment appears too favourable.
[2] SMC, II, 442.   [3] SMC, II, 94 and I, 316.   [4] SMC, II, 122.

King. King Huai-wen reckoned the year 325 B.C. as the beginning of an era. In that year he reformed the sacrifices instituted for the year's close ; but neither he nor his successors dreamt of changing the Chinese method of organization. They limited themselves to following up their victories and extending their fiefs. In 247 B.C., at 13 years of age, Chêng ascended the throne of Ch'in. In 221 B.C., after brilliant conquests, he could declare that China was entirely pacified, and demand of his ministers to find him a title " which was in proportion to his merits." The ministers, pronouncing that now " the laws and ordinances emanated from a single chief, and that *from remote antiquity* there had never been anything of the sort " proposed the title of " Supreme August One " (*T'ai Huang*). Chêng, the better to make clear that he possessed in himself all the Virtue characteristic of the happy age when the Three August Ones and the Five Sovereigns reigned, chose the title of " August Sovereign " (*Huang-ti*). He decided to call himself the First August Sovereign (*Shih Huang-ti*), while his successors were to be called " the second," " the third " " even unto a thousand and ten thousand generations." " By a posthumous venera- tion " he conferred an honourable name on his predecessor (just as the founders of the Chou had done). Having settled the imperial title (the expression Huang-ti is translated Emperor), Shih Huang-ti (we find it more often in history as Ch'in Shih Huang-ti—Ch'in recalling the county of origin of the First Emperor) settled the Emblem and the Number which should stand for the dynasty which he founded. He chose *six* as his " standard-number," and reigned by virtue of the element *Water*. Thus the colour of clothes and flags was fixed—black being the colour corresponding to water and to the number six. The official hats were six inches deep, as were tablets for contracts. Six feet made a step. A carriage had six horses—Water, Black, the North, corresponding to a principle of severity, the policy of the government took thence its orientation. Everything had to conform to Law and Justice, and not to Kindness and Beneficence. In this way the Government was in accord with the elementary Virtue charged with presiding over the new era. Time and the Calendar were altered.[1]

[1] SMC, II, 70, 122, 128 ff.

ATTEMPT TO ASSASSINATE CHÊNG OF CH'IN, THE FUTURE SHIH HUANG-TI

(Bas-relief from Shan-tung. Rubbing by the Chavannes Expedition)

As soon as he had established a new era, the August Sovereign visited all the regions of the Empire. He made pilgrimages to the classical Holy Places ; but the gods received badly a ruler who, governing according to principles worked out in an epoch of tyranny, claimed to establish the reign " of severity and violence." Ch'in Shih Huang-ti was subjected on T'ai-Shan " to a storm of wind and rain." When he wished to go up the mountain Siang, the divinities of the place, who were the daughters of Yao the Sovereign, made such a wind blow on him that he could hardly cross the Yang-tse-kiang. He levelled the forest of the mountain Siang and had it painted red, like a criminal, by 3000 condemned men. Only a tyrant can refuse to bow down before the manifest will of heaven. Indeed, Ch'in Shih Huang-ti had none of the Virtue of a sovereign : he was never able to recover from the river Ssu the royal caldron of the Chou which had disappeared there. Truth to tell, he had not had a miraculous birth. He was not the legitimate son of his father ; neither was he the son of Heaven. History tells us that he was born of a concubine who, when she entered the princely palace, was already pregnant by a former master. Shih Huang-ti had no piety. He forced his natural father to suicide and persecuted his mother.[1] More than this, he persecuted the lettered class.

The wise kings of antiquity, such as Yü the Great, whose body was the standard measure of length, achieved the unity of China by a peaceful propagation of their Virtue. Ch'in Shih Huang-ti achieved it by brute force. It is true that he opened his reign by a banquet of rejoicing and collected all arms to melt them down ; but he did not distribute jewels and conquered territories, and if he introduced uniformity into the laws and regulations, measures of weight and length, the dimensions of axles and the written characters of the alphabet, it was " by monopolizing the whole Empire and avoiding dividing it up into fiefs." Autocrat and revolutionary, he despised the tradition of Kings Wen and Wu. All the traditionalist party criticized his innovations. How could order be maintained without the granting of estates for life ? In 221 B.C., depending on his counsellor Li Ssu (a refugee), Ch'in Shih Huang-ti kept to his decisions. The opposition persisted and a " mandarin of vast knowledge " came, in

[1] SMC, II, 140, 154, 100, 116 ; XII, 89.

213 B.C. to renew the remonstrances fortified by precedents :
" Your subject has heard it said that the reigns of the Yin
and the Chou lasted more than a thousand years. (It is
because the sovereigns of these dynasties) gave fiefs to their
sons, to their younger brothers, to their distinguished subjects,
in order to gain support. Now Your Majesty possesses all
that is within the seas, whilst his sons and his younger brothers
are private individuals. . . . For a person, in any matter,
not to model himself on antiquity, and yet to achieve duration,
—that to my knowledge has never happened." Li Ssu argued
on the contrary : " The Five Sovereigns did not repeat each
other's actions, the Three Royal Dynasties did not imitate
each other . . . for the times had changed. Now, Your
Majesty has for the first time accomplished a great work and
has founded a glory which will last for ten thousand generations. The stupid mandarins are incapable of understanding
this. . . . In ancient days China was divided up and troubled ;
there was no one who could unify her. That is why all the
nobles flourished. In their discourses the mandarins all talk
of the ancient days, in order to blacken the present. . . .
They encourage the people to forge calumnies. This being so,
if they are not opposed, among the upper classes the position
of the sovereign will be depreciated, while among the lower
classes *associations* will flourish. . . . I suggest that the
official histories, with the exception of the Memoirs of Ch'in,
be all burnt . . . and that those who attempt to hide the
She-king, Shu-king, and the *Discourses of the Hundred Schools*
be forced to bring them to the authorities to be burnt."
Ch'in Shih Huang-ti dared to approve the request of Li Ssu.
He decided that those resisting it should be put to death with
their relations. Traditionalist opposition persisted. After an
inquiry " in which the mandarins incriminated each other,"
the Emperor had 460 executed by way of example.[1] This took
place in 212 B.C.

In 211 B.C. there was found on a meteorite this inscription :
" On the death of Shih Huang-ti the Empire will be divided."
A spirit of the waters came to give back to the Emperor the
ring of jade which he had formerly flung into the Yang-tse-
kiang to propitiate the river. Ch'in Shih Huang-ti learnt thus
that he would die within the year. He only pursued more

[1] SMC, II, 131 ff., 171 ff., 181.

harshly the search for strange spells, by means of which, in the absence of the support of the traditional gods, he sought for power. After his accession he had built a sumptuous residence at Hien-yang, in which the palaces of all the suppressed overlordships were rebuilt. There had been crowded the women from the captured harems, the bells and drums of the conquered princes. He transported into his town, to the number of 120,000 families, the richest and most powerful people of the Empire. In his palace of Shang-lin, he made a hanging road, in imitation of that which, above the Milky Way, unites the constellations *T‘ien-ki* (the ridge of Heaven, residence of *T‘ai-yi*, the Supreme Unity) and *Ying-che* (which is the heavenly Temple of Purifications). His 260 [1] palaces were joined by secret passages. The Emperor could move unseen from one to the other. It was necessary that no one should know where he was to be found, in order that the Immortals with whom he wished to communicate might be discoverable. The Immortals only appear on condition of avoiding the Evil Spirits : " If the place inhabited by the Master of men is known to his subjects, the gods are vexed." The Emperor had called together from all parts a great multitude of magicians to seek for the drug that gives Immortality. He wished to become a *True Man*, able " to enter the water without getting wet, to enter the fire without being burnt, to *mount on the clouds and mists*, eternal like Heaven and Earth." He called himself the *True Man*. In 219 B.C. he had sent several thousands of youths and maidens to seek the isles where the Immortals dwell. In 211 B.C. he himself went to the sea-shore. A great *kiao* fish had prevented his emissaries from reaching the Happy Isles. It was necessary to kill it with bow and arrow. No one had had this power. Now Ch‘in Shih Huang-ti dreamed that he was fighting a shark with a man's head ; so he took a bow and awaited the appearance of the great fish. From the heights of the Holy Place of *Che-fu*, where sacrifices were offered to the Masters of Yang and of the Sun, he at last saw a great fish. He drew his bow, and a fish was killed. But then the Emperor fell ill, and died almost immediately. (211 B.C.)

His body had to be brought very secretly into the capital

---

[1] Or rather, 360 : as many as there are days ; see below, p. 392 ; SMC, II, 175. Cf. III, 341 and 355.

and " to mislead people with regard to the smell " the carriages in the procession had to be loaded with a quantity of salt fish.[1] The funeral rites of the Emperor were an apotheosis. Lighted up by inextinguishable torches, made with the fat of the " man-fish " (jen-yu), whilst below, machines caused to flow continually into the sea mercury representing the Blue River and the Yellow River, and above were represented all the signs of Heaven, the tomb, furnished with all the astronomic and geographical mechanisms, had been so deeply dug by 700,000 condemned men, who had been subjected to the penalty of castration, that it went down to the subterranean springs. When the body was placed in it, all the workmen who had set up the machines and hidden the treasures were shut up with it. Further, all the Emperor's wives who had not had children followed him to death.[2] Thus was surpassed the cruelty of Ho-lu, and that of Duke Mu, the ancestor of Shih Huang-ti, of whom it had been said that " Ch'in could no longer govern in the East."

The dynasty of the Ch'in was destroyed (207 B.C.) almost immediately after the death of its founder. In 211, passing over a son of Ch'in Shih Huang-ti, whom they suspected of favouring tradition, the Minister Li Ssu and the eunuch Chao Kao had placed on the throne another of his sons, Hu-hai, known under the name of Êrh-shih (Huang-ti : the Second Emperor). Like his father, Êrh-shih supervised the Empire and lived unseen, " so that no one heard the sound of his voice." He also, multiplying taxes and executions, reigned without being beneficent. The Empire revolted. Thanks to the intrigues of Chao Kao, Li Ssu was executed (208 B.C.), then Êrh-shih was killed, and his nephew Cheu-ying was called to reign. Cheu-ying killed the shameless monster Chao Kao (207 B.C.), but he was obliged almost immediately to give himself up to rebels in the guise of the conquered nobles.[3]

Here is the verdict of history on this period : " Ch'in Shih Huang-ti, brandishing his great horse-whip, governed the World. . . . He destroyed the nobles . . . and imposed his law on the six directions of Space. He handled the whip

---

[1] SMC, II, 126, 152, 177, 180, 190.
[2] SMC, II, 193 ff. ; LXII, vol. II, 400.
[3] SMC, II, 197 and 206, 217 and 224 ; LV, 142, note 3.

PLATE IV

TOMB OF SHIH HUANG-TI

(Photo by Commandant Lartigue)

[face p. 40

and the rod to beat the Empire. His prestige made the Four Seas tremble. . . . In the South . . . the Princes of the Hundred Yue, with bowed heads, handed over their destiny to subaltern officers. . . . In the North, the Hu dared no longer come down to the South to pasture their horses. . . . (But) Ch'in neglected to follow the example of conduct set by the ancient kings ; he burnt the teachings of the Hundred Schools in order to make the people stupid . . . he killed the eminent men . . . (if he melted down the arms of the whole Empire, it was in order to make of them) *Twelve* Men of metal that he might weaken the power of the people. . . . He cherished greedy and base sentiments. . . . He made the foundations of the Empire rest on tyranny. . . . (If he had) administered the realm according to the principles of ancient generations . . . even though one of his successors might have been dissolute and arrogant, Calamity would not have resulted." They scarcely deign to recall the conquests of Ch'in Shih Huang-ti who enlarged the Empire on all its frontiers, and who, even after his death, " remained formidable to foreign peoples." " A man with a very prominent nose, with large eyes, with the chest of a bird of prey, with the voice of a jackal, without beneficence, and with the heart of a tiger or of a wolf . . . (ready to) devour men." [1] In this satirical couplet made up from proverbial sources, is to be found the only portrait which the Chinese have given us of the founder of their national unity.

II

THE HAN

To the tyranny which came to crown the feudal anarchy there succeeded an anarchy equally disastrous. Revolt began in the country of Ch'u (the most redoubtable of the ancient rivals of Ch'in). Its chief was first a man " born in a house where the window was made of the neck of a broken pitcher and where a cord served as a hinge on the door." [2] Rebellion soon spread all over China, and from 208 B.C. the greater number of the feudal States were reconstituted. After the

---

[1] SMC, II, 224 (Extract from *Kia Yi*), 114 ; **LV**, 373.
[2] SMC, II, 219 and 230.

Ch'in were banished their conquerors made a great partition of the Empire.[1] But soon rivalry broke out between the two most powerful chiefs : Hiang Yu and Lü Pang. Hiang Yu is depicted as a bold, generous, and violent soldier. Lü Pang is, on the contrary, a prudent, artful and tenacious person. Hiang Yu won seventy victories and died in battle, after having poured out in song his generous regrets and lamentations on the fate of his wife and his favourite horse. Even in his last moments he would not recognize his faults. He cried (horrible blasphemy) : " It is Heaven which has caused my ruin." [2] Lü Pang was modest. He founded the dynasty of the *Han* (202 B.C.) and received on his death the name of Kao-Chu (Supreme Ancestor).

Kao-Chu was " good and kind ; he loved to show liberality." [3] He was at first a quite small official, despised for his lack of education and his impudence. His fortune began through his marriage with the daughter of the honourable Lu, who immediately recognized in Lü Pang a man predestined for greatness. Kao-Chu had indeed " a beautiful beard and the face of a dragon." Once his mother, on the border of a pond, " dreamed that she met a god. . . . At the same moment there were claps of thunder and flashes of lightning . . . (her husband ran up) and saw a dragon, *kiao*, hovering above his wife. It was after that that she became pregnant and gave birth to Kao-Chu." Later when Kao-Chu was sleeping, a dragon hovered above him. He killed a serpent who was the son of the White Sovereign. An old woman was then heard lamenting ; her child, she said, had been killed by the son of the Red Sovereign. Above places where Kao-Chu stayed there was always a mysterious vapour. Ch'in Shih Huang-ti, uneasy, said constantly, " From the direction of the South-East, there is an emanation from a Son of Heaven ! " But he could not manage to get hold of the rival thus heralded, Kao-Chu was marked out by Fate. It was in vain that Hiang Yu won seventy battles. Lü Pang had on his left thigh 72 black marks. (The sacrifice which commemorates the founding of a dynasty had been made by 72 sovereigns. 72, moreover, is the number characteristic of the brotherhoods.) [4]

---

[1] SMC, II, 285 ff.   [2] SMC, II, 323.
[3] SMC, II, 325.   [4] SMC, II, 325, 331 ff. ; 325 ; LV, 357.

A whole troop of faithful followers attached themselves to Kao-Chu. Eminent men became his counsellors and generals. " He knew how to make use of them, and that is why he got possession of the Empire." When he had conquered and pacified the Four Seas, he divided up at once, among those who had some merit, a territory of which he made them kings or marquises." He only accepted the title of Emperor " for the good of the State," after having declined it three times. When ill, he refused to let himself be looked after, because, he said, " Fate depends assuredly on Heaven." On his death (195 B.C.) his heritage passed peacefully to his son. But, in actual practice, the reign of Kao-Chu was completed by a long regency under his wife. She counted for much in his rise. The Empress Lu, " hard and inflexible," knew, even in her husband's lifetime, how at an opportune moment and under honourable pretexts, to bring to execution the great chiefs who held fiefs and who might have been tempted to revolt. As a widow, with all the authority of a dowager, she gave royal estates to members of her family, thus counterbalancing the excessive power given by her husband to his own relatives (187 B.C.). She chose and deposed nominal emperors. She poisoned and killed. She had inaugurated her power by a dramatic action (the story of which is given as a remarkable example of the precision and truth to be found in Chinese historians). She had the feet and hands of the *fu-jen* Ch'i, Kao-Chu's favourite concubine, cut off. " She tore out her eyes, burnt her ears, made her drink the potion which causes dumbness, and, throwing her into the latrines, called her ' the human sow.' " Several days later (as the *fu-jen* Ch'i was still alive), she showed her to the Emperor, son of Kao-Chu, who wept and declared he would no longer reign. On the death of the Empress Lu (180 B.C.) there arose a violent reaction against her family. It was a " family affair," however, and the Empire enjoyed calm.[1] Then the Emperor Wen ascended the throne and after him the Emperor Wu (civilizer and warrior), under both of whom the prestige of the Han reached its high-water mark.

The Emperor Wen (180–157 B.C.) had " as his sole preoccupation to reform the people by his Virtue : that is why the whole country in the Interior of the Seas was prosperous

[1] SMC, II, 380, 384, 400, 407, 416, 410 and Introd., p. CLXIV.

and flourishing through the execution of rites and justice."
He made his reign illustrious by numerous decrees, the clauses
of which draw inspiration at one and the same time from
ancient traditions and humanitarian cares. These decrees
were given in Council. Did the Emperor fear, perhaps, that
they might be criticized as determined by personal or dynastic
interests ? He took care to present them as imposed by his
Councillors. His was the glory of formulating the principle :
" The Heavenly Way (T'ien tao) wills that Calamity shall be
born of detestable actions and that Prosperity shall come in
the train of Virtue. For the faults of all officials the blame
should be placed on my shoulders." He abolished the office of
secret pleader (167 B.C.) and forbade the use of rites by which
the responsibility for faults was transferred to inferiors. He
also forbade the custom " of making all happiness converge
on his person." If he alone had profited by the good fortune
obtained by sacrifices, and if the people had had no share in
it, it would, in his own words, have been " an aggravation of
his lack of Virtue." He gave liberally to the Gods. He knew
how to humiliate himself. When attacked by the Hiong-nu
(162 B.C.) he confessed humbly : " It is because I am not
perfect that I am incapable of spreading my Virtue afar.
That is why, sometimes, the countries outside my territory
have not had repose, and those who live outside the Four
Desert Zones have not lived a tranquil life." He preferred
" alliances and peaceful relations " to war. When forced to
fight he ordered his soldiers " not to penetrate far into the
enemy country, for fear of harming the people." When the
King of Nan-yue gave himself the title of Warrior Emperor,
far from being annoyed, he heaped gifts on the King's brothers,
" thus replying by conferring favours. The King then
renounced the title of Emperor and declared himself his
subject." Some of the imperial officers let themselves be
corrupted. Instead of sending them before a tribunal, the
Emperor Wen sent them money from his own treasury " in
order to cover them with confusion." When the Empire
suffered from drought and locusts " he redoubled his kind-
nesses . . . lessened the expenditure on his clothes . . .
opened his granaries." He built himself only a modest
sepulchre ; he ordered that his funeral should be without
ostentation, and—far from interring his subjects in his tomb—

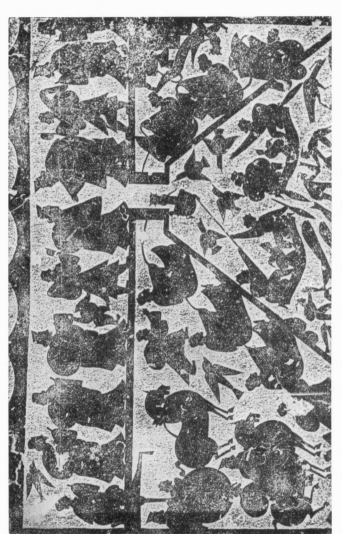

[face p. 44

SHIH HUANG-TI TRIES TO DRAW THE CAULDRON FROM THE RIVER SSŪ. A DRAGON PREVENTS HIM

(Bas-relief from Shan-tung. Rubbing by the Chavannes Expedition)

he lessened for them the severity and duration of the imperial mourning.[1]

The "Civilizing" Emperor took pains to restore in its purity, the sovereign Virtue.[2] It was to the "Warrior" Emperor (140–87 B.C.) that the honour fell of celebrating, after the fashion of the seventy-two ancient sovereigns, the sacrifice *Fong*, which is a symbol of the perfect success of a dynasty. From the first year of his reign " all classes of officials hoped that the Son of Heaven would change the first day of the year and the system of measures and would celebrate the sacrifice *Fong*." [3] [*It is known (a malevolent tradition affirmed) that Ch'in Shih Huang-ti had no better success in celebrating the sacrifice* Fong, *than he had in drawing out of the river Ssu—a dragon preventing him—the magic caldron of the Royal Dynasties.*] The Emperor Wu [*like Shih Huang-ti (the First Emperor)*], triumphed in the South-East over the people on the sea-coast, and in the West, over the people of the steppes. [*The First Emperor had made a number of journeys to inspect the Empire. Like him*] the Emperor Wu travelled (113 B.C.) and [*he also*] sent (in 113 B.C.) an expedition in search of the Happy Isles, where the Immortals dwell. A sorceress discovered (113 B.C.) —an official inquiry proved that there was no question of trickery—a caldron buried in the earth. The Emperor Wu went respectfully to see the marvellous vessel. Thereupon, in the air, in form like a dais, there appeared a *yellow light*. [*Formerly Huang-ti* (the First Sovereign) *who had passed his life in waging war and in travel (he had been in the extreme West, even as far as the Mountain K'ong-t'ong: in 113 B.C. Wu visited the Mountain K'ong-t'ong), after having celebrated at Yong the sacrifice Kiao* (the Emperor Wu in 113 B.C. celebrated at Yong the sacrifice Kiao) *found the magic stalks of the millfoil, and a caldron (or else moulded a caldron), after which he ascended to heaven on a dragon and became immortal. His apotheosis took place in a year in which the winter solstice coincided with the first day of the first month.*]

[1] SMC, II, 487, 473, 474, 482, 486, 487.
[2] Between the Emperors Wen and Wu is the Emperor King (156–141 B.C.) whose reign, a modest carrying on of the preceding one, has deserved to be related in a strictly annalistic form only.
[3] SMC, III, 461. On the Fong sacrifice see below, p. 384. The Emperor Wen in 163 B.C., changed for the first time (the calculation of the years, and made of this year) the first (cf. SMC, II, 481). On the preparation for the reform of the Calendar, see SMC, Introd., xcviii.

In 113 B.C. the winter solstice coincided with the first day of the first month. On the day of the solstice, the Emperor Wu offered, according to the rites of Yong, the sacrifice Kiao, while his assistant pronounced the formula : " *The first of the month has again become the first of the month. The series is exhausted ! It is beginning again !* " The Emperor Wu was not able to make the sacrifice Fong in 113 B.C. because the River overflowed and the harvest failed,—signs of ill-omen. He celebrated it in 110 B.C. on T'ai Shan, accompanied by a single officer. This officer died soon afterwards in a mysterious manner. The sacrifice of the Emperor Wu had been accepted. At the moment of the preparatory ceremonies there was a light during the night and by day a luminous white cloud raised itself from the middle of the hillock." In 113 B.C. at the moment of the sacrifice Kiao, performed according to the rites of Yong [*and under the same conditions as to time which had formerly favoured the sacrifice of the first Sovereign (the death of a mysterious personage is reported at the same time as the sacrifice which was performed in preparation for the apotheosis of Huang-ti, the Yellow Sovereign)*] " there was during the night a marvellous light, and when the day appeared a *yellow cloud stretched up to heaven.*" The Emperor Wu, to perform the sacrifice, had put on yellow garments. The new calendar was only proclaimed in 104 B.C. To accord with it, the dynastic colour was chosen : it was the colour yellow.[1]

The marvellous light and the yellow radiance which appeared in 113 B.C. *were seen* by Ssu-ma Tan, annalist and official astrologer.[2] Ssu-ma Tan, who conceived the idea of the *Historical Memoirs*, was father of Ssu-ma Ch'ien who edited them, and who shared in the work of recasting the Calendar. The *Historical Memoirs*, as we have seen, place at the beginning of Chinese history, Huang-ti, the Yellow Sovereign. The historian Ssu-ma Ch'ien, who lived at the moment when History and Time began afresh, fixed the methods of Chinese historical writing. All his successors imitated him. The same spirit has continually inspired the choice of facts, the processes of exposition, the system of philosophic interpretation.

We will close here our analysis of traditional history.

[1] SMC, III, 481 and 485, 490, 491, 497, 504, 515.
[2] SMC, III, 492. On Ssu-ma Tan, cf. SMC, Introd., VII ff.

With the reign of the Emperor Wu history begins again.[1]
Dynasties are founded, attain their zenith, decline, disappear.
History assigns the same causes to the same effects. " Yao
and Shun practised Virtue ; their subjects were humane and
lived to be old. The last of the Hsia and the last of the Yin
practised violence ; their subjects were barbarians and died
prematurely. . . . When the Kings wish to fulfil their rôle,
they seek from Heaven the principles of their conduct." [2]
The Prince holds his power from Heaven ; and history in
estimating the success of the sovereigns and dynasties,
apprises with exactness their right to reign. It is its task to
judge their virtue. Its judgment, founded on indisputable
principles, is perfectly objective ; judgment and exposition
are mingled, for history is at one and the same time both
moral and natural philosophy. It is engaged in noting in
successive cycles the infallible repetitions. It only knows
typical heroes and stereotyped events. At bottom it has
only to occupy itself with one personage : the sovereign, the
Unique Man, whose Virtue is typical of a particular moment
of time. History does not differ from a Calendar, illustrated
by generic pictures. Equally, it may be said, it is born of
speculations about the Calendar.

---

[1] Here let us limit ourselves to noting that, in the reign of the Emperor Ch'êng
(32–7 B.C.) the last sovereign of the first Han dynasty who possessed effective
power, history calls attention to a rain of stars, in 15 B.C., and in 12 B.C., and in
10 B.C. to the fall of Mount Ming. " All said, ' It is the end of the Han.' "

[2] **CXLV, 455.**

THE CHIEF DATA OF ANCIENT HISTORY

CH'IN SHIH HUANG-TI, who aspired to rebuild everything afresh, burnt the history books. The Han, on the other hand, gave out that they wished to renew a venerable tradition. The Emperor Wu claimed that his reign was not so much a starting-point as a recommencement. He had to prove that in him, restored to its first vigour, the sovereign Virtue was reincarnated. A work of religious restoration was accomplished. It aimed at justifying, by aid of theories of morals and natural philosophy, the establishment of a new Calendar. It was accompanied by a great effort of historical reconstruction. It was in the reign of the Emperor Wu that Ssu-ma Ch'ien, official annalist and reformer of the Calendar, constructed the first systematic history of ancient China. Thus it is from this same reign that works presented as the productions of antiquity began to be examined with some precision.

We have, by Ssu-ma Ch'ien, a grave enough avowal. He recognized that, in fact, the only seigniorial annals that were extant in his time were those of Ch'in. Furthermore he adds : "they are abridged by editing and incomplete." Ssu-ma Ch'ien declares besides, that "if the *She-king* and the *Shu-king* have reappeared it is because some copies of them have been preserved in certain houses." It serves no purpose to note that the prescription of the books in accordance with the edict of the Ch'in could only be enforced from 213 to 207 B.C., and was revoked in 191 B.C. As a matter of fact, the books did not reappear till much later.[1]

Tradition admits, for example, that a part of the *Shu-king* was recited from memory by an old man of 90 years of age, in the reign of the Emperor Wen (179–157 B.C.). Other chapters may have been rediscovered—at the earliest at the close of the second century—when the walls of a house of Confucius

[1] SMC, III, 26 and 27 ; SMC, Introd., CXI. Cf. **CX.**

were broken down. It is a curious fact that the chapters which current tradition says were dictated were, if one believes the most ancient testimony, reconstructed by the aid of a copy which also had been for a long time hidden in a wall.[1]

The ancient works were written in varnish on boards, tied together in piles. It only needed a few years for the ties to come apart and for the characters to become difficult to decipher. Added to this, at the time of the Ch'in, the system of writing had changed.[2]

Ssu-ma Ch'ien says : " The family of Confucius (coming from Lu in Shan-tung) possessed a *Shu-king* in ancient characters. K'ong Ngan-kuo (a descendant of Confucius), *interpreted* it (end of second century) in modern characters." [3]

There is small chance that, in the historical works, the recitations and interpretations were inspired solely by concern for truth.

It is known that the *Shu-king* was recited by numerous learned men of Ch'i and Lu. " Of the great masters of Shan-tung, there was not one who did not use the *Shu-king* for the instruction he gave." Now we have seen that, under the Han, no question was of more importance than that of the sacrifices of Fong. The T'ai Shan, where the Emperor Wu decided to sacrifice, was the holy mountain of Ch'i and of Lu ; it was the chief glory of the maritime province of Shan-tung. In 122 B.C. a prince of the royal house, holding Ch'i as a fief, wishing to pay court to the Emperor Wu, gave the T'ai Shan back to his direct rule. It was an old man of Ch'i, aged 90 years, who persuaded the Emperor Wu in 110 B.C. to attempt the ascent of the mountain. Some mandarins composed a memoir on the sacrifices of Fong ; numberless individuals, described as magicians, claimed to direct this enterprise. " Magicians, with strange practices, came in ever-increasing numbers, to discourse on that which concerns the gods." They were natives " of the countries of Yen and of Ch'i, on the sea-coast." Mandarins and magicians (from Shan-tung) in discussing the sacrifices of Fong, gave differing advice. All sought to gain the imperial favour. All justified their pronouncements by insisting on historical precedents.[4]

---

[1] SMC, Introd., cxv ff.   [2] SMC, V, 448, notes 2 and 3.
[3] SMC, Introd., cxvi. Cf. Pelliot, **CX**, 131 and the discussion, p. 135 ff.
[4] SMC, III, 469, 497, 499, 500, and Introd., clxxxviii ff.

The traditions, like the religious methods, which they claimed to base on truth, were diverse. They tended to give credence and prestige to the representatives of opposed schools and rival countries. They served, however, to constitute a national History the beautiful arrangement of which is impressive. Suspect from their origin, they are still more so from the fact that, in the official versions in which we find them, they succeed in forming a whole, relatively well co-ordinated.

One remark holds for China in all ages. Nowhere have archæological discoveries excited a more passionate interest than in this country, but always, between the date of a discovery and the publication of the " find " there intervenes a long space of time. Writings or objects are produced and shown to the public at the moment when they become the possession of a circle or of a syndicate. These draw from them a means of influence or of fortune. The archæologists who identify the discovered objects are also antiquarians. They provide the objects with good credentials, and it is to them that a purchaser must make application. An exhumed work becomes immediately the property of a " School " ; the same people who, as learned counsellors of State, extract from it profitable, instructive and decisive precedents, take upon themselves also, as scholars, to edit the text and formulate criticisms on it. In proportion as the editions become perfect and as the criticisms become more learned, the work becomes more perfectly in accord with ancient tradition. The antiquities which most resemble the plates of the archæological albums are not necessarily the most authentic. Historical documents can be regarded as so much the more suspect, the better they conform to the canonical traditions. They are specially suspect if it is found that they more and more confirm this tradition, thanks to the critical work of the " School " that patronizes them. The work of the Chinese critic strongly resembles touching-up. It is directed to the purification of the texts and to making sure that nothing contradicts the official version. An infinite amount of erudition has been expended, in such a way as to make all research aiming at what a European historian would call truth almost impossible.

CHAPTER I

THE AGES WITHOUT CHRONOLOGY

I

THE WORTH OF TRADITIONAL DATA

THE Annals of Lu (*Ch'un ch'iu*) begin in the year 722 B.C. Ssu-ma Ch'ien gives dates as far back as 841 B.C. (opening of the period *Kong-ho*). He goes back further than the *Ch'un ch'iu*, basing his work on the lists of reigns furnished with indications of their duration.

With the assistance of the same data, he could have gone back much further still.[1] He did not do so, judging the process to be uncertain. Other compilers were bolder and more logical.

Two chronological systems divided the favour of the historians; one, that adopted and perfected by Pan Ku, the historian of the first Han, places the accession of the Chou in 1122 B.C. According to the other, the victory of King Wu over the Yin was won in 1050 B.C. and King Ch'êng, successor of Wu, ascended the throne in 1044 B.C.

	I	II
Yao . . .	2357–2256 B.C.	2145–2043 B.C.
Regency of Shun	2285–2256	—
Shun . .	2255–2206	2042–1990
Regency of Yü .	2223–2206	—
Hsia Dynasty .	2205–1767	1989–1558
	17 kings = 439 years.	17 kings = 432 years. [or (*Annals*), 471 years.]
Yin Dynasty .	1766–1123 B.C.	1557–1050 B.C.
	28 kings = 644 years.	30 kings = 50 years. [or (*Annals*), 496 years.]

[1] SMC, Introd., CLVI.

	I	II
	I	II
Accession of the		
Chou . .	1122 B.C.	1049 B.C.
King Wu . .	1122–1116	1049–1045
King Ch'êng .	1115–1079	1044–1008
. . . . .		
King Li . .	878–842	853–842
Kong-ho Epoch .	841–828	841–828
King Süan .	827–782	827–782
. . . . .		
Confucius . .	551–479	551–479

1044 is also the date at which, starting from the data furnished by Ssu-ma Ch'ien on the reigns and their duration, the accession of King Ch'êng must be fixed. The chronology of Ssu-ma Ch'ien then agrees with that of the second system. 1044 is, too, the date indicated for the accession of King Ch'êng in the " Annals written on Bamboo." Neither Pan Ku nor Ssu-ma Ch'ien were able to use the " Annals written on Bamboo." They have only been known since the year A.D. 281. They were then discovered in a tomb closed since 299 B.C. The story of their discovery appears authentic.[1]

The agreement between Ssu-ma Ch'ien and the Annals seems to lend some authority to the chronological tradition which is common to them both. In fact, it simply proves that in the second century B.C. a chronological system in vogue in the fourth century still retained some credit. But this system is no less artificial than that which Pan Ku advocated. Indeed Mencius (372–289 B.C.) who employed himself in the fourth century in propagating the glory of Confucius, and whose work served to fix much of the historical tradition, vigorously fathered the belief that a Sage must appear every 500 years ; it is at 500 years' interval that Ssu-ma Ch'ien and the Annals make Confucius and the Duke of Chou, the wise tutor of King Ch'êng, live. Chou-kong and Confucius are the great heroes of the country of Lu (in which Mencius was born), and while one helped powerfully to found the Chou dynasty, the other had proved deserving of the ability to rejuvenate the dynastic Virtue. The Annals (edited in the fourth century) fixed at about 500 years the

[1] SMC, V, app. I.

duration of the dynasties of the Hsia and Yin (471 and 496 years). According to an ancient theory the span of life of a Sage is 100 years ; it is at 50 years of age that the sage is in full possession of his powers. Just as the historians employed much ingenuity in showing that Shun became vice-sovereign and Confucius vice-minister at 50,—so, 500 being a grand total, they wished to make that number play a part in the life of the world analogous to that which they attributed to the number 50 in the life of a man.[1] The chronological traditions from which the *Annals* draw inspiration, were then, from their basic principles, tainted with theoretic prepossessions.

Further, these traditions, since the discovery of the *Annals*, have been worked over more extensively than we can fully appreciate.[2] What we do know is sufficiently serious. When the tomb in which the *Annals* were buried was opened, after almost 600 years, a part of the strips of wood on which they were written served as torches. The remaining bundles were first " scattered at random." The characters which could be read on them were " in a writing long fallen into disuse." The strips, once more gathered together, remained for a long time " in the secret archives." We possess an inventory of them. It shows the *progress* achieved by the successive editions. This inventory teaches us that the *Annals* opened with the Hsia dynasty and attributed to the Hsia a longer duration than to the Yin. The text, as deciphered and put in order by scholars, makes the Yin dynasty, on the contrary, longer than the Hsia, and begins with the reign of Huang-ti. The *Annals*, said the first who saw them, claimed that K'i, son of Yü the Great, had killed Yi, the minister and successor designated by his father, in order to seize the throne from him. This declaration was contrary to the canonical tradition according to which K'i is a saint, and which makes Yi die in an honourable way. The *Annals*, revised edition, state that Yi died a natural death and that the sacrifices to him were offered by K'i. The dates in the *Annals* in their first form were, from 771 B.C., in accordance with the Calendar of the Hsia. The *Annals* are in fact, from 771 B.C., concerned with the overlordship of

---

[1] **LV**, 289 and 600.   [2] SMC, V, 457 ff.

Chin (then in the kingdom of Wei, one of the States formed from Chin by dismemberment). Numerous facts show that the princes of Chin (whom the official history presents to us as being related to the Chou) sought to connect themselves with the Hsia. But—ritual tradition demands it—the Calendar of the son of Heaven was, from the time of the Chou, a law uniformly spread in all that which *ought* to form the Chinese Empire. The *Annals* have in consequence been corrected : the dates in the altered edition are given according to the Calendar of the Chou. In the whole work, a notation of the years figures, in which the sexagenarian cycle is used. This cycle, which Ssu-ma Ch'ien does not use, was apparently not employed two centuries before him and it can be proved by it that the " perfecting " introduced into the *Annals* dates from the seventh century A.D. An eclipse of the sun is mentioned in one of the chapters of the *Shu-king* which counts among the most suspect, and the wording of which is probably much later than the date of the burial of the *Annals*. Now in the *Annals* the eclipse appears again, and very accurately dated (Autumn 2155) ; according to the calculations of Western scholars there was, in fact, an eclipse on 12th October 2155 B.C.). Indeed, the story in which the eclipse is mentioned is, in the *Shu-king*, as in the *Annals*, of a mythical order. The exact date inserted in the *Annals* can only come from a later editing. Only scholars capable of calculating eclipses could have edited the text correctly. Their intervention cannot be much before the T'ang dynasty (seventh century A.D.).

It is evident that the text of the *Annals* has only become correct thanks to the labour of centuries, with the most perfect sincerity. These labours were inspired by the idea that canonical tradition cannot err. On the other hand, errors may slip into the manuscripts in the course of their transmission. To rectify these adventitious errors by using the latest teachings of science is to re-establish the text in its first purity.

The works which the Chinese have preserved have been preserved with an admirable religious piety. . . . Little hope is to be placed in the help which the astronomers might bring to disentangle Chinese chronology.[1] We must resign ourselves,

---

[1] See in JPOS, II, the attempt of Mr S. M. Russel to confirm one of the Chinese chronological systems with the assistance of astronomical data.

as Ssu-ma Ch'ien had already done, to leaving without dates all the periods anterior to the year 841 B.C.

Is it possible to rely at any rate upon the list of reigns ? It seems difficult to place confidence in them. From Yü the Great to King Wu of the Chou, if the sovereigns of the Hsia and Yin dynasties are added there are forty-five reigns ; seventeen generations fill the same period, if we count the princely predecessors of King Wu. In the list of the ancestors of the Ch'in, six generations correspond to the seventeen reigns of the Hsia and ten generations to the forty-five reigns of the Yin and the Hsia. One of the ancestors of the Ch'in is sometimes given as a contemporary of the last of the Hsia, sometimes as a favourite of the last King of the Yin. Moreover, the reign of the last of the Hsia seems copied from that of the last of the Yin. Truth to tell, both are composed with the aid of transposed mythical subjects, and the Yin annals are not less void of facts than those of the Hsia. The few facts which fill up the annals of the last of the Yin are borrowed from the history of the ancestors of the Chou. It is only with the first Chou sovereigns that we get a well-embellished narrative. Is not this because the Chou dynasty is the only one of the three royal dynasties which possesses some historical reality ? As a matter of fact, the history of the first Chou offers scarcely any guarantees. On analysis it is clear that it is made up, not by making use of documents from the archives, but by using the fragments of a poetic tradition. King Wen and his ancestors, like their descendant King Mu, are heroes sung by the poets.[1] If the narrative of the great victory of King Wu over the Yin seems at all exact, it is because it reproduces the scenario of the triumphal dances which, from year to year, commemorated at the Court of the Chou the first glory of their house. (Yet it appears that these scenarios are known, not by the tradition in use at this court, but by that followed, *according to the mandarins of Shan-tung*, by the princes of Lu (Shantung).)[2] The history of the founders of the dynasty emerges from the drama, the epic poem or the romance. That of their earliest successors has drawn its material from discourses which are only the exercises of a " School." It is declared that these discourses were actually pronounced, and the date and the

[1] SMC, I, 215   [2] LV, 113 ff. ; XCIII, 433.

name of the orators are given.   This is intended to prove, above all, that they can be taken boldly as models.   Actually, they contain nothing more than the great themes of an immemorial rhetoric.   The reader never feels that he is in the presence of historical facts, but of an artificially constructed history.   It has been made up with the assistance of literary productions, which, for the most part, are of quite a late epoch, and are all tainted with political or dogmatic pre-possessions.   The whole history of ancient China rests on a system of forgeries, at once ingenuous and scholarly.   For the moment, we have at our disposal no process of sifting out the true from the false, and it may seem as if, thrown back on its own resources, philological criticism might end in negative results.   Does this mean that Chinese tradition has no solid foundation ?   I do not believe it.

It is certainly inexact, even if we are concerned above all to rebut those who have " been so mistaken concerning the antiquity of China " as to write that " civilization is not very ancient in the Far East." [1]   It would be more correct to say : " The Chinese only began to take interest in the facts themselves rather late." [2]   We must add further that the historical sense, and what we call the love of truth, have never acquired among them enough strength to dominate the traditionalist spirit.   But this in itself implies that their traditions deserve *a certain kind* of credence.

They have come down to us in a systematic form.   It is impossible to believe today that the Chinese historians " have not altered the original texts " ;   and it must be admitted that in the system which they have built up there is a large amount of theory.[3]   If, however, in their details, the traditional data have been corrected, the aim was to defend tradition.   Tradition was the basic principle of the political and the religious life.   It was an article of faith.   There is reason for the assumption that it was respected in its entirety.   *On the whole*, we may even believe that by reason of the importance attributed to it, it was known with sufficient exactness.

---

[1] Maspero (in the *Bulletin de l'Association française des Amis de l'Orient*, June 1922, p. 69).   Cf. Pelliot in TP, 1922, p. 441.   At the beginning of his book on *Chine antique*, M. Maspero uses the formula (to my mind more correct) : " The history of Ancient China does not go back very far."

[2] SMC, Introd., cxlvi.

[3] SMC, Introd., cxvi and ccxiv.   Cf. **LV**, 28 ff., 31 ff., 406 ff.

The Chinese, in carrying back their history to the third millenary before our era, lay claim perhaps only to a very moderate antiquity. Their language, however far we trace it, appears like a tongue that has been long in use. It possibly has a long history behind it. It has recently become known that a neolithic civilization existed in China. Perhaps there was continuity between this and the real Chinese civilization. Now not only, as will be seen, do the narratives relating to the Three Dynasties contain features of manners and customs which the historians of the time of the Han or of Confucius could neither understand nor invent, but analogous, nay, even archaic, features are to be found in the history of the Five Sovereigns.[1] Chinese traditions, then, preserve the memory of social transformations which were not carried out in a few years. It can certainly be demonstrated that the stories of Yü the Great are made up of purely mythical elements. That does not by any means prove that Yü is not a historical personage. There is not a detail relating to the Three Dynasties which can be accepted as a historical fact ; but on the other hand, there is no reason to deny the reality of these Dynasties.

A recent discovery has seemed to prove the historical reality of the Yin dynasty.[2] There were exhumed, in 1899, in a little village of Ho-nan, a considerable number of remains of bones mixed with tortoise-shell. The bones bore signs of archaic writing which excited the curiosity of the Chinese epigraphists. The first publication on these documents appeared in 1902 (three years after the discovery) signed by two scholars (*of whom one was to become possessor in 1915 of the first collection of the exhumed bones*). A fairly large number of the reputed bones of Ho-nan are today objects of commerce, and many are said to be fakes. These fakes, however, can, it appears, be detected, and it would perhaps be an abuse of scepticism to refuse to trust in such labours as the learned M. Lo Chen-yu has consecrated to the bones, which he has, no doubt, good reason to declare authentic. He has succeeded

[1] **LV**, 45 ff
[2] **XX**. M. Maspero, who pronounced on the conclusions of the learned Chinese on the bones of Ho-nan, draws from them a knowledge of the Yin dynasty precise enough, as he believes, to permit himself to write, for example : "The sacrifices of the Yin were far more numerous and more varied than those of the Chou." (**XCIII**, 39, note 1.)

in deciphering on them (*amongst other names*), the names of most of the Yin sovereigns, almost as they figure in Ssu-ma Ch'ien and the *Annals written on Bamboo*. The bones were discovered at Ho-nan in a place which *might* have been inhabited, from the third to the fifteenth year of his reign, by King Wu-yi of the Yin dynasty. Chinese scholars consider that the discovered bones were probably buried in the reign of Wu-yi, after divinations, in which the sovereign had consulted his ancestors. This hypothesis has the advantage of identifying the position of the temporary capital of Wu-yi,— a position till then unknown. Indeed, the descendants of the Yin, princes of Song, also reigned in Ho-nan (but, according to tradition, further south), and we might attribute to them or to the princes of Wei the divinations (if divinations they were) to which we owe the bones of Ho-nan. The characters graven on the bones *appear*, it is true, too archaic not to date from an epoch more or less contemporary with the first Chou (unless, in certain cases, as for example, in divinations, it was usual, in all periods, to employ a writing of a particular type, archaic or obsolescent).

In the end we are forced to admit, that the list of the Yin kings, almost exactly as we find it in Ssu-ma Ch'ien and the *Annals written on Bamboo*, conforms to a tradition going back several centuries before the date when the *Annals* and the *Historical Memoirs* were composed. Thus, if the discovery of the bones of Ho-nan does not prove the reality of the Yin dynasty, it *seems* at least to attest the relatively ancient value of the historical traditions regarding the lists of reigns.

It would show little prudence to reject *en bloc* the historical Chinese traditions. But philological criticism by itself has no means of deriving from them a positive history. It must wait for all that other kinds of investigation can contribute. The only thing that, for the moment, it can do, is not to furnish hypotheses in advance of the sciences from which real progress in knowledge can come.

II

CONTRIBUTIONS OF THE AUXILIARY SCIENCES

These sciences, for their part, are not yet in a condition to furnish hypotheses of use to history. The observations anthropology has so far collected in relation to China lack breadth and exactness.

The discoveries of M. Andersson lead to the belief that the neolithic inhabitants of Ho-nan belonged to the same race as the Chinese occupying the same province today.[1] Prehistoric anthropology is only at the stage of its first discoveries. The precise study of the actual types is exactly sketched out. The specialists believe in their diversity and suspect numerous racial crossings. " The Chinese people is descended from a multiple mixture, and there are certainly many types to discover in the Chinese native, which anthropological study has hardly outlined." [2] Basing itself on a very few measurements and on general impressions, the tendency is to distinguish two principal types : Southern and Northern. The Southern Chinese are smaller in build and more clearly brachycephalic.

The poverty of somatological information in no way hinders the advancement of a theory concerning the peopling of China. It is commonly admitted that China of the South and West gathered into its mountains the descendants of the first occupants of the soil, progressively *driven back* by those who are called the ancient Chinese, and usually described as invaders.[3]

This theory is dependent on a general conception of the history of Asia. It is derived largely from theses maintained by Terrien de Lacouperie on the western origin of Chinese civilization.[4] These theses do not rest on any fact of an anthropological nature, but simply on the establishment of Sino-Elamitic parallels, of which the following is an example : Huang-ti is no other than Nakhunte, for Huang-ti is some-

---

[1] I, II, and X.

[2] This cautious indication of Deniker (*Les races et les peuples de la terre*) is taken up and developed by Pittard (*Les races et l'histoire*, p. 487 ff.). China " is not peopled by a ' Chinese race ' in the zoological sense of that word."

[3] Chavannes half accepted this theory (SMC, I, 230, note 1, and II, 61, note 2).

[4] CXXIII.

times described as " lord of *Hiong (You-hiong)* " and his
name can be restored under the form *Nai*-huang-ti
(= Nakhunte)—the character usually read as *hiong* being in
certain cases pronounced " *nai*." Those working out the
parallel, however, omitted to notice : 1, that the purely
fictitious expression Hiong-Huang-ti is not to be found in
any text ; 2, that the character which must then be read as
" nai," is always read as " hiong " by the Chinese, in connexion
with Huang-ti ; 3, that " hiong," " nai," " huang " are
modern pronunciations, far enough removed from the pronunciations most anciently attested.   No sinologist accepts
today the Sino-Elamitic parallels of Terrien de Lacouperie.[1]
Finally, these linguistic parallels would prove nothing as to
the race of the invaders of China.

The theory of the western origin of the ancient Chinese,
however, still holds the field.   At the very outside, it is
limited to making the Chinese come from Turkestan, and to
giving, as the primary cause of their invasion (hypothetical),
a fact (relatively hypothetical), namely :   the progressive
drying-up of central Asia.   The only basis which can be found
for these theories in historical Chinese tradition is the
following :   a note in the *Historical Memoirs* affirms that the
founders of the dynasties of Hsia, Yin, Chou and Ch'in came
from the West.[2]   The historians gratuitously draw the conclusion that " Ancient China was invaded at different times
by barbarians from the West and South-West, and that these
conquests were the occasions of changes of dynasty." [3]   It
will suffice to note that the passage in question from the
Historical Memoirs follows, by way of illustration, the statement of an astrological, mythological principle :   " the East
(the Rising Sun = Spring) is the direction in which creatures
begin and are born ; the West is the direction in which they
end and come to maturity.   (The Setting Sun = Autumn.) " [4]

Prehistoric archæology, which in China is in its earliest
stages, will benefit as much as anthropology and ethnography
by mistrusting imaginative hypotheses.

M. J. G. Andersson [5] published in 1923 and 1924 the

---

[1] On this point see a decisive note of Chavannes, SMC, I, 93, note 3.
[2] SMC, III, 26.   Richthofen (**CXVI,** vol. I, chap. VIII) revived the theory of
the western origin, basing it on analysis of the *Yu kong*.
[3] Note by Chavannes on the passage quoted.
[4] SMC, III, 25.   [5] **I** and **II.**

results from fine fields of excavation in Southern Manchuria, and also in Ho-nan and Kan-su. His findings bear witness to the existence of a neolithic civilization in China. Almost simultaneously, the excavations of Fathers Licent and Teilhard de Chardin, in the upper reaches of the Yellow River, revealed palæolithic beds, in the neighbourhood of classical China.

An ancient native opinion [1] attributed stone tools to man in the period before Huang-ti (? twenty-seventh century B.C.). The age of jade (? jadites) is reputed to have begun with Huang-ti, and with Yü the Great (? 2205–2198) that of bronze. The appearance of iron would date from the Chou (eleventh-eighth century B.C.). Before the recent discoveries, the Chinese theory could be considered as a simple guess. M. Laufer wrote, in 1912, that nothing proved that there had ever been a Stone Age [2] in China.

M. Andersson provided the required proof. He even seems to have demonstrated that there was continuity between the technique of the exhumed neolithic civilization and that of the present civilization. For example, the iron knives used today for the sorghum crop in North China, preserve exactly the shapes of the ancient stone knives, rectangular or curved and pierced with one or two holes, which were found in a neolithic deposit in the neighbourhood of Mukden. M. Andersson points out a resemblance between these stone knives and the iron knives in use among the Chukchee of north-eastern Asia and the Eskimo of North America. But he insists rather on certain differences which he observes between the tools in the deposits of Manchuria and those of Kan-su. He has found everywhere different types of axes of which some recall the bronze axes of the Chou; stone rings which seem to him comparable to the jade rings of the Chou, various kinds of tripods in clay, either of the type of the *li* tripods which under the Chou were made of clay or of bronze; or of the type of the ancient *ting* tripods, which are still made in clay in the region of Pekin, and—as well as numerous objects of coarse pottery of a grey colour—a fine pottery, the red colour of which seems due to oxidization in the firing. The pieces of red pottery are perfectly polished and have designs in black or, less frequently, in white.

---

[1] *Yue tsueh shu*, II.   [2] **LXXXVIII**, 54.

M. Andersson compares this pottery with that which characterizes Western Asia (Anau). Now, whilst the *li* and *ting* tripods exist in great numbers in the Ho-nan sites and are well represented in Manchuria, they are scarcely found in the sites of Kan-su.

On the other hand, fine painted clay pottery is only abundant in Kan-su and only there have there been discovered, as well as some objects in copper, pieces of pottery remarkable for the conventional bird designs, wholly analogous, it is said, to those of certain pieces of the pottery of Susa. M. Andersson deduces from these observations that the origin of Chinese civilization should be sought in the interior of Asia and probably in Turkestan. Waves of emigrants, he holds, transported this civilization into China proper, reaching first Kan-su.

But, as M. Karlgren judiciously remarks, the most archaic being, according to the explorer, those of Ho-nan and of Manchuria, we must suppose that the last waves did not spread as far as the first. So M. Karlgren offers another explanation : the sites of Ho-nan and of Manchuria probably bear witness to a neolithic civilization, indigenous and proto-Chinese. This civilization would, in the West, have been influenced by the technical skill peculiar to a population not of Chinese, but, no doubt, of Turkish race.[1]

As long as the human remains, which would enable us to define the somatological characteristics of populations at present known by some details of their technique, have not been carefully studied, it seems wise to refrain from all hypothesis, and not to transform a problem of technological into a problem of ethnographic history, and above all, not to intervene at too early a stage, with the question of migrations and conquests, in a problem of history proper.

The first problem is to date this Stone-Age civilization. M. Andersson admits that bronze appeared in China in the third millenary before our era. This opinion is not improbable, and it agrees, in general, with Chinese tradition, which makes the Bronze Age date from Yü the Great (? 2205–2198), or which represents Yü and Huang-ti (? twenty-seventh century) as great metal-workers. Are the neolithic sites prior to the

---

[1] Karlgren, Review of the publications of Andersson, in *Litteris*, Dec. 1924.

PLATE VI

NEOLITHIC POTTERY
(Excavations by M. Andersson)

third millenary B.C. ? We may at this stage put a damaging question. It is, in fact, possible to maintain that the objects exhumed in the Ho-nan excavations (even when no trace of copper or bronze has been found) are not necessarily prior to the Bronze Age. Some archæologists insist on the fact that, at the time of the Chou, during the period *Ch'un Ch'iu*, Barbarian tribes lived in proximity to Chinese settlements. May it not be to these Barbarians that we should attribute the neolithic technique which the excavations have revealed ? [1] M. Andersson considers it improbable that the Barbarians imitated, in clay and in stone, instruments which the Chinese beside them made in bronze. A fact of this kind is perhaps not without precedent ; but an argument which may be said to be decisive is brought forward. The earth tripods of the *li* and *ting* types are taller and slimmer than the bronze tripods of comparable form, attributed by the Chinese archæologists to the epoch of the Chou. Now the characters representing the two kinds of tripod appear to the etymologists to represent more slender forms than the form of the Chou bronzes. These characters are borrowed from the Ho-nan bones, and it is not doubted that these bones date from the time of the Yin. The culture represented by these *li* and *ting* tripods must therefore go back at least to the time of the Yin.

There is no advantage in taking sides in the discussion. The solution can only come from numerous and well-conducted excavations which would permit of a methodical classification of the prehistoric sites and tools. The thing to aim at is the extension of the sites discovered in Ho-nan, Kan-su and Manchuria. There is reason to believe that the neolithic civilization to which they bear witness, corresponded all over North China to important groupings of population. There is also a possibility that they were of long duration. For the moment decisive landmarks to guide us are lacking. It will, no doubt, be difficult to find accurate ones. It is known that Asia did not experience the alternative advance and retreat of ice which serves to fix the age of the European neolithic sites. We are thus driven back to pure hypotheses.

---

[1] Andersson (**I**, 30 ff.) has grouped together a certain number of observations forming a presumption against this theory, of which the principal protagonist is the Japanese archæologist, Torii.

E

We will simply note that it is important not to confuse the problems arising from prehistoric archæology with those arising from epigraphy. We will note further: (1) That the bones of Ho-nan, if they date from the time of the Yin, date at the very outside from the end of the dynasty; (2) That there is a large subjective element in the comparison of a character with the object it represents; (3) That the chronological classifications of characters offer no more guarantee than the classifications of the objects on which they are discovered; these classifications are only founded on the impressions of collectors. Further, if the theory, according to which the characters were at first exact ideograms faithfully figuring the objects symbolized, is generally admitted, no one has ever thought of justifying it by proof.

Imagination has always had the freest play in the domain of graphic etymology. The proposals of Chinese scholars (and these are by far the most serious) are derived, in large part, from their beliefs and their archæological theories.

Before attempting to identify and date the prehistoric objects by the aid of alphabetic signs, it would be best to await the compilation of a positive history of Chinese writing.[1] But there is a great temptation to discover a whole unknown civilization without coming out of one's study, by an easy juggling with graphic analysis. P. Wieger has recently succumbed to this temptation. In 1903, he succeeded in defining, with the assistance of the " ancient characters," all the material and moral life of the " first real periods " of China. Thus we learn that " The law was hard, punishments atrocious; " that " the decimal method of numeration was used from the beginning; " and that the Chinese had then as an ideal, " sincerity, some degree of gentleness, mutual co-operation, respect for the old." Finally, having recognized that many of the animals and vegetables depicted belonged to tropical fauna and flora, P. Wieger put forward the idea that the Chinese did not, as had been believed, arrive from the West, scaling the Pamirs on their way, but that, " coming from what is today Burma, they came into China by the South-West, following the route of which the modern stages are, Bhamo, Momein . . . Ta-li-fu, Yunnan-fu . . . and Lake

---

[1] **CXLVI, LXXXVII, LXXXVIII.** See some good critical observations in **CXXV,** 69, and **CVI,** 63 ff.

Tong-t'ing ; " and that they pushed back towards the north the Yi, " a race of archers, armed with flint implements." [1] But in 1917, P. Wieger interpreted the political and religious history of China by means of a secular conflict between the Chinese and the aborigines of the South. He courageously abandoned his first theory, no longer recognizing anything tropical in the fauna and flora of the written characters.[2] Few studies would throw as much light on the history of the " early times " of Chinese civilization as that of the contemporary fauna and flora, and especially that of the domestic animals and cultivated plants. From this point of view, a discovery of M. Andersson's is of great interest. He has found that the neolithic peoples of Manchuria, Ho-nan, and Kan-su kept domestic pigs. Pig-breeding has remained one of the features of Chinese civilization. May discoveries of this kind multiply, and let us await the deduction from them of systematic views by palæobotany and palæozoology. Let us not depend for this on the palæographs only.

Works on the Chinese language are, at the present time, inspired by a more positive spirit than studies of the writing. The science of Chinese linguistics, born about twenty years ago, has already made great progress.[3] Chinese no longer appears an isolated and mysterious tongue. It takes its place in a clearly defined family, to which Tibetan, Burmese, and perhaps Thaïan appear to belong.[4] There is an inclination to admit that the family is divided into two branches ; Thaïan and Chinese forming a first linguistic group, while Burmese and Tibetan form a second group. Perhaps a geographical prejudice plays a part in this division into two groups, one western, the other eastern. In any case the classification can only be put forward provisionally. It would certainly be a mistake to found on it an attempt to explain the ancient Chinese beliefs, by the aid of facts borrowed solely from Thaïan populations. It would be still more unwise to depend on it in describing the migrations of the Thaïs driven back by the Chinese towards the South. As long as we do not

---

[1] **CXLV**, 18.
[2] **CXLII**, 17, M. Forke (**XL**) has taken up the thesis of the southern origin of the Chinese, basing it also on the study of the written characters.
[3] **LXXXIII, LXXXV**, 16 ff.   [4] **CXV**.

persist in confusing *language, civilization,* and *race,* it is
expedient to admit, with M. Pelliot, that the linguistic data
(even if we take them as established) relating to the Thaïs,
Burmese, Tibetans, and Chinese " scarcely teach us anything
about the past history of these various peoples." [1] Here
again, it is best to await the pursuit of studies, each with its
own technique. Every hypothesis of an historical nature
will only hinder their progress, and we are far from the
moment when history could gain anything by borrowing their
hypotheses.

The problem of Chinese origins remains entirely unsolved.
There is little to hope for in the study of the texts, but much
may be expected from archæology and above all from prehistoric archæology. It is desirable that the excavations may
in future be inspired by purely scientific motives, and that
all the prejudices which still dominate the interpretations
may be abandoned. One first fact seems established :
Civilization is ancient in the Far East. A second fact appears
highly probable ; there is little likelihood that this civilization
was strictly autonomous. The idea of a China which in
historical times lived isolated from the world, is long out of
date. But if we frequently speak of the migrations of the
earliest Chinese, there is still a tendency to believe in the
relative isolation of the China of the remote ages. If traditional
history was to be relied upon, this isolation would be held
to have ceased only round about the approach to the Christian
era. From this time would date, with the opening of the
commercial routes, the period of actual contacts, of active
influences, of frequent invasions. Up till then the history
of China would have been made by Chinese alone. There is
no reason to think that the Chinese race (if we can speak of
a Chinese race) was not in its present situation from remote
antiquity. But neither is there any reason to believe that
China knew less invasions and was subjected to less influences
in ancient than in modern times. The most serious criticism
that can be made of the hypotheses concerning these contacts
is that up till now they have always been sought in the same
directions and conceived on the same model. It is possible

---

[1] Preface to Abadie, *Les Races du Haut-Tonkin.*

that waves of people coming from the West, by the North or by the South, may have played a great part in the history of ancient China. But very diverse influences may also have been at work. Neither the steppe, nor the mountain, nor even the sea was, in prehistoric times, an insuperable obstacle.

Chapter II

THE FEUDAL PERIOD

THE feudal régime is assumed by the traditional history to be as old as Chinese civilization. It was practised under the Hsia and the Yin, before the Chou. The system of chiefdoms was, in any case, firmly established by the time when chronology begins ; but hardly anything is known of ancient Chinese history before the *Ch'un Ch'iu* period. Without wishing to prejudge anything concerning earlier times, I name the " feudal period " that epoch which is known to us from dated narratives of the annalistic type, presented as extracts from seigniorial archives. The facts related in these narratives seem, in general, to deserve a certain credence.[1]

I

CHINA IN FEUDAL TIMES

In the eighth century before our era, China appears as an unstable confederation of overlordships. A fairly large number of small nobles are grouped under the nominal suzerainty of a king, the Son of Heaven. What is the extent of this confederation and, first, what are the ideal limits of the Chinese confederation ?

(1) *The Frontiers.* Two works serve to fix the geographical horizon of feudal China. Both, in fact, are attributed to Yü the Great, the founder of the Kingship, for tradition sees in him a great land-surveyor and cartographer. Indeed, the *Yü kong (Tribute of Yü)* in which Conrady persisted in seeing a document of the twentieth century B.C., is a composite work, partly descriptive, in prose, dating *at earliest*, according to Chavannes, from the ninth century; the verses forming

---

[1] The dates given hereafter, after the *Ch'un Ch'iu* or Ssu-ma Ch'ien, are solely by way of landmarks. It would not be at all wise to take them as strictly accurate.

PLATE VII

[face p. 70

LOESS COUNTRY. NARROW ISTHMUSES UNITING THE PLATEAUX

(Photo by Myron M. Fuller)

part of it are perhaps not perceptibly more ancient.[1] The *Shan hai king* (the Book of the Mountains and the Seas) is a miscellany artificially compiled. The first part (The Book of the Mountains: the first five chapters of the classical editions), is the result of a work of compilation which can be dated from the fourth or the third century B.C. These five books are a miscellany of remarks, which formerly were accompanied by maps. They describe, in classes according to position, twenty-six chains of mountains. Although the whole feudal period (eighth to third century) is comprised between the date of the *Yu kong* and of the *Shan hai king*, the horizon of these two works is almost the same, and is hardly more extensive in the latter work.

This horizon is very narrow. It is limited to the regions round about Ho-nan : viz., South of Chih-li, west of Shantung, the continental regions of Kiang-su (like a wave flowing over into Che-kiang), the northern portions of Ngan-huai, of Hu-pei south of Shan-si, and finally, of Shen-si and Kan-su. The course of the Yellow River is well described from its source in the mountains in Kan-su. That of the lower Blue River is sufficiently well indicated, but whilst the *Tribute of Yü* only knows in the South Lake Tong-t'ing, and perhaps Lake Po-yang, the *Shan hai king* has some idea of the mountains of *Che-kiang*. Both works indicate the existence of mountains to the north of Chih-li ; but they are not at all clear as to the direction. Both mention, without much exactness, the deserts of the North-West (the Shifting Sands) ; only the *Shan hai king* describes in any detail the region of T'ai-yuan (Shan-si) which is, however, mentioned in the verses of the *Yu kong*. Finally the *Tribute of Yü* is almost entirely unaware of the whole of Ssu-ch'uan, whilst the *Shan hai king* has valuable notices of the region of Ch'êng-tu.

There are two remarkable examples of ignorance. To the east, the maritime shores seem outside the geographical horizon, whilst the Isles of the Blessed, placed in the western sea, haunt mythical thought, at least from the fourth century B.C. To the west, knowledge comes to an end in the basin of the river Wei. Beyond that is a world of mystery—the *Yu kong* makes a river run there, the Black River, which running in a north to south direction, flows into the southern

[1] See the important note by Chavannes in SMC, I, 102.

sea. The Black River reappears in several places in the
Shan hai king. The chapter relating to the mountains of the
West is filled with the description of a mythical country,
K'un lun, peopled by gods. It is there that King Mu of
the Chou made his " inspired " or legendary " wanderings."
Richthofen, who with a perhaps excessive patience and
satisfaction, has identified all the geographical names of the
Tribute of Yü, finds in the mention of the Black River (and
of the River Jo which in the *Shan hai king* comes out of the
Tree of the West), the proof that the Chinese had retained
an exact memory of the regions crossed by their ancestors
in their journey towards the East.[1] Chavannes, on the
contrary, lays stress on the astonishing ignorance of the
Chinese concerning the places often given as the cradle of
their race.[2] The desert and the sea, indeed, are outside the
geographical horizon of the ancient Chinese ; they are domains
peculiar to mythological narratives.

Within ideal frontiers that were narrow enough, the ancient
Chinese confederation was spread over a territory scarcely
extending beyond the province of Ho-nan and the neighbouring portions of Shen-si, Shan-si and Shantung.   This
territory has as its southern boundary, the Ch'in-ling mountain
range and its extensions to the East—the hills of Fu-niu and
of Mu-ling.   It includes to the north the terraces which border
on the left bank of the middle reaches of the Yellow River.
It ends in the east at the confines of the alluvial zone, marked
by the present lower valley of the Yellow River and a line
prolonging it to the south.

Placed in contact with the loess country, which extends
over the terraced table-lands of Shan-si, Shen-si, Kan-su, and
the immense alluvial basin of the Yellow River, the territory
of ancient China comprises in general, to the west, the first
clay terraces, and to the east, a strip of alluvial soil dominated
by low hills.

(2) *The Country*. The appearance of the ancient Chinese
country is difficult enough to imagine. The regions at present
treeless and entirely under cultivation, formerly contained
immense marshes and important forests.

---

[1] **CXVI**, vol. I, 317. Richthofen believed he could trace, from data furnished
by the *Yu kong*, the route of the march of the western invaders.
[2] SMC, I, 126, note 2.

Dry and salubrious plains have replaced the shifting lands, which, to the east, stretched almost without interruption from the Yellow River to the Blue River. The Hoang-ho emptied itself in feudal times into the gulf of Pechili, but its mouth was situated about where Tientsin is now, for from about the region of Huai-king the River ran more to the north than it does today. About as far as to the present town of Pao-ting, it closely followed the line of the last heights of Chih-li ; then it received, to the north, the whole system of rivers which make up Pei-ho. Further than this, its course was not fixed. In 602 B.C., it shifted towards the East, leaving its former bed occupied by the River Chang.[1] All the eastern plain of Chih-li, where the great Lake Ta-lu was situated, was only an immense shifting delta, traversed by numerous rivers. The Chinese named them the Nine Rivers (which does not mean that there were exactly nine). As far as the River Ch'i (which ran in the present bed of the Yellow River) everything was unstable land, shut in by a network of streams. The fields near the sea were " covered with salt." The uncertainty of the hydrographic system was such that the Chinese could say of the River Ch'i that it flowed into the Yellow River and then came out again. It then formed a lake " with overflowing waters," the Lake of Yong (region of K'ai-fong, Ho-nan). On emerging from the Lake of Yong, it came, more to the East, to the Lake of Ko, which was connected with the great marsh of the country of Song, the Mong-chu (boundaries of Shantung and Ho-nan). To the north-east was situated Lei-hsia, a mysterious marsh, frequented by the dragon of Thunder. To the south-east (along all the present course of the Grand Canal) lakes, of which the best known is Ta-ye, succeeded one another, as far as the region where the Yellow River flowed throughout the Middle Ages and up to 1854. There stretched a plain intersected by the rivers Yi and Huai. It was only an immense swamp rejoining the lower Yang-tse. The mountain chain of Shantung, which is dominated by Mount T'ai-shan, was then isolated, and almost an island.

In the loess region, swamps of less magnitude filled large valley-bottoms with insufficient drainage (the flowing away

---

[1] SMC, I, 108, 109, 113, 144, and III, 521.

of the waters being perpetually stopped by the falling of the terraces). Thus in Shen-si, the " stagnant waters " surrounded by " fields covered with saltpetre " spread over the valleys of the King and the Wei.[1] In the same way, lower Shan-si was covered by swamps between the lower Fen and the Yellow River, and, more to the North, there was again the great marsh of T'ai-t'ai, at the confluence of the Fen and the T'ao (a river which is today dried up). Separated by impassable lands, isolated by canyons with precipitous sides, the loess plateaux were divided up into sections insufficiently connected by narrow isthmuses and difficult passes.

In this cut-up country, vegetation was surprising in its richness compared with that of present-day China. But the records of it are conventional. Such, for example, is the following report of an establishment in the region of the River Wei (Shen-si). T'ai-wang, an ancestor of the Chou (in ? 1325 B.C.) chose there a site on which " the oaks rose majestically," and where " the pines and the cypresses were well-spaced " ; he had " the dead trees cleared away, the thickets pruned and trimmed, the tamarisks and catalpas thinned out, the mountain mulberries and the mulberries used for dyeing, pruned." Some forests, for example that of T'ao-lin (the Forest of Peaches, to the South-east of the junction of the Wei and the River) are given as occupying immense spaces. These forests were inhabited by wild or ferocious animals, boars, wild oxen and wild cats, grizzly bears, brown bears, striped bears, tigers, Russian panthers, white leopards.[2]

Men, in order to settle there, had first to make a clearing by fire, to drain the land and to instal ferries.[3] A passage of Mencius shows that in the fourth century all the work of ordering the country was considered as having been carried out by the founder of the kingship, Yü the Great.[4] Before his time, " the Overflowing Waters flowed at random . . . the grass and the trees were luxuriant, birds and quadrupeds swarmed everywhere, the five cereals would not grow . . . Yi (the great Forester, working under Yü's orders), burnt the Mountains and the Marshes, and reduced (their vegetation) to cinders," whilst Yü got the Waters under control. Only

---

[1] SMC, III, 524.
[2] She-king, C, 361, 336, 406, 407, description of a forest in Chih-li.
[3] She-king, C, 363.   [4] Mencius, L, 126.

PLATE VIII

THE YELLOW RIVER ON REACHING THE GREAT PLAIN

(Photo by Commandant Lartigue)

after that could the Chinese land be put under cultivation and become a country of cereals.

When China was ready for unification, it was believed to have been created by the labours of a Unique Man. But Yü the Great has usurped the glory of numerous demiurges, each one of whom operated in a small canton. It was Nü-kua who, in Chih-li, put the Nine Rivers in order.[1] It was T'ai-t'ai who purified, in Shan-si, the Fen basins.[2] Yü the Great hollowed out the pass of Huan-yuan (Ho-nan),[3] while two giants made a way between the Mountains of T'ai-ting and Wang-wu.[4] In fact, the documents show that a large number of the great mythical labours date, at earliest, from the feudal epoch, and were works undertaken by local nobles. The nobles, in a much cut-up country, where only the ledges of the table-lands and hills were habitable, opened up ways of communication by land and by water. They created at last a territory adapted to a unique civilization and ready for political unification. The uniformity which the China of the loess and of the alluvial deposits presents today is the result of an immense social effort. If, to use the Chinese expression, the rivers have ended by giving themselves up to the sea with the serenity and the majesty of feudatories bringing their tribute, it is because, indeed, the overlordships only achieved alliance and confederation after having tamed nature.

II

CHINESE AND BARBARIANS

(1) *The Chinese Confederation.* In the midst of torrential watercourses, wandering from and piling up the banks of their beds, and spreading themselves over the plains, on the high lands which emerged from the swamps, on the plateaux whose cliffs overhung flooded basins, in ancient days an archipelago of small feudal States was raised up. These were innumerable (ten thousand, it was said) at the time when Yü the Great (? 2198 B.C.) invited the nobles to pay homage to him. There were no longer more than a few dozens by about 489 B.C.[5] In the period between the eighth and the

---

[1] *Lieh Tzŭ*, **CXLIII**, 30. [2] *Tso chuan*, **C**, vol. III, 30 ; **LV**, 560 ; **XCV**, 51.
[3] **LV**, 563. [4] *Lieh Tzŭ*, **CXLIII**, 135. [5] *Tso chuan*, **C**, vol. III, 641.

third centuries, little chieftainships began to collect together and form powerful States. No doubt the movement of political concentration had begun centuries before.

At the beginning of the *Ch'un Ch'iu* epoch, Chinese unity was already sketched out on a federal plan. The expression which, later, was to mean simply *China*, had then the meaning of *Chinese Confederation* (*Chong Kuo*). This confederation brought together overlordships of varied importance, which felt themselves connected less by the force of political relations than by a certain community of civilization. This connexion appeared to rest either on genealogical ties, implying identity of family name, or on a political tradition of intermarriages. Although connexions of this kind are always represented as existing from time immemorial, a shade of difference can be perceived between the expressions *Chong Kuo* and *Shang Kuo*. The latter designates the overlordships (*Kuo*) which were formerly (*Shang*) in confederation, and possessed by virtue of this fact a sort of superiority (*shang*). The House of Wu (Kiang-su) is supposed to have issued from the same ancestors as the royal house of the Chou ; but Wu is an outlying overlordship, and one of its ambassadors [1] calls the central overlordships (*Chong Kuo*) which he visits, " superior " overlordships (*Shang Kuo*). He qualifies as *hsia*—the name of the first dynasty, but this word signifies *civilized* [2]—the music which is used in them. The expression *Chou hsia* (the *Hsia*) before it meant the Chinese, meant exactly the same as *Shang Kuo*. An equivalent of *Hsia* is *Hua* (flower) : the expression *Chong Hua*, the *Central Flower*, is in the end applied to the whole of China. Speaking in the name of Lu, whose princes boasted of descent from Chou-kong, brother of the founder of the Chou, Confucius, in 500 B.C., marks, by means of the words *Hsia* and *Hua*, the moral superiority of his country over the powerful overlordship of *Ch'i*, which was part of *Chong Kuo*, but which bordered on the barbarous regions.[3] The States which boasted of an ancient civilization were those of Ho-nan (more exactly of North-west Ho-nan). The others, round about, were supposed to have a less pure civilization.

The chief States of the Centre were the royal state of the Chou and the overlordship of Wei, which occupied the former

[1] SMC, IV, 15.   [2] SMC, IV, 9.   [3] *Tso chuan*, **C**, vol. III, 558 ; **LV**, 176.

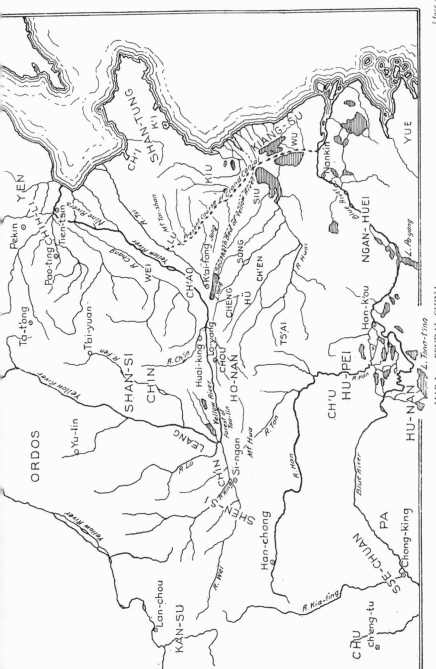

MAP I. FEUDAL CHINA

domain of the Yin, and that of Song, whose princes were
descended from the Yin. To these must be joined the State
of Cheng, although its foundation was considered to be of
recent date, and (in order to respect Chinese traditions) the
State of Lu, situated a little apart in Shantung. The princes
of Lu and of Cheng, like those of Wei, were attached to the
royal family. All round were more powerful states : Ch'i
to the north-west of T'ai Shan, bordered on the plain of
Chih-li ; Chin occupied the south of Shan-si ; Ch'in possessed
the valleys of the Wei and the Lo (Shen-si), which were, it is
said, the first domain of the Chou ; the basin of the Han up
to the Blue River (Hu-pei) belonged to Ch'u. More to one
side, on the mouths of the Blue River, and reaching to the
basin of the Huai, was the principality of Wu, and more to the
south still, extending from the sea to Lake Po-yang, that of
Yue. To the north, far from the centre and hardly in contact
with Ch'i and Chin, the State of Yen occupied northern
Chih-li. Beyond were the Barbarian countries ; to the south
and east, the Man and the Yi ; to the west and north the
Jong and Ti, generic names without precise value.

According to the traditional theory, the Barbarians formed,
on the borders of China, the *Four Seas,—the Interior of the
Seas* being China proper. The Barbarians, indeed constantly
intervene and play a decisive part in the history of the most
central of the overlordships.

(2) *The Countries of the Centre.* Tradition claims that, to
found their power, the Chou depended on the Ti with whom
their ancestors lived. It asserts also that the Yin tried to
reconquer their throne with the assistance of the Yi of Huai.[1]
The *She-king* exalts the exploits of King Süan (827–782 B.C.)
against the Barbarians of Huai.[2] It was, it is said, under
pressure from the Ti that the Chou abandoned Shen-si (the
region of Si-ngan) to go and establish themselves more to
the east on the borders of the Lo, in Ho-nan (under King
P'ing, 770–720 B.C.).[3] The Lo flows in a shut-in valley, in
the very heart of the Chinese country. The Chou kings,
however, in their new abode were not protected from the
Barbarians. In 636 B.C., King Siang, who had married a Ti
princess, was chased from his capital by the Ti.[4]

[1] SMC, IV, 93 ff. ; **LV,** 408.   [2] *She-king,* **C,** 407 ff.
[3] SMC, I, 285.   [4] SMC, I, 293.

From the eighth to the sixth century B.C. there is, practically, not a year in which the Barbarians do not attack some town in the central overlordships. In 715 B.C. the Jong take away a royal ambassador from Ho-nan itself.[1]   In 659 B.C. battle must be waged against the *Jong Dogs*, on the banks of the Wei, and the same year other Barbarians, the Ti, appear on the middle reaches of the Yellow River, near Lake Hiong.[2] They beat the army of the Prince of Wei and take possession of his town.[3]   730 persons escape with difficulty ; in the whole principality there remain only 5000 survivors. In 649 B.C. the Ti destroy a small State, a neighbour of Wei. In 648 B.C. some Jong and *Red Ti* assault the royal city and burn its eastern gate.[4] In 648 B.C. the Ti reappear in the State of Wei, and the year following, Cheng is attacked by the Ti.[5] In 643 B.C. the Jong are in the royal domain, whilst Cheng is invaded by the Ti of Huai.[6]   In 638 B.C. the Ti are again in Wei and, three years later, in Cheng. In 619 B.C., they threaten the western frontiers of Lu. They invade Song in 616 B.C., and Wei in 613 B.C.[7]

Now these Barbarians who appear continually and in all places in central China, are not horsemen, proceeding on rapid raids. They fight on foot, against Chinese in chariots. Such are the Jong of the North, who are found in 713 B.C. attacking Cheng and the Ti with whom Chin has trouble in 540 B.C. in central Shan-si.[8] These last were mountaineers ; other Barbarians, those of Huai, for example, lived in the marshes. Certainly, neither one nor the other, when they suddenly spring up, come from very far. If the Barbarians of the Four Seas could so easily interfere in the central overlordships, it is apparently because they knew the pathways through the woods and swamps, suited for surprise marches ; and also because, in the uncultivated zones, isolating, like so many islands, the overlordships perched on the ledges of the table-lands and hills, they found relays and points of support in settlements occupied by savage populations.

These settlements, in the heart of China, were numerous. In 720 B.C. a Prince of Lu [9] renewed an alliance concluded by his father with the Jong, who inhabited the marshy

[1] *Tso chuan*, **C**, vol. I, 42.   [2] *Ibid.*, 215 and 218.   [3] *Ibid.*, 277.
[4] *Ibid.*, 283.   [5] *Ibid.*, 286 and 290.   [6] *Ibid.*, 312.
[7] *Ibid.*, 326, 357, 484, 498, 515.   [8] *Tso chuan*, **C**, vol. I, 50, and vol. III, 28.
[9] *Tso chuan*, **C**, vol. I, 13.

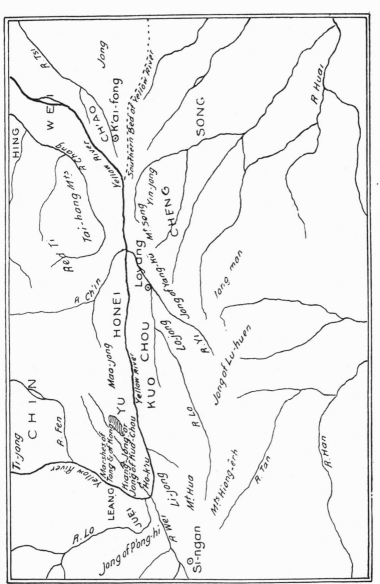

MAP II.   THE ROYAL DOMAIN AND ITS NEIGHBOURHOOD

district separating Ho-nan from Shan-tung, on the borders of the small overlordship of Ch'ao. In 669 B.C. Ch'ao was attacked by Jong Barbarians. Lu attacked some Jong in 667 B.C.[1] In 643 B.C. the Jong committed some misdeeds in the royal domain. It is not known whence they came.[2] But when, in 648 B.C. the Ti attacked the king, they were helped by the Jong of Yang-kü, who were settled in the district of Lo-yang, in the neighbourhood of the capital itself.[3] In 637 B.C. the Jong of Lu-huen, settled in the upper valley of the Yi, a tributary of the river of Lo-Yang, caused trouble to the princes of Ch'in and of Chin ; in 605 B.C. they are attacked by the prince of Ch'u, because they are masters of a region of passes and roads between the tributaries of the Lo and the upper valleys of the tributaries of the Han.[4] To the west are the Jong Man, who occupy the heads of the valleys descending towards Huai. To the east, near the holy mountain of the Centre (Song Shan) other Barbarians, the Yin-jong, are settled. In 532 B.C. they attack the capital.[5] In 618 B.C. Lu makes a treaty with the Lo-jong, who inhabit the country between Yi and Lo, still nearer to the capital.[6] Encircled to the south by different Jong tribes, the Chou kings, in the north of their domain, flung themselves again against other Barbarians, the Mao-jong, who beat them in 589 B.C.[7] These lived in the lower region of southern Shan-si. It is clear that the Four Seas of the Barbarians,—far from there being any need to seek for them on the ideal frontiers of China,—were close to the gates of the royal town.

(3) *The Border Countries.* Quite as much as the domain of the Chou, the feudal States were like bastions shut in by Barbarian settlements.

Let us take for example, the State of Chin, marked out for a great destiny, which might perhaps have realized Chinese unity if it had not been broken up in 376 B.C. into three rival principalities, Chao, Han, and Wei (the three *Chin*). At the opening of the period *Ch'un Ch'iu*, the domain of Chin occupies a narrow country in lower Shan-si, perched high, to the east of the Yellow River, in the district of the Fen. To the south this country dominated the lowlands, covered for the most

[1] *Tso chuan*, C, vol. I, 187 and 189. [2] *Ibid.*, 312. [3] *Ibid.*, 330.
[4] *Ibid.*, 575. *Tso chuan*, C, vol. III, 619. [5] *Ibid.*, 163.
[6] *Tso chuan*, C, vol. I, 490. [7] *Tso chuan*, C, vol. II, 3.

part by stagnant waters (the marshes of Tong and of Kong), which stretch between the Yellow River and the east to west course of the Fen. There was there a regular brushwood undergrowth haunted by foxes and wolves.[1] Jong (Kiang-jong, Jong of Kua-chou) swarmed there, in touch with the Li-jong who, beyond the river, lived in the woods to the South of the Wei, on the border of the country of Ch'in. The Princes of Chin allied themselves with these Jong from the middle of the seventh century B.C. Duke Hien had a Li-jong wife, and in 626 B.C. the Kiang-jong aided Chin in a war against the rival State of Ch'in.[2] In 557 B.C., these same Jong had enough power and autonomy for their chief to be able to force the overlord of Chin to allow them to be present at an Assembly of the Chinese Confederation.[3] To the east, the west and the north, Chin was surrounded by the Ti. Duke Hien (676–651 B.C.) who first extended the frontiers of Chin, had, before marrying a Li-jong, married a Ti woman. She was the mother of Duke Wen, the great Leader ; her brother, Chao Ch'ui, was his chief Counsellor. Chao Ch'ui was the ancestor of the overlords of Chao, the most important of the States which broke off from Chin.[4] The sister of Chao Ch'ui, mother of Duke Wen, was a Ti, or more correctly a Ti *Hu* or Ti *Jong*. The Ti Jong (Jong-ti) seem to be the same as the Great Jong (the names given to the Barbarians have, it is clear, an inde-terminate content) who lived in the north of Shen-si, the west and north of Shan-si. They were masters of the course of the Yellow River above the defiles of Long-men, and separated Chin from its victorious rival, the State of Ch'in. To the north, the Ti occupied both the basin of T'ai-yuan and the high portions of Shan-si, and commanded the defiles which lead to the plains of Chih-li ; they thus isolated Chin and Yen. To the south-east, in the region of the T'ai-hang mountains, lived the most mighty of the Ti tribes, the Red Ti, who claimed to rule over the others, the White Ti.[5] The Red Ti separated Chin from the overlordships of Wei and of Ch'i. Duke Wen and Chao Ch'ui both had among their wives a Red Ti, of the tribe of the Tsiang-kao-ju.[6]

Thanks to a series of alliances with the Barbarian tribes

---

[1] *Tso chuan*, **C**, vol. II, 293 and vol. III, 504.   [2] *Tso chuan*, **C**, vol. I, 431.
[3] *Tso chuan*, **C**, vol. II, 291.   [4] SMC, IV, 259 and 283 ; SMC, V, 12.
[5] *Tso chuan*, **C**, vol. I, 606.   [6] SMC, IV, 283.

which surrounded it, Chin established a contact with the other overlordships. Its endeavours seem to have been directed first towards the south. From the first half of the seventh century, Duke Hien, allied to the Jong, took possession of the small overlordships of Kuo and Yu (654 B.C.) situated in the curve of the River, on the frontiers of the royal domain.[1] From that time, he exercised influence over all the middle course of the Yellow River as far as Ho-nei (the portion of Ho-nan to the north of the Hoang-ho). On this side, contact with the State of Wei become very close, when Duke Wen had acquired Ho-nei, which the Chou ceded to him in 635 B.C. to pay him for his protection against the Ti. Chin was able from that time to intervene in the quarrels of the overlordships of Cheng and of Song, and to balance in Ho-nan the increasing influence of the princes of Chou. At the same time the progress of Chin on the middle reaches of the Yellow River tended to isolate the Red Ti from the central overlordships. These, and especially one of their groups, the Giant Ti, exercise for a long time a strong pressure on the overlordships of the East. They had attacked Song in the middle of the eighth century, and Ch'i, Lu and Wei at the beginning of the seventh century B.C.[2] From 660 B.C. Duke Hien, profiting by the rivalries between the White and the Red Ti, attacked the latter in their mountain strongholds of Eastern Shan-si (Tong Shan).[3] The actual conquest took place at the opening of the sixth century (from 600 to 592 B.C.). It was preceded by an understanding with the White Ti. One of the Chiefs of the Red Ti then had as wife a princess of Chin.[4] After this victory, the State of Wei was no more than a dependency of Chin. It remained to take possession of the passages of the north, towards Chih-li. The first stage was the conquest of the upper basin of T'ai-yuan in middle Shan-si. This was achieved in 540 B.C. " In order to fight in these narrow and steep positions " against foot-soldiers, Chin had to reform its tactics and, not without difficulty, force its warrior nobles to become foot-soldiers.[5] It conquered and made itself master of the great marshy basin with fields covered with saltpetre (*Ta lu*)

---

[1] *Tso chuan*, **C**, vol. I, 253. [2] SMC, IV, 115.
[3] SMC, IV, 261. [4] *Tso chuan*, **C**, vol. I, 592, 593, 606, 654, 660.
[5] *Tso chuan*, **C**, vol. III, 28.

F

where tradition places the capital of the Hsia dynasty. It set out thence, in the middle of the fifth century B.C. to conquer the Barbarian kingdom of Tai (district of Ta-t'ong), whose princes had a dog for ancestor. This country, rich in horses, controlled all the passes to the high plains of Chih-li ; its possessors could put pressure on the northern State of Yen. The conquest was the deed of a descendant of Chao Ch'ui, Chao Siang-tsŭ, whose sister had married the prince of Tai. It had been prepared, from the beginning of the sixth century B.C., by a spear-head boldly pushed northwards into the territory of the Sien-yu (Ti of the North).[1] The expedition, begun in 529 B.C. by a single raid, was continued the following year with the help of an army equipped with siege material. Followed up in 526 B.C., it only ended in 519 B.C. Chin entered from that date into contact with the peoples of the northern steppe.[2]

It was more difficult to acquire, and still more to retain, domination over the countries of the west. From the beginning of the seventh century B.C. Chin extended as far as the Yellow River, built strong places on its borders, and sought to get a foothold on the right bank.[3] It made ties with the Jong of the South of the Wei, whilst to the North of the Wei basin it sought for a political alliance with the nobles of Leang. These, settled in the angle formed by the River and the Lo, attempted to advance northwards, towards the great northern curve of the Hoang-ho. They raised walls and built towns without having enough people to inhabit them.[4] The troubles which the succession of Duke Hien provoked, and which weakened Chin between 651 and 634 B.C. prevented it from taking possession of this easy prey. It fell to the State of Ch'in, which Chin, at that very time, was trying to shut up in the basin of the Wei. Chin, conquered by Ch'in in a battle fought at the vital point where the Yellow River, receiving the Wei and all its tributaries, takes the west to east direction, was obliged to give up its territories to the west of the River (645 B.C.).

Ch'in, advancing first to the defile of Long-men, took possession, in 640 B.C., of the country of Leang. Between the two States thenceforth in contact began a rivalry which,

[1] *Tso chuan*, C, vol. III, 197.   [2] *Ibid.*, 238, 253, 343 ff.
[3] SMC, IV, 266.   [4] *Tso chuan*, C, I, 319

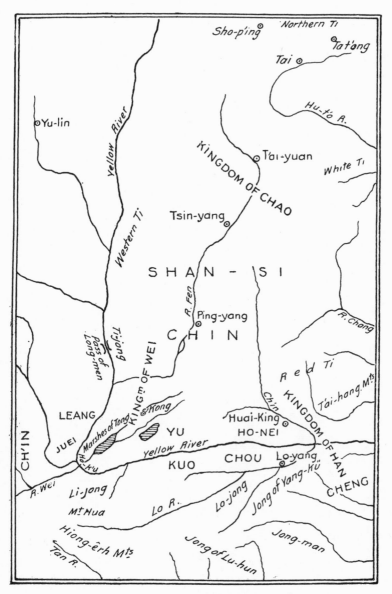

MAP III.   TO ILLUSTRATE THE HISTORY OF CHIN

interrupted by false truces, was destined to last, to the advantage of Ch'in, till the foundation of the Empire. Each of the two rival overlordships sought to establish its authority over the Barbarians, the supremacy going to the one which momentarily gained their alliance. But, from 626 B.C., Ch'in gained the advantage and, in 623 B.C., Duke Mu of Ch'in became the " Chief of the Jong of the West." [1] Chin got back some land at the beginning of the sixth century by forming a confederation with the White Ti under its authority.[2] The Princes of Ch'in finally prevailed when, advancing in the valleys of the King and the Lo, they came in the fourth century B.C. into possession of the plateaux of Shen-si which dominate to the west the north to south course of the Yellow River.[3] Chao, heir of Chin in Shan-si, then finally lost the territories on the right bank of the Hoang-ho. Its attempts to conquer the Hu Barbarians failed, although it tried to adopt their method of combat and created a body of archers on horseback.[4]

Thus Chin, which at first occupied only a small canton in the mountains, obtained possession of the whole of Shan-si, gaining step by step, occupying first the passes and the heads of the valleys. Thanks to its connexions, to its alliances, and to a work of penetration completed by the use of force, it succeeded in forming a federation round itself of the Barbarian groups, whose divisions it exploited, afterwards annexing and assimilating them.

The history of the great feudal States is quite similar to that of Chin. All were, at the beginning of the historic period, little overlordships, shut up in countries difficult of access. The States which obtained the greatest successes were the overlordships on the Borders. They could take into their service the great masses of Barbarians spread over the steppes, the mountains and the marshy districts. They drew them together round about the great basin of the Yellow River, and it is through their solidity that the way was paved for Chinese unity.

The great Leaders of the seventh century were Chiefs of the Marshes. Whilst, with the aid of the Jong and the Ti, Chin and Ch'in created great States in Shan-si and Shen-si,

[1] SMC, II, 41.   [2] *Tso chuan,* C, I, 593.
[3] SMC, II, 63.   [4] SMC, V, 81.

Ch'i, seeking to group, to north and south, the maritime Barbarians, and conquering the mountaineers of the promontory of Kiaochow, made of Shantung a vast overlordship, while in the south, working both eastward and westward, gaining on the marshes of the Huai, the mountains of Ssuch'uan and even those of Yunnan, Ch'u joined in one confederation the Man and the Yi round about Hu-pei, and by the upper valleys of the Han and the Huai seized hold, with increased force, of the central overlordships of Ho-nan. Among these latter one only, that of Song, could think for a moment of becoming a powerful State. It was in contact with the Barbarians of the Huai. At the beginning of the seventh century, it tried to capture their strength in order to exercise the hegemony.

To exercise the hegemony was to command as master the central overlordships. The aim of all the Leaders was to control western Ho-nan. There is the heart of ancient China. There the Chinese nation was formed. A country rather cut-up, but relatively easy of access, where the valleys radiate in all directions, a district intermediary between the tablelands of loess, which are isolated by closed valleys, and the alluvial plains half under water, and eaten into by marshes, Ho-nan was at first divided up between tiny overlordships and feeble Barbarian tribes. All round about, in vaster regions occupied no doubt by less dense and more shifting populations, great States formed, increasing first towards the exterior, seeking (as we have seen in the case of Chin) to cut the communications of their rivals with the Barbarians, mutually forcing each other to change the directions of their expansion, exercising on each other a pressure from behind, and a converging pressure on the central overlordships. All schemed to conquer them. Thus an amalgamation was achieved. Whilst in the centre the Chinese nation was coming into being, on the outer borders States were forming which, aiming at annexing the centre of China, ended by themselves also becoming Chinese.

III

THE FORMATION OF PROVINCIAL UNITY

Through putting together certain facts, we may guess at the importance of the movement of unification which was pursued during the feudal period. In 478 B.C. in Ho-nan, the inhabitants of the town of Jong-chou (or Jong-ch'eng : *the town of the Jong*) revolted against their overlord, the Prince of Wei, who had dared to treat them as Barbarians.[1] No doubt the Prince thought their assimilation incomplete, but they claimed to be and felt themselves Chinese. Some years before (500 B.C.) the people of Lai, in Shantung, who had been in contact with Ch'i for at least a century, and who were conquered, incorporated, and displaced from 556 B.C., were again considered to be simple Barbarians, dancing savage dances.[2] Such was the opinion of those who claimed to represent the spirit of old China ; but the Princes of Ch'i ought not to have despised the Barbarians of Lai, for they themselves, at this epoch, had hardly begun to inquire into the ancient rites. On the other hand, from the end of the fourth century B.C., Ch'i was celebrated for its high culture and the favours which it bestowed on learned men. " They were counted (in Ch'i) by hundreds ; there were nearly a thousand (there)." [3]

If Ho-nan is the *Central Flower* (Chong-hua), it was in the provinces on the margin that Chinese civilization blossomed most fully. It is there that, in more or less stable federations, gathered about a powerful chief, the pride of being Chinese was most strongly felt ; it is there that men were most conscious of superiority over the Barbarians and of the duties thus imposed. At the beginning of the seventh century, during the great struggle against the Ti, who swarmed from all parts, Kuan Chong, Minister of Ch'i, enunciated the principle that all " the Chinese (*chu* Hsia) are related." [4] Then, and often at the common expense, walls of defence were constructed against " the Barbarians (who) are wolves of insatiable avidity." Such, for example, were the ramparts built in 658 B.C. at Hing (in Chih-li) by the soldiers of Ch'i,

---

[1] SMC, IV, 210.
[3] SMC, V, 258, 260.
[2] **LV**, 172 ff.
[4] *Tso chuan*, **C**, vol. I, 209.

Song and Ch'ao, or again those put up at Wei (north of
Ho-nan) in 648 B.C. by the princes in confederation around
the Leader of Ch'i.[1]

In ancient days, an overlordship consisted of a walled
town, surrounded by suburbs protected by other walls.
Inside were the cultivated fields, beyond the uncultivated
regions, wooded mountains, marshes covered with rushes and
brushwood. The seigniorial town served as a refuge and,
according to their distance from it, the inhabitants were
subjected to compulsory labour and more or less heavy dues.
Only those dwelling inside the walls (*fong t'ien*) contributed
to the marriage of the overlord's daughters.[2] The overlordships far from the centre, which grew by assimilating the
Barbarians, pushed their walled frontiers very far. A piece
of the *She-king*, attributed to the end of the seventh century,
celebrates the construction of a wall designed to stop the
nomads of the north.[3] Similar constructions multiplied. The
new walls had as their main object the defence of the great
States against the Barbarians whom a rival overlordship
sought to fling against them in order to outflank them. When
Ch'in, for example, at the beginning of the fourth century B.C.,
put up a long wall at Kan-su, it wanted to protect its newly-
conquered territories against tribes which had not submitted ;
but its advance into these territories is explained by the
desire not to let itself be overrun by the States, the successors
to Chin, who were also expanding their domains towards the
north.[4] Thus Wei (one of the three Chins) carried out a
counter-thrust in 353 B.C., by fortifying the banks of the Lo ;
its wall ran up to the north-east corner of the great bend of
the Hoang-ho. Thus also, King Wu-ling of Chao (325–299
B.C.) raised a long wall to the north of Shan-si. Chao built
fortifications too, to defend itself against Wei (in 333 B.C.)
and others to the east, as a defence against Yen, the State
of Chih-li (in 291 B.C.).[5] In 369 B.C. the Prince of Chong-shan,
another State of Chih-li, had built a wall which protected it
from Chao. In the same way, at the end of the fifth century,
King Süan of Ch'i had raised a wall of more than a thousand
li, ostensibly to oppose the incursions of the Barbarians of

---

[1] *Tso chuan*, **C**, vol. I, 231 and 284.
[2] *Tso chuan*, **C**, vol. III, 323 and 667.
[3] *She king*, **C**, 188.
[4] BEFEO, III, 222, note 4 ; SMC, II, 61 ; V, 71.
[5] SMC, V, 64, 154, 58.

Huai, but actually to isolate him from Ch'u.[1] Finally, Ch'u, on its part, had built to the north-west of Hu-pei the walls of Fang ; they marked the limits of its progress towards the central overlordships.[2]

We can thus trace the process by which the Chinese lands acquired real frontiers. Whilst, under pressure from the Marches, amalgamation of the populations took place, provincial units were formed. There arose first a Chinese civilization and Chinese provinces. Finally, in the new countries on the circumference of ancient China, States attempted to organize themselves.

About the creation of public services and of State domains, we possess only very incomplete information. It is a remarkable fact that this comes almost entirely from the overlordships which exercised hegemony. It is clear that the chief resources of the great lordships were first of all drawn from contributions furnished by the federated nobles. Thus, several times we find Cheng complaining of the heavy tribute exacted by Chin. It consisted of presents of textiles and of horses. It included also compulsory labour.[3] The great princes sought to secure for themselves less precarious revenues. Ch'i is reported as having (from the tenth century, it is said), " made the work of artisans and merchants flourish everywhere, and (having) favoured the advantageous trade in fish and salt." [4] In the reign of Duke Huan (685–643 B.C.), the first of the Leaders, Kuan Chong, reforming the government, " instituted a tax on money, fish and salt, in order to help the poor and reward wise and able men." [5] A work attributed to Kuan Chong shows us this wise minister and his Duke, paying attention to problems of mining, metallurgy, and the currency.[6] In 521 B.C. there existed in Ch'i a fairly complex administration. The monopolies of forest products, the produce of the lakes, of the marshes, and finally, the monopoly of the shell-fish beds and of the salt-pans were shared out for different services.[7] In Chin, the mountains, the marshes, the forests and the salt-pans were also " treasures of the State." [8] The

---

[1] SMC, IV, 406.   [2] SMC, III, 218.   [3] *Tso chuan*, **C,** II, 411, 571.
[4] SMC, IV, 40.   [5] SMC, IV, 49.
[6] The *Kuan ssu*, which uses some ancient data, is a work in which the spirit of the administrators of the time of the Han is apparent.
[7] The chief document is in the *Tso chuan*, **C,** III, 323.
[8] *Tso chuan*, **C,** II, 56.

salt-pans seem to have constituted the chief of the national riches. The mines evidently contributed also. Ch'u had reserves of copper on which it could draw to gain an alliance with Cheng (641 B.C.).[1] Chin possessed iron; and in 510 B.C. it is reported as imposing on each of its subjects a contribution of a bushel of mineral ore.[2]

From the moment when the overlordships included in their walled frontiers the lands which, formerly simple marches, surrounded the walls of their suburbs, it is probable that great works were undertaken to transform into national possessions the forests of the mountains and bog-lands. It is there that political mythology placed the haunts of the demons against which the noble, with the aid of magic arms, protected his people (Demons and Barbarians have a strong resemblance to one another). There is a possibility that the works of land-drainage, the glory of which is attributed to distant ancestors, may have been the deed of rich nobles well enough equipped to furnish their peasants with more fields for culture. These works demanded abundant skill and clever technical workers. They frightened conventional minds. To undertake them was, it was believed, to endanger the overlordship. We have, on this point, a significant document. " The Prince of Han, seeing that Ch'in succeeded in its enterprises, wished to dry it up. . . . He sent thither a hydrographical engineer. . . . This man treacherously advised the Prince of Ch'in to pierce a canal which would conduct the waters of the River King from the mountain Chong to the west, and as far as Hu-k'ou, all along the mountains of the north, to empty them to the east into the River Lo. The course was to be more than 300 *li*. The plan was that the canal should be used for irrigating the fields. The works were half carried out when the trick was discovered." [3] Ch'in had the audacity to persevere; it succeeded in transforming into arable lands the swamps which occupied a large part of its domains : " When the canal was finished, it was used to carry off the stagnant waters, and to irrigate the fields covered with saltpetre, over an area of 4 million acres. . . . Then the country within the passes (Ch'in) became a fertile plain, and there were no more famines. In consequence Ch'in became rich and mighty, and finally subdued the nobles." [4] In the same way Si-men

---

[1] *Tso chuan*, C, I, 317.   [2] *Tso chuan*, C, III, 456.   [3] SMC, III, 523.   [4] *Ibid*.

Pao (between 424 and 387 B.C.) enriched the country of Wei by draining and irrigating the district of Ho-nei between the Yellow River and the River Chang.[1]

We should like to have more information on the great State enterprises which made of China a country of continuous culture, and allowed it to become a land with a homogeneous population. There is reason to think that they date from the time of the "Combatant Kingdoms," and are the work of an epoch which traditional history presents as an era of anarchy. The fact that these enterprises were held to be foolish and ruinous, indicates how far the conception of great and active States was a new and badly assimilated one.

Everything, in fact, which tended to give any strength to a central power was envisaged as an impious innovation. We know as little of the task accomplished by the lawmakers, as of that of the technical workers. There were certainly great legislative achievements during the period of the "Combatant Kingdoms." We know nothing exact about them, except the resistance and the criticisms they roused. Several codes were issued at the end of the sixth century B.C., that of Cheng in 535 B.C., that of Chin in 512 B.C.[2] They were engraved on copper vessels. History begins by affirming that the casting of these would bring about the worst calamities. It would, for example, make the Star of Fire appear in Heaven. After which, history states that the capital of Cheng was indeed destroyed by fire.[3] Thus the crime imputed to the innovators was punished. It consisted in claiming to replace custom by law. It appears that the lawyers wished to augment the importance of rules and to increase the power of the princely administration. They did not limit themselves, certainly, as they are accused of doing, to adding to the punishments inflicted, but probably in legislative matters the progress of the idea of the State translated itself first into a stricter and more severe regulation of crimes of high treason. The codes tried apparently to reduce the power of the local aristocracies and of private *associations*. The administrative innovations of Ssu-ch'an at Cheng were considered as attacks on private rights : "Take our clothes

[1] SMC, III, 511.   [2] *Tso chuan*, **C,** III, 116 and 457.
[3] *Ibid.*, 119 and 122.

or our hats, hide them well! Take our lands, *let us form associations* (to defend them)! Who will kill Ssu-ch'an? We will help this liberator! " But the common people seem soon to have recognized the benefits of State intervention. " We have children and young people; Ssu-ch'an teaches them! We have lands; Ssu-ch'an makes them fertile! When Ssu-ch'an dies, who will succeed him? " [1]

None of the great Chinese States, before Ch'in, was able to overthrow the aristocracy. The only interesting attempt in this direction was made at Chin and succeeded in moderate degree. Duke Hien of Chin had tried to encircle Ch'in, by the south and the north, by getting power over the Li-jong and the country of Leang. Ch'in could only break the hold by taking advantage of the troubles which enfeebled its rival on the death of Duke Hien. Several branches of the princely family disputed among themselves for power, and Ch'in, protecting them each in turn, was able to conclude advantageous treaties. It was then decided in Chin no longer to assign offices and domains to the sons of princes. [2] The idea, however, of making the entire State the direct domain of the overlord was too revolutionary not to appear impracticable. Duke Ch'êng (605–598 B.C.) maintained the adopted principle, but he gave offices and lands, if not to his relatives, at least to his high dignitaries. He took care, it is true, not to reserve their inheritance for their eldest sons. He hoped, no doubt, by the division of estates for life only, to prevent the founding of families as powerful as the families of the princely house had been. [3] In practice it was not possible to avoid distributing lands to the chiefs of the victorious army at each conquest. [4] Six great families arose. They succeeded in 514 B.C., in exterminating the younger branches of the ducal house. The princes of Chin endeavoured to keep up a state of rivalry between these families. They fought, indeed, but, reduced to three (Han, Wei, Chao), finished by turning out the Dukes and dividing up the territory of Chin (403 B.C.). It must be noted that Chao kept the largest part (all the north) of Shan-si, Han and Wei dividing lower Shan-si and the conquests of Chin in Ho-nan. The feudal period ended less in the building up of States than in causing the emergence of provincial units.

---

[1] *Tso chuan*, C, II, 561.   [2] *Tso chuan*, C, I, 573.
[3] SMC, IV, 321.   [4] SMC, V, 133 and 24.

The provinces whose rough outlines then begin to appear, all share the same civilization. The Chinese nation is on the way to its formation ; Chinese land is on the way to becoming tamed by cultivation. There remains the creation of China. There remains above all the building up of a Chinese State.

Chapter III

THE EMPIRE

I

The Founding of Imperial Unity

(1) *The work of the Overlords of Ch'in.* In the first centuries of the *Ch'un Ch'iu* period, political isolation ceases. To resist the raids of the Jong and the Ti, or to repress the internal disorders of an overlordship, temporary alliances were formed, unstable and without much power. They form and dissolve according to the needs of the moment, in response to the interests of the canton. They aim at the maintenance of the local *status quo*. Then the feudal principle of mutual assistance seems the rule.

At the end of the same period, it is provincial interests that control diplomacy. A kind of politics of great Powers seems to appear. These, developing their greatest activities in the Marches, grow away from the centre and assimilate new forces. In the interior of the Confederation, they tend to organize zones of influence. Hence the importance which the small principalities of the centre, such as Lu, Cheng and Song, appear to have in political events. They are, however, only the dependents of the great Border Powers, which often prefer to add to the territory of their protégés rather than to spread too much themselves over Central China. At this time, diplomacy appears to seek equilibrium. It strives to bring about, by means of periodical assemblies, a certain degree of mutual understanding and a sort of agreement.

At the beginning of the period of the Combatant Kingdoms, the excentric principalities achieved the creation of provincial domains which, without as yet having well-defined frontiers, begin to touch one another. At the same time there begins the practice of alliances between great Powers. Chin, made uneasy by the advance of Ch'u into Ho-nan, has no other means of putting direct pressure on Ch'u, unless it is willing openly to fight it in Ho-nan itself. It therefore uses Lu, its eastern dependent, to enter into relations with the barbarous principality of Wu. Wu, from Kiang-su and Ngan-huai, where it is established, can threaten Ch'u on its left and limit its progress towards eastern Ho-nan (584 B.C.).[1] Wu, taught to fight by military missions from Chin, wins a great victory over Ch'u in 506 B.C. But Ch'u has prepared a counter-attack. From 505 B.C. the princes of Yue (Che-kiang) take Wu in the rear, put an end to its success, and at last, in 473 B.C., destroy it. Ch'u, while escaping from a pressing danger, has only changed its rival. It now has to employ all its strength against Yue (339–329 B.C.). Yue succeeds in snatching from it the former territory of Wu, then throws it back towards the south. These events turned the activity of Ch'u towards the east, at the very moment when that of Chin (arrested in the west by Ch'in) was also directed to the eastern countries; hence comes the momentary political importance of the country of the north-east, Ch'i, in Shantung, and of the new power Yen in Chih-li. Political affairs are then directed by the six Kingdoms, Ch'u, Ch'i and Yen, and the three States which had sprung from Chin (the three Chins), Chao, Han and Wei, whilst to the west, the power of Ch'in is increased.

This is the period of the leagues from North to South (*Ho-tsong*), and of the leagues from West to East (*Lien-heng*). [*Tsong* means the warp and *Heng* the woof of a piece of woven material : *Heng-tsong* is also used of strips cut perpendicularly.] At the beginning of the period of the leagues from North to South and from West to East (fourth and third centuries), the confederations of the great Powers are temporary. They aim at limiting the success of one of the great kingdoms. These try to cut each other's communications, and their leagues are attempts at setting up barriers in each other's paths.[2]

Towards the end of the period, the struggle appears limited to Ch'in and Ch'u. Ch'u presides over the leagues from North to South, which aim at opposing the progress of

---

[1] SMC, IV, 5.
[2] SMC, II, 226 : "They founded the confederation from North to South, in order to break the expansion from West to East."

Ch'in. These leagues from North to South tend above all to preserve temporarily the *status quo*. They seem to imply a policy founded on the principle of federation. Ch'in, in practising the system *Lien-heng* (these words come to mean no longer leagues but an extension from West to East) appeared on the contrary to inaugurate a policy of annexation, aiming at the complete absorption of all the overlordships, and the creation of a centralized State. The policy of Ch'in prevailed. It ended in the foundation of the Chinese Empire.

Ch'in had had very modest beginnings. It was at first quite a small overlordship established in middle Shen-si, on the borders of the Wei. Surrounded on all sides by Barbarians, it was threatened by the pincers that Chin stretched to squeeze it to the north-east and to the south-west. It proved possible to loosen the embrace of Chin quickly. This happened when Ch'in, after having fought against the Jong of Tang-she (714 B.C.) and of P'ong-hi (697 B.C.), and annexed the small State of Kuo (Kuo west, 687 B.C.) made itself a corridor giving access to the great bend of the River (Ho-k'ü) and the central overlordships of Ho-nan. It then became difficult for Chin, with the aid of the Li-jong, to turn the flank of Ch'in by the south-east.[1] In 677 B.C., Ch'in entered into relations with the overlordships of Leang and of Juei to the west of the Hoang-ho. It conquered the territory of the Jong of Mao-chin and commanded an important ford of the River, that of Mao ;[2] then it took possession of the country of Leang (640 B.C.).[3] This advance towards the north-west along the Hoang-ho was patiently consolidated by a work of penetration into the upper valleys of the King and the Lo. In 444 B.C., a victory over the Jong of Yi-k'ü opened Kansu and Upper Shen-si to Ch'in. The danger of being outflanked by Chin towards the north-west ceased from the end of the fourth century.[4]

Ch'in intervened in Ho-nan less than Chin and Ch'u. An attempt to dominate Cheng (630–628 B.C.) was rapidly abandoned. Cheng, which commanded the passes towards the eastern tributaries of the Han (Hu-pei) was, between Chin and Ch'u, a region of strife used equally by the two

[1] SMC, II, 19–21.   [2] SMC, II, 25.
[3] SMC, II, 35.   [4] SMC, II, 56.

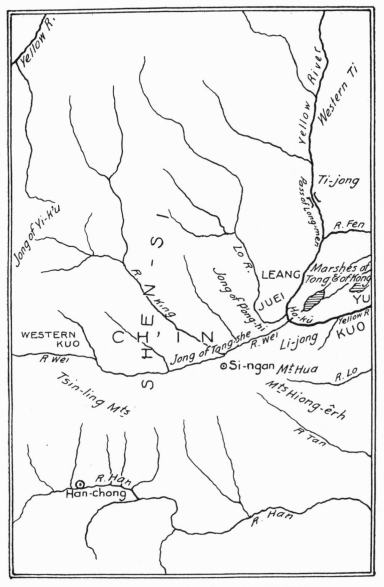

MAP IV.   TO ILLUSTRATE THE HISTORY OF CH'IN

States. Cheng ended by being annexed by Han, one of the three Chin, in 375 B.C. The danger of envelopment by the south-east might again have threatened Ch'in, if Chin had not been from that time divided into States which could not achieve a common policy. As a matter of fact, Ch'in had guarded against this danger in advance by itself proceeding to an envelopment of the basin of the Han from the west. The decisive moment came when Ch'u, which Chin had caused to be attacked by Wu in the east, was obliged to ask Ch'in for an alliance. From that moment, while Ch'u began to slide towards the east, Ch'in was able to control all the countries of the south-west. The alliance granted to Ch'u dates from 506 B.C.[1] From 475 B.C. Ch'in enters into relations with the country of Shu (Ssu-ch'uan district of Ch'êng-tu), and, occupying the passes of the mountain chain of Ch'in-ling, penetrates by the heights into the eastern part of the basin of the Han. In 441 B.C., the region of Han-chong (southern Shen-si) was disputed between Ch'u and Ch'in, which now appears beginning to work along the western flank of Hu-pei. In 387 B.C., the country of Chu is attacked and the region of Han-chong conquered.[2] In 316 B.C., after having conquered (318 B.C.) a coalition of the States of the North (Han, Chao, Wei, Yen and Ch'i), supported by the Hiong-nu (Huns), Ch'in seized the country of Shu, and, soon after, that of Pa (southern Ssu-ch'uan region of Chong-king).[3] Master of Kansu, of Shen-si, of eastern Ssu-ch'uan, Ch'in had become the great power of the West. It set to work immediately on the conquest of eastern China.

This conquest was actively conducted. Ch'in had organized a light and mobile army in which horse and foot soldiers predominated. The other States continued to make use of chariots, and conducted war according to the rules of feudal tactics. They made great demonstrations of strength, then disbanded their troops. Ch'in made war relentlessly. " It pursued the fugitives," and did not hesitate either to kill (" the shields swam on streams of blood "), or to annex.[4] Its adversaries sought either to propitiate the " ferocious Beast " —thus they named Ch'in—and " vying with each other, the nobles pared off territory to offer to it," or had recourse to

---

[1] SMC, II, 51.   [2] SMC, II, 58.
[3] SMC, II, 72.   [4] SMC, II, 228.

old political stratagems : plots, attempts at assassination.[1] Ch'in let them wear themselves out. King Chao-siang (306–251 B.C.) " destroyed " the Chu (the royal domain was divided into two principalities : eastern and western Chu) in 256–249 B.C. ; but his death, then two short reigns and a regency caused Ch'in to pass through a time of arrested progress. King Chêng, who ascended the throne in 247 B.C., was obliged at his majority (238 B.C.) to repress a revolt, and could not free himself until 235 B.C. from the tutelage of his minister Lu Pu-wei (who was reputed to be his real father). In 234 B.C. he began to put his armies in the field. He then acted with decisive rapidity. In 233 B.C. the King of Han " asked to become his subject." But Ch'in wished to finish with feudalism ; it was not content with a declaration of vassalage. In 230 B.C. Han was annexed ; Chao in 228 B.C., and Wei in 225 B.C. Ch'u, since 278 B.C. pushed right to the east, towards Ngan-huai, was conquered in 223 B.C., then Yen in 222 B.C., and finally Ch'i in 221 B.C. " The six kings were subjected to all the penalties befitting their crimes " and Chêng of Ch'in took the title of Shih Huang-ti (221 B.C.). He had required ten years to found the Empire.[2]

(2) *Ch'in Shih Huang-ti.* The first Emperor only reigned eleven years (221–210 B.C.). He had time to give to China the frontiers necessary to allow it to have an external policy. He aimed also at giving it the centralized organization which would have made of it a powerful State.

Ssu-ma Ch'ien and Pan Ku, historians permeated with the traditionalist spirit, wished only to throw light on the harshness of the government of Ch'in Shih Huang-ti. He was bad, because his dynasty did not last. Pan Ku, who chooses to treat him as a bastard, declares that he was wicked and cruel.[3] In order to blacken the man with quite easy consciences, the historians concealed the greatness of his achievements. Undoubtedly, they did not understand it. Ch'in Shih Huang-ti is, for them, only a magnificent example of the king of perdition, whose successes are all shameful. They have distorted all his actions, and made of him a con-

---

[1] **XVII,** 155.   [2] SMC, II, 117–122.
[3] SMC, II, 242. Pan Ku calls Ch'in Shih Huang-ti " *Lu* Chêng," thus declaring that he was the son of Lu Pu-Wei. " Lu Chêng was wicked and cruel. . . . He satiated his passions and loosed the reins of his desires. . . . It seems he possessed the ' prestige ' which belongs to a ' Holy Man.' "

ventional hero. It is difficult to give a just idea of the reign, or to do more than note a few of the traits of the first Emperor.

He was, it appears, of a practical turn of mind. He loved technical experts and specialists. Active and methodical, he knew how to read reports and to pursue inquiries. He took his own decisions. He exercised a strict discipline. He kept faithfully the same ministers. He imposed on them unity of direction and his principles were still followed by them after his death. He did not conceive of his trade of emperor as a ritual and passive function. He wished to found fidelity to the monarch on a religion of the imperial person. An energetic and complete personality, though he had in him the genius of a founder, there were on the other hand traits in his character which were even antipathetic to the Chinese, they seemed so extraordinary in their country. The first Emperor had about him nothing of the risky adventurer or of the placid sage, who seem to take everything from Destiny because they owe all to their surroundings, and who seem to trust entirely to Heaven, because they leave each step to the hazardous expedients of their favourites of the moment. Such are the national heroes whom glory consecrates. But Ch'in Shih Huang-ti saw clearly and saw far. His ruling qualities were, apparently, a reasoned obstinacy and a spirit of like stamp.

He owed his rapid military successes to a consecutive plan. He only attacked Ch'u, his southern enemy, after having conquered his immediate rivals in the north, the three Chin. To reduce Ch'i and push westward, he waited till the defeat of Ch'u was accomplished. Thus he avoided being taken in the flank in his triumphant march to the east. The same spirit of sustained decision is revealed in his efforts to organize the Empire. Shih Huang-ti invented little. He used the administrative creations of the princes of Ch'in, his predecessors, but he had the boldness to conceive them as valid, not only for a single feudal state, but for the whole Empire. He declared out-of-date the theory of the " barrier-vassals " (*fan ch'en*), established like ramparts around the direct domain of the Sons of Heaven.[1] He extended to all the conquered countries the system of prefectures (*Hien*) and of areas of military control (*Kün*).[2] The princes of Ch'in had begun

[1] SMC, II, 131.   [2] SMC, II, 20.

G

from 687 B.C. to establish prefectures in the annexed territories. The division into prefectures became a rule in 350 B.C.[1] But the custom of giving lands for their life-time to the brothers of the prince (for example, one was distributed in 286 B.C.),[2] persisted, and very often a noble without a fief was placed at the head of a newly conquered territory. Thus, Shu was first granted for life to a prince of the country, then it was allotted in the same way to a prince of the house of Ch'in ; and in 285 B.C. he was replaced by a simple governor.[3] In 277 B.C., a new advance to Ssu-ch'uan gave occasion for the creation of an area under military control, that of K'ien-chong.[4] In the reign of Ch'in Shih Huang-ti, after the revolt of Lao Ngai, marquis of Ch'ang-sin (238 B.C.), there is no further question of such grants. Every conquest ended in the creation of fresh areas of military control and new prefectures. Rather than preserve anything of the feudal principles, the Emperor preferred to enter upon a struggle with the traditionalists. In 221 B.C., he decreed that China should be divided into 36 areas of military control. In 213 B.C., he preserved this organization, although the critics declared that it rendered the maintenance of order uncertain. Each area had at its head a civil administrator (*Kün-shou*) and a military governor (*Kün-wei*) ;[5] a third person (the *Kien-yu-she*, or superintendent) exercised a power of control (the scope of which is not clear). The collegiate principle was the rule for the central administration. Ch'in Shih Huang-ti did not let any power exist which was complete or autonomous.

Of all the aristocratic hierarchy, he only kept a single title, that of marquis,—a title which appears to correspond with the existence of a court nobility.[6] The true nobility was made up of the body of functionaries. These were divided into the twenty degrees of a hierarchy which dated back to Ch'in of the fourth century, and which the first Emperor extended to all the Empire.[7] From the fourth degree, the nobles were exempt from rendering compulsory service. Nobility could be acquired by means of gifts made to the State, particularly in times of famine. It was based on wealth and on services rendered, rather than on birth. Sanctions, positive or

---

[1] SMC, II, 65. [2] SMC, II, 84. [3] SMC, II, 78, note 2.
[4] SMC, II, 87. [5] SMC, II, 132 and 531. [6] SMC, II, 529.
[7] SMC, II, 227.

negative,—promotions or degradations—served as principles
of government. They helped to achieve a mixing of the
social classes and were often used to help in the mixing of
populations. From 286 B.C., the conferring of titles, or the
granting of an amnesty for crimes, occurs with the object of
peopling a conquered territory with people from Ch'in.[1]
Shih Huang-ti practised widely the system of transportation
inaugurated by his predecessors. In 239 B.C. he transferred
all the inhabitants of a rebel town from Shen-si to Kan-su.[2]
The next year, 4000 families, under pretext of imposing a
penalty, were transported into Shu (Ssu-ch'uan).[3] There were
further deportations in 235 B.C.[4] On the other hand, all the
powerful families of China were obliged to come to live in
the Capital. It is to be assumed that these displacements had
not as their sole object the desire to terrorize or to possess
hostages. It appears that Shih Huang-ti really aimed at the
result he in fact achieved : to hasten the assimilation of the
various populations of China. Certain legislative measures
(which will be studied in another chapter) reveal the intention
of reinforcing the ethnical unification by the unification of
customs and of law.

At the same time as he laboured to create the Chinese
people, the Emperor laboured to create China. At the end of
the long wars of the Six Kingdoms, the country was infested
with vagabonds and pillagers. In 216 B.C., as the Emperor,
at the end of a tour of inspection, was walking incognito
in his capital, accompanied only by four soldiers, he was
attacked by brigands. He decided to purge the Empire of
them. In 214 B.C. he got them together *en masse*, and made
use of these large bands to add to and defend the territory
of the Empire. One of these bands was sent to the south-
east [5] and completed the conquest of the country of Yue
(or Yu-yue) begun by Ch'u in 333 B.C. The Yu-yue had
been at that time pushed back from Che-kiang towards the
coast regions of the south (Fu-kien, Kuang-si, northern
Kuang-tong). The campaign undertaken by Shih Huang-ti
in the south began undoubtedly in the first year of the Empire.
Fu-kien was first conquered, then the two Kuangs. The
advance of the Chinese, helped by repeated transportations

[1] SMC, II, 84.   [2] SMC, II, 106.   [3] SMC, II, 112.
[4] SMC, II, 116.   [5] BEFEO, 1923, pp. 263 ff.

of the population, reached, perhaps (?) at the time of the
great effort of 214 B.C., all the coast regions of Annam as
far as Cape Varella. Three new areas of military control
were founded. China, to the south, was bounded by the sea
along an immense frontier. In 215 B.C., the Emperor,
inspecting Chih-li, had pushed on to the mountains which
border it to the north. That is where the State of Yen,
after a victory over the Hiong-nu, had put up a long wall.
Shih Huang-ti, who had, in 219 B.C., sent explorers from Ch'i
(Shantung) over the sea sent others in 215 B.C., who came
from Yen. Possibly he had his eye on Korea, quite as much
as on the " mysterious isles." In any case, he sketched out
a maritime policy ; but his immediate preoccupations were
turned to the side where lay the steppes. It was in 215 B.C.,
when he was in the North of Chih-li, that he decided to join
the pieces of the long walls into a great wall which would
protect the Chinese Empire against the Hu. The same year
he ordered General Mong T'ien to attempt a great military
effort in the bend of the River. Mong T'ien was able in fact
to push back the Barbarians to the north of the Hoang-ho.
In 214 B.C., he passed the River and set himself to construct
the eastern part of the Great Wall. The Emperor sent to
him, to carry out the work and colonize the country, a whole
crowd of convicts. The walled frontier of North China
stretches from the river Leao to the region of Lin-t'ao (north-
west of Kan-su). Through it China found herself in contact
no longer only with the Jong, the Man and Me, divided tribes,
but with the great nomad peoples, whom the Chinese called
the Hu and the Hiong-nu. It was exactly at the end of the
third century B.C. that the Hiong-nu formed " for the first
time a united and strong nation." [1] We have less information
on the policy pursued by the Emperor in the West, in the
mountain region ; but there also, contact was established in
the region of Kiang-chong (south-west of Lin-t'ao) with
vigorous and powerful populations. Tibetan tribes, indeed,
then occupied the mountainous valleys of the upper Yellow
River. The territory of Ch'in Shih Huang-ti extended roughly
over what was to be the *China of the Eighteen Provinces*. It
is believed that foreigners called it *China* after the name of
the *Ch'in* dynasty. The founder of this dynasty indeed gave

[1] SMC, Introd., LXV.

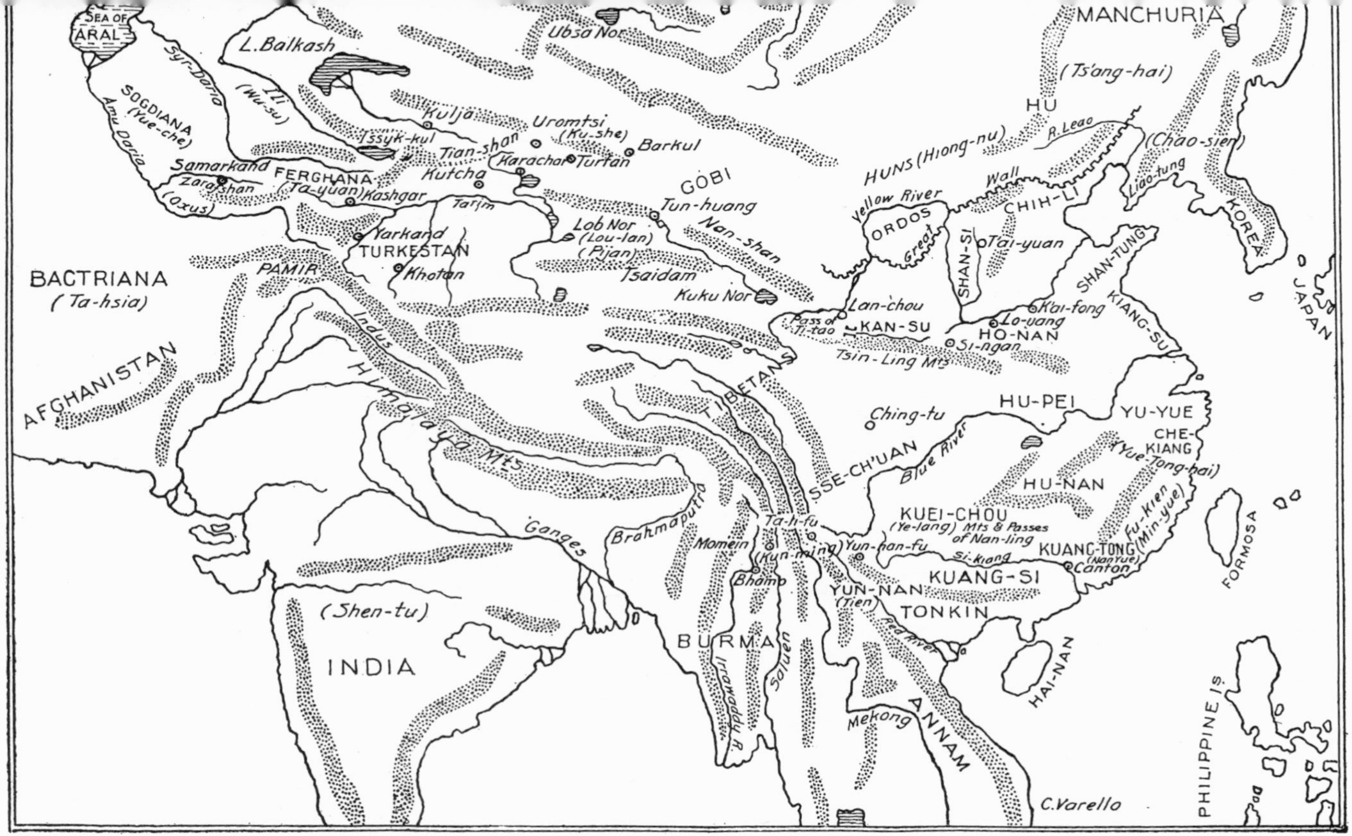

MAP V.   ANCIENT CHINA AND THE SURROUNDING COUNTRIES

[face p. 100

China its traditional limits. He brought it on all sides into contact with great civilizations or great peoples.

In the vast country which he finally provided with frontiers, and which he wished to make homogeneous, the Emperor suppressed internal barriers and local fortifications. He gloried in the inscription which he had raised at the very time when he was engaged in tracing the Great Wall of the North (215 B.C.). " The Emperor has displayed his prestige ; —his virtue has neutralized the power of the nobles ;—he is the first to have established uniformly the Great Peace. He has thrown down and destroyed the internal ramparts and the outer walls (of the principalities) ;—he has made openings through the barriers in the rivers ;—he has smoothed out and suppressed difficulties and obstacles." [1] He had, in 225 B.C., turned the Yellow River towards the south-east below Yong-yang and created Hong-kou. This canal put into communication with one another all the countries of Ho-nan and, uniting the rivers Ch'i and Huai, reached to the territory of Ch'u.[2] It was first and foremost designed for the transport of grain. It was on the borders of Yong-yang (near K'ai-fong in Ho-nan) that the imperial granary of Ngao [3] was established on a mountain. This great centre of distribution, where the armies of the Empire were re-victualled, was, on the death of Ch'in Shih Huang-ti, the stake fought over in the battles which were waged by the pretenders to the succession.[4] Here was the heart of China. A network of roads completed the system of canals. It was begun in the year 220 B.C., when " the imperial highways were traced." Fifty paces broad, planted with trees, raised to be out of reach of floods, with low sides and a central alley reserved for the sovereign, they stretched, it was said, from the capital to the extreme bounds of the Empire, to east and south.[5] In 212 B.C. a great road was undertaken, leading towards the North, as far as the great bend of the River ; " cuttings were made in the mountains, embankments in the valleys and communication was established in a straight line." [6] Here were the strategic roads and (as the construction of the last proves) Shih Huang-ti saw clearly that the danger for China was henceforth towards the North, from the direction of the

[1] SMC, II, 165 ff.　　　　[2] SMC, III, 522.　　　[3] SMC, II, 101 and 302.
[4] SMC, II, 302, 307, 360.　　[5] SMC, II, 139.　　　[6] SMC, II, 174.

Hiong-nu. This gigantic network of roads was like armour to preserve the unity of the country. A collection of verse by Chinese skilled in feudal law contends that the ancient sovereigns, from remotest antiquity, made uniform roads at the same time as they achieved uniformity of writing and customs. Ch'in Shih Huang-ti would not be untruthful if he boasted of having unified the system of writing (the name of his minister Li Ssu is connected with this reform, the importance of which was enormous), nor if he claimed that he had imposed standard dimensions for the axles of chariots, —and finally, had the wheel-ruts placed the same distance apart everywhere, so that the same carriage could travel throughout the whole country.[1]

It appears that the Emperor wished to found the moral unity of his people, by seeking to make them a people of agriculturalists. He aimed at attaching them to agricultural pursuits, through making general the agrarian revolution, achieved in Ch'in from 350–348 B.C. In 216 B.C. the peasants became proprietors, subject to a tax, proportionate to the area of their fields. They ceased to be tenants, bound to furnish, with some compulsory services, a part of their harvest. The Emperor, in an inscription of 215 B.C., declares that " his favours are extended to cattle and to horses (and that) his benefits have enriched the soil of the land." " His bounty has extended to all the patrimonies ;—all have long since taken to the fields,—and *there is no one who is not at ease in his own home.*" [2]   When he granted to cultivators an assured right of ownership, acquired on payment of a fixed tax, Shih Huang-ti was thinking of the stability of the State. He distrusted merchants, whom he saw as speculators and troublemongers. He deported the shopkeepers in 214 B.C.[3] In 219 B.C. he prided himself " on having honoured agriculture and proscribed the lowest of the professions (commerce)." [4] He issued copper money (round with a square hole), but he made it very heavy and difficult of transport.[5] We shall see shortly the importance which commerce and monetary questions assumed under the Han. Ch'in Shih Huang-ti, while increasing in the Empire the facilities of exchange, purposed to hinder the commercial enterprise which these

[1] SMC, II, 135.   [2] SMC, II, 166.   [3] SMC, II, 168.
[4] SMC, II, 146.   [5] SMC, III, 539.

facilities brought with them. He saw in this a cause of social instability. But if the Chinese did not remain, as he wished, a people entirely devoted to agriculture, the opening up of great ways of communication, by which commerce profited, must have helped largely in the progress of national unity.

To obtain unity of thought, Shih Huang-ti tried to spread throughout China a strict domestic morality. Above all he wanted to establish the worship of the Emperor. This part of his work is that which history appears to have misunderstood most. It shows Ch'in Shih Huang-ti as pursuing by magic practices the conquest of personal immortality. It is certain that the Emperor had magicians in his service, but one fact is to be noted. " According to the laws of Ch'in (said one of these magicians, at the moment when he was preparing to flee from the Court) only one art can be exercised at a time and a mistake means immediate death." [1] Shih Huang-ti, when he had the books of *Annals* and political works burnt, as in his view, worthless and dangerous, took care to preserve the works relating to " medicine, pharmacy, divination, agriculture, arboriculture," that is to say the whole of the literature of the technical sciences. The Emperor only trusted in technical specialists and only gave protection to the useful sciences—magic (astronomy, astrology, alchemy, knowledge of drugs) was in his time the source of all knowledge, the hope of the far-seeing. The Chinese historians, in spite of all their ill-will, did not succeed in showing that Ch'in Shih Huang-ti, like so many other sovereigns of their country, was a dupe, who let himself be taken in by trickery. Discipline and devotion were as great, no doubt, among his learned men as among his soldiers. It is difficult to say just what their master expected of them, but it is clear that the whole conduct of the Emperor is explained by the desire to pass for a living divinity. It is to the achievement of this result that his dramatic ascents of holy mountains were aimed, as well as his invisible existence in a palace, constructed after the pattern of the world of the gods. He was informed about everything by reports (he handled a hundred and twenty pounds of them every day) and did not hesitate to go about (though almost alone and without making himself known)

[1] SMC, II, 179.

for the purpose of investigation. Although he rejected out-of-date rites, by which the ancient Sons of Heaven kept up their Prestige while denying themselves all practical activity,—he, like them, wished to make all his subjects feel that he had a divine nature. Thus is explained the mystery with which he surrounded himself and the songs which he caused to be written, to celebrate at the same time his journeyings and those of the Immortals.[1] This positive and powerful mind perceived clearly that for the newly-founded Empire a new religion was necessary, and that to an autocratic power a worship of the imperial person ought to correspond.

Shih Huang-ti died at fifty years of age. He had in a few years brought China to a state of unity and concentration which she was destined never to surpass. Thanks to him, the idea of Chinese unity became an active ideal, but China never again found a controlling genius equal to his, or one who had the audacity to wish to achieve national unity in the form of a centralized State.

II

THE CENTURY OF THE EMPEROR WU

History calls " first Emperor *of the dynasty of Ch'in* (Ch'in Shih Huang-ti) " the man who had wished to be called " first Emperor (Shih Huang-ti)."

It is true that the first Emperor had placed the capital of the Empire at Ch'in, but he did not allow the Empire to be treated as spoil by the people of Ch'in. He succeeded in resisting the provincial egoism of his former subjects. In 237 B.C. he allowed himself to countersign a decree ordering the expulsion of foreigners settled in Ch'in, but he repealed it immediately. His principal minister, during his whole reign, was Li Ssu, a native of Ch'u, who was disgraced and put to death by Shih Huang-ti's successor. The same successor let the soldiers of Ch'in " treat without proper regard " the officers and men of the provincial militias. A revolt of particularist pride explains the rapid fall of the Ch'in.[2]

Eight years after the death of the great Ch'in Emperor,

---

[1] SMC, II, 183.　　　　[2] SMC, II, 272.

the Han inherited his achievement. They seemed, almost without effort, to build up again the unity of the Empire. Under them, China accepted unity, in order to present a single front to the Barbarians. Never, perhaps, was national sentiment more powerful than under their dynasty ; but the attempts of the Han to give internal cohesion to the Empire were extremely timid. In the four centuries of their domination, they did not succeed in creating a State with a constitution suitable for an immense Empire like China.

The epoch of the Han is that of a magnificent start in Chinese civilization. China never had a better chance than in their time to become a political reality. She did not become one. She did not cease to be a collection of provinces, which were related by community of culture, and which could only be united, from time to time, by some danger experienced in common.

(1) *The Consolidation of the Han Dynasty.* The most brilliant epoch of Chinese civilization under the Han is the reign of the Emperor Wu (140–87 B.C.).

Founded (in 202 B.C.) by a fortunate adventurer, the first Han dynasty followed Ch'in modestly. Kao-Chu (202–195 B.C.) installed himself in their ancient fief. He dreamed before all of strengthening himself in the *interior of the passes*.[1] Thus was designated the country of Ch'in " made difficult of access by the girdle formed round about it by the River and the mountains. . . . Its position is so advantageous that when it lets loose its soldiers against the nobles, it is like a man who pours water out of a pitcher from the top of a high house." [2] Kao-Chu would have preferred to establish it " in his native land." To the expatriation to which they reluctantly agreed, the Han owed it that they did not appear as conquerors, bringing to their compatriots the spoils of China.

Less from policy than from necessity, they avoided also being taken for monopolists. Kao-Chu only attained to the Empire by promising a share of the booty to various *condottieri*. In 202 B.C. he distributed kingdoms to them, and appeared to have revived the ancient feudal states. There were again kings in Ch'u, Ch'i, Yen, Chao, Han, Leang

---

[1] SMC, II, 387.   [2] SMC, II, 397.

(the new name for Wei).   Kao-Chu was, indeed, only master of the country of Ch'in, provided with an imperial title.

However, the principles of the imperial administration created by Shih Huang-ti, endured. The generals without a past, whom Kao-Chu had to make kings, had no attachments to the overlordship which was allotted to them. The Emperor profited by this to displace them (201 B.C.). Their kingdoms were only granted for their own lifetime, and their title was precarious. Among the beneficiaries (and in the most important of these estates, at Ch'u and at Ch'i, for example), care was taken to put some relatives of the Emperor. The most powerful of the " fieffed " generals, Han-sin, attempted to revolt, with the assistance of Hiong-nu, who had rapidly reappeared in the bend of the River. Kao-Chu went to meet them in Shan-si. He was surrounded by them in the district of the Fen, and barely escaped disaster.   The fear caused to the Chinese by the Barbarians was not unconnected with the success of the intrigues which permitted Kao-Chu gradually to replace in the fiefs his former companions in arms by members of the imperial family. Yet this new feudal system was no less turbulent nor less dangerous than the other.

It was a pure chance that it did not take on excessive power. On the death of Kao-Chu, his widow opposed her own relations (the Lu) to those of her husband (the Liu). No political idea seems to have guided her (not even the elementary principle : divide in order to rule). She was obeying simply the old popular idea that the chief rôle in guardianship belongs to the maternal relatives. The dynasty nearly foundered (180 B.C.) in the rivalry between the Liu and the Lu. They both found themselves enfeebled by their struggles.

There was, nevertheless, in the reign of the Emperor Wen (179–157 B.C.) a rebellion of the King of Tsi-pei (177 B.C.), and then a rebellion of the King of Huai-nan (176 B.C.). Both of these plotted with the Barbarians. The country of Yue had become independent again, and the incursions of the Hiong-nu were made more and more frequently (177, 166, 159 B.C.).[1] It was high time to secure again some power for the Empire, and for that purpose to ruin the great vassals.

[1] SMC, II, 381, 468.

The Emperor Wen dreamt (perhaps) of lessening the extent of the estates granted for life by multiplying (under charitable pretexts) those nominated to them (178 B.C.). He tried above all to remove the chief intriguers from the capital (179 B.C.).

In the reign of his successor, the Emperor King (156–141 B.C.) the revolt of the chief vassals broke out (154 B.C.). " Forming a league from North to South they advanced from the West." [1] The Emperor only subdued the rebels with difficulty. They depended for support on the Hiong-nu. The Emperor was obliged to sacrifice his minister Ch'ao Ch'o, as guilty of having wished to deprive the nobles of their territory. He barely succeeded, in 144 B.C., in dividing some fiefs whose titular holders were dead, fortunately, at the time when he made the attempt. But the Hiong-nu (142 B.C.) continued to invade Shan-si.

The Emperor Wu [2] ascended the throne in 140 B.C. He was then sixteen years old ; and he was to reign fifty-four years. The Emperor prudently adopted the plan of Ch'ao Ch'o and time worked in his favour. He decided, in 127 B.C., that the estates, instead of reverting to the eldest son, should, on the father's death, be divided between all the sons ; he hoped to secure, in the end, with the automatic breaking up of the fiefs, the extinction of the great vassals.[3] This nibbling policy was sure, but had the fault of slowness (Kao-Chu had distributed 143 such estates ; at the end of the first Han there were 241 ; the breaking-up policy had not succeeded in doubling the number).

The Emperor Wu established near each king or marquis an imperial resident, who had the title of adviser, and who was a censor and a spy. The part played by these persons is shown clearly in the affair which ended, in 122 B.C., in the enforced suicide of the kings of Heng-shan and Huai-nan. On the denunciation of the resident the Emperor sent a legate, whose assassination was attempted. A first penalty (124 B.C.) consisted in diminishing the estate of Huai-nan by two prefectures, and of leaving to the King of Heng-shan only the nomination of the lower officials. An attempt at

---

[1] SMC, II, 509.
[2] On the reign of the Emperor Wu, consult Chapter II of the Introduction by Chavannes to his translation of SMC.
[3] SMC, Introd., LXXXIX.

revolt followed. The Emperor then delegated a functionary with full powers. The princes committed suicide ; their relatives were put to death, as well as a large number of their adherents.[1]

The aim the Emperor Wu had in view was to reduce the feudal system to an outside show only. The military areas of the directly ruled domain were, as in the time of Ch'in, under a military governor and a civil governor. The superintendent was suppressed, and his functions entrusted to *Inquisitors* (*Pu-ch'ŭ-she*), a kind of *missi dominici* of whom there were three for the Empire (106 B.C.). Legates and residents played a rôle with regard to the princes like that of the governors and inquisitors of the imperial domain. The Emperor made it an established rule to name for these posts only plebeians and " new men." These people were imbued with the legalistic principles, which the Ch'in had raised to a place of honour. They waged on the nobility, not without heroism, secret war. Chu-fu Yen (who had caused the principle of the division of the fiefs at each succession to be adopted) was, it is said, a man of low origin. Named resident at the court of the king of Ch'i, he did not hesitate to accuse him of incest. The Prince committed suicide. The Emperor disclaimed responsibility by having Chu-fu Yen put to death.

The nobles dreaded the clerks, who were servants of the autocracy : " The whole Empire is of opinion that clerks ought not to be appointed to high offices," said a conservative writer.[2] The Emperor Wu succeeded, with the aid of his lawyers, in reducing what remained of the old aristocracy to impotence. He favoured the formation of a new nobility, more easily managed, recruited from rich upstarts who had entered on honour-seeking careers. Not only was the hierarchy of the nobility instituted by the Ch'in maintained, but in 123 B.C. it was duplicated by the creation of a nobility, admitting of eleven degrees. It was called a military nobility, for the titles were sold for the benefit of the war treasury. The reforms of the Emperor Wu had revolutionary results. In principle they were only expedients of a financial or political order.[3] In default of interior stability the Emperor used the competition between the old and the new nobility to put an

---

[1] SMC, Introd., xc.   [2] SMC, Introd., xcii.
[3] On this social crisis, see p. 411.

end to the great rebellions. These, combined with the emptiness of the Treasury, hindered a revival of the war against the Barbarians.

(2) *The Wars for Prestige.* The greatness of the reign of the Emperor Wu lies in the struggle he maintained against the Hiong-nu. He limited himself, during the first years, to a simple defensive, but he had the great road to the north repaired and organized great bodies of cavalry,[1] with centres for provisions and studs. It was necessary first of all to contrive a plan of campaign.

In 138 B.C. the Emperor sent Chang K'ien on a mission to treat with a people, the Ta Yue-che, who, according to information (an information service thus existed) were rivals of the Hiong-nu. Chang K'ien (whose Odyssey is not free from the marvellous) was taken by the Hiong-nu, and then escaped. In Ferghana he visited the kingdom of the Ta-yuan, then passed into the valleys of the Syr-daria and Amu-daria. There he met the Yue-che who, fleeing before the Hiong-nu, had first settled in the region of the Ili ; under pressure from the Wu-sun, they had been obliged to pursue their march to the east, as far as Sogdiana, whence, pressing them back to the south of the Oxus (Amu-daria), they had chased the Ta-hia into Bactriana. Chang-K'ien was able in a general way to trace as far as Afghanistan a road of the north, at that time cut by the Hiong-nu. Further, he brought back some rather vague information about Turkestan and its importance. Finally, an inquiry had led him to assume the existence of a commercial route which, escaping from the control of the Hiong-nu, went from Turkestan to Ssu-ch'uan and Yunnan, along the border of the country of Shen-tu (India). Chang K'ien (after another captivity among the Hiong-nu), returned to China, it is said, in 125 B.C.

There could not be any question of employing the Ta Yue-che against the Hiong-nu ; but the Wu-sun, who had replaced them in the region of the Ili, might be useful allies. Chang K'ien left in 115 B.C. on an embassy to them, whilst other envoys went to eastern Turkestan and Ferghana (Ta-yuan). Furthermore, in 135 B.C. a circumspect explorer, T'ang-mong, had divined the importance of the commercial

---

[1] SMC, III, 561.

route which, starting from Canton and going up the valley of the Si-kiang, reached by Kuei-chow (kingdom of Ye-lang) the upper valleys of Yun-nan and of Ssu-ch'uan. This information, combined with that of Chang K'ien, made comprehensible the interest of the routes leading by the Kingdom of Tien (Yunnan-fu) and that of the Kun-ming (Ta-li fu) towards Upper Burma and the country of Shen-tu (India).

After a first period of tentative and scattered efforts [against the Hiong-nu (in 130 and 127 B.C.), against the people of Yue (in 138 and 135 B.C.) and the small principalities of Yun-nan and Ssu-ch'uan (130 B.C.)] a plan of action came to a head, it is said, in 126 B.C.

The first attack was on the Hiong-nu. After two campaigns by Wei-ch'ing (124 and 123 B.C.), which aimed at freeing the approaches to the River, a great cavalry raid was attempted right into the Barbarians' country. In 121 B.C., Ho K'ü-p'ing, general of the light horse, threw 10,000 horse-soldiers 500 kilometres to the west. He beat the Hiong-nu and took prisoner a Barbarian prince of north-west Kan-su (Leang-chou). He renewed his exploit some months later, getting as far as the approaches to the Altai and the Tian Shan. The Kinglets of western Kan-su made submission. The year 119 B.C. was that of the decisive effort. Wei-ch'ing succeeded in surprising the Shen-yu (supreme chief) of the Hiong-nu, to the north of the Great Wall, and threw him back towards the north, whilst Ho K'ü-p'ing, marching out from the mountains north of Chih-li, advanced 1000 kilometres into the interior of the steppes. He returned bringing as prisoners ninety enemy chiefs. These victories gave the Chinese a prestige which, for a considerable number of years, was to assure them relative peace on their northern border. They profited by it to conquer all Kan-su and to establish themselves on the watershed north of Nan Shan (Tun-huang). This gave them an important road-head,— that which commanded the access to the Altai.

In 112 B.C. the effort bore towards the south. The littoral provinces of the south, conquered by Shih Huang-ti had, on the fall of the Ch'in, become independent again. The most northern of them, Che-kiang (Yue Tong-hai) and Fu-kien (Min Yue) were rivals. In 138 B.C. the Chinese, acting as protectors, transported to the north of the Blue River the whole of the people of Yue Tong-hai. In 112 B.C., they dared to intervene in Nan Yue. In 111 B.C. six armies, penetrating by different passes of the Nan-ling into the Si-kiang basin, occupied Canton, and all Nan Yue became Chinese. Tong Yue, isolated, was conquered in 110 B.C. and its inhabitants transferred to the north of the Blue River. China possessed for the first time an immense maritime frontier.

At the same time, she gained control of the roads of Si-kiang. After having obtained the submission of the States of Ye-lang (Kuei-chow) and Tien (Yun-nan), the Emperor Wu, according to the testimony of Pan Ku, hoped to establish a continuous chain of territories stretching as far as Ta-hia (Bactriana). He could not conquer the resistance of the mountaineers of the Ta-li fu region.

This check on a grandiose project of enveloping central Asia by the south perhaps contributed to fixing attention on Turkestan. The principal campaign, preceded by numerous negotiations, took place in 108 B.C. It brought in its train the defeat of the principalities of Lou-lan (Pijan) and of Ku-she (Turfan and Uromtsi). The Chinese from that time commanded the routes of the southern Altai, and found themselves in contact with the Wu-sun of the Ili. They attempted to exploit their success by pushing on to Ferghana (Ta-yuan). The first campaign (104–103 B.C.) failed. The Emperor stopped the retreating army at Tun-huang and forced it, in 102 B.C., to set out again across Turkestan. It finally took the capital of the Ta-yuan. The princes of Ferghana and of Zarafchan sent hostages. They remained faithful to the Han during all the reign of the Emperor Wu. At one stroke, Turkestan fell under Chinese influence and the Hiong-nu, cut off from all communication with it, found themselves threatened by China towards the west.

The eastern raid of Ho K'ü-p'ing (in 119 B.C.) had shown what could be achieved by pressure exercised from the east. The conquest of Chao-sien (between the peninsula of Liao-tung and the north-west of Korea) carried out in 108 B.C. by the combined action of a fleet and a land army, allowed of the formation of four new prefectures which could be a base of operations of great significance for a campaign directed towards eastern Gobi.

As early as 110 B.C. all seemed ready for a decisive blow. The Emperor was not 50 years old. Neither soldiers nor generals were lacking. As soon as " the Barbarians of the south were punished " the Emperor went himself at the head of 180,000 horsemen to attack the *Shen-yu* in the steppe. It was simply a military parade.

In 107 B.C. the Hiong-nu apparently sought alliance with the Chinese, and then again began hostilities. In 104 B.C. an attempt was made to take advantage of their divisions, and a camp was made for deserters ; but a Chinese column, not sufficiently strong, was surrounded in 103 B.C. and the camp was destroyed the following year. In 99 B.C. an expedition which set out from Nan-Shan could with difficulty return to its base, whilst another column was entirely destroyed. In 97 and 90 B.C., the Chinese suffered further serious defeats. The first enthusiasm had died down. The great plan of the Emperor Wu (if, as the Chinese historians believe, he had one) remained unachieved.

The Emperor could at least flatter himself on having acquired one important advantage. Further Kan-su, at last colonized, formed a projection between the Barbarians of the steppe and those of the mountain. [The Tibetans, indeed, began to appear dangerous neighbours, and it was necessary to fight strenuously against them for more than three years (111–108 B.C.).] [1] But there remains, as a charge against the Emperor Wu, that his unreasonable demands upon, and his severity towards his generals, when they did not lead actually to desertions, discouraged their spirit of enterprise.

(3) *The Increase of the Central Power.* Weariness made an immense military effort end in failure. It had been accompanied by a financial effort, remarkable for intelligent flashes rather than for any directing ideas or continued plan.

The most urgent problem was that of money. The Han (in order not to appear monopolists) had allowed the system of free mintage. [2] The fieffed princes of Che-kiang and Ssuch'uan had inundated China with their coinage. Their power frightened the Emperor. He forbade the minting of money. This measure (if it was applied) did not trouble the monopolizers in the least. They enriched themselves in proportion as the imperial Treasury was emptied to pay the military contractors and the contractors for public works. The imperial administration tried first, to establish again in a more scientific fashion the circulation of bills. It tried to acclimatize the system of loans. It set the example by proceeding to make loans of land to ruined and transported people.[1] It ruined itself while " the rich traders and big merchants . . . (gained) fortunes of several myriads of gold pounds : they did not aid the government in its distress, however, and the misery of the common people was doubled." [2] " Money was multiplied . . . merchandise had become rare and grown dear." Then the Emperor after having several times modified the standard of copper money, tried in 120 B.C. to give currency to a new money (an alloy of tin and silver) by using religious artifices designed to create confidence and to make people accept this new standard. Severe measures punished counterfeiting. It did not cease.[3] In 113 B.C. there appeared an edict declaring valueless all money not issued by the imperial workshops (*Shang-lin*). The setting up of the monopoly was mainly of use to test the fidelity of the nobles with estates. It gave opportunity for severe punishments. In 112 B.C. the defrauding princes (to the number of 106 out of a total of 250 at most) were degraded.

To fight against private monopolies, the Emperor Wu set up State monopolies. A service (that of *Shao-fu*) was put in charge of the special revenues of the Emperor, which were drawn principally from the mountains, seas, lakes, and marshes. " The mountains and the sea are the stores of Heaven and of Earth " (that is to say they belong *by private title* to the Emperor) ; he, however, " to favour the public reserves, linked these exploitations to the service of the *Ta-nong* (State Treasury)." This example once given, the monopoly[4] of the salt tax and of iron (119) was instituted, to prevent people without status from " reserving to their sole use the riches of the mountains and of the sea in order to gain a fortune . . . and from putting the lower classes into *subjection* to themselves." Forges and salt pans became public enterprises, and the sale of iron and of salt was entrusted

---

[1] SMC, III, 562.   [2] SMC, III, 546.   [3] SMC, III, 584.
[4] In 98 B.C. a monopoly in the manufacture and sale of fermented drinks was set up.

H

to the service of the State. It was decided at once to subordinate to the prefectoral administration the local officers
of this new public service.

Even more than industry, commerce (which was always
treated as " lowest of the professions ") had given birth to
large private fortunes. Besides this, speculators (" those who
buy on credit and make loans, those who buy to heap up
in the towns, those who accumulate all sorts of commodities ")
tended, by means of *illegal associations*, to become *predominant*.[1] The State defended itself and its people by
instituting (115 B.C.) a public transport system, associated
with an office of control (*Kün-shu*). This had as its mission
to ensure the circulation of " commercial produce " in such
a way as to prevent " sudden variations in price " in the
Empire. It had also to try to secure a certain uniformity in
the markets, where up to then the officials had acted each
" at his own will." [2]   The working of this system (called
P'ing-ch'un—balance of trade) was assured by the aid of
several assistants dependent on the minister of the Public
Treasury (*Ta-nong*) and charged with " going frequently into
the Prefectures to establish there the officials *Kün-shu*, and
the officials for salt and iron." They gave orders for distant
countries to deliver as dues the products peculiar to them
and those which the merchants transported, in order (only
to traffic with them) at the time when they were dear ; they
gave them out and transferred them to each other. In the
capital were set up officials, *P'ing-ch'un*, who had charge of
delivery and transport for the whole Empire. State workmen made the carts and all the means of transport. They were
dependent also on the *Ta-nong*. The *Ta-nong* had the duty
of stocking merchandise ; when goods became dear they
were sold, and bought when prices were low.   " In this way
the rich merchants and large shopkeepers would be prevented
from making big profits . . . and prices would be regulated
throughout the Empire." This system helped to avoid local
famines.   " Transport increased until it reached (for grain)
six million bushels a year . . . and (for textiles) five million
pieces of silk," and this was done while maintaining
" equality of price " and " without increasing the taxes of the
people." The granary of the capital, the granary of Kan-

---

[1] SMC, III, 574, 581, 563.   [2] SMC, III, 579, 597.

ch'iuan (Shen-si) and all the military granaries of the frontiers were filled. (This tribute comes from Ssu-ma Ch'ien, an unfriendly observer.) But a drought having followed the establishment of the system, P'ing-ch'un, it was immediately proposed to boil Sang Hong-yang, its inventor, alive : " Heaven will then give rain." [1]

This advice came from Pu She, hostile to State enterprises and a partisan of the " normal receipts " drawn from taxes on land and duties on textiles (which were classed as peasant productions).[2] Pu She justly found that the iron and salt of the State were of poor quality, and that the taxes on boats, destined to favour public means of transport, had, as a final result, through diminishing the number of merchants, an increase in prices.[3] This partisan of competition and of free trade was a man enriched by a great building enterprise. At least he had a certain fiscal courage. He advocated the system of gifts made by the rich to the State. Of course, the donations ought to be freely agreed to, but they were presented as a duty incumbent on the " rich," and equivalent to that which the " sages " fulfilled in fighting on the frontier. The Emperor stated that the proceeds of voluntary contribution, even when the invitation to give was issued with theatrical forms, and with the support of a virtuous rhetoric, showed only very feeble returns. (" He did not find anyone in the Empire who would give up a part of his resources to assist the provincial officials "—" rich and well-known people vied with each other in concealing their wealth.") [4] The Emperor made contributions on acquired fortunes more productive by instituting fiscal control.[5]

The promoter of fiscal control was Chang T'ang (" he died (115 B.C.) unregretted by the people ").[6] He was an administrator and a jurist. He occupied himself with great works of canal-making designed to render the transport of grain less costly. He made it a recognized principle that the judges ought not to decide on recommendation, but from

---

[1] SMC, III, 596–600.   [2] SMC, III, 600.   [3] SMC, III, 595.
[4] SMC, III, 575, 583, 594. In 111 B.C. there was published a decree raising to the command of the nation, Pu She, who " after having given his superfluous wealth," had wished,—" seized with enthusiasm," " to exercise himself over the management of the boats," and to take part in the campaign against Nan Yue. Pu She did not leave. He was made a marquis and received as a present 60 gold pounds and a fine domain.—(Land and gold ennoble.)
[5] SMC, III, 583.   [6] SMC, III, 584.

personal knowledge of the causes.[1] He advocated the creation of a silver coinage. We have seen that the money policy ended in a great lawsuit which allowed of the decimation of the nobility. In the same spirit Ch'ang Tang and his disciples intervened in fiscal matters. Under their influence, the office of " just denunciators " (*Che-che*) was created and entrusted to pitiless lawyers.[2] They formed itinerant commissions, who went into the areas of military control and kingdoms to judge affairs relating to acquired fortunes. " They took from the *people* riches whose value amounted to hundreds of thousands (of pieces of money), slaves by the thousand and ten thousand, fields in number amounting to several hundreds of *k'ing* in the great prefectures, and to hundreds in the small ones, and dwellings in proportionate numbers. Then the merchants whose fortunes attained to or surpassed the mean, were nearly all ruined. The *people* " delighted in good cheer and beautiful clothes and no one troubled any more to increase and accumulate his patrimony. But the provincial officials, thanks to salt, iron, and levies on acquired fortunes, had abundant resources." [3] The ordinance issued in 119 B.C. instituted a list in which traders were to be inscribed. The investment of their fortune in landed property was forbidden under pain of confiscation, so that they could not benefit fraudulently by the advantages granted to agriculturalists. All had to make a declaration of their fortune. Refusal to make it, or the making of an incomplete one, was punished by confiscation and by the penalty of a year of forced labour at the frontier. The duty levied was one-twentieth of the fortune acquired. Merchandise or raw materials stocked by artisans and merchants was included in the deductions, the basis of deduction being higher for artisans who had in their shops raw material for manufacture. Wheeled vehicles and boats were taxed in accordance with their capacity, which was taken as a sign of the importance of the traffic.[4] Idlers, finally, were struck at : gamblers, hunters, patrons of cock-fights and horse-racing had to choose between penal servitude and entry into an official career—an entry which was obtained with difficulty.[5] Voluntary contributions (in grain) allowed contributors to obtain exemption from

---

[1] SMC, III, 529, 558.   [2] SMC, III, 582.   [3] SMC, III, 586.
[4] SMC, III, 575.   [5] SMC, III, 588.

compulsory labour and access to public office.[1]—The levies
on capital filled to overflowing the treasury of Shang-lin,[2]
to which was attached a special office (*Shuei-heng*). The
confiscated fields constituted the State domain ; the confiscated slaves became public servants and were for the most
part employed in the transport of grain. The convicts
(Ssu-ma Ch'ien estimates their number at more than a
million)[3] were, after an amnesty, either incorporated in the
army or sent as colonists, in company with 700,000 poor
people, sufferers from the flood (120 B.C.) into the newly-
conquered territory (of Sin-ch'in), right to the north of the
great bend of the River (Ordos). After which (in 112 B.C.)
" the denunciations of fortune, *of which use had been made only*
to people the territory of Sin-ch'in, were suppressed." [4]

The fiscal measures of the Emperor Wu are explained in
part by the impoverishment of the State, ruined by its
victories. Private fortunes were raised on this ruin and a
feudalism based on finance added its misdeeds to those of
the great vassals. If, however, the speculators formed
powerful " illegal societies," it must be added that the great
vassals were not the last to speculate. Imperial finance was
inspired chiefly by political aims ; it sought to create royal
rights, while destroying seigniorial rights. This work was
guided by lawyers, by means of financial expedients, the
depreciation of money and the lack of equilibrium in prices
being utilized conjointly to justify the establishment of
monopolies. Thus the public treasury was filled at the
expense of private fortunes (including the imperial fortune).
It was moreover necessary to readjust the budget. This had
been established " by taking count of the appointments of
officials and of public expenses in such a way as to determine
the capitation levy on the people." But wars, large public
works, the expenses of colonization, the growth in numbers
of civil and military officials had increased the budget of
expenses, at the very moment when movable property
assumed importance. The creation of taxation on movable
property was, remarkable to note, advocated by the financiers
belonging to the newly rich classes of the nation (traders
or industrialists), whilst the landed proprietors remained
partisans of taxes weighing solely on the peasants and the

---

[1] SMC, III, 599.   [2] SMC, III, 587.   [3] SMC, III, 580.   [4] SMC, III, 591.

soil.   Taxation, in fact, continued to be indistinguishable from tribute and homage.   It was a way to acquire nobility. The enriched traders and industrialists wished to pay it, and were even disposed to tolerate a restriction of commercial liberty.   They accepted the competition of the State, and the making of laws which restricted their profits, on condition that commerce ceased to be considered an ignominious profession.   They wished to be able to become officials.   To open to themselves an official career, they entered into a struggle with the great proprietors and with those who held to the principle of inherited office.   In these latter, the old spirit of the feudal nobility lived again.   They were opposed to honours granted to personal merit, on the grounds that they might be given to soldiers with distinguished careers or conferred on professional administrators.   They did not admit that valour should be preferred to birth.   Thanks to this conflict of interests, a new order tended to establish itself. The principle of making use of ability entered into competition with the old principle that devotion to the Prince sufficed for everything.   And some minds, passing beyond the idea of the Prince as simply creator of the social hierarchy, advanced to the conception of the State.   They even saw in it, not a simple organ with power to command, but a general office of regulation and control.

The situation, socially, financially, in money affairs, was revolutionary.   If the Emperor Wu had had some kindred spirit, he might have been able to profit by this and create, in a new order of society, the Chinese State.   A particular concurrence of external and internal circumstances might have allowed the public mentality to escape from the feudal outlook.   But the Emperor only saw the most urgent needs. He seems only to have thought of using varied expedients from day to day—rejected when they had yielded sufficient to appear worn out—and new men—sacrificed as soon as they had succeeded well enough to assume a dangerous air of authority.   The restlessness of the despot and the short vision of the imperial law-makers made China miss the rarest opportunity she had had to become a compact and organized State.

(4) *The Task of Civilization.*   Apparently, the anxiety to create a State was less strong than the desire to extend

Chinese civilization. The Emperor Wu worked magnificently to propagate the latter. He attempted to colonize the territory of the Ordos ; he completed the colonization of Kan-su and of Manchuria ; he definitely acquired for China, together with the basin of the Huai and the southern coasts, the whole immense country of the Blue River.

We have seen that in 120 B.C., the northern region of the bend of the Yellow River received a great number of Chinese emigrants. More than 100,000 men were again sent there, with the task of constructing and guarding a long wall. An attempt was made to dig a canal there, in order to irrigate the district and make it habitable ; it cost more than a thousand million pieces of money and several myriads of labourers worked there. Stock-raising was also attempted : " officials lent mares which had to be given back at the end of 3 years, with a colt for every ten mares (lent)." Stewards were charged with dividing the lands into patrimonies, granted as loans. They formed into groups and supervised the colonists. Expense which reached " to incalculable sums " was not shared, so great was the desire to establish a bastion commanding central Mongolia and stopping up the opening of the River by which the Barbarians reached the heart of China.[1]

The colonization of the Manchurian territories of Ch'ang-hai (128–108 B.C.) was carried on with as much persistence, and was not less costly.[2] The interest of this advance towards the north-east was great. It was hoped, thanks to it, to divide the northern Barbarians (the Eastern Hu, enemies of the Hiong-nu, were in fact established all along the great Eastern Wall). Thanks to it also it was hoped to command the gulf of Pechili as well as the communications with Korea. The colonization in the North-East caused trouble in Chih-li and Shantung, for it " ruined the countries of Yen and of Ch'i," that is to say the provinces most loosely attached to China. The great vassals of the east were, indeed, the greatest intriguers. Their leanings towards independence were apparently accompanied by a maritime policy. The Emperor, to reduce them to obedience, had himself to acquire a maritime power and isolate them. He sought to gain control of the Yellow Sea and to colonize the south coasts.[3]

[1] SMC, III, 562, 553, 560, 590.   [2] SMC, III, 549.   [3] BEFEO, 1923, p. 169.

A prince from the south of Shantung had much desired (a significant fact) that the Emperor should renounce the conquest of the Yue country. The Emperor replied not only by proceeding to this conquest, but by colonizing the Huai basin. He took steps to this end by bringing about an amalgamation of populations. In 138 B.C. 40,000 natives of Tong-ngou (Che-kiang) were transported there, and then, in 110 B.C., all the inhabitants of Tong Yue. But in 115 B.C., after a flood, a great mass of Chinese colonists were transferred to the same region, a mass so numerous that the commissioners in charge of the colonization formed with their carriages " a continuous train on the roads." Further, Chinese colonists were sent to the south of the Blue River, and maintained at first by grain imported from Ssu-ch'uan. A canal, that of Hing-ngan, joined up the basins of the Si-kiang and the Yang-tse-kiang. The expedition against Canton was made with the aid of the double-decked boats of the countries of the South. The Empire had now included in its bounds a sailor people. The imperial power was solidly established throughout the Chinese East.[1]

The whole basin of the Blue River was organized into areas of military control (17 new ones were created). " They were administered in accordance with the ancient customs (of the inhabitants) and neither taxes nor dues were exacted from them." The expenses of colonization were borne by the nearest of the old military areas. Assimilation appears to have been made slowly ; " it required prudence, and rebellions were frequent." Great works were accomplished. A canal uniting the rivers Pao and Ye opened communication between the Wei and Hoang-ho basins and those of the Han and the Yang-tse-kiang. A great road was pierced towards the south-west, completing the great cross-system of Shih Huang-ti. " Presents were scattered with profusion among the peoples of K'iong and of P'e (Southern Ssu-ch'uan) in order to win them over." Then " the bold people were invited to go and cultivate the territory of the Barbarians of the South " (money being furnished for this by the ancient military areas of Ssu-ch'uan).[2]

The colonizing effort most pursued, perhaps because, at least at the end of the reign, it appeared the most urgent,

---

[1] SMC, III, 548, 589, 592.   [2] SMC, III, 596, 529, 549, 551.

was that which made further Kan-su Chinese territory.
The Hun-sieh who, after the campaign of 121 B.C., had come
to China to the number of several myriads of persons, were
received into Chinese territory and transported with the
help of 20,000 vehicles. The first idea was to establish them
in the bend of the River, then it was decided to settle them
on the northern edge of the Nan Shan and in the neighbourhood of the Lob-nor. In 112 B.C., the Emperor made a great
inspection of the countries of the north-west and observed
the feebleness of their defences. The same year, the K'iang
(or Lin-k'iang, Tibetans), joined in confederation to the
number of some twenty tribes, allied with the Hiong-nu
(Huns) and penetrated into central Kan-su. An army of
a hundred thousand men was in the field against them from
111 to 108 B.C. Several myriads of men were then sent to
fortify Ling-kü and guard the region of Ti-tao (the road of
the Barbarians) which defended the heights of the valley of
the Wei and might serve as a way of penetration towards
Kuku-nor. " Officers were placed there in charge of the
fields and cultivation, and soldiers supervising the barriers,
who acted as garrison in these places and cultivated them."
This system of military colonization (completed by an
information service, whose agents were taken from tribes
who had formerly given their adhesion, such as the Yi-k'ü)
ended (in 62–60 B.C., in the reign of the Emperor Süan and
under the influence of Chao Ch'ong-kuo) in emptying the
country of its Barbarian occupants. (The Sien-lien tribe
was reduced from 50,000 to 4000 men.) The progress of
colonization on the two slopes of the Nan Shan Mountains
made of western Kan-su the rampart whence Chinese
civilization radiated both into Turkestan and to the borders
of Tibet. From the reign of the Emperor Wu, Tun-huang
was not an advance post, but a military area within the
Empire.[1]

The task of internal colonization was no less brilliant.
It was no doubt in the reign of the Emperor Wu that the
work of setting central China in order was carried on with
the greatest ardour. The journeys and inspections made
by the Emperor involved the making or repair of numerous
roads, especially in the year 112 B.C.[2] Canals for transport

---

[1] SMC, III, 559, 595, 592 (Note 4).   [2] SMC, III, 591.

or irrigation remained the chief of public enterprises. A great canal was dug in Shan-si to irrigate the lands covered with salt. It drew upon the waters of the Lo to the north of the prefecture of T'ong-chou. " The banks of the Lo giving way easily, shafts were pierced, the deepest of which reached 400 feet ; these shafts were made at certain definite distances from one another ; they were connected together at the bottom and water was conducted through them." [1] This was the first of " the canals with shafts." Another canal, using the waters of the Fen, was dug in Shan-si to irrigate the south-west corner of this province. There was nothing there, on the banks of the Yellow River, but uncultivated lands where the common people went to cut hay, and led their flocks and herds to pasture. It was hoped to make fields of cereals, yielding a harvest of two million bushels.[2] A change in the course of the River ruined all these works ; but the peopling of the region was not given up. People from Yue were transported there, who were accustomed to draw means of livelihood from marshy ground. They were exempted from all taxes. A more successful enterprise was the construction of a canal designed to carry the waters of the Wei to the capital. It was entrusted to a specialist, a hydrographical engineer who came from Shantung. It took three years to pierce it. The canal was useful for irrigation, but above all for grain transport. It shortened the distance and lessened the labour. It was very much used.[3] The greatest works of the reign were those rendered necessary by a flooding of the Yellow River. In 132 B.C., it overflowed its banks at Hu-tseu (south of Chih-li), " poured itself out to the south-east in the marshes of Kü-ye, and joined the rivers Huai and Ssu " (following, south of Shantung, almost the course it was to take in the Middle Ages). It devastated part of Ho-nan, of Ngan-huai and of Kiang-su. The breach could only be stopped up in 109 B.C., during a dry year. But wood was lacking, the people of the country having burnt the undergrowth. The Emperor ordered the bamboos in the park of K'i to be cut, and came in person to preside at the construction of the dam. His generals brought their share of sticks in bundles, which were thrown between the poles planted to form the framework of the dam. The

[1] SMC, III, 531.   [2] SMC, III, 528.   [3] SMC, III, 527.

sacrifice of a horse and a beautiful prayer in verse addressed
to the god of the River completed the work, and it was
possible to " conduct the river again towards the north in
two channels, so that it followed the tracks of Yü the Great." [1]
The Emperor was victorious over the flood. His example
led to a great period of rivalry in the construction of canals
all over China. Immense lands were thus gained, according
to Ssu-ma Ch'ien, for cultivation and population.[2] The
Emperor had the right to declare in one of his hymns : " The
Hundred Families are multiplied." [3]

. . . . .

Like Ch'in Shih Huang-ti, the Emperor Wu wished to
acquire divine prestige. We have seen that he celebrated
the sacrifice Fong and represented his reign as the beginning
of a new era. But whilst the first Emperor protected, at one
and the same time, his work and his majesty by a strict
isolation, the Emperor Wu kept an ostentatious court. He
sought less to create a religion of the imperial person, than to
become the high priest of a syncretist worship, abounding
in splendid ceremonies. He called to him the scholars and
magicians of the north-east as well as the sorcerers of the
country of Yue, while he had brought into his palace the
golden idol which the king of Hiu-ch'u worshipped, and into
his stud the celestial Horse taken from the Prince of Ferghana.
He consulted the fates by means of chicken-bones after the
methods of the Barbarians of the south-east, and in the
Chinese manner by using the shells of tortoises. He sacrificed
on flat hillocks as well as on high terraces. He spent great
sums on alchemy, spiritualism and traditionalist literature.
He had hymns composed, classic in form and inspiration,
and patronized the poems in which Ssu-ma Siang-ju imitated,
it is said, the poetry peculiar to the country of Ch'u. The
Emperor Wu had not the forceful and occult genius of the
first Emperor. It was by a dazzling and excessive luxury
that he sought to make his power blaze abroad. " Look all
round about ; contemplate the hall of green jade. A crowd
of beautiful women are gathered together ; here is an
abundant and supreme elegance. Their faces are white like
the flower of the sow-thistle ; (to see them) a million persons

---

[1] SMC, III, 532.   [2] SMC, III, 536.   [3] SMC, III, 617.

press and push. They are clothed with embroidered clothing and in many-coloured gauze, light as a mist. They have trains of fine silk and cloth. They hold in their arms flowers— kia-ye, irises, perfumed orchids." [1]

As well as being magnificent, the Emperor Wu was both suspicious and shrewd. His disfavour was terrible and his favour dangerous. Fear of poison and of witchcraft led him to order the death of his favourite son. The Prince hanged himself, and his children were executed. The Emperor chose another successor. It was a child. The mother was young. The Emperor, to avoid the danger of a female regency, allowed her to commit suicide.

In the reign of the Emperor Wu, Chinese civilization spread widely. The Empire was powerful. Considerations of State predominated over all. It still remained to build up the State. The interest of the dynasty remained the sole principle of government. A crisis over the succession would have been sufficient to ruin the Empire.

III

THE DYNASTIC CRISIS AND THE END OF THE HAN

The Emperor Wu had the successor whom he had chosen. He reigned under the tutelage of three regents named by his father. The chief of these was a brother of General Ho K'ü-p'ing, named Ho Kuang. There were some troubles which were quickly suppressed, but the Emperor Chao died quite young (74 B.C.). Ho Kuang had a descendant in the indirect line put on the throne ; he was deposed immediately, with the support and authority of the Dowager Empress, the widow of Chao, who was a grand-daughter of Ho Kuang and of the one of the two other regents who was still living. A grandson (fictitious without doubt) of the first heir of the Emperor Wu (whose tragic end had made him popular) was named as successor. He was the Emperor Süan (73–49 B.C.). He made the mistake of not marrying a daughter of Ho Kuang. The Empress was poisoned by the wife of the Regent, whose daughter entered the harem. The Emperor already had an heir whom he loved. He had all the Ho family exter-

[1] SMC, III, 613.

minated, for they had become too powerful, and named as Empress a concubine without a child. The reign of his son, the Emperor Yuan (48–33 B.C.) was peaceful. But his wife, the Empress Wang, survived him, and did not die till very old. The Emperor Ch'êng (32–7 B.C.) named as Grand Marshal one of his maternal uncles, whose brothers took possession of all offices. One of them had a son, Wang Mang, who, at 28 years of age, became chief favourite. The Empress was again chosen from the Wang family. The Emperor Ch'êng, not having a child, adopted his nephew, whose legal mother belonged to the Fu family. The Wang at first controlled the Fu queen. She was clever, and wished to possess all the power of a Dowager. In the reign of Ngai (7–1 B.C.) the Fu tried to get rid of the Wang, but when Ngai died, the most ancient of the Dowagers, the Empress Wang (widow of Yuan) blazed forth in supreme authority. All the power passed to Wang Mang. He married his daughter to the Emperor P'ing (1 B.C. to 5 A.D.). He took care to look after the sovereign's mother and her family. He gave them fiefs and kept them away from the Court. He also took the precaution of distributing more than a hundred fiefs to members of the imperial family. In 5 A.D., the Emperor being ill (poisoned, says history) Wang Mang asked of the gods that he might die in the place of his sovereign. Thus had formerly acted Chou-kong, the minister-founder of the Chou dynasty, and great patron of the ritualist school of Lu. The Emperor, however, died. Wang Mang's daughter (at 12 years of age) became dowager. A child of two was named successor. Prodigies then made it clear that Wang Mang had in him the same Virtue as Kao-Chu, the founder of the Han dynasty. The Han had reigned by virtue of the Earth and had taken yellow for their dynastic colour. Kao-Chu, however, was born of a red dragon. The Red Sovereign brought to Wang Mang a mysterious casket. Wang Mang proclaimed himself Emperor (9 A.D.).

The Empire has no other foundation than the Virtue peculiar to a dynasty. Apart from the Emperor the State is nothing. To govern, the sovereign has need of supports. If he seeks them in his own family and practises the policy of granting estates for life, the Empire tends to be only a federation of related overlordships. A sovereign who wishes to strengthen the central power ought to seek to weaken his own relatives and, above all, remove them from the Court. At every succession these relatives may be dangerous competitors. An heir-designate, if he groups a party round him, becomes a rival to the sovereign himself. So, most often, a child of tender years is designated as heir. To assure the succession to him, a party of faithful supporters must then be grouped around him. It is found among his mother's family. Now, old principles of domestic right, favourable to the maternal interests, allow mothers to marry their sons into their own family. A dynasty of dowagers thus tends to oppose itself to the imperial dynasty. The relations of these dowagers form a powerful party, opposed to the party of the imperial relatives. There would result from this a certain equilibrium if the successions were not accompanied by a period of guardianship. When the guardianships are long and frequent (a result which can be secured by assassination or the choice of heirs with poor health), the maternal family provides Regents who are all-powerful. They may content themselves by reigning *de facto*, by founding a dynasty of Mayors of the Palace, but they have every facility for usurpation. To succeed in it, they must dismember the Empire afresh, to the advantage of their own family and supporters. The Empire is dismembered no less if they fall, conquered by a coalition of princes of the imperial family to whom estates have been granted.

Wang Mang only reigned 14 years (9–23 A.D.). He was dethroned by a coalition of Princes related to the first Han. One of them succeeded in founding the dynasty of the second Han (or the Eastern Han—they moved their capital to Ho-nan). It lasted from 25–220 A.D. Its founder, the Emperor Kuang-wu, had to distribute 365 estates (the number of days in the year). He at least laid down the principle that there were to be no more kings, only dukes and marquises. The first successions took place peacefully. It was necessary, however, from 67–71 A.D., to suppress revolts of the princes of royal blood. In 77 A.D. the family of an Empress tried to seize authority. The family of another Empress succeeded in destroying the first. A first regency was exercised by the Tou (89–92 A.D.). Then the Teng family appears. The Empress Teng governs one year (106 A.D.), in the reign of the Emperor Shang, who ascends the throne when a hundred days old. She is still governing in the reign of the Emperor Nan (107–125 A.D.) who, on his accession, was 12 years old. She dies in 121 A.D. Her family is exterminated. The Empress Yen, wife of Nan, tries on her husband's death to have a very young infant proclaimed Emperor. He dies almost immediately and another party triumphs. The Emperor Shun (126–144) is placed on the throne, and names as Empress a woman of the Leang family. Her brother is made Grand Marshal. The brother and sister govern in the reign of Ch'ong, who was two years old, and died in 145 A.D.,— and then in the reign of Ch'e. He was also a child, but a little older ; he was poisoned. The Emperor Huan was then named ; he belonged to the family of the Han, but had married a Leang, younger sister of the dowager. She had no children ; the women of the harem either all miscarried or their children all died young. Soon the dowager died, the Emperor put her sister out of favour and succeeded, aided by a eunuch, in having her brother assassinated. He reigned for twenty years (147–167 A.D.). On his death, there is a fresh regency. The dowager Empress Tou names her father Grand Marshal. He begins a quarrel with the eunuchs of the palace, on whom the Emperor Ling (168–189 A.D.) depends. The father of the dowager was overcome and committed suicide ; the dowager was imprisoned and all her relatives exiled. In 189 A.D. another Empress becomes regent and her brother Grand Marshal. Their family tries to gain a footing in the palace. The dowager's sister is given in marriage, not to the heir to the Empire, but to the son (adopted) of one of the chief eunuchs. The Grand Marshal then tries to take up the quarrel with the people of the palace. The eunuchs win. The Marshal is killed, his sister banished and the little Emperor dethroned. Then begins the reign of the last Han Emperor, the Emperor Hien (190–220 A.D.). He reigned only in name. From 184 A.D. the rebellion of the *Yellow Turbans* upset the Empire. There were again intrigues in the palace. Government no longer existed. From the moment when, refusing the support of a clientele grouped about his paternal or maternal family, the Emperor wishes to be master in his palace, he is no longer anything except the plaything of the courtiers. He no longer counts and the State is dissolved.

The revolt of the *Yellow Turbans* was the occasion of the fall of the second Han dynasty. That of the *Red Eyebrows* at the beginning of the Christian era had been the reason for the fall of Wang Mang, whose reign only prolonged the first Han dynasty. The old idea that the prince is responsible for the order of the seasons and the prosperity of the country remained in force as regards the Emperor. In the vast and varied country, which the China of the Han had become, there was without cessation some canton suffering from flood or drought. As soon as the imperial police grew more lax, or the government no longer looked after local revictualling, a band of rebels formed. When it is no longer capable of being formed into a regiment, to be thrown against the Barbarians, or employed on big public works, it is quickly animated with anti-dynastic sentiments and turned into a gang by some adventurer. The rebellions of the Red Eyebrows and the Yellow Turbans were the consequences of an agrarian crisis due to the development of the large domains. The economists in the service of the Emperor Wu had felt the danger and tried to forestall it, by forbidding the investment in land of fortunes acquired by industry or commerce. But in the same reign, the moralists triumphed over the technical experts. The learned Tong Chong Chu, who advocated the study of the *Annals of Lu*, edited by Confucius, as the only means of forming Statesmen, invited his master to return to the old customs. He advised the restoration of the system of tenure (*ching* system) and of tithes ; from the concession of full ownership there could only result the monopolizing of land and the multiplication of slaves. These evils had become serious by the end of the first Han dynasty. A proposal was made, in the reign of the Emperor Ngai (6–1 B.C.) to fix for each social class a maximum number of slaves and a maximum extent of estates. Wang Mang who, like a good usurper, wished to renew only by retracing old beaten tracks, forbade in 9 A.D., trade in land and in slaves. He claimed for the Emperor a supreme right of property : " The fields of the whole Empire will henceforth receive the name of *royal fields* and the slaves that of *private subordinates*. All property being only held under title of tenure, none could be alienated." The ordinance had to be revoked three years after. Wang Mang had tried to complete it by a system of

control of prices, in which he revived an idea of the counsellors of the Emperor Wu, but the *State* character of which
was clearly determined : the prices were not to result from
the play of economic compensations, but from rates decided
ex officio by State functionaries. It does not appear that the
edicts of Wang Mang were applied in the smallest degree.

In 3 B.C. a great drought caused a vast popular movement,
which took its rise in Shantung. Wandering crowds moved
about the country, singing and dancing to propitiate the
Si-wang-mu (the Queen-mother of the West ; she was a
divinity of the plague ; she became, in Taoism organized as
a religion, the most popular of the divinities).[1] The agitation
diminished quickly ; but the predictions and marvellous
discoveries necessary to accredit Wang Mang kept up a
state of agitation. In 11 A.D. the Yellow River broke its
banks, ruining the plains of Chih-li and Shantung. In 14 A.D.
there was in the north so extreme a famine that people
devoured each other, then famines succeeded each other
from year to year. Then there appeared (again in Shantung)
the Red Eyebrows, bands of brigands who beat the armies
of Wang Mang and who were beaten or formed into regiments
by some princes of the Han blood. One dynasty was brought
down ; another was founded, but perished under similar
conditions, except that the revolt of the Yellow Turbans
had its origin in Ssu-ch'uan. Ssu-ch'uan and Shantung were
provinces with strongly particularist tendencies. They were
both the seats of the first great Taoist sects. The rebellion
of the Yellow Turbans was both a peasant revolt and a
sectarian movement. It was suppressed by some officers ;
but one of them, getting possession of the Blue River basin,
there founded the Wu dynasty, whose capital was placed in
the Nanking region. A second, who belonged to the Han
family, made himself master of Ssu-ch'uan. A third con-
tented himself with *de facto* power, but his son, in 220 A.D.,
deposing the Emperor Hien, founded the Wei dynasty. This
had as its portion all old China of the Yellow River, and also
the basin of the Huai. The Empire was divided into three
Kingdoms.

The work of colonization suffered less than might have

---

[1] *Han Shu*, 98, 86, 84, 27 and 11.

I

been expected from the crises of the Central Government. Certainly, the pressure of the Tibetans assumed sometimes (in 42 B.C., for example), a disturbing violence, and often the Hiong-nu, in spite of their divisions, managed to threaten the route of the Altai. They occupied Turfan from 64 to 60 B.C. But in 60 B.C. the Chinese, following on a successful raid, were able to establish their chief military post at Kutcha. In 49 B.C., the Hiong-nu divided into two groups. A bold and successful stroke (in 35 B.C.) against the more distant group (it had settled in the neighbourhood of Balkash) caused the south-western group, which alone remained in contact with the Chinese, to come and render homage (33) and to demand an alliance. The government had little share in these successes. They were almost always due to the spirit of initiative and adventure which animated those in local commands. That which one might be tempted to call the external policy of China was, at this period, the work of a body of officers possessing in a high degree the colonial spirit. They acted without taking the time to refer things back, and they knew how to find excuses in case of need to justify their successes. It is to this same body of officers that the revival of Chinese power after the dynastic crisis, which took place at the beginning of the Christian era, is due. The submission of Tonkin (42 A.D.) and of Hai-nan, the dissolution of the powerful confederation formed by the Man of Hu-nan (49 A.D.) the pacification of the North-East, thanks to the use made of the Sien-pi tribes in opposition to the Hiong-nu, all these able operations of policy and of war were led to successful issues thanks to personal initiative and intelligent insubordination. The conquest of Tarim, which is the great glory of the second Han dynasty, was carried out by a few men (of whom the most celebrated is Pan Chao) working on a forlorn hope. They proceeded by hazardous sudden dashes, without support or control, at the head of some daring men, but strong with all the prestige of the Chinese name. From 73–102 A.D. Pan Chao [1] taking possession of Khotan, Kashgar, Yarkand and Karachar, threw back the Hiong-nu into the Gobi and the Yue-che beyond the Pamirs, while Tou Hien pushed back the northern Hiong-nu to the North of Barkul (89 A.D.). All the routes

[1] XXI.

of the silk traffic north and south, thus passed under the control of the Chinese, and beyond the deserts of Central Asia, a limited contact was established with Tokharian civilization. The Tokharians and Yue-che were in touch with India, and also with the West.[1] The Chinese, on the other hand, masters of Annam and its coasts, could receive by way of the sea, more distant as well as Indian influences. History declares that Pan Chao conceived the idea of entering into relations with the Romans (97 A.D.) and that, in the second half of the second century, some merchants presented themselves, as ambassadors from Rome, at the ports of the South of the Empire. As much by the south-west, then, as by the east, new ideas and knowledge penetrated into China. Buddhism was installed there at least by the opening of the first century. It made progress there during the period of the Three Kingdoms. Chinese civilization is becoming complicated at the moment when the Empire is breaking up.

. . . . .

On the fall of the Han, China enters into a new era of political division. The Chin (265–419 A.D.) only succeeded for a short time in re-establishing a nominal unity. From the beginning of the fourth century, Barbarians penetrated to the interior of the frontiers. They established unstable kingdoms in North and West China. The Chin only kept the basin of the Blue River and that of the Si-kiang. The breaking-up attains its maximum at the end of the fourth century and the beginning of the fifth. It is only in the seventh century, in order to fight against the Tu-kiu (Turks) that the Empire is reconstituted, raised by the Sui (589–617 A.D.) to whom the T'ang (620–907 A.D.) succeeded. The policy of great schemes, directed towards the steppe, the mountain and the sea, is immediately taken up again. About 609 A.D Tarim, Tsaidam and Tonkin rejoin the Empire, which stretches at one moment to Zungaria and to the Indus. Enriched by the knowledge brought in the train of Buddhism, Manicheism, Nestorianism, and other religious currents, Chinese civilization spreads afresh in China, more broadly syncretist than in the days of the Han, and yet trying still more to attach itself to the past. After a fresh period of crumbling

---

[1] On these routes, see **CXII**.

(907–960) China definitely takes its direction under the Song (960–1279) towards a syncretism of a traditionalist nature. After the formation of the Chinese nation by the Ch'in and the Han, and the creation of the ideal of an imperial unity, it is in the pride which their culture and their traditions inspire in them that the Chinese have, on favourable opportunity, found the strength to appear as a nation or even to play the part of a great power. More than the history of a State, or even of a people, the history of China is that of a civilization, or rather that of a tradition of culture. Its chief interest, if one could define it with some exactness, would perhaps be to show how the idea of civilization has been able, in such a lengthy history, to keep priority, almost constantly, over the idea of the State.

SECOND PART—CHINESE SOCIETY

ORTHODOX history seeks to prove that three thousand years before Christ, and within the classical limits of the country, a disciplined Empire existed in China and a nation which was already homogeneous. On the other hand, from the time that documents appear in comparative abundance, which can be dated with relative certainty and tentatively criticized, the land of the Chinese Confederation is seen as a new and circumscribed country. The soil is not tilled. The inhabitants, penned within small cantons, live isolated lives.

Is it necessary, because of our reverence for dates, to see a kind of primitive state in this condition of China at the dawn of chronology? Is it necessary to make this the starting-point of the history of Chinese society? But who will prove that the Chinese, at the beginning of the *Ch'un Ch'iu* period, were not the remnant of a united and prosperous nation? May we not suppose that they had formerly colonized at least the basin of the Yellow River, and that some cataclysm came to ruin their work? There is no need to imagine an enormous cataclysm: a flood, an invasion of Barbarians would explain the state of partition revealed by the first dated documents. Is it a primitive state? It seems to carry with it a traditional ideal of unity. Can we be sure that this is a recent ideal which has been artificially projected into the past? The existence of an acknowledged sovereign supposes a certain political unity. The relative respect and the consideration which the Chou appear to have enjoyed during the *Ch'un Ch'iu* period seem to bear witness to an authority of ancient date, the mark of a previous state of comparative union. All that can be said in favour of the orthodox tradition has no more than a hypothetical value. But if we rejected these modest hypotheses, preferring an absolute negation founded on the lack of historic evidences, it would be easy to produce some beginning of proofs, insisting, for example, on the importance of traditions relating to stories of a flood, or on the assertions of chronicles which tell of a fierce invasion of the Ti in the seventh century.

We will take no sides. We refuse equally to deny and to accept the orthodox tradition in its entirety. It is probable that Chinese civilization is of great antiquity. It may even be that her history presents a certain continuity : again it is possible that China (or, at any rate, a part of the Chinese country) was possessed in very ancient times of a sort of homogeneity. But what can we make of the traditional theory which sets out to explain the whole of Chinese civilization ? This theory will have it that the society was perfect at its commencement, at the time when the Founders of the national civilization were revealing their Saintship. The idea that the Prince, solely by the observance of certain rites, could regulate his people's morals, and keep the world in order, corresponds with an ideal which is undoubtedly not of recent invention. We recognize indeed that it is the refinement of an ideal : we should like to know, with some precision, its origin and its history. Now for those who embrace the orthodox doctrine, this ideal is one of the necessary data—an accepted fact. It is from this standpoint that the facts of history are explained, nay, that they are related. All the documents have been manipulated and reconstructed by learned criticism. It has accepted the traditional data only so far as they seem to agree with the spirit of the system. Under these conditions, all true research would be impossible, were it not for one fact : the Chinese, when they are systematically constructing or reconstructing their history, think and write only by the aid of consecrated formulas, and within the frame-work of traditional rules. Rules and formulas, once they can be detached from the system, form positive data. It is from these data and these data alone, that the elements of a history of Chinese Society can be extracted.

It is at once evident that these data consist of fragmentary documents which cannot be attached to any chronology. All one's labour consists in classifying them. By this classi-fication, it is possible to relate them to various centres of social life. It then remains to classify these centres. Here we must at first employ a retrogressive method.

We are acquainted, by direct documentation, with the

lettered class, and the nobility of the Empire. The *lettered* class and the officials occupied a place in Imperial China similar to that held by the feudal nobility of China at the time of the tenure by fief. This China is known to us only by what the *literati* have chosen to tell us. But for this purpose they had recourse to traditional formulas. These they interpreted after their manner. But it is not impossible to understand them in the sense in which they were taken by the feudal nobles. To sort out the different values of these formulas is equivalent to relating them to classified centres. Consequently their classification makes it possible to describe an evolution. One may go in the same way passing in a gradual ascent from the Emperor to the feudal lord. But here the passage from one term to another is more direct. As a result of this more continuous evolution, it is possible to trace it almost to its source and discover, under extremely archaic forms, what was the power of the Prince. This power is defined by formulas which are veritable themes of mythology : sometimes we can even connect them with allied ritual acts : the whole reveals the. beliefs and even the data of fact which rendered possible the constitution of chieftainships, and the advent of individual authority. Now there are other themes, chiefly to be found in poetry, which allow us to picture a rustic environment where some of the most important beliefs were nurtured which lie at the root of the authority belonging to the political chief, as well as of that which belonged to the head of the family. Thus by the simple means of referring the rules and formulas in which Chinese beliefs are enshrined to correctly classified centres, we succeed in tracing, in both the political and the family order, a double parallel evolution, which explains the formation of constitutional and of private right.

It will be seen no doubt that if these centres, which were described by the help of formulas borrowed from an immemorial tradition, can be correctly classified, it is only in so far as the rôle of governorship passed successively from one to the other of these centres. We are only stating this fact in other words when we say that the nobility of the Empire was the heir of the feudal nobility, or arose to take its place. This statement does not by any means imply that the feudal nobility disappeared when the nobility of the

Empire arose in its stead to play a similar part in the life
of the Nation. It is possible that groups of the feudal type
still subsisted in China under the Han. On the other hand,
it is possible that a species of nobility existed before the
Imperial Era differing from the real feudal nobility, whose
members were even at that period more like officials than
vassals. In any case, it is certain that in the *Ch'un Ch'iu*
period (and even later) the customs of the peasants remained
almost as they had been at the time when ideas were being
worked out in the rural communities, then representing the
most active element in Chinese society, which were later to
be borrowed and transformed by the founders of the chieftainships at the Revolution whence feudal China emerged.
But it was at that time that the rôle of leadership and creative
activity passed into the hands of the chieftains and their
followers. The beliefs and theories which helped to build up
Imperial China had their origin in the activity of the feudal
courts. Thus we shall study the different centres in which
Chinese civilization was moulded at the moment when they
began their work of creation. And we shall occupy ourselves
more with the fortunes of what they created than with their
own. It would be possible to justify this method by reason.
It will suffice however to show that it is imposed by fact.
There is no possibility of defining the different centres which
must be studied for an understanding of Chinese civilization,
other than through the beliefs and the technology which are
their contribution to that civilization.

It is clear that the evolution, as we are able to define it,
assumes an air of timelessness (for nothing begins and nothing
ends at a fixed date) and a static quality (for there is no
possibility of indicating peculiarities of detail and nothing to
explain whether there were ebbs and flows, if it moved rapidly
here and slowly there, if it was delayed or hastened through
such a cause in such a country).

At first, every attempt at geographical or historical
precision would be a mockery—much more every attempt at
ethnographic precision. Again : the multiplicity and variety
of possible influences render every theory more dangerous
than useful. Nevertheless, I will point out one, solely as a
working hypothesis and because it approximates fairly closely
to an important datum. As far back as we can go Chinese

civilization appears to be a complex civilization. On the other hand, at the beginning of the period known by dates, this civilization has its centre within the borders of two border regions, where the boundary of the fields of loess joins that of the alluvial plains. It is not impossible that the rise of a truly Chinese civilization is explained by the contact of two *principal* (I do not say primitive) civilizations, one of which would be a civilization of terraces and of millet and the other a civilization of rice and of the low-lying plains. The first may have contributed the influences of the Steppe and the other those of the sea. Historical traditions lend some support to this hypothesis. The Chou, who seem to have been powerful in the Chinese west, and were upheld by the Barbarians of the west, are said to have lived in ancient times in caves : for ancestor and god they had Prince Millet. The Yin, their rivals, allied themselves with the Barbarians of Huai in their struggle against them. They inhabited the marshy plains which border the eastern sea. The princes of Song, the descendants of the Yin, with the other princes of the East, always kept up communication with them. On the other hand, it seems certain that the civilization of Eastern China presented a certain unity with individual characteristics. Its sexual customs were more free. Hospitable prostitution was practised, with definite rites of blood alliance.

Before she entered the Chinese union, it is possible that Eastern China entertained relations which were peculiar to herself. It may be that through her, distant influences were brought to bear on Chinese civilization whose importance can scarcely be guessed. It is clear that it will only be possible to write the history of Chinese society in a concrete form when we have discovered how to define the ethnographical or technical influences which acted upon it.

SECOND PART—CHINESE SOCIETY

BOOK ONE

THE PEOPLE OF THE PLAINS

CHAPTER I

LIFE IN THE FIELDS

THE Chinese, from the first day of their known history, appear as an agricultural people. No doubt the raising of crops was of more importance formerly than in our day : but it was by the culture of cereals that the ancient Chinese gained a livelihood, as did the populations bordering their country, whom they considered Barbarians. Certain forays undertaken by the Ti (in 601 B.C. for example) are explained by the drought which had ruined their crops.[1]

Nowadays when one visits the country of old China and sees long row after row of cultivated ground at the side of the roads and canals, one is tempted to think that with their relatively settled climate and apparently rich soil the marshy uplands or alluvial plains must always have invited the inhabitants to live as agriculturists. One would suppose that it had always and everywhere been easy to set up houses and till the fields. As a matter of fact, the Chinese soil has only revealed its fruitfulness canton by canton, and at the cost of heroic labours.

Native legends speak of a time when, ignorant of the art of sowing and planting, men lived with difficulty in the bush. In the high regions of loess, brushwood picketed the steppe. Vegetation consisted of tall, rough plants. Before they could settle on the soil men had " to join together . . . in order to root out and destroy the weeds that covered the land (they must) cut down the flea-bane, the mug-wort, the false hemp, the star-thistle." [2] The peasants knew the cost of these first labours. They loved to sing the merits of ancestors who had cleared the ground : " Thistles in dense

---

[1] *Tso chuan*, C, I, 592.   [2] *Tso chuan*, C, III, 267.

139

clumps !—they had to root out the brushwood.—Why did our forefathers do it ?—So that we could plant millet." [1] It was not enough to make a clearance once for all. On this rich soil, the first rains, at the time of the spring equinox, and above all the great rains of mid-summer brought a swarm of noxious weeds and of insects which devoured or stifled the crops. " Behold the thorns,—and behold the grain ! How stiff they are ! How it is ripening !—No more false sorghum or false millet !—Away with maggots and insects !— and again away with larvæ and caterpillars !—They shall not spoil the growth of our fields !—for the god of the fields is powerful :—let him take them and fling them into the blazing fire ! " [2] The god of the fields, Shên-nung (the divine Husbandman) whom they invited, dancing to the sound of tambourines made of terra-cotta, to come and cleanse the crops, had formerly taught to men the use of plough and hoe. He had also taught them to beat the stalks with a red flail. He bore the title of Flaming Sovereign. The god of agriculture was a god of fire.[3]

To clear the ground in the low-lying parts fire was not enough : one must make use of water. Frequently in the valleys the ground was saturated with saltpetre, or else covered with inextricable thickets of prickly plants. " The farmers must first burn the weeds and the brushwood, then pour water and plant rice : the weeds and the rice grew together : when they were 7 or 8 inches high the whole was cut down and water poured again : the weeds died and only the rice grew : this is what was called clearing the brushwood by fire and hoeing by water." [4] The same procedure was employed in the first century before our era, to tame the vast marshy plains. We have seen above that such great enterprises were long considered foolhardy. Powerful States had to be organized before the risk would be taken. Before venturing to the foot of the great valleys or into the vast plains, the ancient Chinese seem to have confined themselves to the cultivation of hillsides and terraces. But to build in the fields, to contend with the crumbling of moving ground, to construct canals and trenches for drainage,

[1] *She King*, C, 276.   [2] *She King*, C, 285.
[3] SMC, I, 13 ; *Ye King*, L, 383 ; LV, 271 ; *She King*, C, 283.
[4] *T'so chuan*, C, 11, 293 ; SMC, III, 589.

to make them healthy and clean, called for abundant labour
as well as for habits of organization, mutual help and work
in common.

" Ho, there ! clear the weeds ! Ho, there ! stub up the roots
of forest ! let your ploughs cleave the clods ! Thousands
of couples, go and hoe !—there, to the valleys—there, to the
heights !—Here is the master and his first-born !—here are
the younger ones, the children, the helpers and the journey-
men ! " [1] The rituals set forth that the husbandmen must
work in couples at the command of the Overlord. He presided,
they say, at the beginning of the year, over the organization
of the work. He made them " repair the borders and
boundaries of the fields, note the mountains, hills, hillocks,
plains and valleys, decide what crops are suitable for each
ground and in what places one should sow the five cereals. . . .
When the field-work is arranged beforehand, when canals and
boundaries have been fixed by line, there is nothing further
to trouble the husbandmen." [2] In the same way, the dynastic
hymns attribute to Hero-Founders that ordering of the
country which seems to have been renewed with every new
campaign. " He exhorted them and settled them—here on
his left hand and there on his right—setting up boundaries
and ordaining rules—tracing the canals and planning the
fields—setting out from the west and going to the east—
himself undertaking the whole on every hand ! " [3] No doubt
feudal chiefs did not preside at all times over the agricultural
labours, but the subjection of the soil, a hard-won victory
over powerful and rebellious nature, exacted from the Chinese
a continuous effort, an ordered obstinacy, which could only
be made possible by the existence of communities which were
firmly united, fairly extensive and solidly established.

The peasants lived in hamlets or in villages. These were
placed on the heights overlooking the cultivated land. They
were refuges for winter. In the spring, the husbandmen
came down from them and re-tilled their fields. When
autumn was come and the harvest ended, they climbed
again to their dwellings and prepared them for the winter.
" Come, my husbandmen, our crops are gathered !—let us
go up again and go in to repair our homes ! In the day-

---

[1] *She King*, C, 439.   [2] *Li ki,*┌C,┘I, 336.
[3] *She King*, C, 327.

time let us cut the thatch—to bind it in the evening—then to the roof quick, to the top !—When spring comes, we shall have to sow." [1]   The cottages, perched high up, were surrounded with walls or quick-set hedges.   Not only must they be out of reach of floods : they must forestall assault and robbery.   All around the little islets of cultivation which had risen from the efforts of the first peasant communities, surged backward or barbarous peoples, whose home was in the forests or the brushwood of the marshes.   If a numerous and well-organized people had been already required for the conquest of nature, the defence of the harvest demanded an equally powerful combination.   With the appearance of the chieftainships, when the peasants were given masters and protectors, the collection of hamlets grouped round the seigniorial castle, the last refuge, was surrounded by a first wall of defence : territory and suburb were intermingled.[2] From the beginning of sedentary life and peasant civilization, agricultural work, which called for massed labour, was carried on in a confined space, and so to speak, within blockaded bulwarks.   This may be the explanation of certain ancient and permanent features of Chinese agriculture.

The Chinese, by means of human labour, obtain great returns from their fields.   They reap varied harvests from them and cultivate them like gardens.   The hoe, rather than the plough, is their chief instrument.   Such habits might suit a people who had served their agricultural apprenticeship in oases.   As for the Chinese, such an explanation would be very tempting, if it were not a pure hypothesis to look upon Turkestan as their place of origin.   It can be dispensed with if we remember that the predominance in ancient times of a population of relatively powerful groups is attested by documents.   If only because of the difficult conditions of tilling the soil, agricultural life had from the beginning a sort of urban character.   As they were obliged to extract from narrow fields, which they had conquered from Nature and were defending from the Barbarians, all the products necessary to the life of a powerful group, the Chinese peasants adopted the methods of husbandry of the marshlands.   The cultivation of millet and rice is not carried on by the methods

---

[1] *She King*, C, 164.   [2] *Tso chuan*, C, III, 667.

of the larger husbandry. It is carried on, not in great fields, but in squares.[1]

There exists in China today a certain tendency to the specialization of crops in appropriate regions. In ancient times, every canton aimed at producing everything for its own needs. Millet, which is suited to dry soils, was every-where grown beside rice, which requires abundance of water. The distribution of crops around the inhabited heights did not depend only upon the suitability of each, but on the price which they were expected to fetch. The most precious were nearest to the house. At the side of the vegetable garden, which was levelled at the end of the season to serve as a threshing-floor,[2] were found the orchards, which were specially rich in mulberry-trees, and beyond them the first fields, reserved for textile plants, and principally for hemp. This was the department of the women, who were the weavers. The pieces of stuff which they wove, linen or silk, were the chief source of wealth and were used as current coin. Below were ranged the men's crops, first the fields devoted to dry vegetables, then the fields of cereals, and at the very foot, in the low-lying ground which had been won by drainage and irrigation, and was bounded by banks of earth or by canals, the squares of land reserved for rice.

To be complete the cultivated land was ranged, going up in terraces, and the subsistence of the group was only assured when the crops on each of the terraces had all given a good yield. " Creels full in the upper fields !—carts full in the lower fields !—May every harvest prosper ! Plenty ! plenty ! Our houses full ! " [3] To succeed with the various harvests, they had to practise division of labour and to adopt a kind of limited nomadism. The women weavers did not leave the village and its orchards, but the husbandmen must spend busy days in the fields of cereals. They had cabins there in which they slept, ceaselessly keeping guard over their crops. From dawn to dark they worked hard : " The sun is rising : we must get up !—He is setting : we will rest !—Dig thy well if thou wouldst drink !—Work, if thou wouldst eat ! " [4] They worked in close ranks : " The bamboo hats are moving ! —All the hoes are turning up the soil—to

---

[1] *Tso chuan*, C, II, 441.   [2] *She King*, C, 164.   [3] SMC, cxxvi.
[4] *Ku she*, 1. Song ascribed to the subjects of the mythical sovereign Yao.

root out the weeds ! " [1] The only good time was meal time. Women and children brought the food in their baskets. "Hark to the noise ! they are eating now, and bidding their wives welcome ! "

They regaled themselves upon a soup made with millet. Millet was a god. It supplied the main element of food. It was considered the first of cereals. It is interesting to note [2] that millet, according to Mencius, was the only cereal known to the Barbarians in the north of China.[3] The Chinese cultivated many species : one, the glutinous millet, was chiefly used to make a fermented liquor. They also cultivated many varieties of rice, glutinous rice being similarly used to produce a kind of wine. Wheat and barley were no doubt of less importance although in a prayer addressed to the God of Harvests (Hou Tsi : Prince Millet) the cry occurs " Give us wheat and barley." [4] It is observable that barley and wheat are scarcely distinguished in nomenclature. At no time have the Chinese seemed to set great store on barley. It seems that wheaten flour was chiefly used to provide the yeast which was to set up fermentation in the rice or the millet.[5] These were put to ferment, sometimes alone, sometimes mixed. The most valued wine was made of one part black millet and two parts rice. It was prepared in clay vessels, where the grains mixed with water were heated over a well-regulated fire.[6] Certain aromatic plants, particularly a kind of pepper, were used to perfume the liquor, which was filtered through tufts of dog-grass.[7] Brewing it in winter, they began to drink it in the spring. They were also able to produce vinegar from cereals, and used it to make preserves. The grain which was kept for food was crushed in mortars, washed and cooked by steam.[8] Perhaps, in addition to soups, they made some kinds of cakes. For fresh vegetables they ate different sorts of cucumbers and pumpkins. Various condiments, garlic, onion, the mustard plant, served for seasoning : certain herbs and plants, mallows, knotgrass, scented the broth.[9] The chief sauce was made with bruised and fermented beans : they were beans of the type of the soya bean, whose long stems " floated in the wind like

[1] *She King*, **C**, 441.   [2] *She King*, **C**, 439.   [3] Mencius, **L**, 318.
[4] *She King*, **C**, 426.   [5] **XII**, 157.   [6] *Li ki*, **C**, I, 400.
[7] *She King*, **C**, 163.   [8] *She King*, **C**, 352.   [9] *Li ki*, **C**, I, 644.

banners." [1] No doubt cheese made from beans is also an ancient dish. In any case, dried vegetables and peas of different sizes played a great part in food. They were kept in sacks which were easily carried.[2] They served the purpose of reserve rations, and were used during removals. Perhaps their rôle was of chief importance at the time when the Chinese populations lived by cultivating first one corner of the country, then another, and were not entirely settled. Thus the Barbarians of the north and of the west took up new quarters as late as 568 B.C.[3]

The relative antiquity of sedentary life seems to be vouched for by the existence of orchards where a great variety of trees were successfully grown : peaches, apricots, cherries, pears, wild quinces, chestnuts, plums and lote-trees. The plums, the lote-trees and the chestnuts were used in cooking operations. They ate also the fruits of a kind of wild vine,[4] and those of many water and mountain plants. The most useful of all trees was the mulberry. They pruned it carefully. " The branches which spread or climb too much are cut away with a hatchet : only the leaves are removed from the young mulberry-trees." [5] The leaves were given to silkworms, which were kept in wicker stands made of reeds or rushes. " It is springtime, the days grow warm —the goldfinch is singing—girls with their baskets—walk along the little paths—to gather the young leaves of the mulberry." [6] Many kinds of mulberry were cultivated, and likewise many kinds of hemp. The labour of weaving, begun in the autumn, lasted all the winter.[7] Linen stuffs, which were finished by the spring, served for the hot season, as did the shoes made of fibres, of hemp or of *dolic*. Silk, which was warmer and more costly, was chiefly used by the old men. Steeping was done in ditches beside the houses. The women weavers also knew the art of preparing and plaiting nettles and rushes. The archaic garments, which were still used in classical times to drape the effigy of the dead, were made of a matting of reeds held up by a bamboo girdle.[8] [The Jong (the Barbarians of the West), were clothed (557 B.C.) in a straw cloak and wore a hat of bramble.[9]]

[1] *She King*, C, 351. [2] *She King*, C, 360. [3] *Tso chuan*, C, II, 207.
[4] *She King*, C, 163. [5] *She King*, C, 162 [6] **LII**, 49.
[7] **LVI**, 541 ff. [8] *Yi li*, C, 450. [9] *Tso chuan*, C, II, 291.

K

Tradition has it that before Huang-ti the Chinese were dressed only in a short garment of skins. (It was the wife of Huang-ti who taught them the art of keeping silkworms.[1]) Afterwards the Chinese wore a dress made in two parts, tunic and skirt, woven of silk or hemp.[2] Their head-gear was a kind of bonnet or turban.[3] To resist the cold they wore many layers of clothes. They knew how to dye their stuffs and preferred bright colours.[4] They cultivated many plants for dyeing, especially madder and the indigo tree. The weaving women made both plain and flowered materials. The latter were reserved for festival or wedding garments. " In a flowered skirt, in a plain skirt—in a flowered robe, in a plain robe,— come sirs ! come sirs !—take me in the chariot to your home ! " [5]

Nothing could be simpler than the peasants' houses. In historic times, many of the Chinese lived like troglodytes. They inhabited oven-shaped caves, in the sides of the uplands of loess.[6] Huts in the fields were made of branches. One tradition maintains that the Chinese, while still living in the bush, nested in the branches of trees.[7] The cabin of mourning, which was no doubt the reproduction of an archaic form of dwelling, was a sort of penthouse made of branches supported by a few stakes.[8] In proportion as the mourning grew lighter, the gaps were stopped with straw or rushes, then the cabin was plastered with clay, first inside and then out : the door at first remained wide open, but it was surrounded with a palisade of rushes.[9] This type of archaic house, improved little by little, was no doubt common amongst the cultivators of the terraces of loess. They lived like cliff-dwellers. In villages built on the uplands the houses seem to have had the shape of little cubes covered with thatch. The roof was so light that a sparrow could pierce it with his beak, and rats make holes in the walls.[10] They were fragile, being made of mud and clay : heat cracked them : rain undermined them. Climbing plants invaded walls and roofs, and the colocynths threatened to crush them. At the beginning of each winter, the holes had to be stopped with straw. The

---

[1] She appears at the same time as a divinity of lightning and of silk, SMC, I, 35.
[2] **XL**, 132.   [3] **LII**, 57.   [4] **LII**, 57, 70.
[5] *She King*, **C**, 96 ; **LII**, 67.   [6] *She King*, **C**, 326.
[7] *Li ki*, **C**, II, 258.   [8] **LX**, 99.
[9] *She King*, **C**, 20 ; **LII**, 261.   [10] *She King*, **C**, 168.

floor was made of earth beaten and frequently watered. The furniture was reduced to almost nothing. In the hut of mourning, they slept at first on straw, a clod of earth serving for a pillow : towards the end of the mourning they were allowed a bed of unplaited rushes, and then a mat.[1]

The rites no doubt reveal the history of the furniture as well as of the house. The most perfect bed which was achieved was made of rush mats laid one upon another. Some of these mats were decorated with designs. Rich people used a pillow of horn and had coverings of flowered silk. In the day-time, the bedding was rolled up as it is nowadays, and they sat on mats to eat their meals, leaning their back against a stool. The hearth was made of stones placed together : the smoke escaped through a central hole, through which the rain fell into a drain-well. Restricted to one room only, the house was dark, scarcely lighted by one window and a narrow door cut in the south wall, the one opening towards the west, the other towards the east. Doors and windows were made by means of thorns or interlaced branches of mulberry-trees : sometimes the window was a round hole made of the neck of a broken pot.[2] Beneath the window, in the south-west and worst-lighted corner, the seeds were kept and the marriage-bed was laid.[3] It was the holiest spot in the house. But everything in this humble dwelling was sacred, the hearth, the central drain-well, the door beside which were heaped the sweepings from the floor. It was only with precaution that these were swept outside, at the time of the great New Year festivals, for a god lived in them who brought good fortune. His name was Thunderbolt. Owls, creatures dreaded by the thunder, were connected with the doors. Perhaps the bodies of screech-owls were fastened above them, together with bags of protecting herbs gathered at midsummer. The door was not passed without religious terror. " Be careful when thou goest out ! Be careful when thou goest in ! "[4] When crossing the threshold, one should avoid stepping upon it, and should lower one's

---

[1] **LX,** 100 ; *Li ki,* **C,** II, 556, 573.
[2] *Chuang Tsih,* **CXLII,** p. 459. A round clay hut is given as the dwelling of a solitary sage. It is surrounded by a thorn hedge—grass grows on the roof. The door is made of a straw mat fastened to the branch of a mulberry-tree—the windows of the necks of two jars hung with cloths.
[3] **LIX,** 12 ff. ; *Li ki,* **C,** I, 452 and 13 ; *ibid.,* II, 388.
[4] *She King,* **L** (Proleg.), 17.

eyes. Before entering, one should remove one's shoes.[1] No
less respect was shown to the hearth and the well. " Let
the spring water abound !—if a dry time should come it will
cease to flow !—There must be a rule in drawing it—and
good sense in using it ! " [2]

Water was the great anxiety of the Chinese peasants.
Their working capital was very meagre. Of the smaller
tools they possessed hatchets, sickles, hoes and light ploughs
composed of a ploughshare of carved wood and a pole adapted
from a bent branch. They had no large cattle, and nearly
all the work was done by the hand of man, even the transport,
which was chiefly accomplished in baskets and creels, although
the use of carts was not unknown.[3] They kept a few animals,
fowls and pigs, and also watch-dogs, which could be eaten
in emergency. Hunting by means of nets and fishing with
the help of line or bow-net provided a supplement to their
resources. But in these lonely homesteads life depended
chiefly upon the regularity of the successive rains which
assured the success of the harvests of grain and peas. The
peasants built no granaries and scarcely made their calculations
from one year to the next. Famine lay in wait for them.
They could only escape it by dint of hard work and of
agricultural knowledge. The variety of their crops was admirable, and admirable their understanding of the seasons.
Their work was regulated by the help of proverbs in which
rustic wisdom had enshrined precise observations upon the
habits of nature.[4] The agricultural year began with the
first month of spring, when hibernating animals began to
stir, and the fishes to appear, rising up to the ice which was
thinning under the east wind : ploughs were then got ready
and the husbandmen joined together in couples. In the
second month the return of the nightingale announced the
equinox, peach-trees were in flower, the goldfinch was singing :
they knew then that the first rains were at hand : at once
they went to plough and sow. The rainbow appeared again,
the thunder growled anew : thousands of creatures arose
from the earth : the peewit alighted upon the mulberry-
trees : it was time to get ready the wicker stands for the
silkworms. Sow-thistles in flower marked the first month

---

[1] *Li ki*, **C,** I, 16.   [2] *She King*, **L** (Proleg.), 17.   [3] *She King*, **C,** 351.
[4] For these proverbs, see **LII,** 53 ff., and *Li ki*, **C,** I, 330 ff.

of summer, and foretold the great heats which ripened the millet : drought and great storms were then equally to be dreaded.   Then came full summer, when the grasshoppers were chirping and the flowers of the wax-tree appeared. Glow-worms were seen in the grass, which was first dried and then rotted by the heat and the heavy rains of the dying summer.   It was the first month of autumn : they made haste to gather the plants for dyeing.   Migratory birds collected for flight, the cricket chirped at the side of the house : the time of the great harvests had come.   The grain must be reaped and threshed before the hoar-frost lay upon the plants of the field.   In the last month of autumn, when the dead leaves were falling, they hastened to make charcoal : they must go back to the hamlets and there spend the dead season.   The agricultural year ended in the tenth month. The soil, hardened by the dry cold, was no longer amenable to human toil, and ceased to be fertile.   At the time when the rituals were edited, the observations of the peasants served to illustrate learned calendars on an astronomic basis : they were represented as emanating from the princely wisdom. It was even acknowledged that the " good luck of the husbandmen " was an effect of the virtue of the overlord.

It was still admitted that the peasants were simple tenants, the soil belonging from the first to the overlord alone. Nothing could be less clear than the few documents which we possess on the subject of the ancient forms of the appropriation of the soil : they have been obscured at will by native scholarship.[1]   One tradition, which goes back at least to the time of Mencius (fourth to third century B.C.), maintains that during the whole course of antiquity, the fields were divided equally by State management amongst the cultivators.   They were in the form of squares, subdivided into nine smaller squares (fields in the form of *tsing*), eight families cultivating together, for the benefit of the overlord, the central square (the *chou* system, practised under the Yin) or paying into the princely treasury the ninth part of the total produce (the *ch'e* system, practised under the Chou).   Modern scholarship is inclined to admit that the land of each country was

[1] M. Demiéville has given an excellent résumé of the available facts in BEFEO, 1923, p. 491 ff., in a review of a study by M. Hu Shih.

divided between the overlord (*Kong t'ien*, public lands) and the nobles (*Ssu t'ien*, patrimonial domains, or rather estates detached from the public domain). The peasants were only tenants attached to the soil by a sort of serfdom. As to the periodical distribution of land by families and in equal portions, this was an administrative Utopia invented at the time of the Han, or dating at the earliest from the period of the *Combatant Kingdoms*. We have seen that the first great States, and especially the Emperors, strove energetically to colonize the country, creating new lands and peopling them. These immense labours of settlement were completed by an administrative repartition of the land. It is possible that the *tsing* system only answers to an historical Utopia and that it originated in a transposing of the present into the past. It is also possible that the first more modest labours of tilling the soil, which, accomplished by such weak tools, had to be undertaken almost entirely afresh with the beginning of each year, had already led the peasants themselves to institute a periodical repartition of the fields which had been created by their common effort. Under the feudal régime, the husbandmen were no doubt looked upon as simple tenants and accessories to the land. If they belonged inseparably to the soil it was evidently because the ground at first belonged inseparably to the communities which were formed by them. The great reformation of the Ch'in, which, under the Han, was to end in a terrible agrarian crisis, consisted chiefly in the dissolution of the close partnership which existed between man and the soil.

At the time of the peasant communities this close connexion was translated into a proud sentiment of autochthony : " Our ploughshares are sharpened—let us begin work on the southern fields." " Let us sow seeds of every grain ! wrapped up in them is life !—Now let us reap in a crowd, in a crowd !— What abundance at the harvest !—Thousands, a thousand millions—a thousand trillions !—Let us make wine, let us make new wine !—This shall be for offering to our ancestors —for perfect ceremonies !—What a relish has this flavour !— it is the pride of the province !—What a spice has this perfume !—It is the comfort of the old men !—It is not the first time that it has been like this time ! Today is not the first time that it has been like today !—Thus it was in the time of our most ancient elders." [1] To the reverence inspired by the fruitful grain and the fostering earth was added a noble confidence in the eternity of a race solidly planted upon a soil which had at last been tamed. But mingled with the peasant pride was the remembrance of hours of hard work, the consciousness of the flight of time, the fear of less prosperous seasons. And the whole melted into a religious emotion, dominated by the ideas of moderation and temperance : " The cricket is in the hall—the carts in the shed—then why should we not keep holiday ? The days and months are passing ! Let us, however, keep within bounds.—And remember the days of labour !—Let us love joy without folly :—a good man is moderate." [2]

[1] *She King.* C, 441.   [2] **LII,** 188 ; *She King,* C, 120.

PEASANT CUSTOMS

THE Chinese peasants lived a hard and monotonous life from day to day, but at set times great fêtes occurred to awake in them the joy of living. These had the character of orgies. They were condemned from the time of the first philosophers. Yet Confucius acknowledged that they had a beneficent value. He would not have desired that the Prince " after having imposed one hundred days of fatigue upon the people, should not grant them one day of rejoicing " for one must not " always stretch the bow without ever loosing it—(or) always loose, without ever stretching it." [1] Confucius acknowledged that the popular fêtes were an invention of princely wisdom. As a matter of fact, these fêtes date back to an immemorial past, and the general conditions of rustic life suffice to explain them.

I

FAMILIES AND RURAL COMMUNITIES

In all ages, Chinese organization has been governed by one principle : the principle of the separation of the sexes. It is interpreted in the strictest sense. It implies not only strict injunctions, isolating the maidens and youths before marriage. Even husband and wife must live at a distance from each other, and all their relations call for infinite precautions. Amongst the peasants the separation of the sexes was founded upon a division of labour : men and women confronted each other like two rival corporations.

Between husbandmen and women weavers rose a barrier of sexual and technical embargoes. The Chinese myth which has with least difficulty come down the ages (it bears witness

[1] *Li ki*, C, II, 190–191.

no doubt to the most ancient past) relates to two stellar divinities, the (female) Weaver and the Ox-driver. Between them, as a sacred barrier, spreads the Milky Way, the celestial River. The celestial River can only be crossed once a year : on that night the Weaver and the Ox-driver celebrate their nuptials.[1] If to men fell the dangerous task of laying open the soil, at the risk of irritating the mysterious powers of the Earth, and if, on the other hand, only women understood how to preserve in the seeds the principle of life which makes them germinate, it appears that the ritual ploughing by which the earth was initiated into fruitfulness formerly required the joint efforts of a household.[2] The collaboration of the sexes was the more efficacious, because it was reserved for sacred occasions, being looked upon as a sacrilege in normal times.

According to a Chinese proverb the principle of the separation of the sexes is the foundation of exogamy. In all ages in China young people have been able to marry only on condition that they belonged to different families.[3] In addition to establishing a household, marriage serves to draw families together. This drawing-together was accomplished by the help of diplomatic rites. It was necessary to employ a herald. It appears that the axe was the emblem of this go-between who was entrusted with the union of two kindreds : it is used to separate the branches from the trunk, and makes it possible to prepare the faggots in which the branches of different origin may be united. The theme of the bound faggots often recurs in the marriage songs, which went on to sing " How is hemp cultivated ?—the furrows must be crossed !—How does one take a wife ?—the parents must be notified !—How does one cut the branches ?—it can't be done without a hatchet !—How does one take a wife ?—it can't be done without a match-maker." [4] The crossing of furrows and the crossing of families ensured the fruitfulness of households and of husbandry. To inaugurate the work of the fields collaboration of the sexes was necessary. To ensure its full effect it was well for it to bring together not only opposite sexes, but distinct families. While it completed the effects of the separation of the sexes, the practice of

[1] LII, 257 ; LIV, 31. [2] LVI, 543 ; LV, 330, note 1
[3] See, in an opposite sense, XCIII, 117 ff. [4] LII, 126.

exogamy gave an exalted efficacy to the work accomplished in common by the rustic couples.

The rule of exogamy has a domestic bearing : it has a territorial bearing also. It forbids the marriage of young people born in the same hamlet. As soon as he is married, one of the partners, saying farewell to his family, must go and live in a strange village. " The rainbow is in the east !— no one dare point to it. . . . The maid, when she will marry —leaves brothers and parents a great way off." " The spring Ch'uan is on the left, . . . on the right the river K'i. When she will marry, the maid—leaves far away brothers and parents." [1] Listening to the complaints of the young brides, we realize how painful was the abrupt breaking of domestic ties, and the exile which was a prelude to the hard toil of daily life in strange and hostile surroundings. " A daughter-in-law in thy house, these three years . . . never set free from household cares . . . up early and to bed late . . . never could I enjoy my morning sleep." [2] If the verses of the *She King* may be trusted we must conclude that it was always the woman who was expatriated. This may perhaps have been the general custom in feudal times, but there were always husband-sons-in-law who were annexed to the wife's family. The strength of this custom, which persisted in spite of administrative measures,[3] leads one to think that neighbouring villages began by exchanging young boys and not girls. The peasant house was (and in fact has remained) a feminine matter. The man scarcely entered it : the furniture was part of the woman's dowry. In primitive times the village itself belonged to the women ; the divinity which protected it was called the " Mother of the hamlet." The genii of the soil were long in acquiring a masculine form. When chiefs were chosen from the men, they bore the title of " Father " of such a village.[4] The name of the group was also that of the family. Territorial clans formed the smallest group in the population.[5] Thus, in the village, pre-eminence belonged first to the women, then to the men, but the inhabitants were always divided into two groups, according to

---

[1] **LII,** 44 and 97.   [2] **LII,** 127.
[3] **LV,** 17, note 2.   [4] *Lun heng,* **XXXV,** vol. I, 69.
[5] It is still frequently the case in our own days, and peasant marriages generally unite consorts from different villages

their sex, one of which, the group of annexed husbands and wives, was reduced to a subordinate position.

The other group was composed of natives. United by their common name, they formed a clan. An old tradition maintains that a·sort of accord must exist between the dwelling and the name.[1] As the result of belonging to a common soil and a common name, the relationship was of a closer nature than if it had simply been founded upon the ties of blood. Blood is subdivided and is lost : only two brothers-german can possess the same blood. But, marked by the symbol of the name, which all can possess entire, all alike identified with the hereditary land from which all constantly draw the same common elements, the members of the territorial clan form an undivided and singularly homogeneous group. Only age and the difference in generations bring an element of distinction. The old men and the first-born are distinguished. The eldest member of the oldest generation bears the title of Elder. He enjoys a kind of pre-eminence, but it is only by his right as delegate of the group that he retains the vague authority which he exercises ; when he dies, a younger member takes his place, without any succession in the true sense of the word.[2] Identity is absolute amongst the relations of the same generation. They form together one collective personality. None of them, taken singly, has a legal existence. The family nomenclature takes no account of individuals nor of their natural closeness of relationship. It is *classificatory :* it has no need of names except to define the categories of relationship.[3] The word *mother* itself applies to a large group of people : if it be taken in an individual sense, it is used to name, not the woman who has given one birth, but the most respected woman of the generation of mothers. In the same way, the *father* is not distinguished from the *paternal uncles :* the word is even used for a circle which includes far more than the father's brothers. The *sons* are confounded with the indistinct mass of *nephews*. All *cousins*, no matter how distant, are treated as *brothers*. A complete unity is at the base of this organization. It recognizes neither personal ties nor an hierarchy. The affinities of relationship have a universal character.

---

[1] **LV,** 155. Note 1, *in fine.* Cf. *Lun heng,* **XXXV,** vol. II, 410.
[2] **LIII,** 10, 43 and 65.   [3] *Êrh ya,* chap. IV ; **LIII,** 45.

The, family group is all the more self-contained from
being homogeneous. It has no means of absorbing a foreign
element. Essentially relationship can neither be bestowed,
nor lost, nor acquired. It is made up of everyday and
peaceful sentiments. Enthusiasms, or excesses, or connexions
with the world outside, are forbidden to it. Never would
the Ancestors (in the time of Ancestor-worship) accept a meal
except from the family kitchen.[1] Never (when adoption was
practised) could anyone be adopted who did not beforehand
bear the family name.[2] Never (after the State allowed the sale
of land) could a purchaser believe that he had completely
dispossessed the former proprietor.[3] Never did moral sentiment admit that the ties which bound members of one family
together and attached them to the soil, could really be broken.
The family was made up of attachments which were in-
destructible, immemorial and strictly defined. In the constitution of the territorial clans there was a powerful principle
of isolation.

This exclusive character of the clan agreed perfectly with
the retired life led by a family from day to day on the
ancestral clearing. But family sentiments were not the only
strength of the rural society. Chinese peasants were held
within a second system of loyalties involving sentiments
wider, richer and more complex. These are bound up with
the ancient rules of marriage, which, at the same time as the
exogamy of the clan, prescribe a certain *endogamy*. Marriage,
impossible between relatives, was also impossible between
persons who had been complete strangers to each other.
For long centuries it was believed that a conjugal union
could only be happy when it was contracted between members
of families who, from the most distant past, had kept up
intercourse resulting in intermarriages.[4] Custom demanded
that sons should take wives from their mother's family.
Powerful pretexts were necessary to escape from this usage.
" The mother of Shu-hiang wished to make him marry a
daughter of her own family. Shu-hiang said to her : ' My
Mothers (*sic :* system of classification) are many and my
brothers are few. I will beware of the daughters of my

---

[1] **LV**, 157. [2] *Yi li*, **CXXIII**, I, 19.
[3] This holds good even in modern times. See P. Hoang (VS, 11), *Notes techniques sur la propriété en Chine*, pp. 9 and 10.
[4] *Kuo yu*, chap. II ; **LII**, 209 ff. In the opposite sense, **XCIII**, 125, note 2.

maternal uncles [1] (that is to say, I am afraid that they may give me no descendants).' " At the time when Shu-hiang was speaking (513 B.C.) the only relationship recognized (amongst the nobles) was through the male line. Marriages were forbidden between relatives on the father's side. These illegal unions alone were supposed to be unfruitful. To liken such marriages to the union proposed with the daughter of a maternal uncle was to offer an improper excuse at the bidding of passion (Shu-hiang married to his own taste and was unhappy). Such a cousin was never a relative. Whether their descent had been governed by the principle of male or female inheritance, the children of a brother and sister (cross cousins) necessarily belonged to two distinct family groups. Their marriage, far from being forbidden or disapproved, remained a regular custom.

It was at first obligatory. This is proved by nomenclature. The word which signifies *uncle on the mother's side* signifies *father-in-law*, and that which signifies *aunt on the father's side* also signifies *mother-in-law*.[2] This system of naming implies that a principle of endogamy completes the principle of clan exogamy : it implies an organization by which two exogamous family groups, both governed by the rule that relationship. or more correctly the name, is transmitted in one line only, compose a pair which are united by tradition, and regularly exchange the half of their children, boys or girls. It is possible that the nomenclature dates from a period when it was the boys who were exchanged and descent by the female line was given the honourable place : in pronunciation as well as in writing there is little difference between the word by which a man (maternal uncle=father-in-law) denotes the son of his sister (and also the husband of his daughter) and the word which denotes as a whole the family and the family name.[3] But marriage between cousins, children of brothers and sisters, remained possible and correct when the line of descent passed to the male side, no obstacle arising since the name was still transmitted in a single line. It is a most remarkable fact that this custom should have persisted whilst the system of relationship was varied. This fact proves the peculiar solidarity of the associated organization

---

[1] *Tso chuan*, C, III, 437 ; *ibid.*, 752 ; **LV**, 13.
[2] *Êrh ya*, chap. IV.   [3] *Êrh ya*, chap. IV

formed by a couple of families united by one matrimonial tradition. Though it was complicated later, this organization left traces behind it, strong enough to maintain the principal customs which formed an integral part of it. These then should be explained by referring them to the period when a two-fold division ruled the organization as a whole.

While the right to wear mourning and the right to eat food cooked on the same hearth, are the marks of the relation of kinship, the *connubium* is the sign of a second type of relations. These are of a superior order. Thanks to them the characteristic isolation of the local groups may be modified. Domestic sentiments have something exclusive and self-contained, but in every territorial group, marriage introduces motives of altruism. It brings a spirit of fruitful competition, of rivalry, of confidence. For the family (on the father's or mother's side) which receives them, the sons or daughters-in-law are like tokens, continually renewed, of a treaty long ago concluded. They are hostages. Their presence witnesses to age-long solidarities. In feudal times the same word was used to denote the rites of an embassy and those of a matrimonial alliance.[1] Treaties were duplicated almost always by an exchange of wives. Marriage has remained one of the symbols of political friendship. It was from the beginning a principle of peace. It served to maintain an indissoluble union between the pairs of families which made up the ancient rural communities.

In the same way, married couples must remain bound for ever. Matrimonial inconstancy and political instability seemed to imply each other. It was acknowledged that there was a germ of eternity in the marriage contract : " In death, in life, in sorrow—I take thee for my partner !— I take thy hands in mine :—I hope to grow old with thee ! " [2] We divine in this vow a sort of heroic resolve : as a matter of fact, soldiers on a campaign vowed the same vow as husband and wife, taking each other by the hand. The vocabulary makes no distinction between conjugal fidelity and brotherhood in arms. Both have their origin in the same covenant of friendship.

The sentiments upon which the matrimonial alliance is based contrast with the single and simple sentiments which

---

[1] *Li ki*, C, vol. I, 676 ; **LVI**, 36.   [2] **LII**, 207.

colour the family relations. Marriage takes place between cousins, but they are cousins who do not bear the same name. They are not relatives, but they are the children of brothers and sisters. The proximity between them is as close as it can be without attaining virtual identity. This proximity peculiar to those who are called upon to form, not a group, but a pair, rests not upon common, but upon complementary qualities. It is founded on mixed sentiments, in which are found in equal parts, a spirit of solidarity and a spirit of rivalry. One word which means husband and wife, also means rival, and even enemy. A woman introduced in feudal times into a family, whose descent is in the male line, is a friend who, quickly transformed into an enemy, frequently quarrels with her husband in defence of the interests of her own kin. The group of husbands and wives attached to a united family, while it forms a band of hostages, is also a party of delegates representing a rival group.

Rivals and yet united, two groups linked together lived on the soil of a rural community. Each of them had its special territory. But, on this territory, exiled from their own country by marriage, lived also the representatives of the other half of the pair. There again two united and rival groups confronted each other. Even when the organization of the whole no longer rests on the simple two-fold division, this division is found again on the territory of each domestic group. Indeed, marriage does not only unite two partners. It is, in its essence, a collective contract, and never ceases to influence the groups. The bridegroom must have attendants, the bride her maids. " The magpie has built a nest— that nest is full of wood-pigeons !—this girl who is to be married—overwhelm her with one hundred chariots of honour ! " [1] One hundred is an emblem of the whole. The hundred chariots driven by the attendants and maids point out, symbolically, the fact that the groups united by the matrimonial alliance are also pledged to each other without reservation. In very ancient times, the exchange of boys and girls was total, not symbolically, but actually. Households were formed as the result of a collective union which bound together all the representatives of one generation. The word *mother* does not indicate the Mother alone and all

[1] LII, 37.

her sisters. It indicates also all the wives married to the father's brothers.[1] Maternal aunts and wives of uncles are indistinguishable, for they make up the same group of sisters, the same group of wives.

Thus on every piece of land two groups face each other, which are both self-contained in the same degree. They are opposed in sex, in name, in substance, in manner of life. They carry on the ancient rivalry of family pairs and sexual corporations. The principle of the opposition of the sexes, which, translated into laws of exogamy and endogamy, presided over the organization of the peasants, preserves its early vigour and gains new strength in the course of everyday life. Still intact and fresh, those sentiments remain which render the collaboration of the rival sexes so difficult and yet show it to be so fruitful.

II

The Seasonal Jousts

Interdicts, founded upon the conditions of the climate and of the dwelling-place, have for their chief end the setting apart of times and places for the labours of men and women, where they can be carried on without fear of contamination. A seasonal rhythm orders this arrangement. Men and women relieve each other at work but both at the same time change their manner of life.

They change it at the beginning and the end of the agricultural year. In the plains of Old China two moments are clearly marked. The climate is continental and the alternating rhythm of the seasons has an arresting character. Both short-lived, coming between the hard dry cold of winter and the warm summer damp, the spring and autumn, with their gentle rains and their changing sky, are like two wonderful moments. Nature, at one breath, begins or ceases to live. A sudden blossoming and a quick fall of the leaf, the return and departure in a body of migratory birds, the rapid swarming and disappearance of insects, which one by one herald in the fields the pathetic awakening of life or its untoward ending, make a kind of dramatic framework for the changes which the Chinese peasants impose upon them-

[1] *Ĕrh ya*, chap. IV.

selves after the likeness of their own sky. Thus at one blow they revolutionize their habits. Forgetting, in the confusion of the moment, their everyday interdicts, they feel the necessity of coming to the help of nature, and co-operating amongst themselves.

When the Chinese philosophers wished to build up a theory of love they explained that in springtime the girls were attracted by the boys, and in autumn the boys by the girls, as though each of them in turn feeling his nature to be incomplete, was suddenly seized with the irresistible desire to perfect it.[1] Spring was the season of betrothals : in old times the initiative came from the girls. Autumn was the time for setting up house : the wife must come, without delay, to live at her husband's home.[2] In autumn the husbandmen were rich in grain, garnered for the winter: but the women, in spring, had abundance of still more precious riches, stuffs newly woven. At first the women weavers had the means of attracting the husbandmen : then they, in their turn, had the means of making themselves agreeable to the weavers. All, alternatively, had their charms and were able to realize their desire.

Far from avoiding each other then, as they did in the ordinary course, they sought each other out : " Weave your linen no longer !—go to the market-place ! dance ! dance ! " —" Withered leaves ! withered leaves !—the wind will come and blow upon you !—Come sirs ! come sirs !—sing, we will join you." [3] In autumn and in spring, once the labours of the fields and of the weaving were finished, great assemblies were held in the open country, where the boys and girls from the neighbouring hamlets met. Winter was about to imprison each family in its lonely village, or else summer would compel men and women to live apart from each other. Held in autumn or spring, the meetings began by confirming in every heart the feeling of the need for solidarity. Exclusive groups and rival corporations confirmed their alliance while they proceeded to the collective festivals of marriage.

These festivals consisted of communions, orgies and games. After so many days of a life of restraint wasted in self-centred labours and sordid thoughts, a feeling of generous rivalry seized upon the reunited multitudes. Nothing came amiss to feed the passion for sport which was suddenly let loose

---

[1] **LII**, 138 ff.   [2] **LVI**, 543 ff.   [3] **LII**, 43, 122.

in them, it was all turned to account in merry meetings and courteous rivalries.[1]

Great flights of birds passed over the equinoctial skies : they competed for the right to take the eggs out of the nests : the eggs were the foundation of a kind of tournament : in the circles of the shells they found and admired the five colours of the rainbow, the sign in heaven of fertile rains : the girl who got possession of a nightingale's egg during the spring festivals and ate it was conscious that great hopes had sprung up in her, and sang her joy aloud. (Such, it is said, was the origin of the Songs of the North.) Their feet trod upon a fertile soil, lovely in rich green, where blossom was breaking out, with the promise of fruit : boys and girls, in their dances, faced each other for a battle of flowers. They wrestled, plucking bunches of plantain : they sang, kilting up their skirts into a knot at the waist, glad to gather in their lap the thousand-seeded plant. They sang as they plucked on the hillside mugwort with its powerful scent, and ferns with their fruitful spores, or else, on the bank of the rivers, the duckweed, for which aquatic creatures, male and female, gathered together in pairs, were also disputing : or else, again, the large floating plants whose leaves, round as discs or pointed as arrows, grow on the same stalk. Eaten with the joy of conquest, berries seem no less wonderful than eggs. " The King of Ch'ou, passing over the Kiang,—finds a berry of water sagitta !—It is as big as his fist—and as red as the sun !—He cuts it in two, then he eats it : it is as sweet as honey ! " [2]

In the transports of the general rivalry, their hearts rejoiced over the simplest discoveries. They overflowed with lively emotions which gestures and voices were often able to interpret. Games were arranged according to a rhythm under the sway of the common sentiment. Gatherings, assemblies, hunts, became the opportunity for rivalry in dance and song. This may still be found in our own day amongst the backward populations of southern China. Their greatest festivals are those in which the boys and girls of neighbouring villages " form a line abreast and cut the fern, singing extempore songs." [3] On these jousts depend the prosperity of the year

---

[1] **LII**, 203 ff.   [2] *Kia yu,* 14 and *Shu yuan,* 18 ; **LV**, 552, note 2.
[3] **LII**, 283, and App. III.

and the people's happiness.[1] In the same way, in the ancient festivals of China, the young people who gathered for the games believed that they were obeying a command of nature, and working together with her. Their dances and their songs corresponded to the cries of birds seeking a mate, the flights of insects crying as they pursued each other. " The grasshopper meadow and the one on the little hill hops. Until I have seen my lord—my restless heart, ah, how it beats !—but as soon as I see him—as soon as I am united to him—then my heart will be at peace." [2] The grasshoppers which call to one another from the meadows to the little hills, have remained for the Chinese the emblems of fruitful unions and exogamous marriages. They were a reminder to the young people of the imperious law of union to which they were all subject. But, as representatives of their sex and their clan, weighted with the spirit of the soil, full of domestic pride and sexual egoism, they felt themselves at first to be rivals. The courteous struggle which was to bring them together opened with a tone of bravado and mistrust.

Proud of their finery, their flowery robes, their caps dyed with madder, white as the clouds, the young girls opened the fray. Assuming a haughty manner they invited the swains in a mocking tone, and then made as though they would flee. " Here are plums falling from the tree !—fill your baskets with them !—Ask for us, young men !—this is the time : speak then ! " " There are great trees in the south :—but you can't rest beneath them :—Girls walk abroad near the Han :—but you can't ask for them." " If you think of me with love—I shall kilt up my skirt and pass over the Wei !—But if you have no thought for me—are there not other boys—Oh, is it true, most foolish of young fools ? " " The Chen with the Wei—will overflow its banks ! —The boys with the girls—come to pick the orchids—The girls invite them : ' Let us go down ! '—and the boys reply : ' We are coming at once ! ' ' Nay, but how if we go down ?— for across the Wei there stretches a beautiful meadow ! ' Then the boys and girls—play together—and the girls receive the pledge of a flower." [3] As soon as the girls had thrown down the challenge, the party was made up. The chief rôle was taken by the boys. They had to pay their addresses.

[1] LII, 292.   [2] LII, 117.   [3] LII, 49, 98, 104, 105.

In our own day, among the Miao-cheu and the Thos,[1] these addresses are accompanied by a game of ball, mixed with singing. As long as the girl sends back the ball, all is still to do : the swain begins his song again. In the old Chinese customs, when the battle of flowers was one of the chief aspects of the lovers' games, all was over when the girl accepted a sweet-scented flower or a handful of aromatic berries. " You are a marsh-mallow, in my eyes ! "   " Give me those berries ! " [2]

Thus hearts were bound together and the espousals accomplished. Along with the halting couplets, which were invented to suit the rhythm of the dance, according to the rules of traditional improvization, the boy entwined a whole cycle of venerable analogies. Verse by verse, he called up the ritual setting of the festival. Taken as a whole, it was like a solemn command of nature. The sacred images which depicted it in detail, recalled the necessary agreement between the rhythm of the seasons and the human observances. In the time of the classical rituals, Chinese betrothed sent each other a wild goose at break of day. This rite is only a concrete metaphor. They used to sing : " The call of the wild geese is heard—at break of day, when dawn appears !— Man goes forth to seek his wife—Ere ever the ice is melted ! " [3] The geese signify to the maidens that the ice is about to melt at the breath of spring and that the betrothal must not be delayed.

The maxims of the calendar of which the lovers' litany is composed themselves possess a sort of compelling power. As the effect of this long incantation, hearts cast off their defensive shyness. The resistance of sexual modesty and domestic honour vanish little by little. The young people yield at last to the obligation of marriage, and, drawn together by the poetic antiphony, opposing corporations and closed groups, can, in one sacred moment, feel the rebirth of the unity which is their essence.

[1] LII, 286.   [2] LII, 122.   [3] LII, 102, and App. I.

III

The Feasts of Harvest and the Dead Season of the Year

The tourneys of love-songs took place in the open country. They were the principal rite in the federal festivals at which agreement was re-established amongst the peasants. In these open-air gatherings, every group, whether sexual or territorial, forgetting its exclusive spirit, affirmed its solidarity by virtue of communions which put them all on one level. Banquets and drinking parties held in common completed the effect of sexual communion. The festivals were like fairs. The exchange of gifts accompanied personal intercourse. The singing matches had their parallel in a rivalry of presents. " He who gives me quinces—shall be paid with my trinkets ! —That shall not be his payment :—I will love him for ever ! " [1] Verses were exchanged like gifts : but the litany of love has the lilt of a hesitating lament : it lulls to sleep the spirit of defiance. On the other hand a hurried rhythm governs the exchange of material gifts : one gives more than one has received, with the object of compelling a larger return. The value of the presents increases, the excitement of those who offer them increases in the same ratio. This excitement may spread to a communal emotion where all property at last becomes indistinguishable or is swallowed up in a general orgy : " Why do you say you have no garment ?—All mine are yours for the taking." [2] Such is the formula (conjugal or military) of a complete union. And, as a matter of fact, the festivals of the seasons aimed at realizing a union of this kind. But, undertaken in a spirit of usury, the competition in gifts might conduce less to the maintenance of traditional balance than to the victory of the exclusive ideal.

The agricultural year ends with the village festivals, in which the good fortune of their country is celebrated by the husbandmen amongst themselves. In these rejoicings the gift-matches are of extreme importance. These village festivals are harvest-festivals. They coincide with the return of the men to the hamlet. As masculine festivals their im-

---

[1] **LII,** 61, and **LV,** 94, note 1.
[2] *She King,* **C,** 142 ; *T'so chuan,* **C,** vol. III, 518 ; **LV,** 131.

portance dates no doubt from the period when husbands
ceased to be nothing but sons-in-law, and where marriage
was most frequently brought about by the annexing of wives.
It was then that the weaving women lost their pre-eminence
over the husbandmen. This revolution evidently coincides
with the added value which the cultivation of cereals acquired
in the general economy. It is possible that these facts are
connected with the progress of the labours of clearing the
ground, which entailed, with a denser population, the formation of more powerful companies and less simple arrangement of territorial grouping. In this new soil, more favourable
to competition, sprang up the agnatic institutions.

The husbandmen came together at the end of harvest to
spend the winter. The houses in the village still belonged
to the women, even when they became daughters-in-law, but
the men possessed a house in common. The rituals still
preserve the memory of it. They prescribe that the husbands
must retire to it during their wives' confinement. The old
sexual interdicts, even in classical times, recovered all their
authority during the three months which precede and the
three months which follow a confinement.[1] At that time the
old rustic organization resumed all its rights. Various survivals
and a few mythological features witness to the importance of
this house of the men, which was their winter refuge. It was
in this house which they shared in common that the men
gained confidence in their own strength. This confidence
culminated in the assertion of their masculine privileges.

While they were companions in long days of idleness, the
husbandmen kept feasts, from which two classical ceremonies
are derived : the Great No and the Pa Cha. One ushers in
and the other closes the winter, the time of border-line
between two agricultural years. Both tended to approach
the Solstice. Impoverished and systematized, attached to
astronomical dates, they lost their cohesion and their original
value. They were at first connected festivals. Bound up
with the periods of frost and thaw, they marked the two
great moments of a winter liturgy. " The second month has
come : break the ice ! strike ! strike !—And then it is the
third month : put it in the ice-house in the shade !—The
fourth month : rise up early !—Slaughter lambs, offer leeks !

[1] **LV**, 290 ; *Li ki*, **C**, I, 671.

—Ninth month : hoar-frost and cold !—The tenth : a clean, hard threshing-floor !—and two pitchers whose wine tastes good !—Sing, ' Slaughter lambs and sheep ! '—Go to the communal-house !—and raising your horn cups, cry—' Life without end ! and ten thousand years.' " [1]

In the vast plains of classical China, the soil, hardened by the dry frosts of winter, no longer accepts man's labour. The Chinese peasants then considered it to be, as it were, in sanctuary. While they themselves took their rest, they granted rest to " all the creation." They began by inaugurating a season of universal retreat. They sang " O Earth, come back to your place !—Waters ! return to your depths ! —Creatures of the summer, stir no more !—Trees, plants ! return to your pools ! " [2] This invocation can be readily understood from the standpoint of the poor farm-labourers, who were obliged every year to reclaim the fields which had been snatched again by a rebel nature. They explained this resumption as a kind of advance and retreat. Grouped together in species, all creatures came back to rest in a winter refuge. " The water begins to freeze, the earth to harden with the frost. . . . The rainbow is hidden and we see it no more. . . . Heaven and earth no more have intercourse. Winter has set in. . . . Guard the bridges and the fences ! Close the roads and the paths ! . . . Do not uncover what is covered ! Open neither houses nor buildings ! Let everything be closed and everything shut up ! . . . Emanations from the ground might escape and spread ! . . . The hibernating animals might die ! " [3] When the hibernating animals shut themselves up in their retreats, men also shut themselves up, to assist in the universal retirement. " If a peasant has not gathered and garnered his harvests, if a horse or a bullock or a domestic animal be left to wander, he who takes possession of them does no wrong." [4] The rights of property do not hold at a distance, or rather, when winter comes to put as it were the barrier of a divorce between human labour and the ground, every species is put out of the reach of every other. All outside contact is forbidden. There is then a universal ban, a general dispersion, a rupture

---

[1] *She King*, **C**, 165. Upon the feudal aspect of sacrifice to frost and cold, see *Tso chuan*, **CIII**, 71, and **LV**, 330, note 1.

[2] *Li ki*, **C**, I, 596, and **LII**, 185. [3] *Li ki*, **C**, I, 386 ff.

[4] *Li ki*, **C**, I, 401, and **LII**, 187.

of all related life. On the other hand, beings of the same nature who can remain in company, are drawn yet closer together. Penned up according to species, men and things are busied during the retreat in re-establishing their specific genius. Restoring themselves in the company of their kind, they arm themselves with the forces which, when spring has come and the rights of sanctuary have been removed, will allow of a general resumption of contact. Then, with an offering of leeks, lambs, and a black bullock, they can say farewell to the genius of the cold : breaking the ice, they can " remove the barriers which are opposed to the reign of warmth " and call down hail and thunder : they can chase away the genii of drought, and, after a first ritual ploughing, they can once more open up the ground which is renewed by rest.[1]

The festivals of the winter season had a dramatic character. Extreme excitement was general. Even in the day of Confucius, those who took part (on the word of an eye-witness) were all " like madmen " (meaning that they felt themselves filled with a divine spirit). Exorcists played a great part : to them was actually given the name of " madmen." Dances, to the sound of clay timbrels, induced a state of ecstasy. Drunkenness brought it to perfection. The exorcists wore the skins of animals. Animal dances were performed.[2] The husbandmen disguised themselves as cats and leopards. They gave thanks to these enemies of the field-mouse and the wild boar, hoping to gain their favour for the coming season. They sang the labours and the daily life of the past year. They congratulated themselves on the constant agreement of their labours with the rustic calendar : they wished to renew this fruitful agreement between the seasons and the works of man, and hoped to compel Nature to continue her help to them. Drinking and eating, they made haste to consume their harvests : future harvests would not fail to be plentiful. They wrestled to find the man who would most boldly spend his fortune. They staked all on the future : he who staked the most, thought that by giving a larger pledge he would obtain a better reward from fate, a larger return for future labours.[3] Competitions in bragging mingled with the competitions in spending.[4] The protests of the

---

[1] *Tso chuan*, **C,** III, 71.   [2] **LV,** 323 ff.   [3] **LII,** 180 ff.   [4] **LV,** 321.

educated men in the town never had any effect. For centuries, these ruinous meetings continued, no less scandalous than the conditions of folly which went along with them. Perhaps they deserved to be censured after the peasants had learnt to look forward from one year to another, and were familiar with granaries and stocks and a thoughtful economy. Nevertheless these orgies were a fruitful outlay of the first order if by their help the labourers encouraged each other to have faith in their craft and bravely survive the misery of the barren days of winter.

Reunited in the communal house, their idea was to oppose, as with a powerful counter-weight, the influences of dispersal by which the whole world was then assailed : in these powers philosophers of all ages have recognized a feminine nature (*yin*). Men worked to establish the alternating rhythm of the seasons. They succeeded by their own strength, but it was by virtue of the games. Women were excluded from them. Nevertheless an antithetical tendency governed all the masculine orgies. The efficacy of the ceremonies seemed to depend upon the participants confronting each other face to face and performing alternate gestures. There must sit a party of hosts—here, a party of guests. If some were supposed to represent the sun, heat and summer, the principle *yang*, others embodied the moon, cold, winter, the principle *yin*. Before communing, they must confront each other, alternating like the seasons, so that the seasons, alternating also, might bring prosperity to all. The seasons were imagined as belonging to one or the other sex. Nevertheless the actors were all men. But we know by a definite example that when the dancing groups confronted each other, one was composed of young boys and the other of grown men. These games brought together, not delegates from rival sexes, but representatives of classified ages which were variously honoured. Ranks, in banquets and drinking parties, were assigned according to age (literally = according to teeth, that is to say, apparently, according to preferment). The old men presided.[1]

The festivals of winter consisted of a long competition in spending, which was favourable to the constitution of a male hierarchy. Ritual evolution bears witness to the important

---

[1] **LII**, 183 ff. ; *Li ki*, **C**, vol. II, 655 ff.

place taken in it by the old men. The chief part is reserved
for them in the village festival of the Pa Cha which ushers
in the winter liturgy. It is their duty to invite nature and
men to the retreat which is a preparation for the renewal.
The old men give to " things grown old " the signal of repose.
In mourning garments and staff in hand, they lead the year
to its end. The dead season is inaugurated by a festival
of old age.

IV

THE HOLY PLACES

The old men very soon won the privilege of conducting
alone, in the name of their villages, the mourning for the
dying year. For long centuries, initiations were celebrated
in the rural assemblies at the same time as espousals to
inaugurate the new season. Learned rituals still speak of the
spring festivals when " girls and boys rejoiced in a crowd."
The gloss adds : " (then) majority is granted to the boys :
(then) wives are taken." [1] Life can only awake by virtue of
the combined forces of the two sexes. Only a festival of youth
can arouse the spring.

Initiations and espousals were accomplished under the
control of the whole community. They held their sittings
in places set apart from domestic occupation and profane
uses. In a wide untrammelled landscape boys and girls,
freed from customary restraints, learnt contact with nature.
When she welcomed their first meeting, she was glistening
with new-born freshness, overflowing with creative life.
Waters flowed in the brooks set free by the melting of the
ice : springs which had been bound by winter burst from
the fountains which had once more come to life : the thawed
ground opened to let the grass appear : the animals peopled
it, all springing from their retreats. The times of seclusion
were over, and that of universal interpenetration had come.
Earth and Sky could " commune," and the rainbow was the
sign of their union. Closed groups could now enter into
alliance, sexual corporations encounter each other. In a
landscape which was at once venerable and new, where
from time immemorial their ancestors had been at once

[1] *Petit calendrier des Hia,* 2nd month.

initiated into social and sexual life, the young people were united. The sentiment of profound solidarity arose, blossoming from their rediscovered youth, in the midst of a nature which was itself rejuvenated, fertilized and brought again into common use. These unions in the fields were susceptible to sudden and collective emotions, in the highest degree contagious. By an effect of transference, this intercourse in contact with the soil was intercourse with the soil itself, and rendered it sacred. Clothed with an august majesty, the traditional site of the festivals seemed to all to be their country's Holy Place.[1]

In all the customs of the festivals, the young people sought in the most intimate way possible to have contact with the Holy Place of their race. They assigned to it a power of fertilization to which in the remotest corners of the country they hoped to lay claim. These sentiments lie at the root of beliefs which were destined to long life.

One of the most important games of the spring festivals was the crossing of rivers which was performed half naked and immediately before the unions in the fields. Shivering from contact with the living water, the women then felt themselves to be penetrated, as it were, with floating souls. The sacred fountains, long dried up, awoke anew as though the coming of spring had set free their waters from an underground prison where winter had enchained them. From these touching images the idea arose that the souls of the dead, seeking a new life in springtime, escaped on the stream of the spring floods from a deep hiding-place where death had shut them in. So there was invented a country of the dead, neighbour to man's earth, and communicating with it at sacred moments. This underground dwelling, which was called the Yellow Springs, could only be the winter refuge of the Waters. By the act of crossing the rivers their deliverance was celebrated, fertile rains were drawn down upon the land, and upon oneself the spring of fertilization.[2]

The Chinese never ceased to pray at the same time and by the same rites for births to enrich their families and rain to make the seed to spring. Rains and reincarnations were at first obtained by the sexual games. But in the end it was believed that water possessed a female nature, and that

[1] **LII, 191 ff.**   [2] **LVIII and LIV, 23.**

inversely women alone could retain the virtue by which it is possible to obtain rain.[1] In the same way they imagined that virgins could become mothers by simple contact with the sacred rivers.[2] It was in fact a time when births were acquired at the sole profit of the wives and when the only reincarnations were those of maternal ancestors. It was the time when houses and villages belonged to the women. They ruled there, bearing the title of mothers. Guardians of the seeds, they kept them in the dark corner where they spread their mats for the night. The men, who were like strangers, only drew near the marriage-bed in an almost furtive manner. In the house, by the contagious effect of communal emotions, unions upon the soil were, as in the Holy Place, unions with the soil. This soil was the land of the women. They conceived, in the house of their birth, at the contact of the seeds which seemed to hold life in themselves. Between the mothers of the family, the garnered seeds and the domestic soil, a community of attributes was established. Near the seeds and the bed a confused multitude of ancestral souls seemed to dwell in the maternal soil, waiting for the time of reincarnation, while at the same time the Earth itself appeared to be a Mother, giving fertility to women, and receiving it from them.[3] Thus there was a period when the earth which had been inhabited and claimed had none but female attributes. Organization was then almost entirely matriarchal. Then when the husbandmen, in creating agnatic institutions, became the masters of cultivation, the spirits of the soil seemed to be endowed with masculine traits. On the other hand, in all ages, the Holy Places remained the object of a universal reverence which scarcely allowed of distinctive attributes.

In every feature of the ritual country-side of the festivals something sacred was embodied. The feudal States reverenced the vast forests, the great marshes, the hills and the rivers. They did not imagine them to be simple nature divinities. They saw in them the dispensers of rain and of drought, but also of abundance and of poverty, health and sickness. They believed them to possess a combined power similar to that of the overlord. The hills and rivers did not owe this

---

[1] *Ch'un ch'iu fan lu*, 17.   [2] **LII**, 156.
[3] **LIX**, 55, and **LIV**, 26. Cf. in the contrary sense, **CIII**, 161 ; **LXIX**, 35 ; **XVI**, 524·

sanctity to a majesty which overawes the imagination. They owed it to the games, in which hunting and picking of flowers led the young people to the banks of streams and the mountain-sides. The Hills and Rivers were honoured as the guardians of the natural and the human order because, in their open-air festivals, the peasant communities had sealed their alliance with nature while they renewed the social compact. The sentiment of reverence which sprang up in the course of the seasonal gatherings was called out indiscriminately by the streams and the rocks : likewise by the flowers and the animals, by the most beautiful trees as well as by the meanest plants. One common Virtue was in everything. Equal hopes were aroused by picking a berry and by crossing a river. Every flower produced pregnancy, removed evil influences, united hearts, ratified vows. There was not one whose discovery was not a miracle, but none had a virtue peculiar to itself. Their virtues belonged to them all because they had appeared at the time of the Festivals, because they had been plucked, or given, or won in the games. They were as it were a portion of the indivisible power of the Holy Place. Flowers and animals, rocks and plants, land and water, things and people of the festival were sacred by the same right. The Holy Place was each and all, each and all were the Holy Place, for a common bond united the whole.[1]

As the sacred witness of the federal festivals in which, to a rhythmic measure, the treaty was renewed which bound men group to group, and all to Nature, the Holy Place was a tutelary power with unlimited properties. In an age when only isolated specks of land in the country of China were inhabited, when men and women formed close groups, when there existed scarcely a first rough draft of the hierarchy, the Holy Place was looked upon as the guardian of the most vital solidarities. It played the sacred part of a Chief. Year by year, when its prestige and authority were renewed by means of a magnificent hierogamy, it became, through the collective marriages, the divine regulator of the rhythm which actuated the seasons and the life of man.

[1] **LII**, 173 and 192 ff.

BOOK TWO

THE FOUNDATION OF THE CHIEFTAINSHIPS

CHAPTER I

HOLY PLACES AND CITIES

FROM the most remote past which documents allow us to picture, the inhabitants of old China have lived collected together in fairly powerful groups. It is probable that the density of these groups increased in proportion as the area of the soil under cultivation spread by means of deforestation, clearing and drainage. Local cataclysms (floods, invasions by nomads) may here and there have retarded this progress : we have no means of tracing its curve. As a matter of fact, the existence of rural communities formed simply by the union of two territorial groups can be detected only by the help of the family nomenclature and of the traces which dualism has left in the customs of law and religion. We may suppose that from the dawn of historic times, the territorial groups were of a relatively complex nature : more than two exogamous and compact groups entered into their composition. In the villages themselves, as at the present day, would be found on the one hand those who bore the same name or at least who did not intermarry, and on the other those who belonged to distinct families. In either case the documents invariably reveal a China of the towns, side by side with a China of the villages.

The sharpest distinction exists between citizens and villagers : the one are *rustics*, the other nobles. The latter pride themselves on living " according to the rites " which " do not descend to the common people." [1] The country people, on the other hand, refuse to have anything to do with public affairs : " It is the *meat-eaters'* business to discuss them " they say.[2] The two have neither the same interests,

---

[1] *Li ki*, C, I, 53.   [2] *Tso chuan*, C, I, 148 ; LV, 8.

nor the same food.   They differ to the point of following
opposite systems of orientation :   the nobles prefer the left
and the peasants the right.[1]   The village has at most an
Elder.   The nobles are vassals of an overlord who is the
Master of the Town.   At his side they lead a life entirely
taken up by court ceremonies.   Grouped round the Master,
they chant their contempt for " the people of the field, the
clownish people—who live for nothing but to eat and drink
. . . .—But they, all the nobles, they, all the vassals,—are
gathered together to make the Virtue of the chieftain ! " [2]

The peasants are supposed to be tenant-holders.   Are the
citizens their conquerors ?   There is no overlord without a
town, and every town is said to have been founded by an
overlord.   Is he the descendant of a victorious race which
at one stroke introduced the feudal system and urban
organization into China ?   There is no reason in the order of
history which allows us either to accept or to reject this
hypothesis.   History brings no witness in favour of an
invasion :   but why should China have suffered fewer invasions
in unknown antiquity than in historic times ?   Inversely, the
opposition of nobles and peasants is an established fact :   but
what right have we to affirm that the supposed invaders
were feudally organized ?   Their opposition might be the
result of a different evolution of manners in two centres
which, though distinct, were of the same origin.   It is possible
that invaders were introduced into China, but the appearance
of the chieftainships can be explained, apart from every
hypothesis of an historical order.   The power of the chieftains
seems to be based on beliefs which were first adumbrated in
peasant centres.

The Chieftain possesses an authority identical with that
which the peasant communities ascribe to their Holy Places.
He wields this authority in a Town which is looked upon
with respect as an Ancestral Centre

Great festivals which were also fairs were held in the
Holy Places :   there one communed with one's native soil :
there one invited one's ancestors to come and be reincarnated.
The nobles' town is holy :   it contains a market, an altar to
the Soil, a temple of Ancestors.   The city of the founder of
a seigniorial dynasty bears the title of *Tsong*.   This word is

---

[1] *Po hu t'ong*, 12 ; **LIII**, 41.   [2] *She King*, **C**, 184.

also used to designate groups of people who are united by the worship of the same Ancestor. In an expression like Chou-*tsong*, it can scarcely be understood but as : *Ancestral Centre* of the Chou. But the same word appears again in the expression Ho-*tsong*. Now this serves to denote at the same time the Hoang-Ho (the Ho—the River *par excellence*) and the god of the Hoang-ho. It is used again to denote the family group set apart for the worship of the Yellow River as well as the dwelling-place of that group. This latter is looked up to as a Town, as an ancestral Centre. It is indistinguishable from the Holy Place where the divine power of the River is manifested.[1]

The seigniorial town is the successor of the Holy Place. The Chieftain is the *double* of a sacred power, impersonal at first, which called for the reverence of a community. Materialized later, under the likeness of an ancestor, it received the worship of a hierarchized group.

The sanctity of the peasants' places of Festival descended intact to both the Chieftain and his Town. It was incorporated in the person of the overlord, in the ancestral temple, in the altar of the Soil, in the ramparts and gates of the City. There is a significant passage in the Mei-ti.[2] In an eloquent sermon Mei-ti gives decisive proofs of the avenging power which belongs to divinities. He shows the gods punishing the guilty upon an altar of the Soil in an ancestral temple, in a marsh, and finally in a place, called Tsu, no doubt less well known or less definite. Then he exclaims : " And Tsu, for the land of Yen, is as the altar to the Soil and to the harvests is for Ch'i, it is as *Sang-lin* (the Forest of mulberry-trees) is for Song, it is as (the marsh of) Yun-mong is for Ch'u : *it is there that boys and girls gather and come to be present at the Festivals !* " The connexion is clear between the urban worship and the peasant festivals. It is particularly instructive in the case of *Sang-lin*. *Sang-lin* appears in the sermon of Mei-ti as ancestral temple of the princes of Song. It appears elsewhere as god of the Soil, and it is also the name of one of the gates of Song.[3] Again it is the name of a demiurge and of a Holy Place whose genius commands

[1] **LV**, 469, note 2.
[2] *Mei-ti*, VIII ; **LV**, 447.
[3] *Shu chuan*, in **XVI**, 475 ; *Tso chuan*, **C**, III, 335 ; **LV**, 444 and 452, note 2.

M

rain, drought and sickness : [1] by consecrating himself in this Holy Place, the founder of the Yin, the ancestors of the Princes of Song, obtained the right to assume his authority.[2] The princes of Song alone possessed the cult of *Sang-lin*. The core of this cult is a dance, the dance of *Sang-lin*.[3] Now, Mei-ti maintains that *Sang-lin* is the place of Festival for the land of Song, where girls and boys gathered together. A continuity was therefore evident between the festivals of the peasant communities and the cults of the feudal overlords.

The cults of the towns were the result of the breaking up of a rural cult which addressed itself to undefined holy forces. The virtue of the Holy Place was transferred (sometimes, as we have just seen, with its very name) to the altars where differentiated gods were honoured. The Holy Place itself was affected very often by the process of differentiation. Outside their town, the overlords pay worship to such a mountain or such a river. The efficacy of the places consecrated to the peasant assemblies is found again intact in the Mountain or the River. They are the regulators of the natural as well as of the human order. The Chief is also a regulator no less than they. He rules over nature as he rules over his own followers. The power which he possesses, he holds in partnership with the Holy Places of his country. In them he sees as it were the exteriorized principle of his own power. This has no efficacy if the Mountain and the River prove to be powerless, and Mountains and Rivers are powerless if the Virtue proper to the seigniorial Race is exhausted. " An overlordship ought to have the support of its Mountains and Rivers. When the Mountain crumbles or the River dries up, it is an omen of ruin." [4]

The Power of the Chieftain and the power of the Holy Place have the same duration, the same extent, the same quality, the same nature. They are indistinguishable in so far as the feudal Hero and his Holy Place are each as it were the duplicate of the other. It is as the effect of the Virtue of a Founder, such as Yü the Great, that the sacred Rivers flow and the foundations are laid of the everlasting Hills. Inversely, while Shên-nung and Huang-ti could each

---

[1] *Huai-nan tsih*, 7 ; *Tso chuan*, **L**, 665 ; **LV**, 442, note 1, and **LII**, 193.
[2] **LV**, 450 ff.   [3] **LV**, 457 ff. ; *Tso chuan*, **L**, 446.
[4] SMC, I, 278 ; **LII**, 195.

acquire from a river the specific genius which fitted them to reign, it was " from the Holy Mountains (that) the sacred powers descended which caused the birth of (the Princes of) Fu (and of) Shen." [1]

Between the Holy Place and the Chieftain there exists a bond of interdependence which may be represented under the guise of a filial relationship. Considering it in that light, the Holy Place of a peasant community appears to be the ancestral Centre of a feudal dynasty.

[1] *She King,* C, 396 ; **LII,** 198.

DIFFUSED POWERS AND INDIVIDUAL AUTHORITY

Every ruling race is attached to a Founder. The birth of this latter is due as a rule to a miracle.

The only expounders of its worship and masters of its dance, the owners of *Sang-lin* (the *mulberry* forest) are descended from a woman who conceived after swallowing the egg (*tsih*) of a swallow. She had gained it in a tournament the very day of the spring equinox.[1] Some say that she conceived after having sung in a place called the Plain of the *Mulberry-trees*.[2] If the Hero born of her was given for patronymic the name of *Tsih* (egg) it was *mulberry-trees*, grown by miracle, which announced to his descendants a renewal or a decline of the Virtue proper to their race.[3] Thus the emblematic name and the actual emblem are both attached to an analogous myth : that of a birth obtained in a Holy Place in the course of a seasonal festival.

In the peasant centres, a symbolism fed on strong and confused emotions was the soul of all faith and all worship. The sights which appeared in the festival countryside were taken as manifestations, signs, and symbols of a creative power which was materialized in the Holy Place. Now parenthood, implying the exogamic obligation, rested solely on the symbolic bond of the name, and on the possession of a common essence. This essence, which was nourished by the right of eating at the same table, was derived from the food taken from the family land. A kind of agreement, we are assured, must exist between the family land and the family name. These facts lead us to suppose that the peasant organization was founded on a principle analogous to the totemic. Totems or, more correctly, emblems were chosen to all appearance from among the animals and vegetables which

---

[1] SMC, I, 173 ; *Annals written on Bamboo*, 5 ; **LII**, 166.
[2] LV, 449.
[3] SMC, I, 450 ; LV, 360 ; *Lun heng*, **XXXV**, vol. II, 22 and 340.

were found in the Holy Place at the time of the Festivals. There are certain motifs of the ancient songs which can only be understood if we see in them the themes of an incantation designed to make an associated species increase and multiply. " O winged grasshoppers,—how numerous you are !—May your descendants—have great virtues." [1] The jousts, dances and songs sought to secure the prosperity of each group with that of the emblematic species. The plants and the animals, whose seeds and eggs they consumed in order to assimilate their essence and, by communion, to ally themselves with them, must often have been humble plants and humble animals. Yü the Great, the first King of China, was born from a plantain seed.

History only concerns itself with great families. We know scarcely any but princely emblems. These are not usually common animals, but mythological beasts. Their composite nature betrays an effort of the imagination which is an offshoot of the art of heraldry with the dance as its point of departure. Amidst these heraldic beasts figures the Unicorn, who was summoned by the aid of verses closely resembling those of the " Grasshoppers." [2] The most famous of these symbolic animals is the Dragon. The Dragon, before becoming the symbol of sovereign power, was the emblem of the first royal dynasty, that of the Hsia (or rather, one of the emblems which tradition ascribed to the Hsia).[3] One of the ancestors of the Hsia transformed himself into a Dragon in a Holy Place. This metamorphosis took place after he had been cut in pieces. It is therefore the sequel to a sacrifice. Dragons appeared when there was a renewal or a decline of the generic virtue by which the Hsia were empowered to reign. One branch of their family had the privilege of breeding dragons and knew the art of making them thrive. One King of the Hsia fed upon dragons to make his reign prosperous. Finally, two dragon ancestors procured a birth for the descendants of the Hsia. Remarkable to relate : they fought with each other before they disappeared, leaving nothing behind them but a fertilizing foam.[4] Duels between dragons, male and female, were a sign of rain, and

---

[1] LII, 35. [2] *She king*, C, 115 ; LV, 115, note 1.
[3] For the Hsia and the Dragon, see LV, 554 ff.
[4] *Lun heng*, XXXV, vol. II, 163.

had for their stage the marshes formed by two rivers which had overflowed their banks.[1] In such a case it was also said that the rivers were wrestling together, no doubt in sexual duels, for the gods of two rivers which mingle are thought to be of different sexes.[2] Two rivers which mingle are, moreover, a symbol of exogamy. Their junctions were, in fact, places sacred to amorous jousts. In time of spate, the boys and girls believed that by crossing the water they assisted the reincarnations and called down the fertilizing rain.[3] Now it was believed that the crossing of the water by companies, meeting and dancing, was practised in imitation of the duel of the dragons, male and female. They were thus instigated to unite and to send down the fertilizing waters.[4] It is obvious that before becoming the princely emblem, the dragon was the motif of popular dances. The dragons were at first a projection into the mythical world of the rites and games of the seasonal festivals. But as soon as they are regarded as the patrons of a race of Chieftains who alone are able to feed upon them and make them thrive, these dragons, from being simple emanations of the Holy Place, take shape as Ancestors. All the virtue of the Holy Place, all the virtue of the Festivals is in them. It is also present, though diffused, in the race of heroes. It is actually incarnate only in the pair of Great Ancestors who themselves render the reincarnations certain, and who, alone, are both dragons and men.

The mixed genius of the species can be still further individualized. During the spring festivals of the land of Cheng, young men and girls met in a place where scented orchids grew. They plucked them, and waving them on the waters, they called upon the ancestral souls to come and be reincarnated. They believed they were thus summoning a soul-breath (*hun*) which is not distinguishable from the *personal name*. When the game of rivalry was finished, the girl received a flower as a pledge from the boy to whom she was united. The orchid of the Holy Place thus served to procure births for all the people of Cheng. It ended by becoming a princely emblem. " Duke Wen of Chêng had a wife of the second rank whose name was Yen Ki. She dreamed that a messenger from heaven gave her an orchid

---

[1] *Tso chuan*, L, 675.   [2] **LV**, 480, note 3.
[3] **LII**, 105.   [4] *Lun yu*, L, xi, 15 ; *Lun heng*, **XXXV**, vol. II, 333.

(*lan*) saying to her : ' I am Po-yu : I am thy ancestor. Make thy son of that. Because the orchid has a princely perfume (or, alternatively, *because the orchid has the perfume of the country*) he will be recognized to be a prince (of Cheng) and people will love him.' *Hereupon*, Duke Wen came to see her. He gave her an orchid and lay with her. Asking his pardon, she said : ' Your servant has no talent (= no prestige). If by your favour I have a son, people will not believe me : dare I take this orchid as a proof ? ' The duke said ' Yes.' She bare (him who was) the duke Mu, whose *personal name* was *Lan* (orchid). . . . When duke Mu fell ill, he said : ' When the orchid dies, behold I shall die also, for by it I live (or, alternatively, *for of it I was born*).' When they cut the orchid, the Duke died (686 B.C.)." This anecdote implies that the personal name, the exterior soul or pledge of life, the proof of paternity, the taking in marriage, the principle of maternity, the title to power, the ancestral throne and *emblem* are indistinguishable equivalents.[1] The emblematic species alone is associated only with a single individual, and corresponds, not to the family, but to the personal name. The genius of the Holy Place, incorporated in a characteristic plant, is the property of the reincarnated Ancestor and animates him alone who is worthy to be a Chieftain. It is only when the Holy Place where the plant is gathered takes shape as an Ancestor who gives the plant, that the emblem appears as a princely emblem and ceases to be the affair of a group. The Chieftain then, and none but he, possesses the genius of the Holy Place and looks upon the latter as an ancestral Centre.

One fact should be kept in mind : the Ancestor who is substituted for the Holy Place is a *maternal* ancestor. In peasant centres, the women were the first to acquire authority, with the title of *mothers*. At the time when the idea of the Earth-Mother was elaborated the notion of parenthood seemed to be more important than that of alliance by relationship, from which it was an offshoot. Conceived as a bond uniting a child to the maternal race, parenthood appeared to depend upon uterine filiation, and to implicate one side of individual relationship. It was then no doubt that the bond of universal

[1] *Tso chuan*, **L**, 294 ; SMC, IV, 463 ; **LII**, 200 ff.

relationship, which united a whole community without distinction to the sacred place of its festivals, was imagined in the guise of a bond of filiation which united the Chieftain, in whom all power was centred, to a maternal ancestor invested with all the authority of the Holy Place.

CHAPTER III

MALE GODS AND CHIEFTAINS

INDIVIDUAL power and the hierarchy are dated, in their first beginnings, from the epoch during which matriarchal right held sway for a time. The theme of the Great Ancestresses, the Queen-Mothers, fills an important place in Chinese mythology. Every seigniorial race springs from a Hero, but it is the Mother of the Hero who receives the greatest honour. Nothing in the feudal town is more sacred than the temple of the Ancestress of the race. The most beautiful of the dynastic hymns are sung in her praise.[1]

Nevertheless feudal organization depends upon the recognition of the masculine privilege. It appears that from father to son the princes alone command the seasons: they only are judges and keep peace between men. But various themes, juridical or mythical, reveal that the most archaic attributes of the princely authority, before they were ascribed to a male Chieftain, belonged to a princely couple, of whom the wife did not at first play the more self-effacing rôle.

The Chieftain, being Master of the Calendar, determines by simple monthly proclamations from his town that collaboration between men and nature which was formerly achieved through the equinoctial marriages in the Holy Places. Such is the ritual theory. But the Rites affirm, on the other hand, that the Prince's marriage is the most important of State matters.[2] The course of the world and of society depend upon it. The universe is out of joint when the union between king and queen is not perfect. If one or the other oversteps his rights, there is an eclipse of the Sun or the Moon. " The Son of Heaven directs the action of the male principle (*Yang*), his wife that of the female principle (*Yin*)." [3] A good understanding between them is indispensable. A king is nothing

---

[1] *Tso chuan*, **C**, II, 436 ; *She king*, **C**, 347 and 462.
[2] *Li ki*, **C**, II, 367 ff. ; *ibid.*, 651.   [3] *Li ki*, **C**, II, 650.

without his queen, a lord is nothing without his lady. Sacrifices are only valid when they are celebrated by a wedded pair. The principle of the necessary opposition of the sexes has its counterpart in the principle which demands their collaboration.[1] A chief (whether of the State or of the Family) cannot remain without a wife. Sexual life in fact affects the universal order. It must be meticulously regulated. When the Moon is quite round and faces the Sun, the king and queen must be united.[2] Now the full moon is a ritual equivalent of the equinox. In feudal thought the union of the chief and his wife is not less powerful than on another plane the collective marriages of the federal festivals which were celebrated in the equinoctial months of autumn and spring. The Prince has substituted his authority for that of the Holy Place. He acquits himself of his task by celebrating fruitful hierogamies at stated times. He appears to be the only master. And, as a matter of fact, although legal opinion still grants a certain authority to the woman, it does not belong to her in her own right. The queen is said to possess only a reflection of the marital authority. The Moon borrows its light from the Sun. Nevertheless, in the beginning the power was retained by a princely couple. One formula shows this clearly. The Chieftain does not say that he is the father of his people. He claims to be their " father and mother." This is an admission that the authority is concentrated in him which was formerly indivisible and was shared by a household.

In like manner the Prince alone wields the authority of judge and peacemaker in his town. The judicial debates over which he presides are battles of words, and have the appearance of a cursing-match. These judicial tournaments took place usually in the town and on the altar of the Soil. But the most serious cases must be judged (at Lu at all events) on the banks of the river, where with the help of dancing jousts, the spring festivals were also celebrated.[3] Furthermore, the same word denotes the official complaints of the pleaders and the litany of the amorous duels.[4] A Founder, the Ancestor of the princes of Yen, is famous as a dispenser of justice. The debates over which he presided were matches

---

[1] *Li ki*, **C**, II, 320 ff.   [2] **LIII**, 39.
[3] *Tso chuan*, **C**, III, 390 ; **LII**, 159.   [4] **LII**, 263.

of verse-making in which boys were opposed to girls. His
sentences were not pronounced in the town on an Altar of
the Soil, but at the foot of a tree. This was worshipped for
long centuries—equally with the judge. It was apparently
the most sacred tree of a Holy Place. Under its shade the
Great Ancestor of Yen presided over the sexual festivals
which were the source of peace and good order. This hero,
as a matter of fact, was endowed with a significant title :
Great Mediator.[1] The same title was borne in feudal times
by an officer whose duty was to preside " at the unions in
the fields," which it is said that princely wisdom permitted,
in the second month of spring (equinox). He also presided
at certain nuptial purifications. The same title is also
bestowed on a hero, Kao-sin, who is one of the first Chinese
sovereigns. Men and women went to celebrate the feast of
Kao-sin in the open country, and precisely on the day of
the spring equinox. This was not, we are told, a popular
festival. It was limited to a request for children in the
reigning house. Kao-sin deserved the confidence which was
placed in him. In old times two of his wives each gave birth
to the Founder of a royal line. It is true that they both
conceived in the open fields, the one while she placed her feet
in the foot-mark of a giant, and the other, after bathing and
games of rivalry, while she was swallowing an egg. It was
later admitted that Heaven was the true Father of these
Sons of Heaven. However, a temple was built for Kao-sin
no less than for the Mothers of the race, which was dedicated
to him under the title of Supreme Mediator.[2] Comparing
these data we gather that the Prince, in imitation of the
Holy Place, is the author of fruitful marriage. This attribute
is periodically renewed when he himself unites with his wife
in holy wedlock. He derives his authority from a Hero-
Founder. This latter presided formerly over the collective
marriages of the seasonal festivals. But he did not preside
at them alone. He even took a subordinate place beside his
wife, the Great Ancestress.

Men took precedence over women when they learnt to
obtain the alliance of the Holy Place by other means than
human marriage.

The sexual duels were finally replaced by dances in which

---

[1] *She king*, **C**, 20.   [2] *Li ki*, **C**, I, 341 ; **LIX**, 24 ff.

only men took part. Formerly there existed a Pheasant
Dance. Like the men and women of the country, pheasant
cocks and hens danced in the spring of each year. These
dances aimed at the multiplication of the species. They
were the prelude to pairing. As in the country festivals, it
was the females who by their songs called to the males.
They had the initiative. Perhaps even, at an agreed moment,
the Pheasant Dance was a female dance : women of all
periods borrowed their head-dress from the pheasants : some
also bore their name. But in the end it was the males who
played the chief rôle. Their dances, instead of ensuring
prosperity of the species, were intended to time the appearance
of thunder. Thunder hides itself in the winter and should
be heard when spring appears. But first the pheasants
must " sing their song and as it were beat a drum with their
wings." Thus they create the thunder. They are also its
emblem. Thunder is a pheasant. Only, in feudal times, he
was seen not as a couple of pheasant dancers, but as a cock-
pheasant. Thus at Ch'en-Ch'ang, in the Ch'in country, a
cock-pheasant was worshipped which came to roost at night
beside a sacred stone. Then the muttering of thunder was
heard. The stone which attracted it was a hen-pheasant
metamorphosed. It had been originally a young girl who
appeared at the same time as a young boy. Both were
changed into pheasants. Whilst the cock became a god, the
hen was turned to stone and it was said that he only would
become king who could catch the cock.[1]

A similar myth will show still more clearly how masculine
authority was imposed in the end. At the time when the
world needed a Hero to set it in order a pheasant dancer
appeared at Yu Shan. Yu Shan is a holy mountain where
pheasants' feathers were sought for the dancers' costumes.
It was also on this holy mountain that, by a metamorphosis
following a sacrifice, Kun was changed into a bear. Kun is
the father of Yü the Great. As soon as the pheasant dancer
appeared at Yu Shan, Yü, the son of Kun, was brought forth
for the happiness of the world. He founded Chinese royalty.
He made peace between the Earth and the Waters. These
were the works of a demiurge. They can only be effected
by dancing. Yü the Great, in fact, like the pheasant of

[1] LV, 569 ff.

Yu Shan, was a dancer. He even invented a famous *step*. Thus he danced to reduce the floods of waters to their rightful bounds : he stamped upon the stones while he danced. A country is known to have existed in China where boys and girls stamped upon the stones when they forded rivers swollen with the spring floods in the course of their festivals. They produced a kind of intermittent rumbling with their stamping, and thus drew down the rain which is accompanied and heralded by thunder. And during the feudal epoch they knew that it was enough to dance the dance of Shang-yang to obtain the regular rains. This also was danced by couples of young people. They must shake their shoulders (as the pheasants who produced the noise of thunder shook their wings). They must also stand on one leg, for the Shang-yang is a divine bird who has only one foot (as the pheasant dancer who appeared at Yu Shan had only one foot). Yü the Great, when he danced his step, hopped likewise, dragging one leg after him. So he hopped in his dance when he took in hand the ordering of the straying Waters. It is not said that like the dancers he wore at that time feathers taken from Yu Shan, that holy mountain haunted by his father, the Bear. It is said that Yü affected the appearance of a bear. Bears hide themselves in winter, like the thunder. They might be emblems of the thunder as well as the pheasants. To open the pass of Huan-yuan, the Head of the State danced a Bear Dance. He was careful to dance it alone. Solely because she had seen him perform his divine work, piercing the mountains, stamping upon the stones, his wife was turned to stone. After being turned into stone she had still to be opened, for Yü demanded from her the son of whom she was pregnant. It is related also that Yü cleft in twain his wife with one stroke of his sword.[1]

The sexual dance of the peasant festivals was changed into a masculine dance. The man who dances is identified with the Holy Place, the abode of the animal emblem from which he takes the emblems which are symbolical. He possesses, by his right as an ancestral Centre, the holy place which is haunted, in animal form, by the soul of an ancestor, and where the birth of a son may be obtained. But in order that the Chieftain, while he dances, may be identified with

[1] **LV, 563 ff.**

his emblem, that an intimate union may take place between him and the Holy Place, a sacrifice must be made to complete the dance. The victim is the dancer's wife. When he sacrifices his wife to it the Chieftain is allied to the sacred power, whose double he becomes. A hierogamy is required as soon as the desire is felt for the appointment of a sacred authority. This authority possesses complete efficacy on condition that it unites within itself the antagonistic forces (*yin* and *yang*) which in the human and natural world are in opposition and alternation the one to the other, but only in conjunction are able to create. When the chieftains rested their authority, not only on a Holy Place, a principle which was exterior to their power, but also on dynastic talismans, drums, cauldrons, and arms, this creation of a *palladium* seemed also to demand a hierogamy.[1] For example, the fabrication of metal objects was a holy work. It was done by means of alloys. Metals, like all other things, being male and female, enchanted articles were obtained from their union, whose power extended to men as to all other creatures. They contained in themselves a principle of universal concord. Thus the mixture and fusion of metals could only be accomplished according to the rites of marriage. Virgin boys and girls in equal numbers acted as the bellows. They gave their breath (that is to say, their soul) that the fusion might be attained. When the casting was made they baptized the metal, all together throwing water upon it. Where this produced a blister, the metal was male. It was female where a hole was formed. The founder then knew whence to obtain and how to combine the warring elements whose union would produce a perfect work. The principle of perfection lay in the collaboration of the sexes which had each given all their vital force. To work the bellows, not less than three hundred girls and three hundred boys were needed. Three hundred is a supreme total. The sexual corporations gave themselves entirely to the sacred work, as in the peasant festivals. But the fusion and the alloy could also be obtained if the master forger and his wife alone gave themselves to the work. Both had no other duty than to throw themselves into the furnace. The cast was then made at once. The sacrifice of a household, when it is a princely household, is as

[1] On the hierogamy of the founders, see **LV**, 498 ff.

powerful as the collective marriages. The complete pair however was not always sacrificed. The master smelter might be satisfied with giving his wife to the divine furnace which produced the alloy. To lend adequacy to this economical proceeding it was enough to assert that the deity of the forge was of the same sex as the smith. The woman thrown to this male deity was given him as his wife. Her sacrifice was looked upon as a marriage with the god of the furnace. In giving him his wife the smith, by a sort of sexual communion, allied himself with his patron. This rite of union preserved all the validity of a hierogamy. The metal which came out of the mould was always considered to be bi-sexual.

The gods assume a masculine appearance in proportion as male privilege is established. The history of the divine furnace is also the history of the Holy Places.

To obtain a correct alternation of the seasons under the rule of the Han it sufficed to throw into the water, at an acceptable time, two spirits of drought, male and female, Keng-fu (the Ploughman) and Nü-pa : a household of ploughmen might also be sacrificed in effigy.[1] Formerly, the feudal lords had to pay in person. They only merited power when they were able to identify themselves with the antagonistic forces which dispense drought and rain. To realize in themselves (and in nature) a perfect equilibrium of virtues, it sufficed for them to go and live in the open fields, exposing themselves to both sun and dew.[2] Nevertheless they preferred to expose the witches. They made them dance till they were exhausted. If necessary, when the drought was too severe, they burnt the witch as a sacrifice.[3]

Witches have a virtue which renders them powerful. Their power lies in the fact of their being emaciated or quite dried up. Now, it happens that two Founders of royal dynasties, T'ang the Victorious and Yü the Great, are represented in history as dried-up beings. Both inaugurated their reign by sacrificing themselves for the good of their people, the one to put an end to drought, the other to stop a flood. At that time they cut off their hair and their nails and presented them as a pledge to a divinity. Thus, to obtain the fusion of metals, the smiths, instead of flinging

---

[1] *Tong king fu ; Shan hai king*, 17.
[2] SMC, IV, 361.   [3] *Tso chuan*, C, I, 327 ; *Li ki*, C, I, 261.

themselves into the furnace, might simply throw their nails and hair into it. Husband and wife threw them together. When the deity possessed pledges given by the two halves of the couple it possessed the entire couple with its double nature, for to give part is to give all. Yü and T'ang the Victorious devoted themselves entirely. Nevertheless the deity only took half of them. They were only half dried up. We can see why Yü the Great hopped and danced his step dragging one leg : he was paralysed down one side. The *Step of Yü* is only the half of a sexual dance. The devotion of Yü is only the half of a devotion. The complete devotion would have been that of a household—like that of the Masters of the Forge as long as the deity of the furnace was not thought to be masculine. T'ang was devoted to the Forest of Mulberry Trees (*Sang-lin*) where girls and boys assembled together for the jousts. Yü the Great was devoted to Yang-yu. Yang-yu is the Holy Place where the Count of the River has his capital (*Ho-tsong*) but the Count of the River is married, and even the name he bears (*Ping-yi*) belonged originally to his wife. If Yü devoted himself alone, it was perhaps because his sacrifice dates from a time when the goddess took precedence of the god. The god conquered her. He ended by taking from the goddess even her name. From that time the sacrifices at the River, which had always been inspired by the idea of hierogamy, henceforth had women for victims.[1]

The River, during the feudal epoch, was honoured at two places in particular, at Lin-tsin and at Ye. At Ye, in the country of Wei, it was the object of a popular act of worship presided over by witches and invokers of spirits. Every year a beautiful girl was chosen. Fed and adorned like a bride, she was laid on a bridal bed. This was launched on the water and borne to a whirlpool where it sank. Thus the chosen one went " to be married to the Count of the River." [2] There is no doubt that the worship of Lin-tsin was also a popular religion. But, in 417 B.C., the lords of Ch'in (Shen-si) conquered the region. They annexed the Holy Place. One of their greatest ambitions was to snatch from their neighbours of Shan-si the protection of the God of the River. It was their duty to gain his alliance. They gained it less for their country than for their race. Every year they married a princess of their blood to the Count of the River.[1]

Sexual dances and collective marriages clothed the Holy Places with an august authority. This authority was seized in the end by a race of Chieftains. The sacrifice of a household, the half-sacrifice of the Founder, the sacrifice of the wife, the sacrifice of virgins served to cement an alliance and in themselves to form a union. The Holy Place, even when it becomes an ancestral Centre and its divinity acquires masculine features, preserves its complex authority, thanks to the hierogamies. In the same way, when masculine privilege is established, the Chieftain remains in possession of a double authority. His power extends over the antagonistic forces which form the universe : *Yin* and *Yang*, Heaven and Earth, Water and Fire, Rain and Drought. But it was only at the cost of most terrible sacrifices that this mixed authority was able to centre itself in him.

----

[1] SMC, III, 452 and xv ; **LV,** 477.

CHAPTER IV

RIVALRIES OF BROTHERHOODS

IT appears that the first male authorities were set up—in the course of the winter-season ceremonies—during the reunions of the brotherhoods.

In the course of wintering in the common house, the husbandmen, by dint of jousts and expensive orgies, learned to have confidence in the virile virtues. Their prestige increased in proportion as their clearings extended. But the Founder Heroes did not derive their glory solely from the fact that they had subdued the soil and conquered the brushwood with fire. In yet another manner they are the Masters of Fire. They are potters or smiths. They know how to make the divine vessels by means of holy and tragic unions. All the dynastic virtue is incorporated in the magic caldrons cast by Yü the Great, exactly as it might be in a Holy Mountain or River. These latter crumble away or dry up when the Virtue of a Race is exhausted and totters. In the same way, when this virtue is too much enfeebled the caldrons lose their weight. They depart, of themselves, to another master to be charged anew with prestige.[1]

Yü the Great, the first King of China, was a smith. Huang-ti, the first Sovereign, was also a smith. Huang-ti was the god of the thunderbolt. Yü commanded the thunder. It was thanks to the thunder that he brought the Virtue of his Race to its plenitude. First, in a dancing match, he had conquered gods or chieftains (the terms are interchangeable) who were related to *bulls* and roared like the *winds*.[2] Huang-ti, likewise, arrived at power after he had " enkindled his virtue " in a match where he got the victory over Shên-nung. Shên-nung is sometimes shown to us presiding over the festivals of the forge (and it is related that his daughter was burnt to death—or drowned). But he is in the first instance the

---

[1] *Mei-ti*, 11.　　[2] *Po wu che*, 2 ; **XVII**, vol. I, 79 ; **LV**, 343 ff.

god of *burning winds*, the god of the fires of the clearing. He is the god of the husbandmen. Huang-ti fought with Shên-nung : he fought also with Ch'e-you. Historians confuse the narrative of these duels. Truth to tell, Ch'e-you and Shên-nung have little to distinguish them. Both bear the same family name. Both are men with a bull's head. Ch'e-you, however, is not a god of field-labour. He is the Master of War, the inventor of arms. His bones are concretions of metal. He has a head of copper and a forehead of iron : in the same way one of the tools used by the ancient smelters was made of copper and tipped with iron. Ch'e-you, who invented the casting of metals, feeds upon mineral ore. He is the forge, the forge deified—and yet the resemblance between him and the god of field-labour is complete. The juxtaposition of these facts suggests a hypothesis. Brotherhoods of artificers from the body of husbandmen became the guardians of magic knowledge and masters of the secret of the primeval powers.[1] The existence of rival brotherhoods presupposes a centre whose organization is no longer founded on simple bipartition. Now, according to the most ancient Chinese conceptions which are known to us, the Universe (the Universe is not distinguishable from Society) is made up of sections whose Virtues are in opposition and alternation. These Virtues are materialized under the likeness of *Winds*. The Eight Winds correspond not only to divisions of the human and natural world, but also to magic powers. Everything is divided in the domain of the Eight Winds but together they preside over music and dancing. It is the function of dancing and music to tame the world and to subdue nature for men's profit. In most of the mythical dramas, in which the legend of a foundation of power is commemorated, beings with the traits of dynastic ancestors or heraldic beasts, are represented as ruling a section of the world, and these, in many cases, appear in the form of Winds. We have then the right to suppose that a division into marshalled groups was substituted for, or rather superimposed upon, the twofold organization of society, each being appointed to one department of the Universe and all working in concert—dancing, playing games, rivalling each other in prestige—for the upholding of a single order. From these rivalries and these

[1] **LV,** 351, 354, 492, 504.

games, sprang a new order of society, a hierarchical order, founded upon prestige. Consider, for instance, the way that Huang-ti gained his power. He only obtained it after having conquered Ch'e-you, the great rebel. Both faced each other in a duel where each had two acolytes. Ch'e-you had requisitioned the Count of the Wind and the Master of the Rain. Drought and the Dragon of Rain (Dragon Ying) fought for Huang-ti. The Dragon Ying gathered the Waters together. Ch'e-you stirred up the Rain and the Mist. Starting from the River of the Ram, he climbed as high as the Nine Marshes and attacked K'ong-sang. K'ong-sang is the hollow mulberry-tree where the sun rises, and it was from it that Huang-ti set out to climb to the place of sovereignty (which is that of the sun at his meridian). Ch'e-you had locks of hair upon his temples crossed in the form of a lance. When he rushed forward *with his horned head* no one dared oppose him. But, *blowing a horn*, Huang-ti sounded the note of the dragon, and came out victorious from the duel. (Horn-playing was employed as an ordeal even in classic times : the vanquished was worthy of death.) The Dragon Ying cut off Ch'e-you's head. (In feudal times, the head of the vanquished was cut off and fixed on a standard.) Huang-ti seized his rival's standard. On this standard was Ch'e-you's effigy. From henceforth, Huang-ti reigned in peace, for this effigy terrorized the *Eight Regions*.[1]

It is evident that this myth is nothing but the rendering in the form of a fable of a drama which sets forth a struggle between rival brotherhoods, carried on by means of religious dances and magical situations. In fact, the dance of Ch'e-you was well-known. The dancers, who faced each other by twos and by threes, wore a bullock's horns on their heads and fought with their horns. Ch'e-you, moreover, is not only the name of a dance and the name of a play : it is the name of a brotherhood. Ch'e-you was not one : he was 72 (8 × 9) or 81 (9 × 9) brothers. He was prince of the Nine Li and the eighty-one brothers represented the mythical Nine Provinces of China. He had eight fingers and eight toes, and held the Eight Regions in awe. (The Winds are Eight. Ch'e-you is the god of one of the points of the compass, and he is a god of the winds.)   The 72 brothers thus represented a section of the earth as well as a fifth of the days of the year. $\left(\dfrac{360}{5} = 72\right)$.

Finally, 72 is the characteristic number of the brotherhoods.[1]

In the rivalries between brotherhoods which preceded a hierarchized organization of society, the leading rôle belonged to the brotherhoods which were masters of the arts of fire. Indeed their emblems became royal emblems.   There is no doubt that the dragon was one of the coats-of-arms of the Hsia dynasty.   Now the dynastic caldrons are guarded by dragons.   In the same way the royal swords are dragon-swords : they vanish in the rivers and play there like lightning or else, when they are used in the tournaments, they cause dragons to ascend to heaven amidst terrible thunder-claps. Moreover, a personification of the forge is called the Dragon-torch.   This Dragon-torch, which bears in addition the name of Drum, and was born on the Hill of the Bell, is also an owl. The owl was the emblem of the Yin, the second royal dynasty. The owl is the bird of the Solstices, the favourable days on which magic swords and mirrors are made.   He unites the genius of the forge and the bird of the thunderbolt.   Again he is the symbolic double of Huang-ti, the Master-Smelter, the god of the thunder and the first Sovereign (with whom all the royal lines are connected), for Huang-ti (the *yellow Sovereign*) was born of a flash of lightning upon a hill whose sacred bird, called the *Yellow Bird*, was an owl.   The Yellow Bird figured upon the royal standards.[2]   In the same way, the *Red Bird* emblazoned the standard of the princes of the third, Chou, dynasty.   The Red Bird is a raven.   He appears to the Chou before a victory or when a saint is about to be born of their race.   One branch of the Chou family is called the Red Ravens.   Like the owl, the red raven was a bird of the Fire, but, as a Raven with three feet, he was the bird of the Sun rather than the bird of the thunderbolt.[3]   Sovereign authority is based upon the possession of talismans and emblems inherited from mythical smiths.   With the help of these emblems and talismans, the Kings, Masters of the Sun and the Thunderbolt, can command nature.   All the prestige which the most wonderful of magic arts gave to the

---

[1] LV, 357.   [2] LV, 523, 536 ; 548, note 2.
[3] LV, 387 ; 548, note 2 ; 603.

Masters of Fire is concentrated in the person of the sovereign, the Son of Heaven.

The concentration of power, which was the object of the rivalries of brotherhoods, one coat-of-arms waging war against another, seems to have had its starting-point in the jousts which occupied the masculine gatherings during the winter. A royal festival was in fact celebrated during the long winter nights. On that occasion the Chieftain underwent a great trial. By it he showed that he was worthy to govern Heaven.[1]

Yao, the Sovereign who " appeared like the sun " had to aim arrows at the sun before he could become a Son of Heaven. Thus he succeeded in overcoming his celestial double. ' As soon as he had conquered the emblem of the sun, he was worthy to reign.[2] Archery is an inaugural ceremony by which one can reveal one's virtue. But an unworthy Chieftain will see the proof turn against him. The penalty which overtakes the incapable magician is the result of a reflex action, the arrows which are aimed at Heaven fall back in the form of lightning. The bowman himself is struck by lightning, and perishes, because without possessing the necessary qualifications, he has attempted to awaken and capture the energies of the Fire. Such was the case of Wu-yi, a king without Virtue. Wu-yi shot an arrow aiming at the sky, or rather at a leather bottle full of blood which he called the Sky. Made of the skin of a bull, it had the shape of an owl. The king drew his bow after he had won *the owl's move* at a game of chess which gave him the right to try his fortune. Wu-yi belonged to the family of the Yin, who owned the emblem of the Owl and bore the name *Leather Bottle*. But, being degenerate, he had not the virtue in himself which empowered him to be worthy his coat-of-arms and to remain master of his mythical double. It was quite otherwise with Huang-ti. Huang-ti (the yellow Sovereign) was able to catch Owls (Yellow Birds). A true sovereign ought to be able to shoot them by using twisted arrows. Like the lightning, these are the bearers of fire. Huang-ti, who fed upon owls, knew how to identify himself completely with his emblem. By means of sacraments, all the virtue of the celestial fires

---

[1] Throughout the following passage, I make use of the facts which I intend to study in detail in a work which I have in preparation (*Le Roi boit*) in which I propose to analyse the antecedents of the idea of Majesty.

[2] *Huai-nan tsih*, 13 ; **LV**, 377.

was incorporated in him. He was thus enabled to ascend to heaven by apotheosis in a hurricane.

Huang-ti was thunder. He was also identified with a celestial Leather Bottle, under the name of Ti-hong. The leather bottle Ti-hong is a bird as well as a bag made of skins and a drum. There is even an owl (his name is Drum-of-the-Night) who is a bag, and from whom thunderbolt and arrows will rebound. And finally, there is a drum who is an owl, producing the wind when he breathes. Completely red and with immovable eyes, he represents a forge and its bellows. The Celestial Leather Bottle is red also, like mineral ore in fusion, and at the summit of the Hill of Heaven, which is rich in copper. It bears the name : Chaos (*Hun-tun*). Chaos dies when it is pierced seven times by the Lightning. But this death is only a second birth. It is an initiation. As a matter of fact, every man has seven apertures in his face. But only a respectable (*i.e.* a well-born) man has seven to his heart. Hun-tun, the Leather-bottle Chaos, when he was personified, was represented as a stupid busybody. He had no aperture : he had " neither visage, nor eyes," that is to say, he lacked *face*, or respectability. In a mythical drama in which he figures, he is born anew in the end, by means of execution. In his right as celestial Leather Bottle, he takes part in a dance, and he is shown besides offering a banquet. It is precisely to the Lightnings that he offers it, and if they pierce him seven times, it is not with evil intent and in order to kill him : they mean to pay him for his kind reception.

The theme of the shooting of arrows against the sky and the myth of the Leather Bottle shaped by the Lightnings evidently preserve the remembrance of the rites of initiation and of the ordeals by which mastery in a brotherhood of smiths is acquired by the dangerous manipulation of fire. These same ordeals were imposed upon a king, the Son of Heaven. He must know how to tame and mould the world after the manner of a demiurge. Above all, at suitable times he must restore the celestial Fires in all their glory, and at the same moment, possess himself of their virtues.[1]

Now, at any rate, when it figures in the legend of Shou-sin, the most sinister of the kings of perdition, the shooting of arrows against the sky represented by a leather bottle seems

[1] **LV,** 536 ff. ; 523 ff. ; 543, 544, notes 2 and 3.

to be connected with a winter festival called the " *carousal of the long night.*" The Lightnings pierce seven openings in the Leather-Bottle Chaos. Shou-sin (famous for having wished to verify the fact that the heart of a sage has seven apertures, by disembowelling his uncle, Pi-Kan) shot arrows at a Leather Bottle filled with blood. He had prepared himself for this archery by the slaughter of men and domestic animals of " the six species." The first six days of the year were sacred to the six domestic animals. The seventh was sacred to man. Shou-sin is said to have continued his carouse for seven days and seven nights. One author relates that Shou-sin made the Carousal of the Long Night last for one hundred and twenty days, but that, he says, is an exaggeration. Let us suppose that his prowess was simply multiplied tenfold. The twelve last days of the year were a religious period, and even in classical times the year closed with a dance of the Twelve Animals, which were taken to represent the twelve months. Whether the winter carousal lasted seven or twelve days, it is obvious that it occupied a marginal period placed between two successive years. The religious year of the Chinese comprises three hundred and sixty days and twelve lunar months. If these revolutions of the moon were originally all counted as twenty-nine days, as appears to have been the case, there remained at the end of the year a period of twelve days which could be held sacred to the Twelve Animals. If the lunar months, alternately long and short, lasted some for thirty and the others for twenty-nine days, six days remained to make up the year, which could be dedicated to the six domestic animals. The seventh day, the Man's day, began the year. It must be the day of a supreme sacrifice. The cannibalistic feasts of Shou-sin have justly remained notorious. Moreover, the blood which filled the Leather Bottle representing the sky, was doubtless that of the individual, who when he played chess before the shooting match had played for the sky against the king.

The carousal of seven or twelve nights (which has its equivalents in European folk-lore as well as in the Vedic customs) is connected with the old habits of the Chinese peasants. During the long nights of winter, they too drank without ceasing. They too tried their fortune at the game of chess. They still played at the game of bottle-neck, the game for which bent, so-called serpentine, arrows are used, like those which the king shot at the Sun or the Owl. It was a question of shooting these arrows into the mouth of a large pitcher. As one would expect, the Chinese pictured Heaven to themselves in the guise of a broken pitcher, the lightning escaping through the fracture. Like the pitchers, the bottles of ox-leather which are shaped like an owl and represent the sky when they are filled with blood, are also used to hold wine. The peasants also keep wine in pitchers, and the nobles in bronze bells. Both accompany their carousals by playing the drum on the pitchers or the bells. Thus they produce the sound of thunder so effectually, it is said, that the pheasants begin at once to sing in the night. Thus was revealed the energy of Thunder, of Fire, of the male Principle (*Yang*). Thunder has no longer strength to utter its voice in winter : the Sun scarcely succeeds in showing itself. The Chinese believed that during the cold season the *Yang*, the male principle, was tricked and imprisoned by the adverse forces of the *Yin*. Is it not the period when the husbandmen, reduced to inaction, retire into the communal house, in the heart of the village which belongs to the women ? During this retirement, they concentrate their energies, and are able at last to help in the restoration of the male forces of nature. Therefore their winter festivals ended with an orgy in which men and women, formed into opposing groups, struggled together and tore off each other's garments. This match took place in the night, after the torches had been put out. In the same way, in the royal festival, men and women pursued each other, quite naked. Singing a song which treated of the death of the sun, they then danced round dances. [The end of an eclipse of the solar forces is symbolized (as we know from other sources), by the dance of a naked boy revolving by himself.] At the end of the ceremony, the torches were relighted. The match which had been danced by men and women facing each other (in the royal feast, the sexual orgy appears to have been accompanied by the ritual murder of the queen, who is afterwards communally eaten) had procured a victory and a rejuvenation of the male principles of the Fire. Immediately, as soon as dawn appeared, the torches were raised in the air. Also a very young boy was procured whose body was blood-red and who was exhibited quite naked. This little child represented the new-born Sun. They called him the god of Heaven. In the legends of the Kings of perdition the entrance of the red child symbolizes the arrival of a new Chieftain succeeding to the power of the old who has not been able to renew his failing virtue. As a matter of fact, the winter banquets and carousals served to renew the vital forces of the old men. The festivals of the communal house consisted above all else in a drinking orgy. Then the new wine was relished, brewed in winter and stored in leather bottles, jars or bells. This orgy ended in the drinking of healths and in wishes of endless life : Ten thousand years ! It accompanied the game of the bottle-neck and was rounded off by boasting matches. Victuals had been accumulated in heaps higher than a hill ! No river could hold so much drink ! Shou-sin, when he celebrates the winter festival, piles up a mountain of food. He digs a pond which he fills with wine. In such a pit of drink it is said that boats could be turned about. A chariot race could be run on the mound made by the victuals. In these entertainments, every one present is expected to drink to satiety, lapping up the wine and wallowing like a bullock. The king, who must give evidence of his capacity by various ordeals, must prove it above all by filling himself like a leather bottle. Afterwards, wearing a cuirass of bullock skin, he is able to shoot at the Leather Bottle which is itself the skin of a bullock. He may cause the blood of Heaven to rain upon him, a marvellous baptism which is equivalent to a rebirth. When his inaugural archery is successful, the vassals proclaim his glory : " He has conquered Heaven ! No one surpasses him in talent ! " And the healths and the good wishes : " Ten thousand years ! ten thousand years ! " go the round of the circle and echo far away—as soon as the king drinks.

The royal festival of the long night seems to be a development of the festivals of the communal house. It is rich in dramatic, not to say horrible rites, for it marks the culminating point of a winter liturgy, in which by the help of jousts, ordeals, sacrifices and sacraments, merits are classified and the hierarchy is founded. Some of these jousts and ordeals are remarkable. There was the test of a see-saw, which was used to weigh talents, and the test of a greased pole whose victims were consumed in a funeral pile. Shou-sin, the sinister king, who forced his subjects to drink after the manner of bullocks (and of Nebuchadnezzar) died on a funeral pile (like Sardanapalus). As a good smith, he could stretch an iron bar in his powerful hands, and (as strong as Samson) he could hold up the lintel of a door and take the place of one of its columns. He cast and chased tall pillars for the test of the see-saw or of the ascension. He also built a tower, which, after the manner of Babel, was intended to reach the sky. It was from the top of such a tower that the bloody Leather Bottle would be hung to represent the sky, and Shou-sin shot arrows at it (like Nimrod). We have already seen that the celestial Leather Bottle was a drum. Now, not far from China lived a people who every year sacrificed a man whom they called the " Celestial Lord." On the occasion of these festivals, it was customary to suspend a drum from the top of a wooden pole fixed in the ground (*Kien-mu*). On their part, the Chinese knew a divine tree which was called *Kien-mu* (the fixed tree). This tree stands exactly in the centre of the world, and marks the point of noon, the moment when everything which is perfectly straight casts no shadow. The tree *Kien-mu* is the hand of a sun-dial. It is also a greased pole. By its aid the Sovereign, that is to say, the Sun, ascends to Heaven. Thus it is as straight as a pillar, but there are at its foot and at its summit nine roots and nine branches : that signifies, I suppose, that it reaches to the Nine Heavens above and to the Nine Springs below. The Nine Springs are the underground Springs, the Yellow Springs, the abode of the dead, the Great Abyss. One plunges into the Great Abyss when one gets dead-drunk in a carousal of the long night. This carousal takes place in an underground palace. The sun only rises into the sky after it has issued from the Great Abyss. The Yang, whom the Yin keeps in prison during the winter, retires into the Nine Springs. Before appearing on the morning of New Year's day like a risen and victorious Sun, the Chieftain too must submit to a retreat. He is imprisoned in an underground chamber as deep as the Seven Springs. After which he may rise to the Nine Heavens in a triumphant ascension. Intended for the ordeal of the ascension the high tower or the sculptured column of Shou-sin mark the place where the Chieftain can proceed to his apotheosis. They mark the capital which is regarded as the centre of the world.

The Chief's power took its rise in the festivals of the men's house and the jousts of the brotherhoods. He is a founder of cities and a leader in war. Ch'e-you, the smith who invented arms, is the chief of a dancing brotherhood and a war god. Huang-ti, his fortunate rival, another smith, is also a god of battles. Both, when they tourney together, tourney three against three. The number three is at the base of military as well as of urban organization, for the town is scarcely distinguishable from a camp. It is composed of the residence of the overlord surrounded on the right and on the left by the houses of vassals. The army normally comprises three legions, the central legion being that of the prince, and manned by his relatives. The royal army alone comprises six legions. In the ceremony of archery, which is perhaps the most important of the feudal rites, the shooting match is inaugurated by two bands of archers vying with each other, three against three. Three, according to Chinese traditions, is the old number of the dancers (who were formed afterwards into bands of eight). The spirit of rivalry which animated the male brotherhoods, and during the winter season, set them face to face in dancing matches, lies at the root of the institutional progress, thanks to which the *tributary* organization characteristic of feudal cities issued, together with the hierarchy, from the old organization, which was *dualist* and segmentary.[1]

[1] LV, 617.

Chapter V

THE AGNATIC DYNASTIES

When the rustic games in which competing sexes were opposed to each other were superseded by rivalries between societies rich in technical secrets and newly-won prestige, male authorities came into being, and an active hierarchy was evolved from amongst them. But the principle of alternation which presided over the seasonal games did not immediately lose its force. With this principle dualism maintained its rights—even after the social order was no longer founded on simple bipartition, and society was tending to assume the tributary organization which is favourable to the concentration of authority. Thus it was only with difficulty that the authority which the male chiefs had won became the property of a line of princes who, from father to son, transmitted to each other the right to govern by themselves and for their lifetime, the assemblage of forces which make up the world of men and things.

The mythical heroes whom history represents as the first sovereigns of China, are uniters of the people, strong by reason of their knowledge. Shun was a husbandman, a fisherman, a potter, and " at the end of a year, in the place where he lived, a village had grown up. At the end of two years, a market-town. At the end of three years, a city." [1] Whatever may have been his wisdom and renown, neither Shun nor Yao, his predecessor, transmitted his authority to his son. They did not even keep it to the end of their own lives.

For both there came a time when they had to efface themselves before the growing prestige of a Sage whose genius was better suited to the new times. The *Annals* have preserved the memory of some of the prodigies which notified to a Chief that he must retire and *hand over his authority (jang).* [2] The

---

[1] SMC, I, 74.   [2] *Annals Written on Bamboo*, 2.

Shu King gives a vague description of palavers in which one tried to gain the precedence while pretending to grant it (*jang*).[1] According to the historians who are their mouthpiece, the rivals had no thought but to make a parade of the purest civic virtue. As a matter of fact, antagonistic geniuses which were made to alternate came to grips in these duels of eloquence. Yao the sovereign could order the course of the Suns. He had to fight with Kong-kong, who was able to make the waters rise, and led them to the attack of K'ong-sang, the hollow Mulberry Tree,—the pole which is climbed by the Suns : also, with a thrust of his horn, he broke open the mountain Pu-chu, which is the pillar of Heaven, so that all the stars had to take flight into the west. Kong-kong, who disputed the rank of Sovereign with Yao, only succeeded in getting drowned at the bottom of a chasm.[2] Possessed by the geniuses of Water or of Fire, informed by Yin or by Yang, animated by the spirit of Earth or the spirit of Heaven, right-handed or left-handed, fat or tall, big-bellied or strong in the back, planted solidly on earth by their great feet or stretching their round head up to heaven, the candidates obtain authority only when their essence answers to the alternative requirements of Nature and their body can serve as a standard of measurement for the order which is imposed at the moment.[3] We may presume that there was a time when the Chiefs, representing opposite groups and conflicting geniuses, alternated in authority with the seasons. The legends of Chinese tradition only inform us of the epoch when authority belonged to two chieftains, one of whom, the Sovereign, took precedence of the other, the Minister. The Sovereign possessed the Virtue of Heaven, the Minister the Virtue of Earth.[4] They worked in partnership—perhaps taking the first rank by turns, each commanding in the places and times suited to his genius. They were also rivals. As in Nature, at certain dates, the Yin and the Yang succeeded each other at work, so when the Minister had reached a certain age, the Virtue of Earth was replaced by the Virtue of Heaven—always supposing he issued victorious from certain tests, such for example as exposure in the brushwood or marriage with the daughters of the Sovereign.[5] In this

---

[1] *Shu King*, in SMC, I, 150 ff. [2] *Huai nan tsih*, I ; **LV**, 359.
[3] *Chun ch'iu fan lu*, 7. [4] **LV**, 272. [5] **LV**, 273 ff.

case he could oblige the latter to *cede the authority (jang)* to him after which he drove him out of his city *(jang)*. When only an ageing Virtue was left in Yao, Shun, his Minister and son-in-law, hastening to banish him,[1] celebrates his elevation to the rank of Sovereign by offering a sacrifice to Heaven. It is said that Tan-chu, the eldest son of Yao, was present, doubtless in the capacity of victim, at this inaugural sacrifice, which took place in the outskirts of the capital, for we know from other sources that Tan-chu was banished or put to death.[2]

According to another tradition, Shun inaugurated his authority by opening wide the four principal gates of his square city. On that occasion he banished to the four poles of the earth four personages who were endued with an anti-quated and maleficent virtue. These four monsters split up (for the tributary organization of society is always dominated by dualism) into two groups of three (formerly dances were performed in groups of three). In fact, one of the banished monsters bears the name of Three-Miao (San-Miao). Three-Miao, who was a winged creature, was relegated to the Extreme West upon the Hill of the Feather, where the birds go every year to renew their plumage. On this hill, which has three peaks, live three birds, or, it may be, an owl with one head but a triple body. Three-Miao is also identical with the caldron Glutton, which is a tripod.[3]

Facing Three-Miao, the one and the three, the other monsters form a trio of accomplices. The chief personage in the band is Kun, the father of Yü the Great. He was banished to the Far East, upon a Hill of the Feather where the pheasant dancers are wont to appear. There he is said to have trans-formed himself into a tortoise with three paws. Others maintain that he was changed into a bear : his son, at a later time, could dance the Bear Dance. The most unvarying tradition has it that Kun, by order of Shun, was cut in pieces, which proved no obstacle to his becoming, in animal form, the Genius of the Mountain, or of the Chasm of the Feather.[4] Thus Shun could not reign until he had executed Kun or conquered Three-Miao, that winged creature who, it seems, was guilty of having upset the calendar. But when, shield

---

[1] SMC, II, 70, note 1 ; **LV**, 293. [2] **LV**, 413, 427.
[3] **LV**, 242 ff. [4] **LV**, 245 ff., 265 ff.

and lance in hand, Shun had danced a Feather Dance, he was able immediately to renew the Season.[1] In the feudal courts an exorcist, and not the prince, was required to dance to inaugurate the New Year. This figure, wearing a mask with quadruple eyes and surrounded by four acolytes called " the fools," danced, shield and lance in hand, clothed in bearskin. The ceremony was concluded by quartering the victims at the four chief gates of the square city.[2] At the time of Confucius, the Chinese still thought that in order to establish the authority of a chieftain and to disperse an order which had grown old in process of time, it was well to sacrifice a man, and fling his members to the four gates: the victim was a dancer, but a dancer substituted for a chieftain.[3] The rites employed to expel the old year and instal the new, bear the name of *jang*. *Jang* signifies to banish : the same word also means to renounce, but to renounce in order to have. The Chinese sovereign scarcely exists, who, at the moment of assuming his authority, did not act as though he desired to renounce it. The personage upon whom he then seems to wish to devolve the duties incumbent upon a chieftain, immediately goes and commits suicide, usually by flinging himself into a chasm whose genius he then becomes.[4] The inauguration of the New Year and the enthronement of a new chieftain were accomplished by means of rites which can scarcely have altered from the time when, in order to rule over the world and the seasons, Sovereign and Minister divided between them the Virtues of Heaven and Earth. The word Minister is equivalent to Three-Dukes. The ceremony of accession seems to have comprised a dancing match (three facing three) pitting two chieftains against each other, who were surrounded by their seconds, who formed a square.[5] The chieftain of the defeated dance paid for his defeat with his death, or with his expulsion from the city, or else his eldest son was sacrificed in the outskirts, as was the fate of Tan-chu.

Kun, who, being hewn in pieces and changed into a bear, became the Genius of the Chasm of the Feather, had first received from Shun a command to govern the Waters. He

---

[1] LV, 243, 269.　　　　　　　　　　[2] LV, 299 ff.
[3] LV, 213 ff.　　　　　　　　　　　 [4] LV, 294.
[5] See above, the duel between Huang-ti and his Minister Ch'e-you.

was the victim of misplaced ambition. He wished to make
his Sovereign *resign his authority* in his favour. He professed
to possess the Virtue of the Earth which qualifies one to be
minister, and subsequently to take rank as Sovereign, if later
one can obtain the Virtue of Heaven. It was in vain that
he proclaimed his titles in the course of a palaver, and danced
madly in the open country, like the exorcist in the bearskin.
His defeat shows that he was qualified neither to be a Minister
nor to succeed to the sovereignty. Kun, in fact, who was the
father of a Sovereign, was also (like Tan-chu) the eldest son
of a Sovereign.[1] He belonged to a generation which was
debarred from power. He had to be sacrificed. It was to
his son, Yü the Great, that the right reverted to be the
Minister and successor of Shun. It is an important feature of
Chinese legends that they preserve the memory of a time
when authority was transmitted from grandfather to grandson,
skipping a generation in the agnatic line. This system is
characteristic of a right of transition and marks the moment
when the principle of filiation by women yields to the inverse
principle. In a society where relationship is of the classificatory
type, and where marriages, uniting two exogamic families,
are necessarily between cousins the offspring of brothers
and sisters (cross cousins),—such was the Chinese organization—the agnatic grandfather and his grandson (referring
to the plan below) bear the same name, *even at the time when
it is transmitted in the uterine line*. As a matter of fact, the
agnatic grandfather [2] is at the same time a maternal grand-
uncle. The grandson inherits from him inasmuch as he is
his uterine great-nephew. But if the agnatic grandfather and

---

[1] *Mei-ti*, 3 ; **LV**, 273.

[2] Suppose three generations in a couple of exogamous families which in each
generation are united by marriage (marriage of cross cousins). The capitals
represent the women. The men are represented by small letters. The figure
marks the generation. The arrow unites a husband and wife.

$$a^1\ A^1 \longleftrightarrow b^1\ B^1$$
$$A^2\ a^2 \longleftrightarrow B^2\ b^2$$
$$a^3\ A^3 \longleftrightarrow b^3\ B^3$$

(The name is transmitted through the women.)

I am b^3. My mother, who has transmitted her name to me, is B^2, wife to a^2.
a^2, who is my father, bears a different family name from me.
My father (a^2) has for mother A^1, wife of b^1, who is the father of my father.
b^1, my agnatic grandfather, has the same family name as I.
My agnatic grandfather (b^1), brother of B^1, has for uterine nephew b^2 (son of B^1).
b^2, brother of B^2, my mother, is maternal uncle to me (b^3). I am at the same time
grandson in the agnatic line to b^1 and his great-nephew in the uterine line. b^1 is
my agnatic grandfather at the same time as he is my maternal great-uncle.

o

grandson belong already to the same group, the father and son belong to opposite groups. Indeed, the Chinese traditions reveal an astonishing antagonism between fathers and sons. A father and a son are inspired by antithetic geniuses, and where one is a Saint worthy to rule the Empire, the other is a Monster who deserves to be banished. But when the son is banished who will hold the estate in trust until the time when the grandson (in whom all the virtues of the grandfather should reappear) can inherit ? In the uterine system, transmission occurs from maternal uncle to uterine nephew. Now, since the marriage was made between cousins (the offspring of brothers and sisters), the father of the wife must be her mother's brother, and every man has the son of his sister for his son-in-law. [As a matter of fact [1] the same word denotes the maternal uncle and the father-in-law (*Kiou*). Inversely, a man calls by the same name (*Sheng*) his uterine nephew and his son-in-law.] Every man, therefore, by uterine right, has for successor the son of his sister, but when the inheritance passes from maternal uncle to the uterine nephew, *everything occurs as if* the inheritance was transmitted from father-in-law to son-in-law. Thus, as long as filiation is settled in the female line, the son, who belongs to a group in opposition to his father, cannot be his successor and the rôle devolves upon the son-in-law, because he is a nephew, the sister's son.

In a system founded upon male descent (but where marriages are still made between cousins, the offspring of brothers and sisters) the son-in-law is also a uterine nephew. He belongs, however, to a different group from his father-in-law (whose successor he became, to the exclusion of the son, in the other system). As long as the son, being the victim of the survival of sentiments inherited from the uterine régime, still seems to be endowed with a genius opposed to

---

[1] Suppose three generations in a couple of families. The same figures as in the preceding plan.

$$A^1 \; a^1 \longleftrightarrow B^1 \; b^1$$
$$A^2 \; a^2 \longleftrightarrow B^2 \; b^2$$
$$A^3 \; a^3 \longleftrightarrow B^3 \; b^3$$

(The name is transmitted by the women.)

I am a^2, the son of A^1 : I am the husband of B^2, the daughter of B^1, and B^1 is the wife of a^1 : a^1, who is the father of (B^2) my wife, is also the brother of my mother (A^1).

I am a^2, husband of B^2, mother of B^3, and B^3 is the wife of a^3. a^3 (the son of my sister A^2) who is my uterine nephew, is also the husband of (B^3), my daughter.

that of his father, as long as it is not yet decided to consider him as a possible successor, and he is supposed to be eliminated, it is to his brother-in-law, the son-in-law (who is already fully qualified to receive the inheritance) that it will be given in trust, for, being the uterine nephew of him whose succession falls vacant, the son-in-law is also the maternal uncle of him (the agnatic grandson) who will finally take it up.[1]

Thus then, when the son is banished, the son-in-law must succeed. And, as a matter of fact, in the only example which is related to us in detail of Chinese succession in ancient times, we see that Tan-chu, the eldest son, was banished, and Shun, who succeeded, was Yao's son-in-law.

Shun, being the son-in-law of Yao, was qualified, not only to succeed him, but also first to be his minister. As a matter of fact, if, in the uterine system, the father-in-law (maternal uncle and sister's son) belonged to the same group, they belonged to opposing groups as soon as the name was transmitted in the male line. Now, the Sovereign and the Minister (the Virtue of Heaven and the Virtue of Earth) ought to possess opposing geniuses. They form a couple of rival and yet united geniuses, as the families coupled together by a tradition of matrimonial alliance are rivals though united. Thus the dualism of the political organization and the dualism of the domestic organization are closely related. But, in both organizations, this dualism is in process of disappearing : little by little the sovereign absorbs the powers proper to the minister, while the son, who was at first sacrificed to a uterine relative, succeeds in supplanting him.

---

[1] Suppose three generations in a couple of families. The same figures as in the preceding plans. The members of group aA are repeated to show the double marriage which unites it at each generation to the group bB.

$$a^1\ A^1 \longleftrightarrow b^1\ B^1 \longleftrightarrow a^1\ A^1$$
$$a^2\ A^2 \longleftrightarrow b^2\ B^2 \longleftrightarrow a^2\ A^2$$
$$a^3\ A^3 \longleftrightarrow b^3\ B^3 \longleftrightarrow a^3\ A^3$$

(The name is transmitted by the men.)

I am b^3. My father is b^2 (of the same group as myself) and my agnatic grandfather is b^1 (as in the uterine system).

b^1 (my agnatic grandfather, brother of B^1 who is the wife of a^1 and the mother of a^2) is the maternal uncle of a^2. b^1 has for his daughter B^2 who is the wife of a^2. Therefore he has for son-in-law his uterine nephew.

a^2 (uterine nephew and son-in-law of b^1, my agnatic grandfather) is the brother of A^2, the wife of b^2 who is my father (I am b^3). a^2 is also the father of A^3 who is my wife. I am the uterine nephew and the son-in-law of him (a^2) who is the uterine nephew and the son-in-law of my grandfather.

Chinese traditions show that the concentration of power in the hands of the chieftain is the result of a parallel progress in the development of the agnatic right.

At the time of Yao and Shun (the two Sovereigns mentioned by the *Shu king*) the Minister succeeds and expels the son. The Minister being a son-in-law, everything happens as though two agnatic groups (allied by marriages in every generation) were to occupy the throne in turn. But in the history of the founders of a royal dynasty we see that the son succeeds and the minister is sacrificed. The same agnatic line is perpetuated in power, and forms a dynasty. This line possesses the supreme authority. It does not possess the whole authority. The king can only reign with the concurrence of a minister. At first, he is not taken from the agnatic group which provides the royal line. He is taken from an opposing group. The family group which gives the sovereign his wife, gives him his minister also. T'ang the Victorious, the founder of the second royal dynasty, obtained the princess who was his wife from the family of Sin, and Yi Yin, who was to be his minister, came in her escort. The succession was by the male line, but the agnatic descendants of T'ang the Victorious had the sons of Yi Yin, the minister and brother-in-law of T'ang, for their ministers. It is acknowledged that the function of Three-dukes (minister) involved the task of bringing up the heir presumptive. For whom (admitting the rules of the ancient organization) was this duty more fitting than for a maternal uncle ? Yi Yin undertook the office of Guardian to T'ang's successor. It is in the mother's family that a guardian is found for him who will succeed by agnatic right. Of the two groups which formerly duplicated each other and governed by turns, one now occupies a purely subordinate position, but something remains nevertheless of the principle of alternation. The minister, who by duplicating the sovereign was formerly preparing himself to be clothed with the sovereign authority when his turn came, is no longer the successor. But he is still entrusted with the regency. When that is ended, he resigns his power, as before, to the representative of the agnatic line. Now, however, it is the son who takes the power which is resigned (*jang*) to him, and it is the minister (such was the lot of Yi Yin) who is banished (*jang*), sacrificed.

A Chieftain by maternal relationship, the minister has sunk to the rank of herald in the agnatic dynasty.[1]

At the death of King Wu, the founder of the Chou (third royal dynasty) there was a regency (as at the death of T'ang) and the regent, on this occasion also, had to undergo banishment. But, although King Wu had his uterine uncle as principal minister (minister of War) it was neither he nor his son who was the guardian of King Ch'êng, son and successor of Wu. Too many traces remained of the opposition which at first existed between the agnates of two successive generations, to make it thinkable that a son could be *immediately* capable of succeeding his father. On the other hand, in family as in town, the first honours were entrusted to the old men. Each group had for its president the oldest representative of the oldest generation. Even when the agnatic principle was adopted, the Chinese family remained an undivided family. It was subject to one authority (in the strongest sense of the word). It began to assume the patriarchal form only when the right of primogeniture was at last recognized. As the son had had to struggle against the old prerogatives of his maternal uncle, so the eldest son had to destroy the ancient rights of his father's younger brothers. Thus the younger paternal uncle is seen to succeed the maternal uncle in the ungrateful rôle of dynastic Herald. The custom of the regency, the remains of an old obligation of alternation between two duplicate powers, allows of respect for the old sentiments, which, making two rivals of father and son, necessitates an interregnum. The rite of cession (*jang*) by which the power is placed in deposit with a third person, renders possible the transmission of authority.[2]

One last step remained to be taken, which was the suppression of the interregnum. It was taken when without the interposition of either maternal uncle or father's younger brother, the son succeeded immediately to his father by right of primogeniture. A prince (in 489 B.C., at the very end of the period *Ch'un ch'iu*) who wishes to leave the power directly to his eldest son, begins by calling round him on his death-bed, his own younger brothers. Following the order of their birth, he resigns (*jang*) the power to them. The elder brothers refuse it. The youngest feels obliged to accept it. But, if he

[1] **LV**, 417 ff.　　　　[2] **LV**, 404 ff.

must accept it, he must also, as soon as the prince is dead, invest the son of the deceased with the power.[1] There is no longer an interregnum. The rights of each of the younger brothers have been suppressed (to all appearance) for the profit of the youngest. This recognition of the minority appears to be a judicial fiction used to suppress the principle of fraternal succession and to replace it by the principle of succession in the direct line. The eldest son succeeds immediately and almost by simple prerogative thanks to the device of the cession (*jang*) which has the appearance of a last will and testament made *in extremis*. While the cession had at first the value of a rite it served to bring about a real alternation of powers, and later made possible the interregnum by which the principle of alternation was kept alive. Made at the moment of death, it became no more than a trick of procedure intended to ensure the continuity of an agnatic line of first-born sons.

While it preserved its first value, and its full force, the practice of the cession was split up into two ritual acts. The sovereign, when he grows old, retires, and before doing so he *resigns the power* (*jang*) to the minister, who assumes it. The chieftain's abdication is the signal for his period of retirement whose length in theory is thirty years (for old age begins at sixty-six years and a sage dies in his hundredth year). The sovereign employs his retirement by preparing himself for death. This death begins a period of retirement for the survivors which is occupied with mourning and whose length in theory is three years. In the third year, the minister resigns the power to the son, who does not assume it, but is, on the contrary, eliminated. When, as the result of a reversal of the operation it is the minister who is eliminated, that also happens at the end of the mourning. Yü, the founder of the first royal line, had *resigned the power* to Yi, his minister. When Yü the Great died, and the three years of mourning were ended, Yi, the minister, *resigned the power* to K'i, the son of Yü. K'i took the power and Yi had to leave the capital. One tradition (rejected as heterodox) holds that Yi, the minister, was killed by K'i, the son of Yü. When T'ang, the founder of the second dynasty, died, Yi Yin, his minister,

---

[1] *Tso chuan*, C, III, 478 ; LV, 614.

began by *banishing* T'ai Kia, who, by agnatic right, should have succeeded T'ang. Yi Yin governed the Empire for three years, the regulation time of mourning. One tradition (rejected as heterodox) holds that T'ai Kia, returning from exile, killed Yi Yin. Again it is in the third year following the death of King Wu, the founder of the Chou dynasty, that the *banishment* of the duke of Chou, the regent of the Empire, took place. Thus the regency lasts during the time of mourning and ends fatally for the minister. But the death of the minister or the end of the interregnum are normally marked by miraculous storms which have all the character of an apotheosis, and it happens that these storms break at the moment when the regent and the new king meet *in the outskirts*. We have seen that Tan-chu, Yao's son who was sacrificed, represented Heaven at a sacrifice celebrated in the outskirts by Shun, the minister who succeeded him. When the sons succeeded in supplanting the ministers, these, in their turn, were doubtless *sacrificed in the outskirts*, at the end of the mourning.[1]

The sacrifice which ended the mourning retirement (which in theory lasts three years—the first three months being the strictest period) cannot have differed materially from the sacrifice by which the winter retirement (lasting three months) was brought to an end. Both served to remove the interdicts imposed by the death of the Sovereign or by the winter season. Winter is the time of competitions in which opposing groups strive for pre-eminence. In the same way the period of mourning is occupied by a long competition in which the minister and the son oppose each other, both struggling for virtue and striving to issue victorious from the test. Thus struggled Shun and Tan-chu, Yi Yin and T'ai Kia, and " the noblemen unanimously gave themselves " to him who, minister or son, was most capable of acquiring the genius of the deceased.

At all times, in China, mourning has been considered as a test which qualifies for the succession. This test was not endured by the son alone, even in ages dominated by the agnatic law. During the feudal period, each family possessed a steward, a kind of domestic minister, *alter ego* to the head of the family. He was bound to this latter, intimately, by

[1] LV, 291, 424 ff., 413 ff., 580 ff.

a bond as close as that which unites a wife to her lord. The
duties of the steward, during the period of mourning, were
scarcely less important than those of the son. At the end of
the mourning, other duties, still more arduous, were incumbent
upon him. Frequently the steward is known to be the con-
fidant of the widow in her choice of companions in the tomb
for the dead man. Both try to depute their own duties to
substituted victims. In point of fact, the master should be
followed to the tomb by the vassal who was closest to him
and also by his wife. The duke Mu of Ch'in had three friends
(Minister is translated Three-Dukes) who had been devoted
to him personally. They were sacrificed at the death of the
duke. The sacrifice took place at the time when the deceased
took possession of his last resting-place.[1]

The actual burial marks the end of the strictest observance
of mourning. The sacrifice which accompanies it ensures the
apotheosis of the dead, who, transformed at last into an
Ancestor, mounts in triumph to Heaven, escorted by a train
of the faithful. This actual burial is preceded by a provisional
burial which in theory should last for three months. The
provisional burial takes place in the house. The dead is
disincarnated in the midst of his relatives. As long as the
period lasts during which the impurity of death is being
dissipated, they must in all things share the condition of the
dead. They must purge him from his infection, for his
infection is theirs. Among many peoples who practise the
system of twofold burial, it is the first duty to eat the decom-
posed flesh of the dead. The ancient Chinese used to impose
the duty of consuming the corpse upon him, who, in the hope
of succeeding him, aspired to acquire the virtues of the
deceased. At the death of Yi, the Great Archer, the prince
of Kiong, " they boiled his flesh and gave it to his sons to eat.
The sons could not take it upon them to eat (their father).
They were put to death at the *gates* of Kiong." [2] If T'ai Kia
succeeded in acquiring the virtues of his father T'ang, it was
doubtless because, less fearful than the sons of the Archer,
he took upon himself the duty of delivering the bones of the
deceased from the infection of death. As a matter of fact, he
only succeeded in acquiring the paternal virtues after Yi Yin,

---

[1] SMC, II, 45 ; *Tso chuan*, C, I, 470 ; LV, 219.
[2] *Tso chuan*, C, II, 205 ; LV, 164.

the minister, had banished him for the period of mourning to T'ong, where T'ang was actually buried. Yi Yin, when he resigned to T'ai Kia the duty of purging the funeral impurities, put him in the way of succeeding, and, after T'ang had attained the rank of ancestor, T'ai Kia, on his part, when he *resigned* to Yi Yin, whom he slew, the honour faithfully to accompany his master, was the instrument of his obtaining the glory of being the Herald of a dynasty which was about to be founded. Formerly, as a good nephew on the mother's side, the minister would doubtless have claimed the duty of purging the bones of the deceased, and would have sacrificed the son in the outskirts to bring the mourning to a close.

The continuity of the royal lines was assured, and the agnatic right established from the moment that the son heroically had the courage to claim relationship with his father. Huang-ti, who was born on a Hill of the Owls, was able to sustain his emblematic genius by eating owls. It appears that it is a custom with owls to devour their mother. To feed on the flesh of one's mother (when the filiation is on the mother's side) is merely to confirm in oneself the virtues of one's race.[1] The endo-cannibalism which permits a family to preserve its substantial integrity, is a perfectly simple duty of domestic piety. Whoever accomplishes it takes part in a pure communion. He sanctifies himself without trying to exceed the order of sanctifications permitted to his original genius. When it is not a case of endo-cannibalism, cannibalism is, on the contrary, an act of faith and an act of pride. The hero who is capable of eating the flesh of him who is not his relative shows an ambitious virtue which does not flinch from annexing and exceeding. Such is properly the Virtue of a Chieftain. Chinese history shows us the sons of the Archer, a race of usurpers, perishing because they have not courage to drink the broth made from the corpse of their father. It shows us also two great sages, who, thanks to their courage, founded two glorious dynasties. Defied by a rival, King Wen, the founder of the Chou, drank the broth of his son. The founder of the Han, Kao-chu, gave proof of no less heroism when in 203 B.C. he calmly agreed to drink the broth of his father.[2] It is significant that these anecdotes have their

---

[1] LV, 162 ff., 536 ff.
[2] SMC, I, 202, note 2, and II, 307

place in the history of the founding of two dynasties. They reveal the cannibalistic test as a sort of rite preliminary to enthronement. When, face to face with his rival, the chieftain drinks, no one can doubt that, thanks to this act of triumphant annexation, he now possesses the twofold virtue of Heaven and of Earth, formerly shared between prince and minister, between father and son.

CHAPTER VI

THE INCREMENTS OF PRESTIGE

FEARFUL rites alone had the power to draw together the father and son who had been members of two different stocks and were endowed with virtues of different nature. Agnatic infeudation was not unlike triumphant annexation. At first, however, no victory could be won and no battle fought to a finish within the domain of the family and the city. It was in the marches that martial law came into being by which alone substantial increments of prestige could be won.

The Chieftain is a warrior, a tamer of beasts, a civilizer of Barbarians. Master of fire, with whose help the brushwood is cleared and arms are forged ; he can control the world. He can quell the wild beasts, the demons, the savages who surround the town in the waste marches and beyond the tilled fields. He has endured the test of exposure in the brushwood, whether at his birth, like Hou-tsi, or like Shun, before he assumed authority. Like Yü the Great, he can dance the steps which make the Ch'e-mei harmless, those fierce spirits of the marshes and hills, or the dance which, taming the Three Miao, those winged creatures, forced them to abandon barbarism and bring their tribute to the capital. He knows the name of the monsters : this name is their very soul. When he pronounces it, he sees the most terrible beast run to him, enslaved.[1] The Chieftain is a provider of game, a conqueror of names, a hunter of emblems. The soul of captive beasts floats in his standards, echoes in his drums. He sallies forth to capture in his swamp, the divine Crocodile, who plays the drum upon his belly and bursts into sudden laughter, or, in the brushwood, K'uei, bullock and dragon, who makes the noise of thunder : with their skin and with their bones he makes himself a drum which commands the thunderbolt.[2] He goes into the marshes, where the Wei-t'o

[1] LV, 257 ff.
[2] *Lu che ch'un ch'iu*, 9, par. 6 ; *Shan hai king*, 5 and 14.

crawls, clothed in violet as befits a prince, and sinuous like
a floating flag : he takes him and eats him, for the Wei-t'o
conceals a princely Virtue and commands the Drought.[1]
The Chieftain is a hunter, but he hunts by means of music,
and dancing, and beating the drum, and brandishing like a
banner the tails of animals,[2] he captures animals, eats their
flesh, wears their skin, clothing himself with their nature and
assimilating their genius. He gives his men the name of
conquered monsters to bear or their skin to wear. He van-
quishes emblems and distributes them. Nature and men
obey him, thanks to these emblems. But he can only vanquish
them in the desert marches, the land of the chase and of
war. There live the Barbarians, who are the prey of the
Chieftain.

It is a fact that war was formerly forbidden between the
Chinese. It seemed to be impossible. All the Chinese were
allied [literally : *Kiou-sheng*—fathers-in-law and sons-in-law)
or brothers (*hiong-ti*)]. If they bore different names, they
were united by marriage or by vendetta, living in a state of
agitated equilibrium which was radically different from the
state of war. As a prelude or as a crown to their vendettas,
union by marriage corresponded to a truce in which rivalries
may have been rather accentuated than calmed. The vendettas, which were regulated competitions in insult and
challenge ending in solemn communions, profited by the
general sentiment of solidarity equally with the exchange of
hostages or wives. On the other hand, all is held in common
between relations. Exchanges are impossible. The vendetta
would be as immoral as marriage. War is not to be imagined.
He whose ambition drove him to such folly would be frightened
by the first reprimand. " To destroy an aristocracy bearing
the same name is not in accordance with the rites ! " [3]　In
the same way, another being, warned of the sinister designs
of a relative, is unable to believe it. " We bear the same
name ! It would not be proper for him to attack me ! " [4]
It is true one may fight against a family or an aristocracy
" of fathers-in-law and sons-in-law "—or rather one may
measure oneself, not without brutality, but one never aims

---

[1] *Chuang tsih*, **CXLIII**, 363 ; *Kuan tsih*, 14 ; *Shan hai king*, 2 and 3.
[2] *Lu che ch'un ch'iu*, 20, par. 6 ; **LV**, 269 ff.
[3] SMC, IV, 307.　　　　　　　　　　　　[4] SMC, IV, 268.

at a definite victory or an annexation. The lord of Chin (583 B.C.) sets out to exterminate the whole family of Chao. He looks upon the Chao as rebel vassals, but they are in reality a rival family which has its own place in the State. People ask him : " Is it possible to interrupt their sacrifices ? " Whereupon he immediately restores their family inheritance.[1] A family and its lands are one unbroken whole. In case of necessity, a family may mortgage (*hsia*) a part of their domain : they cannot transfer the ownership.[2] They cannot alienate it. They cannot be alienated from it. If they are criminal, they are altogether criminal and their domain with them. When a divine family deserved punishment, the mountain belonging to them was shaven and painted red, like a criminal : but such a chastisement is the act of an autocrat (219 B.C.) and deserved reprobation.[3] There was not and could not be, in a strict sense, a penal law, before the State was in the hands of a truly sovereign authority. To be able to punish, one must be able to destroy utterly, and how can one destroy a family ? One cannot leave the fields without masters, nor confiscate what is still inhabited by the genius whom one cannot assimilate. Neither the penal code, nor the commercial law, nor the State can make the slightest progress while they still hesitate to disturb the ancient equilibrium which renders inviolable both inheritances and families.

It is a significant fact that the first codes are supposed to have been promulgated during the hunt, that is to say, in the Marches which are the home of Barbarians. The penal code, while it exceeds simple family justice or the procedure of the vendetta, is like martial law, or the right of war. The codes were engraved on caldrons, whose metal was dug up in the mountain gorges, as the emblems which adorned the dynastic caldrons had been conquered in the Marches. In the same way, the public treasury was originally a spoil of war. It consisted of " feathers, skins, teeth, and horns," [4] which gave their potency to the instruments of war or of the dance (the terms are interchangeable) and were originally the first method of paying tribute : but this tribute was the tribute of Barbarians and not of vassals. Finally, the first

---

[1] SMC, IV, 323.
[2] *Tso chuan*, C, I, 66.
[3] SMC, II, 154.
[4] SMC, IV, 288.

landed property belonging to the State consisted of the forests and swamps of the Marches : the products of the marshes and the forest, salt, minerals, precious stones, foreign riches, these were the first resources of the State, and the sole objects which obtained a large circulation.[1] Neither grain nor stuffs were originally objects of commerce nor of tribute. They were only used for the purposes of covenant-making. They were the subject of competition. They were lent on condition of repayment. They could neither be sold nor freely circulated. As agricultural products, they belonged to the domestic fields and partook of their inalienable character. The family or sexual group which, raising the grain and weaving the stuffs, incorporated in them with its labour something of its own soul, ate them or wore them, after having caused them to be de-consecrated by an allied group. Portions of them might be given to this group, but in the same way that one gives or rather lends oneself when one wishes to take part in a communion and draw near to another person, without allowing oneself to be annexed. On the other hand, the objects and creatures of the marches are matter for spoil, matter for trophies, matter for triumphant annexations. There is nothing to prevent their being destroyed. He alone who has the right to destroy can possess the whole. He alone has the right of alienation.

The Barbarians are by nature capable of the sole crime which is a true crime. They live outside the order of civilization illuminated by the virtue of the prince. Also, from the time that there were chieftains and that they punished the crime of rebellion, its penalty was banishment into the un-cultivated marches. When the exile was exposed, alive or dead, in the country of the Monsters, his soul was banished from the world of human beings. Banishment to the land of the Barbarians was equivalent to a sentence of death, for they have the nature of beasts and not of men.[2] Two human beings, two Chinese, if they are related, possess an identity of genius : if they are allied, their geniuses are complementary. With the Barbarians, no relationship is possible and no rivalry recognized. They are different in their food and their clothing. Neither grain nor stuffs can be exchanged with them. They cannot make an alliance by marriage or vendetta.

---

[1] SMC, IV, 40 and 49.   [2] *Tso chuan*, C, I, 413.

No communication is possible with them as with commensals. They are left " to live with the foxes and the wolves " or else they are driven away.   War is made upon them.[1] Captives are furnished by the Barbarians and trophies by their land.   From trophies and captives comes that increase in prestige which is glory.   A triumph is held to consecrate it.

When his army has won glory, the warrior chief dances the dance of triumph.   " He holds the flute in his left hand. He holds the battle-axe in his right.   He marches at the head of choirs of victory.   He offers up the spoils."   The spoils include the left ears which are cut off from fallen enemies and those which are cut off from the captives who are dragged in the show.   To cut off the ear is a dedicatory gesture which opens the battle.   It also opens the warlike pomp which commemorates it.   The first blood drawn from the ears by a knife hung with little bells summons the gods who are looking on to a banquet.[2]   The dance of triumph is ended by a cannibal feast at which victorious men and gods may glut themselves.   The Barbarians are nothing but game.   By devouring them, one can assimilate foreign virtues, and complete conquest.

Infeudation may be obtained and a frontier wiped out by a cannibal feast.   The feudal and agnatic order came into being as soon as the military code had permeated the relations between families and between cities.   Then those men would be treated as enemies who were formerly counted rivals. Instead of dividing to form a vendetta they faced each other for conquest.   Where they would only have claimed the right to obtain a restitution of prestige, they sought now for complete victory.

At Ch'in and at Chin [3] reign rival families.   They exchange their grain and their children.   But Duke Mu of Ch'in affects hegemony.   He takes prisoner Duke Huai, the prince of Chin, in battle (644 B.C.).   He treats him as a captive, and leads him in triumph.   He lodges him in the tower Ling, the dwelling of prisoners destined for sacrifice.   He orders preparatory purifications.   But the wife of duke Mu is Huai's sister.   She climbs straightway into another tower, that of condemned women.   She shuts herself up in it and her children follow her.   A messenger, clad in mourning, goes to carry to

---

[1] *Tso chuan*, **C**, II, 292 ff.   [2] **LV**, 136 ff.   [3] *Tso chuan*, **C**, I, 300.

her husband the threat of a collective suicide. The conqueror is obliged to renounce the triumph which he intended to celebrate, not over a Barbarian, but over an ally. He returns to the old customs. He confines himself to restoring the old alliance of the rival countries, in an equalizing banquet. The vanquished is neither sacrificed nor eaten like a Barbarian. He is invited to share with the conqueror a banquet of seven bullocks, seven sheep and seven pigs. The old order is respected. But, almost at the same Date (640 B.C.), Duke Siang of Song was himself aiming at hegemony. He convokes an assembly, in the Eastern marches, on the pretext of uniting the oriental Barbarians under his authority. Only, to strengthen his prestige, he offers a sacrifice whose victim is not a Barbarian, but an aristocrat, an ally. And he does not hear the rebuke : " If a man is sacrificed (a *Chinese* is understood) who (of gods or men) will be willing to eat him ? " [1]

Formerly, when he wished to found a dynasty and " bring to perfection the prestige of the Hsia," Yü the Great convened an assembly in the Marches of the South.[2] He too sacrificed one of the aristocrats who was summoned to the meeting. This sacrifice was connected with a dancing match. It seems to have been the crowning point of a dramatic competition. Geniuses bellowing like the winds were conquered by dragons who ascended to Heaven in a storm of rain and thunder. Wind against thunder and dragons against bulls, the tournament of Yü the Great, which ended in an apotheosis, was a triumphal dance, a dance of accession. But the conquered is called a Barbarian and history abstains from relating that Yü ate him : Yü is in fact a hero of whom no ill must be spoken. The Duke Siang of Song is on the contrary represented as an ambitious man mad with pride. There is no hesitation in relating the cannibal feast which he celebrated. Was it not indispensable if, pursuing victory to triumph, its object was to obtain a real increase of prestige by an annexation ? The acquiring of the substantial qualifications necessary for a new authority is the only means of effacing a frontier.

When the tournament pursues a similar end it ceases to be a simple fencing-match of courteous rivalries. The spirit

[1] *Tso chuan*, **C**, I, 319–321 ; **LV**, 146.   [2] SMC, V, 312 ; *Shu yi ki* ; **LV**, 348.

of rivalry becomes incensed and is turned into a desire for domination. Instead of ending in a banquet and marriages which reveal profound solidarities and re-establish equilibrium, the triumphal tournament is closed by an incorporation. The two chieftains who confront each other do not commune by eating together in a banquet of equals, but the victor communes as a ruler with the vanquished. He makes them into vassals by assimilating, with the flesh of his fallen rival, all the virtues belonging to the subject group. Henceforth, the barriers are broken down between countries and families of different essence. Passages and exchanges become possible. The times are past when equilibrium was the ideal but exclusion was the rule. On the contrary, groups and families penetrated each other with a violence which was the more impetuous, as they had been originally closed to each other. A spirit of war had entered into the tournament : a will to conquest presided over the communions. The communal proceedings aimed at obtaining, no longer a simple and distant solidarity, but an infeudation. Only by trying to excel them were they united to the others. A passion for expenditure, for outbidding, for destruction, the spirit of a wager, inspires the whole of social life.

Chapter VII

THE PRINCIPLES OF INFEUDATION

At the time of the peasant agreement and the equalizing communions, the solidarity of the families who were gathered together in rural communities was obtained by the help of payments in kind which were at once alternative and total. As long as the rule of alternation governed the social organization payments in kind were in principle total. When Shun marries the daughters of Yao and becomes minister, with future succession, Yao presents him, in addition to his daughters, with bullocks and sheep, instruments of music, the shield and lance which will be used in war and the dance, the granary which will enable him to show his generosity, all his vassals and all his sons.[1] Shun, who receives all Yao's inheritance, will in his turn give all his inheritance to his own minister. If he restores everything he does not give more than he has received. It is otherwise in the feudal order. At any moment any possession may have to be restored to the Chieftain. Nothing is possessed which has not first been resigned (*jang*). " When a man of the people has a possession, he gives it back to the head of the family. When a dignitary has a possession, he makes an offering of it to his lord. When a lord has a possession, he gives it back to the Son of Heaven. When the Son of Heaven has a possession, he resigns (*jang*) the *Virtue* (*tô*) of it to Heaven." [2] A thing can be made use of only after the gift has lifted its tabu, but the gift becomes profitable as soon as it is made to a superior. It is then equivalent to a consecration. The gift gains in value in proportion to the authority of the chieftain to whom it is made. The Chieftain, on principle, must not monopolize. He must be able " to communicate his fortune and to distribute it from top to bottom of the scale of creatures, thus causing gods, men, and all things,

---

[1] SMC, I, 53 and 73.   [2] *Li ki*, C, II, 313 ; LV, 88, note 1.

to attain their supreme development." [1] Property becomes valuable when it is used for gifts. The circulation of things creates and defines values, at the same time that it defines and creates a social hierarchy. The virtue (*tô*) of things is the result of their consecration by the chief when he resigns (*jang*) them to Heaven, the supreme authority. Fortune is the result of sacrifice, abundance (*jang*) the result of the sacrificial oblation (*jang*).[2] Thus every gift attracts to itself in return the gift of increased value. The benevolence of the god or the generosity of the chief responds to the sacrifice of the believer or the vassal. Presents serve in the first place to show respect and to enhance the prestige of the receiver, then to reflect respect and prestige upon the giver. Emulation, made up at the same time of disinterestedness and of ambition, is the common principle of homage and of tribute, of the feudal system of payment, and of the nobility.

This generous and grasping emulation is strong enough to break down the ancient barriers. It is possible to enter the family of a chief if one's devotion to it is great enough for a total sacrifice. Chao Kien-tsih conspires (496 B.C.); he is too powerful to be punished; he is asked only to sacrifice his most devoted follower : the latter himself embraces death : after his suicide, he receives offerings in the temple of the Chao family.[3] The bonds of a vassal's fidelity (personal ties) are stronger than domestic ties. They are stronger also than territorial bonds. Two brothers, personal vassals of Ch'ong-êrh, the future Duke Wen of Chin, accompany him on his flight into foreign parts : their father is a vassal of the reigning prince of Chin : Ch'ong-êrh receives an order from him to send back his sons : he refuses: "*When a son is capable of holding office, his father teaches him fidelity : he then inscribes his personal name* (which is identical with his soul and lays it open to capture) *upon a tablet, and presents an offering as a pledge.* (The ritual of homage is related to the ritual of self-devotion. In making an offering, one gives oneself *entirely :* henceforth one would be incapable of serving a second master.) *To reveal a double* (soul), [which my sons would do if they returned to you] *is a crime.*" [4] The principle that one belongs entirely to a single group preserves its force,

---

[1] SMC, I, 269 ; LII, 189. LV, 336, note 3.   [2] LV, 336, note 3.
[3] *Tso chuan*, C, III, 583.   [4] *Tso chuan*, C, I, 339.

but the group which possesses the individual is no longer of
the family or territorial type : it is a feudal group.   The
vassal belongs entirely to his liege-lord.   His lord marries
him as he thinks well.   He cannot even profit by the exogamic
rule.   Kuei and K'ing-che bear the same name : but the
ties of family seem insufficient to them both : Kuei then
becomes the vassal of K'ing-che (544 B.C.).   K'ing-che gives
him his daughter in marriage (this gift is like a counter-move
to the taking of the oath of homage).   Then when Kuei is
asked :   " Why do you not refuse to marry your relative ? "
he replies :   " When we sing verses, can we separate the
couplets ?   I had asked for what I am now receiving (by
declaring myself a vassal)." [1]   The feudal régime entails a
movement of things and of men, which results in new and
constantly changing classifications.   Individuals are no longer
bound for ever to their family or country.   On the other hand,
no group, family or country is any more hermetically closed.

Henceforth the barriers which surround a domain may be
removed.   Duke Huan of Ch'i comes to the help of Yen
(663 B.C.).   The lord of Yen, to show his gratitude, is at
pains to accompany him home, and even goes too far with
him.   He penetrates into Ch'i's territory.   This was treating
Duke Huan like a sovereign, or a Son of Heaven.   Huan
was striving at that very time to usurp the royal authority.
But he that humbleth himself shall be exalted.   It is by
resigning one's possessions that one's fortune grows.   It was
Huan's duty to decline the homage he had received, in order
to make it more evident, but he would have to pay it back
before he could boast of it.   " Separating it by a ditch he
detached the territory which had been reached by the prince
of Yen, and gave it to him."   This moderation, this apparent
generosity were the calculations of an ambitious man : no
one was deceived by them : the lords, learning of the adventure, all follow in the train of Ch'i. [2]   The gift of land
as a compensation for homage is one of the principles of
infeudation.   Ch'i appears to incorporate a piece of his
domain with Yen : he does in fact give Yen in fief to Ch'i.
Inversely, an act of homage may compensate for a gift of
land.   Chin exercises hegemony, Song is his ally : they
unite and together suppress a small manor (562 B.C.).   Chin

---

[1] *Tso chuan*, C, II, 507.   [2] SMC, IV, 51.

resigns the land to Song, but not without mental reservation. He establishes in his own domain a representative of the conquered family, which alone is qualified to observe the regional religious rites. Thus he gives up the tenure, but keeps the important rights. Song will only come into possession of the territory conceded to him when he goes to Chin to ask for the religious ceremonies which are necessary before he can exercise his new rights. Nevertheless the gift lays an obligation upon him and he must discharge it. So the prince of Song invites the prince of Chin to a banquet. He proposes to him to have the dance of Sang-lin performed for him, the dance of T'ang the Victorious, the founder of the Yin. This dance is a kind of royal blazon of which it has been impossible to dispossess the descendants of the Yin. In addition to the Yin themselves the Chou alone are able to have the dance performed, which belonged to the Yin whom they conquered. To dance the dance of Sang-lin in honour of Chin is equivalent to treating him as a sovereign. The prince of Chin only half accepts the homage of the dance. He is conscious that Song is giving him too much, and that by displaying to him the living emblem of a royal race, he offers him communion which is as formidable as an ordeal. Bearing the standard from which floats the genius of Sang-lin, the chief dancer appears. Immediately the prince of Chin takes to flight. Nevertheless he falls ill. A clever vassal fortunately succeeds in averting misfortune from him. Otherwise, in order to exorcise it, Chin would have been reduced to applying for the religious services of the prince of Song. In the duel of gifts and homage, Song took the first place while he seemed to resign (*jang*) it. He did not hesitate to bring the very essence of his authority in question. He sacrificed everything. Chin could not exceed this sacrifice. If he had accepted it in its entirety, he would have been beaten in the wager, and become the obliged and infeudated.[1]

Arising and resulting from such gambling with fate, the feudal hierarchy was established by means of bravado. Grain, being the sacred gift of the soil, was produced for the reapers to eat on the spot, and not to be stored or sent out of the territory (except in the case when the equilibrium between neighbouring groups has been broken by a famine

---

[1] *Tso chuan*, **C**, II, 254; *ibid.*, I, 257; **LV**, 457.

and must be re-established). But when the feudal order was founded, grain was exchanged as tribute or wages: it was gathered into granaries, and even the word " granary " came to mean " treasure." Drinks extracted from grain, being drunk in common, gave a substantial basis to contracts of alliance. But, while a man and wife (even at the time when the husband is master) drink together out of two halves of the same calabash, the feudal drinking-bouts which were the original of the infeudating communions, begin with a gesture of distrust in the offer of a cup. Before the battle, a cup is offered to the enemy. Let him take what comfort he can ! He will find he has met his match.[1] After the victory, a cup is offered to the vanquished. This is treating him as guilty, for defeat has revealed a criminal in him and he must be compelled to purge himself of the evil spirit. But it has besides the object of rehabilitating him by blotting out the past, and also of avoiding reprisals by proposing communion. Finally, its purpose is to emphasize one's own triumph.[2]

In the archery tournaments, the vanquished, holding their bows, unstrung, receive a horn cup from the victors. They drink and expiate their defeat. Afterwards the victors expiate their victory : they drink in their turn, but it is out of the cup which is used at investitures. Once the hierarchy was created, solidarity was confirmed : all shared in the communion by drinking in turn. To distribute cups and to distribute honours is expressed in the same words.[3] In the same way, to receive grain to eat is equivalent to receiving a fief. He who consents to nourish himself with grain from which others also derive their life, binds himself to his companions by a bond of complete solidarity. It is his duty to refuse if he recognizes a harmful genius in them which would infect him with its uncleanness. " I will no longer eat what they eat ! " cries Kie Tsih-ch'uei : the other vassals his companions seemed to him to be too greedy and consequently disloyal.[4] Thus alimentary communions succeed in binding together individuals of different family and different virtue. But in the gift of food, as in the gift of drink, one is conscious of a desire to impose an ordeal and attempt an annexation. An invader appears : the first gesture which one attempts

[1] *Tso chuan*, **C**, II, 139.
[3] *Yi li*, **C**, 124 ff.; **LV**, 91, note 1.
[2] *Tso chuan*, **C**, II, 431.
[4] *Tso chuan*, **C**, I, 356.

is to offer him victuals. The object is not to appease him. On the contrary, the intention is " to treat him like a victim who is being fattened." The army of Ch'u (536 B.C.) penetrates into the territory of Wu. The prince of Wu sends his own brother to bear the gift of victuals. This piece of bravado is answered by another. Ch'u immediately makes a point of sacrificing the messenger : his blood will serve to anoint a military drum.[1] The gift of food or drink is equivalent to a challenge which entwines fates and binds destinies together. It is intended to be the prelude to an annexation.

The speculator who, while he makes a parade of moderation (*jang*), is bold enough to make a habit of renunciation, he who gives the most, he who seems to pledge his all in the competition of wagers, he alone is capable of annexations which will authorize him to found a government. At Ch'i, the T'ien family is preparing to usurp the princely authority. They are striving to steal away the vassals of the reigning house. They wish to put the whole country under their protection. (From 538–485 B.C.) they practise the system of double measure : they use unequal measures in taking and receiving : they give 5 and only claim 4. So there is a song made : " When an old woman has millet—she carries it to T'ien ch'êng-tsih." The princes of Ch'i possessed only a useless granary where the grain was allowed to rot. The granary of the T'ien family on the contrary was a veritable treasure-house. The T'ien family gave alms to the poor. They increased the number of their clients and of their guests. They bound them to themselves by gifts and alimentary communions. They also made use of the sexual communion as a principle of infeudation. T'ien Ch'ang had a harem peopled with one hundred tall women. He allowed his guests and his hosts to penetrate inside it. Through this exercise of hospitality he gained sixty-six sons. It also brought him a still greater benefit. Those who, uniting themselves to women who were his vassals, united themselves to him through them, contracted a bond of dependence upon him. They did not become allies, as is the case with sons-in-law : they became vassals. " The people of the country sighed for the arrival of the T'ien to power." " The people celebrated the

[1] *Tso chuan*, **C,** III, 113 and 671.

generosity of the T'ien in their songs and their dances."
These formulas of the historians mean, no doubt, that the
T'ien had succeeded in making the whole people share in the
glory of their family. The treasure of their dances and
domestic songs, like their treasures of grain and of women,
had become not exactly a public treasure, but the treasure
of a seigniorial house.[1]

He who, by dint of defiances, bravadoes, wagers, expendi-
tures, cruel sacrifices, warlike jousts, infeudating communions,
succeeds in breaking down the old domestic and territorial
barriers, he is a Chief, for, by conquest after conquest, he has
built up a treasure of emblems, of grain, of men and women
vassals. This treasure in its entirety is his fortune and
that of his fief. Nothing has value or weight (*chong*) until it
has been dedicated to a powerful personage, and become
part of a treasure which has been enhanced by many gifts.
The overlord distributes emblems, women and grain. He
gives back in the shape of salary and fief what he has received
in right of homage and tribute. Tribute gives power to the
Chief. A salary gives nobility to the vassal. A new order
is created, which is founded entirely upon prestige. Human
groups are no longer hermetic. Men and things circulate, and
while they circulate they take their place in a hierarchy.
They cease to possess the specific virtues which isolate them.
As a compensation they acquire a value which classifies them.
The genius of a group was formerly embodied in a standard :
the feudal banner signifies only a degree of dignity : what
was a domestic emblem has become a titular ensign. Instead
of being divided up into groups which were jealous of their
independence, society is composed of graded classes. It
tends less to the equilibrium of forces than to the concentration
of powers, or at least, to a hierarchy of prestige.

[1] **LV,** 583 ff.

BOOK THREE

THE SEIGNIORIAL TOWN

IN the course of the feudal period, which lasted a long time, the various chieftainships met with varied fortunes. Some remained very humble, preserving a completely rural appearance. In certain tiny lordships, that of Yu, for example, in Shan-tung, the overlord (in 513 B.C.), went in person to preside over the work of the fields.[1] This was (so it appears, at least, from the account in the *She king*) the principal function of the chieftain.[2] Religious and public life was reduced to a few great rustic festivals. They kept the feast of Shên-nung, the divine husbandman, the god of the clearing fires and the purifier of harvests. Again they kept the feasts of the spirits who animate the four seasons, while they preside over the four points of the compass. To those of the North (Winter) and the South (Summer) were offered, as the most important, a black bullock (Water) or a red bullock (Fire). Dualism reigned in society as in thought. The chieftain had two seconds, the inspector of fields and the forester. In mythical times, Yü the Great had for his companions K'i, the Master of the harvests (Hou-tsi: this title was kept up, as a royal title, by the Chou, who derived their genealogy from K'i), and Yi, the tamer of wild beasts, the great forester, whose orders were obeyed by four acolytes: Fir-tree, Tiger, Bear, and Striped Bear. We know that Yi the Forester was sacrificed by the son of Yü, to end the mourning for his father.[3] In the seigniorial courts, the Grand Forester, the leader of the princely Chase, was charged to summon and lay the superior ghost (*hun*) the breath-of-life of his dead master: this ghost, when it was not laid by worship, might go and embody itself in a fierce animal in the forests. As the Hunter of Beasts and Barbarians, the Forester owned dreadful privileges: he was charged, in case of crime, with

[1] *Tso chuan*, C, III, 289. [2] *She king*, C, 285.
[3] SMC, I, 154; *ibid.*, I, 85.

the execution of the prince's parents : in case of misfortune, he must take the ill luck and the mistakes upon himself.[1] Compared with this distant predecessor of the ministers of war and justice, the Steward of the fields seemed to exercise a more peaceful sway, although it may have involved him in heavier responsibility.   He seems to have acted at the beginning of the mourning a part which balanced that acted by the Surveyor of Forests at its close.   Charged with planting the banner of the dead chief upon a rough effigy which covered two pots of rice, it was doubtless his mission also to preside over the rites which allowed the corpse to decompose and the inferior soul (*p'o*) to be reabsorbed into the sacred forces from which the soil draws its fertility.[2]   Upon these humble seconds, the rural chief laid the most strenuous duties of expiation which fell to the overlord.

Great lordships make their appearance at the end of the feudal period.   Their chiefs, branded by history for their lack of moderation, are described as tyrants.   Under the influence of lawyers, the idea of the State was vaguely elaborated at their court, while an administrative system was sketched out.   Potentates ruling over a large territory sought to base their authority on a newly discovered prestige.   Even when they seemed to care only to surround their person with a glory of apotheosis, one is conscious in the midst of their pride, of the idea that the supreme power is made up of expiations and devotions.   The powerful ministers who are their favourites preserve the appearance of expiatory victims which connects them with the humble stewards of former times.

But, if one can believe the rituals and the chronicles, between the age of rural chieftainships and the epoch of the tyrannies (*The Combatant Kingdoms*), there was a long period during which China knew a stable and well-regulated order. The chances are great that at all times the feudal order had been singularly unstable.   There is certainly a great mixture of historical Utopia in the collections of regulations which profess to describe the customs actually practised under the feudal lordships.   Nevertheless, by the side of the Chieftainships which preserved a truly rural character, and the powerful States which the tyrants attempted to build up, lordships

---

[1] *Chou li,* **VII,** I, 85.   [2] *Yi li,* **C,** 443, and **LV,** 159.

of a strictly feudal type do appear to have held an important place. The hierarchy was relatively stable in them, hereditary rights were recognized. The posts of ambassador, judge and recorder remained in the same family. Amongst the lordships, which like the vassal families, were always seeking to rise in the scale, a certain order of registration was maintained.[1] One must not copy the feudalists who edited the *Chou li* at the time of the Han, and perceive in the feudal customs a fixed juridical system born of a constitutional charter. But the ideal which inspired the feudalists and guided the chroniclers in their attempts at historic reconstruction is not altogether of their invention. It was shaped in the seigniorial courts established in the little towns, which seem sometimes to have resembled citadels and sometimes hamlets. There a few vassal families leading a noble life grouped themselves around a hereditary overlord. Their chiefs were at the head of a militarily organized group, and lived by the labour of a subordinated group of peasants, called people of naught or villeins. From their course of life, at the court or the army, and from their domestic discipline is derived the code of morals which was later to be imposed upon the ruling classes of the nation as a whole. It was the code of *decent men* who were originally gentlemen (Kün-tsih) leading a life entirely dominated by the worship of honour and etiquette at the court of an overlord.

[1] *Tso chuan*, C, III, 478.

CHAPTER I

THE TOWN

SOME verses of the *She king* give an idea of the ceremony of founding a town. The founder, wearing all his jewels, jades and precious stones, and bearing a magnificent sword, proceeds first to inspect the country. To ascertain the points of the compass, he studies the shadows (with the help of a gnomon ?). He examines the declivities, in sun and shade, the *yang* and the *yin* of the country, to know how the chief constituents of the world are divided. Finally he takes account of the direction of the running water. It is his duty to recognize the religious value of the site (what will be called later the *fong-shuei*). In the end he consults the tortoise, and learns from her whether his calculations are correct.[1]

When the site has been chosen, the founder gives the order to build. For that he waits for the propitious moment, the culmination of the constellation Ting (Pegasus ?) (in the evening ?), that is to say, in the tenth month of the year. It is indeed expedient that the season of rustic labours should be over. Not before then can one begin to build. At the winter solstice the work must be finished. There is a settled order in which one must proceed. The ramparts are first raised : they are the most sacred part of the town. Afterwards the temple of the ancestors (*Miao*) is built. Care is taken to plant trees meanwhile (hazels and chestnuts) whose fruits or berries will be offered to the ancestors, and those trees (pauloconias) which are used to make coffins and sonorous drums.[2] " In ancient times when the plan of the capital was traced, they did not fail to choose the most important rising ground in the kingdom and constitute it the ancestral temple, nor to select trees of the finest growth to make the

---

[1] *She king*, C, 57, 346, 361.
[2] *She king*, C, 57 and 397 ; *Tso chuan*, C, I, 200, and II, 330.

sacred forest." [1] When the walls, the altars and the planta-
tions which are to give sanctity to the town are finished, the
palace and the houses are built.

The dignity of an overlord and of his town are seen by
the ramparts of the city. They are made of beaten earth
when the town does not contain the ancestral temple of the
princely line (*tsong-miao*) : it does not then merit the title
of *tsong :* it is called *Yi*—a small borough. A real town
possesses ramparts of masonry : it may be called *tu*, a capital.[2]
The ramparts were built by forced labour, furnished by the
field-workers. Those who were liable worked to the sound
of a drum, keeping their ranks, under the orders of a noble :
the latter was armed with a staff of office to keep up the
courage of his men and, above all, to suppress ill-omened
talk. The workmen sang as they worked : the discontented
were able to cast ill luck upon the ramparts with a bad verse.[3]
The terrace-makers brought earth in hods : they heaped it
between planks which, resting upon stakes and placed every
one in line, formed a long shell. They rammed the first layer
of earth with care before raising a second.[4] If they had not
laboured conscientiously the rains, digging breaches in the
walls, would have exposed the town to surprise.[5] The most
serious business was the construction of the gates. Girdled
with moats, armed with towers, furnished with portcullises,
they formed a veritable stronghold, a sort of fortification
with redan, which was the chief entrenchment of the defence.
It was upon these that the assailants concentrated their
efforts. They were entrusted to a caretaker who must never
open them before the cocks had crowed to announce the
dawn. The post was given to a tried vassal who was consecrated for his office by a kind of hall-mark : his feet were
cut off. In no case should he desert his trust. For the rest,
the gates were protected by their own sanctity, except from
a determined enemy. They owed their consecration to the
heads of the vanquished which had been duly buried there.
He who brought an excess of sanctity to a gate by his severed
head deserved to be its guardian : the tolls were collected
for his profit.[6] On the towers of the gates the head of the

---

[1] *Mei ti*, 8, and **XVI**, 472.   [2] *Tso chuan*, **C**, II, 494, and I, 198.
[3] *Tso chuan*, **C**, II, 330.   [4] *She king*, **C**, 221.
[5] *Tso chuan*, **C**, II, 472.   [6] *Tso chuan*, **C**, I, 502, 503, and II, 471.

traitor who had hoped to see the enemy obtain an entrance into the town was exposed out of bravado. Also in a spirit of bravado, captured corpses were exposed upon the walls and at the gates were hung trophies, arms taken from a rival chief and also, no doubt, the flags of the conquered, which after a battle in the open country were at once set up at the tent doors. On the other hand, a city knew itself to be conquered when the besieger planted his chief's standard upon its walls. The divinity of the town is lodged in the gates and walls.[1] To the gods of the city were given other dwellings : the Altar of the Soil and the ancestral temple. The Altar of the Soil [2] was formed, like the more humble ramparts, by a simple elevation of beaten earth. This eminence, which was square (for the earth is square, and in principle, the town also) should be covered, so the rituals ordain, with earth of one colour : it is in fact an admission that every fief is held by investiture : this is done *per glebam :* the recipient is given land of a colour conformable to the orientation of his fief : he should make use of it to erect his Altar of the Soil. In fact (as may be seen by a quotation from Mei-ti) the sacred eminence is already in existence, covered with trees, when the city is founded, and it was actually because of it that the site was chosen. The Altars of the Soil are marked by a sacred tree, or, at the least, by a wooden tablet. This tablet, taken (in theory) from a tree whose essence must be in keeping with the orientation of the fief, is the central and divinest portion of the altar. The chief carries it in his baggage when he sets forth to war : before it he sacrifices the vanquished and the guilty. It is stated that in certain countries it was made not of wood but of stone. The tablet, tree, stone, memorial plinth, or stake, seem to have been used in primitive times at the consecration of trophies, men and animals. They were fastened to a post that they might be offered to the gods of the native country. In proportion as the Altar of the Soil remained broken-down and barbarous looking, the Temple of the Ancestors grew in magnificence. Yet in the beginning it was indistinguishable from the wooded hillock which had been chosen to be the heart of the town. Even when it was made a splendid edifice, the trees destined to

[1] *Tso chuan,* **C,** I, 51 and 533, and III, 611.   [2] **XVI,** App., 437 ff.

support it and to cover it were taken from the rising ground enclosed within the walls. The walls were made of clay. All the magnificence lay in the woodwork. " Let us go up to the mountain *King*—the forest of firs and cedars !—Now let us hew and carry—let us square and saw with care !— The rafters of firwood are long—many are the tall pillars." The architect Hi Ssu built at Lu (between 658 and 626 B.C.) a temple which remained famous, for the strength of its columns and the length of its rafters allowed of generous proportions in the halls, which were great and lofty. They aimed at elegant lines in the roofing " like a bird with new plumage." The edges of the roof were curved " like the wings of a pheasant in flight." [1] The wainscoting was richly painted. All this magnificence, however, was not of old date. Conservative men cried scandal when (in 669 B.C.) it was decided to carve the rafters and to paint the pillars red in an ancestral temple at Lu. According to the old regulations, it should have had only a thatched roof.[2] It ought to have been so lightly built as to be destroyed without difficulty when the deceased had no longer right to regular sacrifices. But the lords, when they became heads of large governments, would have liked to possess eternal ancestors. They no longer demolished the temples of distant ancestors. Heaven itself had to undertake this duty by a thunderbolt or by fire.[3] Formerly a humble building of earth was thought sufficient to house the small number of tablets needed to propitiate those who were lately dead—who alone were entitled to receive personal offerings, together with all the ancestors who came, for example, in the form of serpents, two by two, to share in family mourning.[4] As in the case of the gods of the Soil, these wooden tablets were the centre of religious ceremonies. To hold them all one only needed a small stone box, which could be closed and carried in a sack if one was forced to leave one's country.[5] With the tablet of the Soil, the chief bore the tablets of his ancestors to the war. In front of these he bestowed rewards. But positive and negative penalties were dispensed at one and the same ceremony, that of the triumph. The agrarian and ancestral gods ended by

---

[1] *She king*, **C**, 438 and 222.　　[2] *Tso chuan*, **C**, I, 185 and 70.
[3] *Tso chuan*, **C**, III, 615, and I, 293.　[4] *Tso chuan*, **C**, I, 583.
[5] *Tso chuan*, **C**, III, 287 and 719.

sharing attributes which were formerly inseparable. The connexion between them was never entirely lost. In the towns which conformed to the ritual plans, between the Altar of the Soil and the ancestral temple, but close to the latter and screening it, there must be the Altar of a god of the Soil, which was especially terrible and venerated. To this, the triumphal dances led, as a supreme trophy, the chief who had been conquered and was destined for the sacrifice. Now the victim, even if he were sacrificed to the god of the Soil, must be consumed by the Ancestors. There is no doubt that the altar of the Ancestors and the altar of the Soil were formerly one and the same. Perhaps the tablet of the Soil which was later to serve as a screen to the ancestral temple at first formed part of its gateway.[1] It is possible that originally it was identical with the central post of this gateway. There the trophies were consecrated.

Perhaps indeed this sacred post was at first that of the town gate—the sacred wood of the gates (like the Forest of Mulberry-trees at Song) was not less holy than the wooded hillock embraced by the walls—at a time when the city was identical with the dwelling-place of the chief and the latter was still no more than a citadel.

The seigniorial residence is represented (in lyrical writings) as an immense and gorgeous dwelling. " As the successor of ancestors and ancestresses,—I have a palace five thousand feet long—windows to the south—to the setting sun!— There I live, there I dwell,—there I make merry and there I hold council! " [2] And the poet celebrates the court of audience, perfectly level, surrounded by very high columns, halls which are vast and extensive, or else light and brightened by the sun, roofs with flowing lines, and above all, compact walls which cannot be pierced by rats and birds like those of a cottage. It is stated that in 606 there were princely palaces whose walls were decorated with paintings.[3] When, adding greatly to the misconception which already existed, the legends of the cycle of Shou-sin were transformed into historical facts, that king of perdition was credited with a fairy palace whose halls were beautified with ivory and its gates garnished with jade. The very imagination of such

---

[1] LV, 126 ff. [2] *She king*, C, 221.
[3] *Tso chuan*, C, I, 568.

Q

magnificence dates at the earliest from the period of the fighting kingdoms. A few great potentates were then aiming at sumptuousness. In 541 B.C. the Duke of Lu was universally condemned when he deserted the ancient dwelling of his fathers and had a palace built for himself in the style of the palaces of Ch'u. This act was looked upon as a sort of betrayal of the fatherland, an actual treason which would be expiated by an unlucky death : "If the prince does not die at Ch'u he will certainly die in this palace." [1] It is possible that the modes of construction were not everywhere the same. It appears however that in every country the princely residences were usually humble dwellings, quickly built and rapidly demolished. In 502, for example, a highly placed personage had a house of beaten earth made for his son, at the side of his own palace. [2] There was no hesitation in throwing down entire houses to make way for a funeral. [3] An old ritual rule (which is explained by the constitution of the family) required that sons should not have the same abode as their father : fathers and sons resided (in alternate generations) on the right or left of a building which was supposed to have been the house of the founder of their line. The same disposition held good for the chapels of the ancestral Temple which were consecrated to the most recent ancestors. All these ephemeral dwellings, enclosed within low little walls and separated by narrow alleys, were crowded around a sort of fortress. In time of revolts and vendettas (for example at Chin in 549 B.C.) attackers are seen to leap over the low walls. When they have hoisted themselves upon the gate of the palace, they can rain arrows into the prince's chamber : but a fortified tower serves as an entrenchment for the defenders. At Ch'i, in 538 B.C., under a prince famous for his ostentation, the chief minister resides in a low quarter containing the market. He inhabits "a low and narrow house, exposed to the dust." The prince is alone in possessing "a piece of ground which is well lighted, high and dry." Built upon an eminence and flanked by towers, the seigniorial residence looks like a fortified village dominating the low-lying outskirts of a market. [4]

The chief's citadel, as it grew in dimensions, ended by

---

[1] *Tso chuan,* C, II, 565.
[2] *Tso chuan,* C, III, 547.
[3] *Tso chuan,* C, III, 291.
[4] *Tso chuan,* C, II, 293 ; III, 59, 60, and 736.

becoming a town. The city walls enclosed the residences of the great vassal families together with the castle of the overlord. They too possessed their keep, which was surrounded by parapeted walls.[1] The towns, even in the great States, were at first nothing more than a collection of buildings crowded one against the other. Thus the first care of nascent town-life was to guard against the dangers of fire. At Song, which had just been partially burnt down, the owners of large houses were obliged (in 563 B.C.) to rough-cast their walls, and it was agreed to knock down the small dwellings.[2] It was a problem how to obtain a little air, for shops, either private or owned by the overlord, emporiums of archives, arsenals, stables, temples, and harems, were jumbled against each other. From the height of his tower, whence his eye plunged into the little yards of the neighbouring houses, anyone might perceive the wife of a rival, set up an intrigue with her, or even conspire to rob her of her beautiful head of hair.[3] This promiscuity, which is explained by the survival of domestic communism, could last as long as the inhabitants of a town look upon themselves as the members of one family. In 634 B.C., rather than submit to an overlord to whom they did not feel themselves related, we see the inhabitants of Yang-fan choose to expatriate themselves *en bloc*.[4] Nevertheless, the town, when it really deserves the name, is the result of a synœcism, a treaty (*meng*) sworn during the sacrifice of a red bull, by the chiefs of a few families (*sing*) and the overlord to whom they declare themselves infeudated. The overlord and his descendants have the duty of presiding at the city sacrifices : the chiefs of the family provide the victims and are endowed, in return, with hereditary offices.[5] Henceforth the town begins to be distinguished from the citadel. It is divided into quarters which have their chiefs who are themselves placed under the authority of the chief of the district of the left or of the right. These latter are also the chiefs of the legions of the left or right. The central legion is known to have been that of the prince. The organization of the city is tributary, like that of the army. The town tends to imitate the arrangement of the camps,—which is

[1] *Tso chuan*, C, II, 496, and III, 713. [2] *Tso chuan*, C, III, 613, and II, 233.
[3] *Tso chuan*, C, I, 486, and III, 737. [4] *Tso chuan*, C, I, 371.
[5] *Tso chuan*, C, II, 265.

itself indistinguishable from that of husbandry,—the fields are cultivated in squares. The square town is pierced with straight avenues which end at the chief gates. Towns of this type make their appearance as new establishments. They are built after an exodus or a conquest. They appear to be cities of the plain, the antithesis of citadels. They are built on ground which has scarcely been tamed for human habitation, where water still rises to the surface.[1] Taken as a whole, they must date from the era of the first great clearings. They seem to have been built in the marches which had been won from nature and the Barbarians. In the seventh century the progress made in subduing the soil was not yet accompanied by a sufficient increase in population to people the walled cities which were being built in great numbers to break the onslaught of the Barbarians. These cities of refuge were surrounded by a double ring of walls : they were agricultural and military, permanent camps built to house the warriors and in case of need to shelter the entire population of husbandmen. One wall was properly speaking the city wall (*kuo*) the other surrounded the suburbs, that is to say, all the cultivated fields and the whole country (*Kuo*).[2] But the cultivated fields extended into the town, which must be able to feed itself in case of siege. To high-perched, cramped and ungainly citadels succeeded spacious and airy cities whose architecture may have been rectilinear and which were built by the line.[3] But, just as a mercantile suburb had clung to the walls at the foot of the citadel, so, at the cross roads which lead from the gates of the square town of the plains, suburbs arise which are reserved for merchants and artisans.[4] The town, agricultural and military, is also a centre of exchange. A synœcism of a peculiar kind presides over the constitution of these new cities. When he has cleared the brushwood and wishes to found a town the overlord joins himself to a merchant. Each, for himself and for his descendants, takes the oath (*meng*) of a treaty of alliance (*sin*). The merchants will not rebel against the lordly authority, but the chief will buy nothing from them by force. " If they profit by the sale of precious objects " the overlord " will know nothing of it." From that time, the power of the provost

---

[1] *She king*, **C**, 327, 362, and *Tso chuan*, **C**, II, 233.
[2] *Tso chuan*, **C**, II, 549.   [3] *She king*, **C**, 328.   [4] *Tso chuan*, **C**, I, 197.

of the merchants grows side by side with the power of the prince.[1] Artisans and dealers ply their trade by hereditary right. The provost at their head keeps his office from father to son, but he receives his investiture from the prince.[2] It is his right and duty to take part in the embassies sent by the overlord to the neighbouring courts. But, in time of war, merchants and artisans are not, like the labourers, expected to take arms under the leadership of the overlord, and it is evident (for example at Wei, in 502 B.C.) that the nobles and their chiefs are obliged to bargain with them to induce them to join in their military undertakings.[3] The men of the corporations grouped together in the suburbs, are not, like the peasants who remain in the hamlets, bound by a complete solidarity to the warriors living in the town.

Sheltered behind the sacred ramparts of the city, the overlord and his followers live nobly together. In the ideal town (conforming to the ritual plan) the seigniorial residence rises in the exact centre. Square like the town, and surrounded by walls, it is a town in itself. Its walls must be very high, its gate beautiful and majestic. On the flat ground its one-storeyed buildings spread far abroad, perched on high terraces. Its plan was made with the line. Each building had its assigned place. In the centre, the hall of audiences opens upon an avenue, which, passing between the altar of the Soil and the ancestral Temple, runs direct to the gate of the South. By this avenue arrives the procession of vassals whose homage the prince receives with his face to the south. Like the princely residence, the dwellings of the great families are each a town in themselves, a town grouped around the great hall where the chief of the family receives the homage of his relatives, turning towards the south. And inside all the little walled towns which make up the city, more walls are raised to enclose the dwelling of each chief of a small domestic group. For each son of the family, as soon as he marries, must possess a hall of reception beyond his enclosed courtyard. This edifice is always conceived in the same style. At the back is a wall pierced with little doors. Through them one enters the long and narrow rooms which are entirely shut in by walls : these are the living rooms. To right and left two lateral buildings project as far as the courtyard. Closed

---

[1] *Tso chuan*, C, III, 267.   [2] *Tso chuan*, C, II, 239.   [3] *Tso chuan*, C, III, 543.

in by the wall at the back and by those of the lateral buildings, sheltered by a great roof, whose central beam rests on two isolated columns, the hall of reception is entirely open towards the south and forms a kind of elevated verandah reached from the courtyard by two staircases at the corners. That on the east is reserved for the master of the house, who, taking his stand a little behind the steps, does the honours of his house with his face to the east, like a prince. The chief of the smallest domestic group has an altar to the Ancestors and a god of the Soil in his home. The gate which leads to his court of honour is not less sacred than one of the town gates. In his own home he is a master and a chief. But when he is received by the chief of the family or the master of the city, he must, when he presents himself in the court of the latter, stand at the foot of the steps, with his face to the north, in the posture of a vassal. In the great city each of the special dwellings is not a building set apart in a castle, or a house attached to intermediate houses, but a seigniorial residence. And all these residences are towns complete in themselves. They are all enclosed, however, within the seigniorial walls. In the same way, their various owners are united by the bond of dependence upon the common overlord, the master of the city and of its walls. Formerly, when the Founder had finished building the ramparts, when he had distributed dwellings to right and left, and set up his great hall for himself, he called together all the chiefs of the families which were bound to him by oath and whom " he assembled to obtain glory." He set mats and stools for them. He offered them a great banquet as an initial communion. " He had a pig chosen for the sacrifice—he poured wine into the calabashes—he made them eat and he made them drink :— Lord of vassals. Chief of the family ! " Whilst before the master, all " bore themselves with deference and gravity." [1] Court life, the life of the nobility, was inaugurated.

[1] *She king*, C, 362.

CHAPTER II

THE OVERLORD

ACCORDING to the theories elaborated late in the day by the feudalists, the overlord is he who, having received the investiture of the king, the sole master of the whole country of China, is charged with the government of a fief. He governs it in the name of the Son of Heaven, enforcing the regulations laid down by him. In every fief the seigniorial authority belongs to one family. Nevertheless, at the death of the holder of the position, his successor only assumes the emblems of his dignity after having received the king's investiture.[1] As sovereign of all the overlords of China, the king wears a dozen symbolical emblems upon his robes. The three first (sun, moon and constellation) are strictly reserved to him alone. The right of wearing others (or rather a certain number of them) is granted to the various invested overlords. The number of emblems allotted to each varies with the quality of the investiture. This determines the rank which he holds in the feudal hierarchy. The overlords form five classes (dukes, marquises, counts, viscounts, barons), the extent of their fiefs varying (according to the theory) in proportion to their title. The domain proper of the Son of Heaven measures one thousand *li* in length and in breadth. One hundred *li* are the measure of the domain of a duke or marquis, fifty *li* that of the fief of a viscount or baron.[2] A smaller domain is still a fief, but it is not held directly from the king (at any rate in his capacity as king). Its titular owner is the vassal of the master of a particular domain. The overlords and the king distribute not only the hereditary fief of the domain, but also its offices or fief salaries. The titular holders of salaries belonging to the fief are divided into five classes and bear the title of grand-officers (*t'ai fu*) or officers (*she*). Originally these titles, like all feudal titles,

---

[1] *Li ki*, **C**, I, 328.   [2] *Li ki*, **C**, I, 264 ff.

had a military signification : all implied the idea of command. Each of them came in the end to correspond to a settled rank, and then to a degree of the feudal hierarchy. The word *officer* (*she*) denoting the lowest order of nobility, acquired the general sense of noble. The word duke (like the word *prince*) is a title applicable to every overlord, at any rate within his own lordship. Each one is master in his own house. The feudalists, however, credit the king with the right of promoting or degrading the overlords according to their merits.[1] These merits are displayed in the careful maintenance of the altars of the Soil and of the Ancestors, and in the suitable enforcement of the royal edicts relating to morals, to music, to measurements, and to clothes. Nominations and promotions (by the king and the princes) must be made in Council and after a debate requiring the agreement of the vassals. Punishments (or at any rate, the most serious punishment : banishment or death) must be proclaimed on the public square and submitted to the approval of the whole people.[2] The constitutional theory implies the idea that authority is only retained through an investiture granted by a sovereign and the consent of vassals and subjects. The king-sovereign himself holds his throne at once from Heaven and from the people. It is his mission to maintain an order of civilization whose worth is appraised by the help of natural signs and the sentiments of men. He wields his authority from above, delegating to the various feudatories authority of a lower order but the same nature. The overlords, attached by their genealogy to the reigning dynasty or to one still more ancient, are only qualified to rule in their fief by virtue of an investiture received in past times by an ancestor and confirmed at every succession.

As a matter of fact, if the annalistic documents *seem* to show that, during the period *Ch'un ch'iu*, the overlords when they succeeded to power invariably asked for the royal investiture, this was of no advantage beyond fixing their place in a hierarchy which was much more fluid and singularly less well-ordered than orthodox traditions admit. Contrary to the assertions of feudalists who were inspired by an administrative conception and a lofty and original idea of the central power, it is certain that the foundation of the

---

[1] *Li ki*, C, I, 276.   [2] *Li ki*, C, I, 274.

seigniorial authority is to be sought elsewhere than in the investiture of the sovereign. The word (*ming*) which signifies *investiture* and *commission* is identical with the word (*ming*) which means *destiny* and is the same as the word *ming* which means *name*.[1] The name expresses the being, and makes the *destiny*,[2] so that any man born a Prince will become a stable-boy if he has been given the name of " Ostler " while it is impossible that another should fail, who has been called " He will succeed." Furthermore, a child predestined to the name of Yü, who bears on his hand at birth the signs which make the character Yü, will come into possession of the fief of Yu,[3] *even in spite of the royal will.* Family names, connected with the soil, were held from ancestors : personal names were given after a trial of the voice (the voice is the soul and also the name) but also after a consultation with the ancestors. Authority, like the name, is derived from the ancestors, and every special act of authority must be pre-ceded by a consultation of their will. An overlord has the right to act only upon a *commission* from his ancestors. As a matter of fact, his *destiny* and that of his race are strictly dependent upon the Virtue of its founders. It is indistinguish-able from a sort of destiny, with a settled quantity of power whose value is fixed by this same Virtue. Shun, a perfect sovereign, who lived for one hundred years, transmitted to his descendants the power of offering seigniorial sacrifices : an enemy who wished to exterminate the race of Shun before its allotted number of princely generations was exhausted, could not by any possibility succeed.[4] No human endeavour has the power to shorten the duration of a family destiny. As long as the family retains a stock of virtue, it cannot be torn from the land in which this virtue has taken root. The *destiny* of a race is in fact bound up with a certain country, a capital, or a Holy Place. It corresponds with the possession of genealogies, legends, dances, religious privileges, talismans and jewels. In short, it corresponds with a collection of emblems and powers indicative of a certain specific genius, whilst the emblems conferred by the investiture of the sovereign indicate only a dignity and a rank.

[1] On the import of the word *Ming* see a different interpretation in Maspero, **XCVII.**
[2] **LV**, 159, note 2.　　　　[3] SMC, IV, 250, and *Tso chuan*, **C**, I, 317.
[4] SMC, IV, 179.

The sovereign when he gives the investiture (*ming*) confirms a decree (*ming*) of Heaven : this has first " *opened the
way.*" *Way* is a translation of the word *tao*. This word is one
of the richest in the old Chinese language. In the language
peculiar to the old *Taoist* philosophers, it denotes a certain
power of realization, which, whether it remains indistinguishable from the efficacious principle of all things (often called
the *Tao*) or whether it animates a distinct individuality,
never ceases to be entire and the same in itself.[1] In ordinary
language, the word *tao* had less force. It was most frequently
employed in combination with the word *tô*. *Tô* and *tao*
correspond to twin ideas which are nevertheless opposed to
each other. They denote the two aspects of an efficacious
power, *tao* indicating pure efficacy, concentrated, so to speak,
and quite indeterminate, while *tô* describes the same efficacy
in the act of spending itself and becoming particularized.
The word *tô* denotes, for example, the kind of genius which
is acquired (together with a *name*) by living in a specified
country : this genius is itself the qualification for commanding there as a master.[2] Used independently or in
conjunction, *tao* and *tô* express the joint ideas of authority
and of power, of efficacy, force and fortune. The expression
tao—tô can scarcely be translated except by the word *Virtue*.
Virtue, the *tao—tô* conceived as an animating force of universal
essence even when it resides in an individual, is the characteristic of a Chief whose way (*tao*) is opened by Heaven and
who is invested by it (*ming*) with a specific genius (*tô*) while
it bestows upon him the destiny (*ming*) suitable for an overlord. The overlord is, if I may so put it, the sole and
universally powerful spring of action in the country over
which his specific genius destines him to rule. There he
commands nature and men, or rather he causes nature and
men to be what they are. He dispenses to men and things
their destiny. He gives them a certain potency of being
which is the measure of his own power. The formula must
be taken literally : like overlord, like subjects, like prince,
like country. Rushes and chrysanthemums grow thick-set
and vigorous when the princely genius is in full strength.
Does it decline, is it exhausted ? the people of the country
die off prematurely. Millet thrives and has no lack : men

[1] **LIV**, 143 ff.   [2] **LII**, 197.

and women vassals increase and multiply, the plantain yields thousands of seeds, or else harvests fail upon the exhausted soil, men refuse to marry, the ground crumbles, the wells dry up, the stars fall—according as the virtue of the seigniorial race is decadent or vigorous, powerful or exhausted.[1] The *tao—tô* of the Chief is the principle of all success. It is the luck of the fief. The fortune of all things, the morals of men, depend upon it, upon it alone. Orthodox theorists (who are moralists and have scarcely any thought but for humanity) believe that this dominating action of the prince may be explained by imitation : the prince is a model for the whole country, he teaches while he acts. As a matter of fact, the princely genius is of a religious and magic nature. This genius rules and regulates all things by immediate action, the action of spirit upon spirit. It acts by contagion. " The prince's thought is boundless in extent :—he thinks of horses, and they are strong ! . . . The prince's thought is tireless : he thinks of horses and they break into a gallop. . . . The prince's thought is quite correct : he thinks of horses and they run straight." [2] The overlord draws his power from a mystic force which is in him in a concentrated form, but which, diffused, animates his whole country. The genius of the country exists in its entirety in the overlord. The latter in fact, strengthens his authority and lays its mystical foundations while sharing most intimately in the life of his domain. In his fief, it is he who profits by all and suffers for all. His entire life is spent in relation to the group which he aspires to govern, which is a human and natural group. He devotes himself to the country and acts as its scapegoat on every occasion. He pays for the crimes, the successes, the mournings, the disasters, the victories, the favours, the severities of the weather, the good harvest or the bad year, the least good and the least ill fortunes, fortune of things and of people. He neutralizes the dangerous side of every event : he releases its fortunate side. He takes upon himself the misfortunes of each, and embodies in himself the fortune desired by all. He incurs all the risks. He assimilates the luck of the whole community. Every spring he first breaks open the ground : he first tastes the fruits of every harvest. The seigniorial tasting, the princely ploughing, remove the ban for the

[1] LII, 79.   [2] *She king*, C, 447.

profit of all, from the earth which had returned to its virgin state, and from the first fruits which it was still forbidden to gather. But the whole success of the work is ascribed to the overlord, as the entire substance of things is in the first fruits which he consumes. When any vassal dies, and when, for all men, "the corpse is still nothing but an object of horror," the prince, first of them all, embraces the dead man, clasping him to his heart. At the end of the mourning which was inaugurated by this sign of devotion, the dead man's family may have gained an ancestor, for he has gone to swell the train of princely ancestors, to augment their prestige and that of the overlord. The warriors have taken to flight, the army is defeated : the chief mortifies his body, is troubled in spirit and eats gall. When he has eaten the gall, courage re-awakes in the soldiers and the seigniorial territory gains in the end.[1] The conquered enemy humbles himself : good fortune should be met with fear and trembling. Success would be short-lived if the conqueror on his side did not know how to be humble. The army accomplished less, when it won the battle, than the prince when "he mourns and sighs" and secures victory to his country by confessing his own unworthiness.[2] If, in time of drought, he confesses his faults, if he lays the blame upon his lack of virtue, if he calls down celestial chastisement upon himself alone, as soon as the ordeal has been surmounted, as soon as Heaven is reduced to repentance by the princely contrition, the overlord will have the right to call himself the sole author of the natural order. When, clothing himself in mourning, depriving himself of music, abstaining from food, lamenting for three days, he expiates the crumbling of a hill, the crime committed by a parricidal subject, the loss of territory, the disaster of a fire, when he claims for himself alone the impurity left by a crime or revealed by a misfortune, and when, in the end, he purges it with the aid of privations and lustrations, his penitence, which purifies his country and his subjects together clothes himself with purity, re-born, shining and august.[3] His sanctity is asserted when he wipes out evils and lifts tabus. He spends himself for the profit of all, but the daily sacrifice which he makes of himself feeds the holy force in him which he received from his ancestors. Like theirs,

---

[1] SMC, IV, 424.   [2] SMC, IV, 304   [3] *Tso chuan*, C, II, 50.

expiation and devotion are the foundation and principle of his authority. It is even supposed to have its historic origin in a famous expiation : the foundation of princely power was accompanied by a heroic and complete sacrifice, that of the Great Ancestor, who, by the sacrifice of his body and soul, allied his race to a Holy Place.

But the overlord is not related to his country solely by a life of sacrifice. He succeeds in infeudating it to himself thanks to a system of positive hallowings. He causes all its beneficent influences to converge upon himself. He assimilates them, and thus creates for himself a princely soul. His capital is a centre which aims at being the centre of the world,—the ideal would be, that at noon on midsummer day the hand of the sun-dial would cast no shade—but it must at the least be a climatic centre. " There, Heaven and Earth are united : there, the four seasons are at one : there wind and rain meet together : there, the *Yin* and the *Yang* are in harmony." [1] The overlord lives at the heart of the region, in a place of convergence and union. When he holds a reception and stands with his face to the south, the luminous principle (*Yang*) clothes him with all its brightness. He can also capture the energy of the *Yang*, if he has a high tower and climbs to the top of it. Living in a vast and lofty chamber, he will assimilate the energy of the *Yin*. But he has no need of a splendid palace : simply by exposing his body in turn to the sun (*yang*) and to the dew (*yin*), the overlord can nourish its substance with the constituent forces of the universe. When he is nourished by them, his country is also fed, through his intermediation. His benevolence extends over all things. Like a dew falling upon the plants in the fields, it waters the whole. But everything is also warmed by it, for it acts in addition like gentle sunshine dispersing the excess of dew.[2] At the beginning of spring the prince is careful by breaking and collecting the ice to remove " the barriers set up by the frost " against the reign of the principles of warmth. He keeps it in a deep ice-house which is opened with infinite precautions. Thus he prevents the

---

[1] *Chou li*, **VII**, vol. I, 201, and SMC, I, 243 and 247. A good capital is one round which the measurements of distance " remain constant," that is to say, which is in the centre of pure Space.

[2] *She king*, **C**, 196.

cold from escaping during the summer. He prevents it from going to call forth the devastating hail to clash with the adverse forces whose time it is to rule. But at the same time, he preserves the principle of the cold, whose reign must one day return. And he is also able, by eating and distributing the ice, to temper the excess of heat for himself and his people. Thus he secures for his country, his men and first of all for himself, an even distribution of the forces which sustain the life of the world. Henceforth, there can no more be " unseasonable warmth in winter, nor destructive cold in summer, nor icy wind in spring, nor disastrous rain in autumn . . . and no one again will perish of a premature death." [1] In the first place, the overlord must watch over his own health. His health is that of the country. Nothing is of more importance than his manner of feeding. " Let the prince alone have costly food ! " A prince is fed upon essences. By extracting these essences from things at their proper times his diet is so regulated as to embody in him a collection of specific qualities, each suitable to a season, and each also indicative of an orientation. Thus he acquires the soul of a Chieftain : a virtue which is efficacious at every time and in every direction. He makes the flocks increase in the territory, he makes the fruits of the earth to prosper, when he is careful in spring to eat mutton (an animal of the East) and wheat, in summer beans and fowl (South), in autumn dog (East) and oleaginous grain, in winter millet and pork (North).[2]

But if he is a chief who is not perfect, if he forgets proportion (*tsieh*), if he despises harmony (*ho*), if he cannot combine in himself " the bitter, the acid, the salt and the sweet," if above all he compromises the male vigour (*yang*) which is in him, by a thoughtless approach to women (who are *yin*) he will become the victim of *ku*—which is the penalty of all excess, the harmful result of improper tabus, misfortune and sickness (more powerful the greater the soul) maleficence in its full force.[3] And if he is a criminal and unworthy lord, he will no longer be able even to endure the obligatory tabus which give vigour and virtue to the just man, but for him will be turned into deadly poison. Prince King of Chin, who exceeding his authority wished totally to wipe out one of the

---

[1] *Tso chuan*, **C**, III, 71.   [2] *Li ki*, **C**, I, 332 ff. ; I, 641 ; *Tso chuan*, **C**, III, 37
[3] *Tso chuan*, **C**, II, 85.

families of his lordship, was told by a soothsayer that he would not be able to eat new wheat. When the season had come, and he had to eat it, " his belly immediately swelled : he retired to relieve himself, fell down and died." On the other hand, a good prince " brings peace to his heart " by eating broth which is a mixture of " water, fire, vinegar, minced meat, salt, plums, and raw fish." " The head-cook harmonizes (all these ingredients) determining the proportions according to their odours," adding what is lacking to certain foods, modifying what is too much in others. Thanks to these precautions, the overlord avoids the evils which would render him incapable of " keeping guard over the altars of the Soil and of the Harvests." [1]

The altar of the Soil, a simple square of earth contained (?) within the princely residence, holds in itself all the virtue (*tao*) of the seigniorial land.[2] It is identical with the father-land. The fatherland ceases to exist when this altar is turned into a morass. All vassals, and the prince first of all, should be willing to die in its defence. But vassals are not obliged to die for the prince except in cases when he by living as a true overlord has identified his soul with that of the fatherland. The altar of the Soil is duplicated by an altar of Harvests.[3] Chief of warriors and master of labourers, the overlord ensures the survival of the fatherland and the subsistence of its inhabitants, when, with all the forces of a great, complete and well-balanced soul he secures a fortunate succession of harvests for the country. The weather will perform its tasks in rightful order, the ground will give abundant fruit if the overlord, from the midst of his town, has been able to share in the rhythm of the seasons and of the produce of the fields. For this reason an urban god of Harvests appertaining to the overlord suffices to make the fields fruitful.[4] The overlord enriches his territory by his sacred labours. On the other hand, the whole territory contributes to enrich the soul of the overlord. He draws an abundant supply of virtues from the fields and their produce. He draws others, not less abundant, from the hunting and fishing grounds, from the distant marches where he owns reserves of game and nurseries. He is an " eater of meats." While the soul of the peasants,

---

[1] *Tso chuan*, **C**, III, 325. [2] *Tso chuan*, **C**, III, 38 and 325.
[3] *Li ki*, **C**, I, 587. [4] **LIV**, 68 ff.

meagrely nourished on fruit and grain, has not the strength
to pass through death, and returns to matter, mingling at
its last breath with the powers of the soil and of germination,
the soul of the overlord, " which has become vigorous through
the use of a multitude of essences of creatures " is able to
acquire " an essential robustness " which enables it to sur-
mount death and to live on in the state of a " spiritual being "
(*shen ming*).[1] A man or woman of the common people loses
all individual existence when he dies at the natural end of
life. Death, if it should come while a supply of breath still
remains to them, with this short-lived breath sets free a soul,
whose puny strength only suffices for the acting of a few evil
tricks. It is very different with a lordly soul. Strictly
speaking, the overlords alone have a soul in the true sense
of the word. This is a soul which old age cannot wither. It
only enriches it. The overlord prepares for death by gorging
himself with savoury meats and life-giving drinks. He eats
" fish richly fried," he drinks wine mingled with pepper
which " sustains the strength of old men with bushy eyebrows." In the course of his life, he has assimilated quantities
of essences. The vaster and richer his domain, the more he
will have assimilated. He has added to the substance bequeathed him by his ancestors, rich as that was, since they
themselves were overlords full-fed with meat and venison.
When he dies, his soul, far from melting away like a soul
of the vulgar, escapes full of vigour from the body. Instead
of being dissolved and mingling with the indistinguishable
forces of the parent soil, it may take possession of the bodies
of those animals who are a noble quarry : the bear or the
boar.[2] It will be of fierce nature if the overlord was an
intemperate being, and if he suffered the premature death
which he deserved in that case. But if the chief has led
according to rule the life of an overlord, if, at the end of a
long career, he died in his own country, his town, his palace,
his chamber, according to the rites, his soul, further ennobled
and purified by the expiations of mourning, possesses after
death an authority which is venerable and serene. It
possesses the beneficent power of a tutelary genius, while
preserving a lasting and sacred personality. It is the soul of
an ancestor.

[1] *Tso chuan*, **C**, III, 142 ; **LV**, 18.   [2] *Tso chuan*, **C**, I, 143, and III, 138.

Worship will be paid to it in a temple situated not far from the altars of the Soil and of Harvests. Seasonable ceremonies will enable it to share the life of nature and the life of the country. Its festival is held in spring when the ground is wet with dew, and in autumn when it is white with hoar-frost.[1] It eats when the hunting has been good. It fasts when there is a poor harvest. The ancestral soul subsists and endures, fed upon grain gathered in the sacred harvest-field of the overlord, upon meats brought from the parks of his domain and prepared in the princely kitchen, upon game killed in the marches and dedicated by the hunters at the altar of the Soil. But, however rich in personality a chief's soul may be, a moment comes when this personality is scattered and extinguished. At the end of a few generations, the tablet to which this soul has been attached by appropriate rites, ceases to have the right to an individual sanctuary. Like the tablets of more ancient ancestors whose memory has already vanished it is relegated to a stone coffer kept in a hall dedicated to the most ancient ancestor. The ancestor which it represented and whose name it bore is no longer fed like an overlord and as a tutelary genius possessed of a strong and distinct individuality. His career is over, his rôle as an ancestor is played out. Through the worship paid to him he has escaped for long years the fate of the plebeian dead. At last he too joins the multitude of impersonal and indistinguishable forces which is the joint destiny of the fief and of the princely race. Like the nameless powers of the Soil, he is now nourished with raw meat alone. He has been re-absorbed into the stock of holy things which are the universal soul of the country, but to the overlord he appears in the guise of a First Ancestor with the mythical traits of a Founder Hero. To him he ascribes all the merits of an inventor and a demiurge. By subduing the ground, harnessing the waters, conquering the fire, expelling monsters, clearing the arable land, producing new cereals, domesticating horses, the Great Ancestor gave proof of a virtue (tö) which was inherited by his race and endowed them with their emblems, their fief, their name, their destiny. Official history, on the other hand, represents this ancestor as a deserving vassal who received a title from his sovereign. As the heir of an heroic ancestor,

[1] *Li ki*, C, II, 270.

whose glory, sung in the sacred hymns of the family, is reflected upon himself, the master of the altars of the Soil (many founders are called gods of the Soil or gods of Harvest), the possessor of a temple where seasonal ceremonies revive the vigorous personality of his immediate ancestors, the overlord is clothed with a sanctity which imposes a formidable etiquette upon his followers as well as upon himself.

The august force which informs the chief is a mystical force whose tension is extreme and which is strangely contagious. As a rule, it acts by simple radiation, but to this end it must be kept concentrated and pure. On exceptional occasions it must operate with its full vigour, and for this reason it is advisable to preserve it from any diminution through lapse of time. The overlord leads an isolated and passive life in the midst of his court. The vassals " form a barrier." They protect their master from any contaminating approach. They act in the chief's stead, enhancing a prestige which is preserved intact. The court labours to keep the overlord in a sort of splendid quarantine radiating glory.

Strictly understood, the overlord is the man to whom no one speaks, even in the third person. " His servants " only are spoken to, so that the expression " (those who are) *at the foot of the steps* (of the throne, and to whom alone I dare address myself) " ended by signifying " Your Majesty " in imperial China.[1] One does not speak to the overlord, one speaks in his presence, and when one offers him advice *indirectly*, it must be done " in a *round-about* manner." [2] The breath of a vile voice must not come to sully the princely purity : the sanctity of the chieftain must not be exposed to the insult of a reproof or of a direct counsel, no matter how just : for they come from beneath. " To look fixedly over the head, is arrogant : to look below the girdle is to show vexation : to look sideways is to display evil sentiments." The eyes of the vassal may not be fixed on the prince " higher than the point of the chin," but they must always be directed straight upon him.[3] Every one must let himself be directly penetrated by the virtue which illuminates the eyes of the Chief. No one would dare to endure its brightness. The most exact discretion is imposed upon a prince's servants. An officer, in his master's presence, must " stand with body

---

[1] *Tso chuan*, C, II, 206.   [2] *Li ki*, C, I, 96.   [3] *Li ki*, C, I, 104.

bent, the ends of his sash hanging to the ground, his feet seeming to tread upon the hem of his garment. The chin must be stretched out like the gargoyles on a roof : the hands must be clasped together, as low as possible." The scribe who in the prince's presence should dare " to shake the dust off his books " or simply " to arrange them," the soothsayer who " should hold the sprigs of yarrow upside down " or who " should lie down beside the tortoise-shell " would deserve chastisement.[1] Where the prince is to live, all must be order and cleanliness. His most intimate vassals (the grand officers) never fail to wash their hands five times a day. Before appearing in the master's presence, " they purify themselves by severe abstinence : they do not enter the women's apartments : they wash their hair and body." [2] He who offers ready prepared meats to the Overlord is careful to arm himself " with plants of bitter taste, the branch of a peach-tree, and a besom of rushes." [3] The bad influences which he in his unworthiness cannot fail to bring with him may thus be deflected from the food which is destined to enter the sacred substance of the Chief.

The prince, sheltered from every contamination which might come to sully his holiness by a court governed by a meticulous etiquette, himself submits to an etiquette which is even more minutely regulated. He lives surrounded by his whole court, and each of his followers must at the least breach recall him to order. Annalists are there to note down his slightest gestures, his most trifling words. He lives under the menace of history. Coming from an overlord, the most futile action is weighed with incalculable consequences. A chief may neither play nor jest : what he has done, is done, what he has said, is said.[4] He must hear nothing but strictly regulated music : he must carry himself exactly upright : he must seat himself correctly only upon a mat which has been correctly arranged : he must only eat meals which have been put together according to rule : he may only walk with an exactly measured step. Circumspection is his first duty. In circumstances when a simple noble takes a stride of two feet, and a grand-officer of one, the length of the overlord's stride must not exceed six inches.[5] Whilst his followers,

[1] Li ki, C, I, 704 and 76. [2] Li ki, C, I, 685. [3] Li ki, C, I, 715.
[4] SMC, IV, 251 [5] Li ki, C, I, 719.

inspired in his presence by the greatness of the princely service, make haste and hurry, and seem to fly " walking with their elbows spread out like the wings of a bird," the master, condemned by his prestige to an inert gravity, must remain immovable, inactive and almost dumb.[1]

The Chief in Council confines himself to saying " Yes," but this princely " Yes " is a decree which controls destiny, and if the prince, when he speaks, can only express himself with the help of consecrated formulas, history shows that the fortune of States was altered because at a certain date a certain chief had chosen to designate himself by one of the personal pronouns permitted to an overlord, which on that occasion happened to be suitable or unsuitable.[2] Song deserved to become prosperous because in a time of flood its prince in reply to condolences had the happy idea of using the expression " little orphan " to denote himself, rather than the formula " man of small virtue " : but (a significant fact) it was not the prince who himself made this choice : he was obeying one of his counsellors.

The elusive and fugitive virtue of the chief only dwells in him when it is preserved by the life of the court and by etiquette. Imprisoned by the court, bound by etiquette, the overlord reigns only on condition of remaining passive, of ordering nothing in detail, and of not directing an administration. He acts only through the simple efficacy of his prestige. The real activity is carried on by the vassals. Princely power is founded upon the possession of a Virtue of religious and magical essence. It is less a power of command than a power of inspiration. The overlord is the chief of a hierarchy and not a Chief of State.

[1] *Li ki*, C, I, 720.   [2] *Tso chuan*, C, I, 153.

CHAPTER III

PUBLIC LIFE

THE overlord presides over the Court of the Vassals and sends them to war. The two great obligations of a vassal are counsel and service. As a result of court life the nobles' code of morality assumed a refined character. It was formed in the life of the camp. Military order lies at the foundation of civil order.

I

THE NOBLES IN THE ARMY

The predominance of the military order is shown by a significant rule. The census of inhabitants by which the ranks and tribute of land and men are determined, is a military undertaking. Precisely on this account it appears a formidable and almost sinister task. It decides the fate of the country. Only a prince who is too much enamoured of war, dreams of himself undertaking a numbering of the people, which is equivalent to a brutal snatching at command and possession. The responsibility for so bold an act should normally be left to a man whose life has been devoted to war. The minister of war (" that is the proper thing ") [1] is charged with fixing the rate of contributions, and counting coats-of-mail and arms. To this end, he enters in a register the account of arable land, of mountain forests, of marshes and lakes, hills and hillocks, low-lying or salt land, flooded marches, and weirs. He partitions the level ground which is contained within dikes, and makes a new allotment of pasture-land and ground which can be cultivated. He then decides upon the contributions which must be made. He fixes the number of chariots and horses as well as the number of warriors mounted in chariots, of foot-soldiers who escort them, of coats-of-mail and of

[1] *Tso chuan*, **C,** II, 439.

shields. The operations of the property-register and of the census are interchangeable. Military duty has a bearing upon land as well as upon men. It seems to be incumbent upon men in proportion to the land which they hold in direct ratio to its nature and value. Husbandmen furnish the army with foot-soldiers only. Vassals who possess a domain comprising hunting- and pasture-grounds, must equip a settled number of chariots of war. This number gives the measure of their fief and of their dignity.

The act of numbering the people devotes the country to war. This act of bravado which undertakes to force the hand of fate must be counterbalanced by a gesture of moderation. The taking of the census is accompanied by liberal and expiatory measures. The most characteristic is an amnesty. " When the great census had been taken, the debtors were set free, alms were given to widows and to the poor : the guilty were pardoned : the army had its full complement." [1]

The army is composed, on the one hand, of men to whom some punishment was remitted on condition that they devoted themselves to the works of death, and, on the other hand, of vassals who are warriors by birth and are bound to the chief by perfect loyalty. As soon as the army is assembled the arsenals are opened and arms are distributed. In theory, the arms belong to the overlord in whose keeping they are, carefully shut up—and this not as a simple police precaution : arms exhale a dangerous virtue.[2] They are not assumed until a period of abstinence has prepared men for this formidable contact.[3] Fasting takes place in the ancestral temple and such an emotion is aroused by it as induces the conviction of communion with the ancestors. Presentiments received during the vigil of arms seem to forecast the fortune of the campaign. He who then feels his heart unquiet knows that he is destined to death. A bloody unction clothes the armies with new power. The chief performs a sacrifice. The armed bands gather round the hillock of the Soil. The gods of the highways are first propitiated, and then the army takes the road.

The foot-soldiers are poorly armed. They act as trench-makers and valets. They go " without hope of return,"

---

[1] *Tso chuan*, **C**, II, 29–30 and 241.   [2] *Tso chuan*, **C**, II, 412
[3] *Tso chuan*, **C**, I, 133.

marching and camping full of fear, on the edges of the woods. All their time is taken up with the care of the horses, which they feed, like themselves, upon sow-thistles. Overjoyed to reach a halting-place, they congratulate themselves that they are not yet dead, bent under the weight of baggage, hustled about, groaning in a spiritless voice—gagged as soon as they are formed into ranks.[1] The nobles set out, mounted in their chariots of war, calm and playing upon the lute. Their chariots, which are short and narrow, are formed by a box open at the back and mounted on two wheels.[2] In front is a curved coach-pole to which two shaft-horses are fastened : on each side two outside horses are kept at a distance by side-straps. The four chariot horses are provided with bits to which two little bells are fixed. The reins are attached to these bits : the inner reins of the two outside horses are fastened behind to two rings placed right and left of the board which forms the front of the chariot : the other six reins are held by the driver. He stands in the centre of the chariot.[3] On each side, balancing each other, stand an archer on the left (the place of honour) and a lancer on the right. The horses are armoured, and often caparisoned with the skins of wild beasts. The three men of the equipage wear a leather jerkin made of one or more bullock (or rhinoceros ?) skins. These cuirasses are glazed with varnish. In front of the chariot, protecting all the warriors, are placed three shields of light wood. The archer keeps two bows at hand in the same quiver, unbent, and tied to a brace of bamboo that they may not get out of shape. Within reach of the lancer stand several weapons with long handles which end in hooks or tridents of metal. They are used for piercing and above all for hooking and pulling down the warriors from the enemy chariots, after which they are slain on the ground or taken prisoner. On the way, the men-at-arms repose, sitting upon a double mat or on a tiger skin spread in the body of the chariot. Standards float over them. The cuirasses of the warriors are covered with ribands or with silk.[4] Varnish shines upon them. The archers have finger-shields of ivory. The tip of the bows is of ivory also. Bows, quivers, armlets, knee-pieces are painted in bright colours. The shields are

---

[1] *She king*, C, 35, 167, 185.
[3] For the chariot, see *She king*, C, 124.
[2] *Tso chuan*, C, II, 189.
[4] *Tso chuan*, C, II, 189.

decorated with painting. Embossed ornaments hang on the breast of the horses. The chariots move forward majestically, guided by drivers expert in handling all their reins as one, careful to keep their four horses abreast so that their ornaments and bells may ring in unison. The army pursues its route, always by the compass, in an unvarying and commanding order, facing the south on its march, as a chief would do. The banner of the Red Bird (South) is borne before it; behind that of the Dark Warrior (tortoise and serpent: North); on the right wing (West) that of the White Tiger; on the left wing (East) that of the Blue Dragon.[1] On the right of the chariots the foot-soldiers' duty is to keep watch over the chariot-poles: those who march on the left gather herbs along the route.[2] Orders are given by means of flags. The marching orders of the army must be signalled with dog-grass (dog-grass is used as a litter for the wounded), as dog-grass must be found at the head of a funeral procession, and also before a chief who is devoted to death.

The army encamps, as it marches, by the compass. The camp is a square town where wells are dug and hearths are built. It has its gates at the four points of the compass, and holds within its enclosure the tablets of the Ancestors and the geniuses of the Soil. In the centre is the legion formed by the prince's familiars: it is encircled by the legions of the left and right.[3] Temporary camps are surrounded by simple fences, but when an army wishes to leave behind a monument of its glory and to take possession of a country, it builds an entrenched camp, a fortified place.[4] If several armies encamp together, each takes care to place itself at that point of the compass which corresponds to its native country.[5] When the army is encamped, life goes on in every particular as though the seigniorial city, armed with all the sacred forces of the native country, had been bodily removed. Facing it stands the enemy city, the opposing camp.

In each camp, a sort of retreat is begun which is the preparation for battle. Attempts are made to tire out the enemy's patience, to discover if he is disposed to make a great effort, to divine if he has brought great stores of grain and dried vegetables in sacks, to see, in short, if he intends to

---

[1] *Li ki*, C, I, 55. [2] *Tso chuan*, C, I, 614. [3] *Tso chuan*, C, II, 132 and 468.
[4] *Tso chuan*, C, III, 214. [5] *Tso chuan*, C, II, 479.

gain a victory or simply to make a show of his forces. Sometimes, the armies range themselves in battle order without either advancing to fight. Each is waiting for the favourable day looked for by their soothsayers. They exchange messengers to fix the time of the encounter. One may gauge the determined spirit of the enemy by the firm or faltering voice of the ambassador.[1] In each camp, warlike meetings follow each other, for the other camp to see : religious and military parades which raise the hopes of victory.[2] " In the army of Chin (which the prince of Ch'u and one of his officers watch from their camp, mounted upon a tower) men are running right and left. What are they doing ?—They are summoning the officers.—They are meeting in the centre of the camp (around the chief).—They are going to take counsel. A tent is being set up.—They are going to consult the tortoise before the tablets of the dead princes of Chin.— They are taking down the tent.—The prince of Chin is going to give his orders.—They are shouting. . . . A cloud of dust is rising. . . . They are stopping up the wells. . . . They are destroying the hearths. . . . They are forming rank. . . . When they have mounted the chariots, the archers to the left, the lancers to the right, all grasp their weapons and get down again. . . . They are going to listen to a speech (from the chief). . . . Are they going to fight ? . . . There is no means of knowing. . . . They mount the chariots a second time, to left and right, and then all descend once more. . . . They are going to pray for the issue of the fight."

This prayer (*tao*) accompanies a tragic gesture and oath by which the chief definitely devotes the army to battle. He gives precious stones to the ancestors : this is the pledge exacted from him who, when he asks for protection, ought to offer up his most precious possessions as an equivalent and be willing to stake his body and his life. The chief begins by justifying his expedition. Its sole object is the punishment of the guilty and the disturbers of the peace. " Ready for battle, I hold my lance in rest ! I dare to give you warning ! May our nerves be unshaken ! May our bones be unbroken ! May our faces escape scars ! Our end is to accomplish the great work ! It is our wish not to dishonour you, our ancestors. It is not long life (*ming : destiny)

---

[1] *Tso chuan*, **C**, I, 509.　　　　[2] *Tso chuan*, **C**, II, 132.

that I ask for! I dare not keep back the jades from my girdle!"

When the warriors, harangued by the chief, bound by his oath, see that they are devoted at last to a terrible fate, the bravest compete for the first fruits of glory. They go and defy the enemy, in whom already they recognize a guilty party, the enemy whose defeat will testify to his crimes. The battle is a trial of Fortune. The first passages of arms are effectual omens. The first necessity is to secure precedence. As soon as the battle is joined, fortunes are intermingled. Again one may learn from the outset what is at stake in the battle, and whether it will be a courteous joust with the object of ranking the combatants in order of honour or else an ordeal to the death, ending in a complete victory and a defeat from which there can be no appeal.

If the adversary appears not as a rival, but a real enemy, if the object is to declare him outside Chinese law, and to punish him as a Barbarian, if the intention is to suppress an outworn and harmful dynasty, a decadent or savage race of overlords, then heroes, devoted to death, are sent to *join* the battle.[1] This is the rôle reserved for pardoned criminals, led, in theory, by the minister of war. On meeting the adversary, they must cut their throats with a great shout. A furious soul exhales from this collective suicide. It fastens itself like an evil fortune upon the enemy. The duel will be terrible, though not necessarily a duel to the death, if, as an invitation to the adversary, a chariot is sent to him bearing a lancer who " finds his way within the entrenchments, kills a man, cuts off his left ear, and returns." [2] (At the beginning of a sacrifice, to ensure the attention of the gods and to consecrate their victim, the first blood is drawn from the ear, by a knife hung with bells.) By the first blow, the enemy is marked out as the expiatory victim of the battle. Yet he is not destined irremediably to a total sacrifice. The gods permit the substitution of victims. The conqueror may consent to the ransom of the conquered. But there are also more humane methods of inviting to battle. They reveal not a will to conquest, or at the least to infeudation, but a simple desire for honour and glory. If the contending forces approached each other in neighbouring encampments, or if

---

[1] SMC, I, 233, and IV, 25. [2] *Tso chuan*, C, I, 626.

one of them came to set up his camp opposite the walls of the rival town, the two opposing armies are considered to be each in their own town, a town whose entrenchments are as sacred as those of their own home. To inflict the first most decisive and keenest wound upon the enemy, it will suffice for a fully harnessed chariot to go with lowered standard " to skirt the enemy entrenchments." Or else the trees of the sacred thickets which surround the rival town may be set on fire.[1] Less serious, but still sufficiently insolent, would be the gesture of the warrior, who calmly exposing himself, counts with his riding-whip the boards of which the gate is made.[2] As soon as he realizes that he is defied, as soon as he has seen his walls insulted, there is no more to be said : the enemy resigns himself to endure the fortunes of war.

When it is begun by boastings in which spiritual strength is affirmed with more or less brutal stoutness, the battle or siege or struggle in open country is reduced to a combat of moral forces. Having the unstable minds of serfs, the foot-soldiers carry no weight in the fateful struggle, whilst the noble equipages of the chariots are clashing standard against standard, and honour against honour.

The vassals of the two armies are not strangers one to the other. Almost all have been the bearers of missions in the rival country. There they were received on the footing of guests. When they recognize their respective standards, they exchange distant civilities. Failing a feast for the men of his suite, they send the enemy a pot of wine, which he is asked to drink for his comfort. This wine is tasted with fitting ceremony while acts of politeness in time of peace are called to mind.[3] The enemies salute each other, not on their knees (for they are armed) but by bowing three times. They descend from their chariots. They remove their helmets when they see a great chief among the enemy.[4] They dare not attack an overlord, " for he who would touch him would deserve to be chastised." They dare fight only amongst equals.

They must fight politely. An equipage, which is on the point of capturing another, will let it escape if one of the enemy warriors has the good taste to pay a ransom of homage on the spot. An archer of Ch'u, in an unfortunate position,

---

[1] *Tso chuan*, **C**, I, 625.   [2] *Tso chuan*, **C**, II, 339.
[3] *Tso chuan*, **C**, III, 392.   [4] *Tso chuan*, **C**, II, 135 and 136.

saw his chariot held up by a stag. At this stag he shot his last arrow. His lancer immediately gets down from the chariot, takes the stag which he has killed and offers it to the warriors of Chin : " Because it is not the hunting season, the time has not come for making presents of wild animals. Yet I venture to present this one for your followers to eat." The enemy, checking his attack, explains : " Here, on the left, is a worthy archer and on the right a well-spoken lancer : these are gentlemen ! " [1]

Gifts of arms are exchanged in the same way as gifts of food and drink.[2] Prestige grows by generous actions, rather than by stubbornness or military wisdom. Such warriors, as in the preparatory exercises have been able to pierce seven cuirasses at once with their arrows, and make their boast of it, hear the chief say to them : " You will bring great dishonour upon the country ! Tomorrow morning, when you shoot arrows, you will die the victims of your own proficiency ! " Even when victory has proved the righteousness of the cause, and one has only to reckon with the fugitives, that is to say, the guilty, a noble warrior cannot make up his mind to slay more than three men. Again when he lets his arrows fly, he shoots with his eyes shut : they will hit the enemy if fate wills.

In the thick of the battle, prudence should always give place to courtesy. Two chariots advance to meet each other. One turns aside. The enemy chief immediately calls out the name of the charioteer who seems to be avoiding the struggle. He, being defied, returns to the combat, and tries to shoot. He sees that he is subdued, for the other, who is ready, lets fly his arrow, invoking the miraculous virtue of his ancestors to shield him from harm. But when the other is about to shoot a second time, he cries : " If you do not let me make an exchange (of my arrows with yours) it will be an ill deed ! " Recalled in his turn to the laws of honour, the enemy plucks back his arrow which is already upon the bow, and' awaits motionless the deadly shot.[3]

It is a great thing to spare the enemy. It is a fine thing to expose oneself foolhardily. The supreme action is to devote oneself to death for the sake of the chief. If the

---

[1] *Tso chuan*, C, I, 626.   [2] *Tso chuan*, C, II, 136.
[3] *Tso chuan*, C, III, 340.

latter's chariot is stuck in the mire, or closely pressed, the faithful vassal will attempt at once to take his master's place. He will personate him in the vehicle which is always made conspicuous by the chief's standard.[1] A noble warrior does not consent to lower his standard even to escape pursuit.[2] Whilst the standard floats, one must go at a foot pace or march forward to the enemy entrenchments. It would be a supreme disgrace to flee with the standard unfurled, for if one goes to battle it is to do honour to one's flag. To run the risk of being the laughing-stock of an enemy who may cry your name aloud, or even to be haughtily spared by him—these are the worst misfortunes that can happen. To avoid them calls for as much cunning as bravery. In a battle between Chin and Ch'u (596 B.C.) one of the Chin chariots is stuck in the mire and cannot go forward. The situation is desperate. The enemy amuses himself by giving advice. " A Ch'u warrior told the driver to raise the transverse bar (upon which the weapons were hung). (When the bar was removed) the chariot (could) move forward, but only a little. One of the Ch'u warriors (then) told the driver to remove the standard and lower it over the yoke. (When the standard was removed) the chariot would be able (at last) to get out of the hole. The driver, turning his head aside, said (in return for the insulting advice which he had just received, and the clemency which it was dishonour to him to accept) " We are not practised in (the art of) running away, like the inhabitants of your great country ! "

The great game, during the battle, is to bully the enemy. One bullies one's fellow soldiers also, in the act of helping them. " Chao Chan gave his two best horses to his elder brother and his uncle to assist them to fly. He himself returned with his other horses. He met the enemy, and was unable to escape. Abandoning his chariot, he went away on foot through the forest. Fong (another warrior of the same army) passed (near him) mounted in his chariot with his two sons. He told them not to look behind them (to turn their heads and see Chao Chan fleeing on foot, would have been to humiliate him). But they turned round and said (calling the fugitive by name) ' Old Chao is down there behind us ! ' Chao, seized with fury, ordered them to get

[1] *Tso chuan*, C, II, 13.   [2] *Tso chuan*, C, III, 749.

down (from their father's chariot) and showing them a tree, he said to them : ' You shall stay in this spot, stretched out as corpses ! ' (They were obliged to get down and) their father (immediately) presented the cord to Chao Chan (to help him to mount his own chariot) and so escape. The next day the corpses of his sons marked the spot which had been pointed out. Both being taken prisoner (the enemy) had (killed them and) bound them to the tree." [1]

The battle is a confused mêlée of boasts, generosities, homages, insults, devotions, curses, blessings and sorceries. Much more than a clash of arms, it is a duel of moral values, an encounter of competing honours. One tries to qualify oneself by disqualifying others, not only the enemy but also, and in equal measure, those of one's own side. The battle is the great moment in which each warrior proves his nobility, while in addition they prove to all present the nobility of their prince, their cause and their country. Often aggressive and always marked by the ambition of taking first place, the spirit of solidarity which animates a body of vassals is shown in the ordeal of battle as well as in its preparatory ordeals. A vassal loses rank if he allows himself to be beaten by a comrade in the peaceful wrestling match.[2] A minister of war is no longer worthy of his position, if he allows a cord to be thrown round his neck, in jest, as though to take him prisoner.[3] He who, not daring to kill a prisoner in bonds, lets fall his lance, will not be a lancer. His place will be taken, at the right of the chariot, by the loyal man, who refusing to be terrified by the loud cry uttered by the victim, calmly cuts off his left ear. He is not afraid of drawing down upon himself the avenging visitations of an enemy spirit : he is bound till death to his comrades in the equipage.[4]

The solidarity of the equipages is indeed the foundation of honour, to such a degree that it is sufficient for a chief to slay his charioteer to be ever afterwards disqualified to be the headman of a chariot.[5] This solidarity, which forms the strength of the armies, is made up of elements held in common, but conceals a sentiment punctilious on the point of honour. Chang-ko and Fu-li, great officers of Chin, are commissioned

---

[1] *Tso chuan*, **C**, I, 633.
[2] *Kuo yu*, 15 ; **LV**, 356, note 2.
[3] *Tso chuan*, **C**, II, 214.
[4] *Tso chuan*, **C**, II, 449.
[5] *Tso chuan*, **C**, II, 194.

to go and provoke the enemy : they require a charioteer who is familiar with the country and the road : they make request for him from Cheng, a little lordship joined with Chin in a war against Ch'u. The tortoise being consulted points out She-Küan, a great officer of Cheng. The rank of the three warriors is equal : but not the prestige of their countries. She-Küan, warned of the danger which he runs of being snubbed and treated as an inferior, makes up his mind to uphold his honour and that of his country. He will prove the falsity of the proverb : " A little hill has neither cypress nor fir-tree." The equipage sets out. While Chang-ko and Fu-li were in their tent they left She-Küan to sit outside (refusal of communion by domicile). They gave him food only after they had eaten themselves (infeudating com- munion). When they were in presence of the enemy, She- Küan, *without giving them warning*, made the horses gallop. The two (others, who having laid aside their armour, were calmly playing the lute, hastened to) uncover their helmets and put them on their heads. When they were within the enemy entrenchments they got down from the chariot, seized each one a man, threw him to the ground and took him in their arms to carry him away captive. (But She-Küan) had (already) left the entrenchments, *without waiting for them*. They too went out, leaped into the chariot, drew their bows from the sheath and let fly some arrows. When the danger was past, they sat down again and played upon the lute [wishing before all things to appear perfectly calm]. (After which) they said to She-Küan : " *My lord* (they addressed him by the title which was due to him, his family coming of princely stock, for She-Küan, by his conduct, had just effaced the distance which they desired to mark between themselves and him), *we make up part of the same equipage : we are brethren*. Why have you twice acted without consulting us ? " She-Küan replied [his prestige being restored, he has nothing to do now but make a show of modesty] : " At first I thought of nothing but getting inside the enemy's camp, and then *I was afraid* [I do not pretend to equal you in bravery : this formula disarms anger]." The two others began to laugh, saying : " Your lordship is very prompt ! " [1] It is evident

---

[1] *Tso chuan*, C, II, 414.

that in the trials imposed by the point of honour, loyalty is content to appear like treachery.

The brotherhood of arms has something equivocal about it, for, equally with the victory or the defeat of the country, the battle results in the enhancement or the lowering of personal prestige. Inversely, friendly sentiments no less than hatred may be felt towards the incidental enemy whom one is fighting chiefly with a view to classifying him in his proper camp.

Except in extraordinary cases where war is a war to the death, the end of the battle is not by any means the destruction of the adversary. It ought to be a courteous combat. Duke Siang of Song is waiting for a pitched battle while the army of Ch'u is crossing a river.[1] He is told : " They are many : we are few : let us attack them before they have got across ! " The duke does not follow this advice. When the crossing was accomplished, but before Ch'u had yet disposed its troops to battle, the duke was told " We must attack them ! " He replied " Let us wait till they are drawn up in battle array ! " At last he attacked, was beaten and wounded. He then said : " A chief worthy of the name (*kün-tsih*, prince, gentleman, good man) does not (seek to) overcome an enemy in misfortune. He does not beat his drum before their ranks are formed." Although they made answer to Duke Siang that success alone was praiseworthy, history has pardoned his many and grave faults because in this instance he thought only of keeping his honour intact.

Victory is only to be had when the chief's honour issues enhanced from the battle. It is enhanced less by the pursuit of success (and above all, when it is pursued to the bitter end) than by the evidence of moderation. Ch'in and Chin are facing each other (614 B.C.). The two armies are ranged and do not fight. At night a messenger from Ch'in comes to warn Chin to get ready : " There is no lack of warriors in the two armies ! Tomorrow I engage you to meet us ! " But the people of Chin notice that the messenger has an unsteady gaze and that his voice has no assurance. Ch'in is beaten beforehand. " The Ch'in army is afraid of us ! It will take to flight ! Let us hem them in against the river ! Certainly, we will beat them ! " Yet the Chin army does not

[1] *Tso chuan*, C, II, 334.

move, and the enemy can decamp in peace. It has sufficed for someone to say : " It is inhuman not to gather up the dead and wounded ! It is cowardly not to wait for the time arranged, or to press upon the enemy in a dangerous passage." [1]

And these are the words proper to a conqueror when it is proposed to celebrate his glory by building a camp on the scenes of his successes, and by raising a monumental mound over the bodies of his slain enemies.[2] " I was the cause that two countries exposed the bones of their warriors to the sun ! It is cruel ! . . . (No doubt) in ancient times, when kings resplendent with virtue fought with men who had no respect (for the celestial order) and when they took prisoner (those who, like) whales, (devoured the weak, those kings) might then raise a triumphal mound (*fong*) to expose (for ever) the bodies [of the guilty : those of the wicked chief and of his followers, wicked by contact]. But now ! there are no guilty [= I am not qualified to conduct a war to the death !]. There are only vassals who have been faithful to the end ! They died, uniting their destiny [*ming :* life, destiny, order, investiture] with that of their prince ! Why should we raise a triumphal monument ? "

While the vassals confront each other in a confused mêlée, the chief alone bears the responsibility of the battle and its consequences. It is the chief alone who conducts the fight. Victory is won by his virtue alone. He ought to permeate all the combatants with the strength of his spirit. He ought to spend himself without reserve. K'i-K'o commands the central legion of Chin ; Huan is his lancer, Chang-hou is his charioteer. At the beginning of the battle (588 B.C.) [3] " K'i-K'o was wounded by an arrow : the blood ran down to his shoes : *he did not cease to beat his drum.* (But at last) he said : ' I am in pain ! ' [Chiefs under arms must respect etiquette. Their followers are bound to recall them to duty.] Chang-hou said to him : ' Since the commencement of the battle, two arrows have pierced me, one in my hand, the other in my neck. I pulled them out to drive the chariot. The left wheel has turned purple. Did I dare to say I was in pain ? My lord, be patient ! ' Huan said to K'i-K'o : ' Since the beginning of the battle, as soon as there was

---

[1] *Tso chuan,* C, I, 509.   [2] *Tso chuan,* C, I, 635.   [3] *Tso chuan,* C, II, 10.

S

danger, I got down from the chariot and led the horses. My lord, have you (once) given a thought to me ? And yet, my lord, you are in pain ! ' Chang-hou continued : ' *The eyes and ears of the army are turned towards our flag and our drum.* From them they take the word to advance or to retire. This chariot of ours will be able to fulfil its task as long as there is a man to drive it ! Because you are in pain, would you lead the great work of our master to destruction ? *He who puts on a breastplate and takes up arms must march forward without faltering, even to death.* You are suffering, but not unto death. My lord, conquer your suffering ! ' Then Chang-hou, gathering the reins into his left hand, took the drumstick in his right, and beat the drum." But Chang-hou was not qualified to act as chief : his horses became entangled, and the battle was lost. A chief is worthy of his rank when he can exclaim after the battle : " I was thrown down over the sheath of my bow ! I vomited blood ! *And yet the sound of my drum did not grow faint !* Today, I have been a chief ! " And because he was truly a chief, his lancer was able without difficulty to make a way through the enemies while his charioteer, with reins so worn that they would *infallibly have broken* with the least attempt at pulling, was able to drive his chariot at full gallop in the mêlée.

The voice, the breath, the spirit, the ardour, of the chief are communicated to his chariot companions and to the whole army, but they inspire in the first place his drum and his standard. The flag represents the whole of the fatherland. The overlordship is lost if the flag is destroyed. The flag *is* the prince himself. He who touches the ensign-bearer is guilty of lèse-majesté, and the overlord is seen in person, wherever his pennon is carried.[1] Only on exceptional occasions does the prince expose his person and his standard together. As a rule, he entrusts the flag and delegates his command. Few, however, are those who are willing to accept the dangerous honour of a complete *imperium*. A prudent general at least cuts off the fringe from the princely standard. He fears to be too completely identified with the overlord.

All the vassals are in principle devoted to death when at the setting-out of the army a bloody unction breathes a soul

---

[1] *Tso chuan*, **C,** I, 219 ; III, 173 ; I, 57. For the flag, see **LV,** 385 ff.

into the flags and drums. But the general to whom are confided the drum and flag of command is actually devoted to death, if, by accepting the *imperium*, he becomes the overlord's double. When, after a consultation with the tortoise and severe abstinence, the war chief, holding the axe in his hand, is presented with drum and flag, he must proceed to take a habit which cuts him off from the world of the living. He puts on a funeral garment and will only be able to leave the city through a breach made in the northern gate : thus at the time of burial the dead go out by a breach from the ancestral temple.[1] The general must cut off the nails of his feet and hands, as the custom is when devoting oneself entirely to a sacred power. Henceforth he is " devoted to death," and " must look no more behind him." Held by a bond of absolute fidelity, no longer capable of " having a double heart," he becomes the soul of the work of slaughter inaugurated by his taking of the habit. This resembles the exorcists' taking of the habit, when they are charged with the expulsion of hurtful powers, on behalf of the overlord. The exorcists, when they put on their consecrated costumes, swear not to return till they have " fought to a finish." The war chief, however, sometimes renews his vow in the course of the campaign. Chong-hang Hien-tsih, general of Chin (554 B.C.) cast precious stones into the River and pronounced this oath : " I will not permit myself to recross the River ! " Hien-tsih was only half victorious and yet he recrossed the River. He then fell sick. His eyes bulged out. He demanded a successor and then died. When he was dead, he continued to look through his bulging eyes with his mouth wide open. Someone said : " Perhaps it is because he has not finished his work ? " His second in command, laying his hands upon the corpse [a communal gesture] then cried aloud : " My lord, you have made an end ! but if I do not follow up your work, be witness, O River ! " The corpse then consented to shut its eyes and it was at last possible to close its mouth. Hien-tsih's funeral oration was : " He was a man." [2]

Gentlemen, as a rule, prefer half victories, or tempered defeats. In this case, they may expect terrible threats from an ambitious prince : their master will not feel satisfied even

---

[1] *Huai-nan tsih*, 15 ; *Li ki*, C, I, 157.   [2] *Tso chuan*, C, II, 334, 346.

when he has eaten them.[1] All faithful vassals can quote the proverb: "Conqueror: minister of war; Vanquished: boiled in the caldron!" They know too that their master, if they let themselves be beaten a little, or even taken prisoner, will quickly pardon them and will pay their ransom, only too happy not to see them pass into the service of another. One is still necessary as long as one is not so imprudent as to finish one's task at one blow. The good general knew how to fly, lightened of his armour. At most it cost him a mock triumph and the annoyance of entering the city again to the good-humoured accompaniment of songs:—"Bulge your eyes!—Blow out your belly!—Throw off your breastplate and come home!—Oh beautiful beard! oh beautiful beard!—Here you are back again without your breastplate!" "The bullocks have still got their skin!—and there are many rhinoceros!—I have thrown off my breastplate: and what next?" "It is true, the skin is still there: but where shall we find the red varnish?"[2] On the other hand, after a great victory, the chief re-entered the town amid boastful songs of triumphal pomp: "We are climbing their hills (they are ours!)—they cannot make a stand upon their hills (they are ours!).—Ours are the hills! ours are the mountains!—They shall never again drink from their springs! (they are ours!).—Ours are the springs, ours are the lakes!"[3] In the first rank of the triumphal dancers the conquering general marched with his battle-axe still in his hand, on that day of glory.

The difficulty was to lay down the battle-axe and not to lose life itself with the *imperium*. Tsih-wei (540 B.C.) acts as chief in command on behalf of Ch'u. His master allows him during the whole time of his charge, to wear a prince's robes and to be guarded, like an overlord, by two lancers. This costume is not more than is required to impose the hegemony of Ch'u upon all the rival countries. But, says a foreign diplomat, "Tsih-wei has borrowed it for a moment. He will never give it up again!" and all the chiefs of the other countries make haste to give way to Tsih-wei, glad to enhance his fortune, for they hope to condemn him to a terrible fall. Tsih-wei did in fact keep his two lancers. He overthrew the prince of Ch'u, assassinated his sons and

---

[1] *Tso chuan*, **C**, II, 432. [2] *Tso chuan*, **C**, I, 566.
[3] *She king*, **C**, 335.

seized the power for himself : but, after celebrating extravagant triumphs, he died in misery.[1]

An alternative is imposed upon the war chief who seeks too great fortune for his arms : he must either usurp or perish. Disgrace follows the triumph if rebellion does not forestall it. A loyal and wise general avoids the responsibilities of victory and divides those of defeat : " Instead of taking the blame upon yourself alone, you will share it with your six legionary chiefs : will that not be better ? " [2] Such is the formula of the military mind and morale. They were formed, with scarcely a variation, in the course of those interminable jousts which made up the feudal period. Officers and chiefs detest brutal war and discourteous victories for which one must hazard one's fate on too decisive a throw. They prefer the beautiful alternation of warlike parades and armed truces which allow reputations to be founded and talents to be used to advantage.

Feudal battle (when the game is nobly played) is an ordeal which allows of appeal. Consecrated by success, the victor holds in his hand for a moment the fate of the vanquished. This latter, who is counted guilty, then begs for mercy, but begs with provoking humility. His supplication, if it is perfectly humble, his confession, if it is complete, his avowal of weakness, if it is striking, absolve him from his fault and are sufficient to re-establish the equilibrium of fate. While he delivers himself without reservation to the master of the hour, he is offering him for the future a challenge which is too compelling, a wager whose stake it is wholly to the interest of his partner to lessen. The victor is careful only to exact a moderate compensation. He hastens on his part to restore the vanquished and to rehabilitate the guilty.

Song is besieged (593) by Ch'u. It has no hope of relief. The enemy disposes himself to encamp till the place falls. The best that one can look for is an accepted surrender or at the most a treaty, sworn (hateful disgrace) under the very walls of the town. Then plundering the past and destroying the future, the besieged burn the bones of their dead and eat their children. They send word to the besieger. This horrible confession of weakness does not encourage the latter : it terrifies him. Ch'u's army retreats thirty furlongs. An

---

[1] *Tso chuan*, **C**, III, 7, and SMC, IV, 357.   [2] *Tso chuan*, **C**, I, 619.

honourable peace is concluded.[1] After seventeen days of
siege (596 B.C.) the inhabitants of Cheng learn from the
tortoise that their sole resource is to abandon their town
after lamenting their fate in the Ancestral Temple.   The
enemy's army retires, conquered by this funeral rite.   The
besieged, taking heart again, put the town again in a posture of
defence : the enemy, being defied, surrounds it anew.   Soon
he enters the place. All seems lost. " The prince of Cheng,
bare to the waist (a rite of mourning) and leading a ram by
a cord [in the ceremony of triumph, when the vanquished
was not sacrificed, a ram was substituted for him] went to
meet (the conqueror). He said : ' There is no longer a Heaven
(for me) ! I have not had the talent to serve you (as a vassal),
my lord ! I have caused you, my lord, trouble and anger !
This anger strikes my poor country ! *It is my fault !* Shall
I not have the courage to accept your decree (*ming*) ? If you
wish to send us, your captives, to the borders of the (Yang-tse)
Kiang and of the sea [banishment to the uncultivated marches]
we will obey that decree ! If you wish to divide us as spoil
among your feudatories, if you will that (both men and
women) we shall be all reduced to the state of servants [penal
servitude] we will obey that decree ! But if you deign to
recall the ancient bonds of friendship, if you desire a share
in the good fortune which can be granted by our royal and
princely ancestors [this good fortune (*fu*) will be acquired
by the consuming of sacrificial meats which the speaker will
always be able to send as a present (*che fu*) if the sacrifices
to his ancestors are not interrupted by the destruction of the
overlordship], if you do not destroy our altars of the Soil and
of Harvests [by reducing them to a slough], if you transform
me [that is to say, if you communicate your virtue to me]
to such a degree that I shall be able to serve you as a vassal
on the same footing as those Barbarians (nine of whose
districts you have been able) to incorporate (in your country)
it will be a good action (*on your part*) ! That is not what I dare
to hope ! (But) I dare open my heart to you ! My lord, it is
for you to decide ! ' "   The prince of Ch'u, vanquished by
this irresistible confession (" An overlord who can humble
himself is certainly capable of winning entire loyalty from
his people ") made his army withdraw thirty furlongs and

---

[1] *Tso chuan*, C, I, 653.

granted an honourable peace.[1] The army of Cheng enters victorious into Ch'en (547 B.C.). The minister of war straightway carries the sacred vessels of the ancestors to the conquering generals. The overlord of Ch'en puts on a mourning headdress and takes the tablet of his god of the Soil in his arms. The people of Ch'en, all their ranks confounded, but divided into two bands, men and women apart, stand waiting, bound in advance like captives. The enemy generals appear. One has been careful to provide himself with a chain : but it is not to bind the captives but to answer humility with humility. He salutes on his knees and presents a cup to the vanquished prince : this is to let him know that his victory will have no further consequence than that of the archers, in the ritual tournaments of archery. These tournaments serve to classify merit, but are a prelude to communal rejoicings. Another general comes forward in his turn : he confines himself to numbering the captives, reducing his taking possession of the city to a symbolic act and the triumph to a simple affirmation of prestige. Instantly, the inhabitants of Ch'en resume their privileges and their ranks : the god of the Soil, purified by the care of him who invokes him, takes his place again as the centre of a fatherland restored and rehabilitated, while the army of Cheng returns home, clothed with the glory which is the gift of moderation, a pure glory which is not embittered by the fear of a turn of fortune. Its generals have not at once exhausted their share of happiness. We are told that their favour and their renown will long endure.[2]

Triumph is the crown of victory. It authenticates it. The conqueror scores a point. He adds to his assets, in addition to the glory of having shown mercy, all the spoils by which the vanquished have paid for their defeat and their absolution. These spoils, captives taken during the battle, hostages or territory pledged as a guarantee of the treaty, women handed over to renew the alliance, jewels offered as gifts to restore friendship, these have a value as trophies and a price as booty. The conquerors at the time of the triumphal return, share them out, *pro rata*, according to the merit won by each of them in the martial tournaments. This division becomes the occasion of a tournament in which rivalries are opposed as sternly as on the field of battle.

---

[1] *Tso chuan*, C, I, 61.　　　　[2] *Tso chuan*, C, II, 431.

When for the glory of his arms, a prince creates an Order of Heroes, and, pointing with his finger to two of his warriors, he says : " Those are my heroes (literally : my males, or more precisely, my cocks) ! " the vassal who considers himself to be unjustly deprived of this badge of honour, will exclaim : " If those two were wild animals, I would eat their flesh ! I would make my bed of their skins ! " [1] It is the virtue of the overlord which has made and won the war : it is the overlord who reaps the trophies : but he ought immediately to share the glory, and this distribution engages his responsibility to a frightful extent. The vassal who is dissatisfied with his share of honour and profit has only one weapon and one resource against his overlord, but they are the strongest possible : he can curse. He can even, by committing suicide, fasten a creditor soul upon his master. Kie-tsih Ch'uei, whom the Duke Wen of Chin had forgotten to reward, does not protest, but he makes use of the power of song : " A dragon [the overlord] desires to ascend to Heaven !—He has five serpents [five faithful vassals] to sustain him !—The dragon has ascended to the skies !—Four serpents only found a resting-place !—The other, sad and solitary, was never seen more ! " Whereupon, he flies to a wooded hill, whence fire cannot expel him. He is burnt to death with his arms around a tree. To expiate this sinister death, which threatened to attach itself as a blot upon his fortunes, Duke Wen was reduced to giving Kie-tsih Ch'uei a posthumous fief : the mountain on which he died was consecrated to him, as much to reward him for his past devotion as to turn away his future sorceries.[2]

A vassal who wants to be rewarded, but who knows how to make effective play with the recompense to be obtained, will confine himself to suggesting to his master that if he has received no favours it is doubtless because he deserves a chastisement.[3] As the effect of coercive curses, as well as of demands for punishment, which are only disguised threats, the overlord is reduced to keeping nothing of the benefits of victory, but glory, naked and unadorned, stripped of material advantages. He consecrates the trophies to his

[1] *Tso chuan*, C, II, 373.
[2] SMC, IV, 296 ; *Tso chuan*, C, I, 357 ; **LV**, 81, note 4.
[3] SMC, IV, 296–297.

ancestors, but he shares them amongst the vassals. If he is of a virtue so material as to wish to realize his success by annexations of territory, he is riding for a fall, for the conquered lands will go to swell the fiefs of his vassals. They, when they grow rich, are tempted to become rebels. The feudal prince has an equal or greater interest in sparing the vanquished than his seconds in command. A triumph pursued to the end would be his ruin.

The chief or only benefit which accrues to the overlord in a campaign lies in the fact that it enables him to test his vassals. The triumph gives him the opportunity of punishing those " whose heart is double." [1] He spares, less readily than he spares the conquered, the chiefs and warriors whose loyalty is doubtful. He chastises those who have lost their standard, the prisoners released by the enemy (whom also he can restore or deliver to the jurisdiction of their family chiefs), the cowards who were incapable of giving their lives at the same time as their comrades of the equipage, and above all, those bold men who are inclined to insubordination, —at least, if they have received wounds which seem to render them incapable of service and to leave them without defence. War " makes for the disappearance of turbulent men." Woe unto him who would abolish it ! Thanks to the executions of the triumph, it has actually a purifying value.[2]

The great potentates who created provincial unity and a species of small nations in China, made an industry of war. That time marked the end of the feudal period. The prince keeps the material gains of the war for himself. He annexes territories to his own domain. He also annexes populations. Henceforth the army has nothing in common with a feudal group which sets out with great pomp and in a religious spirit to take part in a tournament. The overlords of the period of the *Combatant Kingdoms* lead their men into the Barbarian Marches which they are striving to appropriate. Against the tribes which live outside Chinese law, they conduct wars of conquest in which the old rules of battle are no longer valid. They undertake colonial wars, wars of civilization : they make real war, bitter and without quarter. They incorporate the conquered into their armies. They adopt their technique. The mass of their warriors is no

---

[1] *Tso chuan*, C, I, 407.   [2] *Tso chuan*, C, I, 388, 406 ; II, 38, 492 ; III, 441.

longer made up of cavaliers, but of adventurers, bravoes, strangers from the colonies. Their army which fights not for the glory of taking prisoners and the one gain of ransoms, but in order to kill and to pillage, figures as a national army when it marches against the army of another potentate, who is himself the creator of a provincial unit. In China proper, struggles between princes appear to be conflicts of civilization, West against East, South against North. Between the combatant Kingdoms, the campaigns are veritable wars, where the enmities of provinces, cultures, races, techniques clash murderously together.

When Ch'in (540 B.C.) wished to conquer the country of the Jong of the mountains, who fought on foot, he abandoned the system of chariots, and organized companies of foot-soldiers for a new method of warfare. At that time there was a hero who preferred death to the dishonour of being dismounted.[1] The old order of feudal battles, the nobility, and the feudal system were themselves struck down with this gentleman. It was worse still when the overlord of Chao (307 B.C.) in order to fight the warriors of the steppe, adopted their tactics, and created a corps of archers on horseback. He had to encounter a desperate resistance on the part of his vassals and friends.[2] It is a significant fact that it was by a group of simultaneous reforms that Ch'in (who was to found the Empire) created an army of foot-soldiers and of light horse, modified the system of land tenure, and, no longer distributing fiefs, established a military hier-archy founded on services rendered. From this hierarchy was to issue a new nobility.[3] But from that time begins the reign of technicians, military engineers and professors of tactics. Then machines of war are invented (the sage Mei-ti owes a great part of his glory to the inventions which are ascribed to him). Then the art of siege is brought to perfection, in which water, catapults and rolling towers can be employed. Then are devised innumerable stratagems of war, and ambuscades.[4] The object of war is the destruction of the enemy. Ch'in does not invite the prisoners to pay a ransom for their restoration : he executes them. Immense massacres add to his prestige. The battle is no longer an ennobling tournament.

---

[1] *Tso chuan*, C, III, 29.
[2] SMC, IV, 69–84.
[3] SMC, II, 64 ff., and chap. LXVIII.
[4] *Tso chuan*, C, III, 355.

Success alone counts. It seems to be the result of magic art
and not the consecration of religious merit. The miraculous
replaces the epic in the military annals. The heroic strain
is exchanged for the romantic. A *morale* of power tends to
supersede the old *morale* of honour and moderation.

Formerly war bestowed honour, but it was necessary to be
already honourable to become a warrior. Only a man, a
major in point of age, had the right to bear arms. He who was
admitted to the battle, even when very young, attained his
majority by that very act. Inversely, children, old men,
and women, all who were stained with the defilement of
mourning, all who through illness were impure to the touch,
were excluded from the game of battle and its consequences.
No one would have dared to kill a man infected with plague,
to lead an old man into captivity, or to expose the virile
trophies of ears cut off the enemy to female contagion.[1] All
who could not take part in a vendetta were likewise incapable
of suffering or profiting by military tournaments. Care was
taken to shut out the great officers of a demolished overlordship, the chiefs of a beaten army, and those who had
passed by adoption into a strange family, from the preliminary
ordeals of archery.[2] The battle had the value of a test of
purity, limited to the nobles and to the pure.

On the contrary, the ambitious wars of civilization spare
no living soul : " All who have or keep any strength are our
enemies, even if they are old men. . . . Why should we
refrain from wounding a second time those whose wound is
not mortal ? " [3] War which aims at conquest and annexation,
refuses to acknowledge the old laws of feudal encounters :
it is a useful trade, a plebeian occupation : it repudiates the
art which was waged with religious valour but temperate
restitution by the noble soldiers of former days.[4] Yet the
old principles of the age of tourneys are rooted in the Chinese
mind : there they form a deep stratum which does not
disappear with the disappearance of the feudal nobility.

Except when he encounters Barbarians who are strangers
to the Chinese law, the Chinese is inspired by a sentiment of
honour which includes, in a characteristic mixture, the taste
for a wager and a spirit of moderation, both of a singular

---

[1] *Li ki*, C, I, 462 and 219.   [2] *Li ki*, C, II, 674.
[3] *Tso chuan*, C, II, 30, and I, 336.   [4] *Tso chuan*, C, I, 335.

quality. Fortune is constantly challenged, though care is always taken not to exceed one's destiny. But, no sooner does one exceed it, than mad extravagance takes the place of moderation. Without any transition, the sense of honour, of registered values, of equilibrium maintained by slow movement, gives place, in these extreme cases, to an urgent, inordinate and unrestrained appetite for power. He who transgresses the code condemns himself, and acts as one condemned, who has lost all he has to lose.

II

THE NOBLES AT THE COURT

The principles of military morale inspire the nobles even in their civil life. At the same time, under the influence of court life, these principles undergo a change. A pretty anecdote clearly shows the relationship and the antagonism between civil and military virtues, and also, if I may so express it, the part played by romanticism in a life which tended more and more to be governed by red tape. A personage of Cheng (540 B.C.) had a very beautiful sister. A noble of princely blood asked her for his betrothed. [The rites of betrothal are diplomatic rites : with cultivated courtesy they flatter the dignity of the two families who are about to be allied.] ,Another noble of princely blood forced the girl's family to accept the wild goose which constitutes the first step in betrothal. [The marriage contract is by right two-sided : but the presents, the expression of one-sided desire, are used to make contracts binding.] The brother, alarmed at having to decide between two powerful rivals, consults the minister of Cheng, Ssu-ch'an. Ssu-ch'an is a sage. He advises him to let the girl make her own choice. [The future wife has no legal right to give her opinion : she ought neither to see nor know her future husband : but in peasant custom betrothals are made in the course of a tournament of love songs and dances.] The two aspirants accept this ruling. One, having dressed himself in magnificent garments, comes with extreme politeness and pompously spreads out his presents in the courtyard. The other arrives in his turn : he is wearing his panoply of war : he shoots arrows to all the points of the compass : he leaps into his chariot and departs : " He is a male ! " As is right and proper, the girl chooses the soldier. Nevertheless, speaking of the civilian who is beaten in the amorous quest, she says, " Truly, he is handsome ! " [1]

In the overlord's circle it is the correct thing to be hand-some. At court assemblies, " a perfectly beautiful toilet *opens the way (tao)* and allows you to go far," for : the coat makes the noble. The toilette is the vassal's first duty. He dresses for the prince.

It is evident he cannot remain naked like a savage, nor half-clothed like a labouring man. Such people do not draw near to a chief, and they have no soul. A soul which is already powerful dwells in the body of a noble. He would surrender it, if he let himself be seen naked. Therefore he will never strip himself, except on extreme occasions, to receive a chastisement or to dedicate himself without reserve to a sacred power.[2] A woman, who (unless she is a witch) conceals harmful or debilitating charms in her body (*nü tö* = a feminine virtue) will never show herself naked.[3] In presence of his lord, whose sovereign soul he wishes neither to weaken nor contaminate, the vassal ought as a rule to clothe himself as hermetically as a woman. " Even while exerting himself, he will keep his arms covered : even in the hottest season, he will keep his under-garment lowered." His tunic must be " short enough not to drag in the dust," " long enough to hide the bare skin." [4]

But it is not enough to be clothed when one goes to court : one must know how to dress, to be received there. Tseng-tsih and Tsih-kong, disciples of Confucius, present themselves at a house where a prince is on a visit. The porter tells them : " The prince is here : you cannot come in ! " As a matter of fact, the two personages, when they got down from their carriage, had not taken time to arrange their garments. They went straightway into a corner of the stable to tidy themselves. At once the porter, making way before them, told them " You are announced ! " and when they came forward, the most distinguished personages came to meet them. The prince himself to mark his esteem (their toilet

[1] *Tso chuan*, **C**, III, 21.   [2] *Li ki*, **C**, I, 246.
[3] SMC, I, 282.   [4] *Li ki*, **C**, I, 28, and II, 586.

did him honour) paid them the compliment of descending one step of the staircase.[1]

Elegance is obligatory : it consists in wearing clothing which corresponds to the rank which one occupies, which is suitable to the season, appropriate to the circumstances and in keeping with the dignity of those to whom the visit is paid. The costume, moreover, ought to make up a harmonious whole, in which all the details are in secret accord. " An officer who possesses the right to a single emblem wears knee-pieces dyed with madder and a black clasp." " The sash is only two inches broad, but appears to be four, as it goes twice round the body." " It is of dressed silk, simply hemmed at the edges, and bordered only at the ends." " It is fastened by means of buckles through which a silk ribbon is threaded." [2]

The prince's guards, when they stand at his right, wear a tunic trimmed with tiger skins, and when they stand at his left, a tunic trimmed with wolf skins. " Over a (first) tunic which is trimmed with blue fox and its sleeves decorated with leopard skin, a (second) tunic is worn, which should be of dark silk. Over a tunic which is trimmed with doe-skin and its sleeves decorated with the bluish fur of the wild dog, a tunic of yellowish green is worn. Over a tunic, which is furred with black lamb, and its sleeves decorated with leopard-skin, a black tunic is worn, and finally, over a tunic of yellow fox a yellow tunic." On the other hand, " over a tunic (vulgarly) trimmed with dog- or sheep-skin, it is forbidden to wear a second tunic, . . . (for) this is done to show off the beauty of the costume." In visits of condolence, a third tunic must be added, in order not to be too perfectly elegant. But, *in presence of the overlord, one always appears with the second tunic, the most beautiful*—unless one is holding the shell of a tortoise ; whose sanctity (like the sacred character of people in mourning) demands a triple breastplate of clothing.[3]

" The tunic of an officer must be of one of the five fundamental colours, his under-garment (a sort of cotton drawers) of one of the corresponding intermediate colours." Different head-dresses are worn in time of mourning, of abstinence, of disgrace, when one is dealing with business and when one is

[1] *Li ki*, C, I, 254.   [2] *Li ki*, C, I, 700–702.   [3] *Li ki*, C, I, 693 ff.

resting. There is a special head-dress which is used to confer
the majority, for the head-dress is the noblest part of the
clothing : the head-dress is never removed in a chief's presence.
One does not die unless the head-dress is well set upon one's
head, and the chapter of the head-dress opens the most sacred
of the ritual books, the *Yi li*.[1] Before entering the court, the
garments must be adjusted in correct colour and proportion.
A tablet must also be held in the hand, which, for an officer,
is of bamboo decorated with ivory, and for a great officer, of
bamboo decorated with little barbels. Finally he must
deck his girdle with precious stones. " Those which are on
the right side should give out the fourth and third notes
of the scale : those on the left side should give out the first
and fifth notes." " In presence of the overlord, no one (not
even the heir-apparent) allows the precious stones of his girdle
to hang down freely and to make a sound." Only the tinkling
of the princely trinkets must be heard. But, when the
noble is in his chariot, he hears a harmony of bells, and
when he walks—always with measured speed and movements
—" he hears the sound of the stones hung at his girdle : then
neither error nor fraud can enter his mind." [2] The noble
must be brave and pure. In battle, he must prove himself
to be good (*shen jen* or *leang jen*). At court he must take
pains to be beautiful (*mei jen*) for beauty (*mei*) and purity
(*kieh* = clean, of good alloy) are interchangeable terms, and
moreover, valour is indistinguishable from a fine carriage.[3]

He is noble who bears himself nobly. When one is wearing
a garment " made of twelve strips as the year is made of
twelve months "—whose " round sleeves, made like a circle,"
invite " to graceful movements "—whose " square-cut neck "
and " seam down the back, as straight as a measuring line "
recall " uprightness and correctness,"—finally " whose lower
edge, horizontal as the beam of a balance in equilibrium, sets
the feelings at rest, and the heart at peace," [4] it is possible
to preserve the noble bearing (*Yi*) which causes " a man to
be truly a man." Being well dressed, there is no risk of being
compared to a rat who has only his skin, to a beast whose
movements are irregular and wild.[5] He has a soul, which

---

[1] *Li ki*, C, I, 690 ff. ; I, 28.   [2] *Tso chuan*, C, III, 715.   [3] *Li ki*, I, 707 ff.
[4] *Li ki*, C, II, 588 ff.   [5] *She king*, C, 59.

is moulded by his garment, correctly, solidly, which can endure. He will not then be told: " A man who has no deportment!—he would be better dead!" On the other hand, it will be said of an accomplished gentleman who wears jewels in his ear and whose cap sown with pearls " shines like the constellations," that " he will never be forgotten." His manners must inevitably be " grave, majestic, imposing, distinguished." [1] " When the garment is all that it ought to be, the carriage of the body may be correct (*cheng*), the aspect of the face sweet and calm, the forms and dispositions conformable to the rules." [2] Then only can he be looked upon as a vassal by his prince, as a son by his father, and by all as a complete man. The ceremony of majority is the taking of a habit which consecrates a gentleman and devotes him to elegant duties. As soon as he is dressed and covered nobly, he can take part in those tourneys of lofty bearing, physical or verbal, which make up the life of the court.

The great test of nobility is the archery tournament (for the nobles are first of all warriors) : it preserves none of the brutality of a test of skill or of courage (in the vulgar sense of the words) ; it is a musical ceremony, regulated like a ballet, in which one must prove oneself skilful in fine salutes and grand in one's clothes. Every movement must be made in cadence, and the arrow which has not left the bow at the right note can never hit the mark (or at least, does not count).[3] " The archers, whether advancing, retiring, turning or returning, must *express the heart* (*chong*) of the ritual rules. Within a correct (*cheng*) attitude of mind, without, an upright (*che*) attitude of body—these are necessary before bows and arrows can be grasped firmly and with care. He who grasps bow and arrows firmly and with care will be able to say that he has hit the centre (*chong*) of the target. And it is thus that virtue (*tö*) may be recognized," not only the virtue of the vassal who shoots, but also the virtue of his overlord— which, alone, can direct the arrows to the mark : thus it is said that the sovereign reduced the fiefs of those overlords whose vassals, disqualified nobles who displayed the uncertain integrity of their master, could not hit the bull's-eye.[4] But a prince who shoots arrows all day without " one arrow

---

[1] *She king*, C, 63.   [2] *Li ki*, C, II, 636.
[3] *Li ki*, C, II, 699.   [4] *Li ki*, C, II, 672 ff.

missing the mark " will be said at once to be capable of
reigning : (" Oh ! he is worthy to be praised !—his fine eyes
shine with a pure brilliance !—and how upright is his bearing
(*yi*) ! ") ; he is handsome, he is pure ! " he can dispel misfortunes ! " [The ancient chiefs are known to have chased
away defilements by shooting arrows.] At the court of the
virtuous overlord the vassals shoot one against another, all
with the most exquisite courtesy : " The bells and the drums
are ready !—the great target is set up !—Bows stretched and
arrows fixed,—the archers take their places by two and two ! "
" I offer you [*hien :* a term which is equivalent to the gifts
set aside as offerings and the challenges flung to a rival] to
prove your art ! " " I will go then, and prove you—and you
will drink to my prayer [*K'i*, a prayer addressed to a holy
power, humbly, but with the intention of compelling him
to answer the petitioner]." [1] The refinement is such that the
cup (imposed upon the vanquished in view of a repentance
and a reconciliation) is presented to him only as an act of
homage. The gentleman " when he exerts himself to hit
the mark," should make believe that he is trying for victory
out of pure humility, " so that he may ' decline the cup ' and
let the honour go [honour and cup are expressed by the same
word]." [2] To the other is generously passed on the honourable
consolation (*yang*) of the healthful cup of drink (made to
restore declining strength, but) reserved for old men who
deserve to be respected. The duel with bow and arrows,
which is held at court between men of honour, soothes sus-
ceptibilities in the most exquisite way. It allows of an
infinite number of genuflexions. It is a test of deportment
and of fashionable discipline. Every trace of brutal savagery
is carefully eliminated. Behind every target is a man, but
he is not posted there to be shot at : it is simply his duty to
cry " hit ! " in a true and harmonious voice, upon the note
given by the musicians. He is a recorder who marks the
points, and there is besides a director of archery. He verifies
the number of arrows belonging to each pair of archers, and
sees that order is respected : he undertakes to recall delinquents
to duty, by means of a little cane. Thus the rules of honour
will be upheld, and all being inspired by them, they will be

---

[1] *She king*, C, 112 and 296.   [2] *Li ki*, C, II, 680, and *She king*, C, 297.

T

taken for the guide of daily life.[1] If two rival archers decide to meet on the plain, they will shoot one with the other, both at one time, as at the behest of music. And their arrows, both being well aimed, will meet in mid-air—without harm to anyone (provided they have the same number of arrows). It may happen that one of the two, being too much enamoured of victory, will conceal a supplementary arrow. The other will ward off this criminal shot with a cane. Whereupon, " both, weeping (out of pity for each other) and laying down their bows, will make genuflexions upon the spot, facing each other, inviting each other (to live henceforth as live) father and son " and binding themselves each to the other by an exchange of blood (taken from their arms).[2] These regulated tournaments of archery serve to purge the spirit of vendetta. An old fountain of violence and treachery is thus diluted and diminished, greatly to the encouragement of loyal exploits : it is so altered that it seems to disappear. Everyone fashions his looks to a noble exterior. The official soul of the nobleman is this vestment of loyalty [*chong* : *chong* (loyalty) is written with the sign *heart*, and a drawing showing the arrow in the bull's-eye]. He is the civilized being (*wen* = distinguished), the man who is truly a man (*jen*), he who, even in an encounter with savages, is able to maintain his deportment. " The rules of the ceremonial (*li*) teach us, some to control our feelings, others to try to excite them. To give free course to one's feelings, to let them follow their bent (without hindrance) is the way (virtue : *tao*) of Barbarians. The way imposed by the ceremonial is quite different. . . . The ceremonial fixes degrees and limits (to the expression of senti-ments and in consequence to the sentiments themselves)." [3]

From deportment, from the consciousness of deportment, result control, and the mastery of self. The life of the court, with its obligations of etiquette and the perpetual menace of the vendettas, is a school of moral discipline. Minutely ordered by the register, gestures serve to hold impulses in check : " Rites obviate disorder, as dykes obviate inunda-tions." [4] The vassals, instead of having an unruly heart, learn to have a mind which is under control. They prove the quality of their soul and of their destiny in these cere-

---

[1] *Yi li*, **C**, 238 and 125.   [2] *Lieh Tsih*, **CXLIII**, 147.
[3] *Li ki*, **C**, I, 215.   [4] *Li ki*, **C**, II, 359.

monies, which are tournaments of elegant movements. If
two gentlemen, offering each other their tablet, take it, one
too high and the other too low, if they hold themselves, one
too upright, the other too much bent, it may be said at once
that they are going to die or lose their rank, for "ritual
gestures (*li*) are the bodily substance (*ti* : the body, the
foundation, the material basis) of (that which causes) life or
death, the keeping or losing of one's fief. The future is judged
by the manner of walking to right or left, of turning, advancing,
retreating, bowing and drawing oneself up." [1] The exercises
of civility allow of the definition and classification of destinies :
thus in addition to their value as tests, the tournaments of
ritual acts may present the attraction of an assembly of
mimic oracles. When the tortoise is consulted, to discover
which of the sons of a father who has just died, is worthy to
succeed him, it may have the facetious cunning to reply :
" Let them all wash their hair and body, let them hang
precious stones at their girdle, and you shall have a sign ! "
Five of the brothers bathe and adorn themselves straightway,
but the sixth well knows that those are acts forbidden by
the state of mourning; he takes care to remain unwashed and
without ornament; to him the inheritance belongs (without
need of a supplementary sign given by the divinity); [2] if he has
discovered the worldly snare of the tortoise, it is because he is
impregnated with a sense of the proprieties. It is clear that
he possesses the virtues required of a son. Knowing the value
of rites, he is able to prove that he was born a gentleman.

The virtue of the soul is strengthened in the mimicry of
the court, as it was formerly acquired in the sacred dances.
They sang while they danced, the efficacy of the rites being
complete only if the voice accompanied the actions. But
the voice is the soul itself, and if that be so, the soul is moulded
by song, even more than by the carriage of the body.
Ceremonial does less than music to perfect the good man.
Military life or court life, warlike ballets or fashionable ballets,
are a school of intonation rather than of deportment. Nevertheless, if invective and prayer inspire the gesticulation of
the fighting man, this latter (technically) may be supposed
to play the essential part. Warriors first of all, the nobles

---

[1] *Tso chuan*, C, III, 589. [2] *Li ki*, C, I, 225.

proved their worth when they gave *service* to the prince : thus the first in date of the liberal arts are archery and the driving of chariots. Nevertheless, the science of beautiful language ended by ranking first in the noble arts, and *counsel* by being more valuable than *service*. Court life is spent in ceremonies and palavers, but, more than any other tourney, the oratorical tourneys seem to be rich in efficacy : they are also tourneys of song. In 545 the overlord of Cheng received at dinner Chao Mong, a powerful personage of the country of Chin, from whom Cheng wished to obtain favours.[1] The duke of Cheng was surrounded by the chief nobles of his court. Chao Mong asked them to sing " to complete the favour which he was receiving (from the prince of Cheng : for songs are a kind of homage), and also, to let him understand their sentiments." As a matter of fact, they all revealed their minds, not by inventing verses, but by choosing to sing some verses of the *She king* with secret design, the intonation of the singer adapting them to the circumstances of the meeting. After each song Chao Mong replied by a brief commentary emphasizing the interpretation which he *personally* knew how to give to this homage rendered in verse. Ssu-chan, the chief personage of Cheng, was the first to pay his tribute. He sang: "The meadow grasshopper is chirping. —The hill grasshopper is hopping—till I have seen my lord— my restless heart, oh, how it beats !—But as soon as I see him—as soon as we are united—then my heart will be at peace ! " [It is a love-song, but understand : Cheng only asks to be united to Chin, obedient to the first invitation of this rich country governed by you, my lord, whose prestige gives my heart no rest.] And Chao Mong replies : " (That would be) perfect indeed ! But you talk of a chief (worthy to administer) a State, and certainly, as far as I am concerned, there is nothing in me which can be compared to him." [=I accept your praise for my country : I decline it so far as it concerns myself.] Po-yu (he was a powerful noble, well-connected and turbulent) sang : " The quails go in couples—and the magpies go in pairs.—Shall I take for my brother—a man without kindness (*leang*) ? The magpies go in pairs, and the quails in couples. Of a man without kind- ness—shall I make my lord ? " [This is a love-song again.

[1] *Tso chuan*, **C**, II, 489.

Po-yu suggests (the indirect meaning being apparent in the diplomatic interpretation) that it is fitting to make a good match : understand, if you will (it is all that I can say officially) " I hope that an alliance between Chin and Cheng (as it is governed at the present moment) will be a good thing ! " But (the indirect meaning being concealed) understand (if you accept the idea of a secret alliance with me) " Cheng is governed by people of no virtue whose authority I do not recognise."] And Chao Mong replies [he has no confidence in the success of Po-yu's intrigues] " Nothing which relates to sexual matters should ever cross the threshold (of the private apartments), much more when it is in the open field ! These are things which cannot be listened to ! [= I am not listening, not wishing to be suspected of even half-understanding your hidden meanings.] " It was the turn of Ssu-si : " The glorious labours of Sie—are directed by the duke of Chao !—The terrible chiefs of the army—are inspired by the duke of Chao ! " [A military song praising the chief of an expedition : will Chao Mong be imprudent enough to take all the praise to himself ?] He replies : " Truly we talk of a prince [it is to a prince that all the merits praised by the song must be referred : in the same way, the glory of the present successes of Chin (where I am only the minister) must be set to the account of the prince of Chin alone] but I, what have I been able to do ? " [= You shall not get the better of me by overcoming my loyalty.] Then Ssu-ch'an [who will become chief counsellor of Cheng ; Ssu-ch'an is on good terms with Ssu-chan : he effaces himself and takes up a theme which the latter had given out, but if I may say so, in a lower key] : " What strength in the mulberry-trees of the valley !—what beauty in their foliage !—As soon as I see my lord—what is my joy !—He whom I love from my heart— he is too far away to remember me !—He whom I respect from the depths of my heart—when shall I be able to forget him ? " [= I am not qualified to tell you my joy in an alliance maintained by your intervention, but I can tell you that you are a true gentleman (*kun-tsih* = lord) whom I shall never forget.] Chao Mong [who has just given clear proof of his loyalty, did not depart from his prudent attitude, but he does not go so far as to reject homage which can be accepted without danger. He] replies to Ssu-ch'an : " I allow myself

to accept on my own behalf [certainly not the verses in which
the expression *kun-tsih* is used, but] the last strophe [in which
I understand that you assure me of your personal friendship]."
Yin-tuan then sang : " The cricket is in the hall—and the year
draws to an end !—Why then should we not keep festival ?—
days and months are flying.—Nevertheless let us be temperate
—and remember our position !—Let us love joy without
folly !—A good man is circumspect ! " And Chao Mong :
" Perfectly true indeed ! There is a man who will keep his
domain : as for me, it is my own desire [so I will be (in all
circumstances) moderate and circumspect !]." And finally
Kong-suen Tuan sang : " The yellow-hammers of the mulberry-
tree are fluttering !—how bright their plumage !—These
gentlemen are amiable—they will receive the gifts of Heaven ! "
This was a feasting-song and worthy to close the evening.
Chao Mong replied : " Neither turbulent nor proud ! Could
the gifts of Heaven take wings and fly away ? " . . . The
joust was ended : those who were present counted up the
marks. Merits were classified, destinies could be foretold.
" Po-yu will be executed under circumstances of infamy.
Songs tell the sentiments of the soul.—His sentiment (has
driven him) to speak ill of his prince. . . . The families of
the other six (singers—who have shown a loyal spirit) will
remain (flourishing) for many generations. That of Ssu-chan
(who has sung like a wise minister) will disappear the last.
He was in the highest rank and knew how to humble himself.
The family of Yin-tuan [Chao Mong said " Perfect " after
Yin-tuan's song as after that of Ssu-chan] will only disappear
before (that of Ssu-chan) for he praised moderation in
pleasure." The vassals, by their singing, honoured their
prince and his guest, but at the same time that they competed
in intelligence with the representative of a neighbouring
lordship, they were rivals amongst themselves, deceitful or
loyal, greedy or prudent, and once this singing-match of
verses with diplomatic double meanings was ended, each of
them, having spoken his mind, had decided his fate and that
of his family. Faithfulness is proved, nobility is acquired in
the oratorical tourneys. Does not one chapter of the *Shu King*
(one which has been most irritatingly modernized, but fragments of song still adhere to it), show us Yü the Great (a
future sovereign) victorious over Kao-yao (a future minister)

after having had a fencing match of eloquence with him in one of the great palavers at which Shun presided ? [1]

Words control destinies. He only is noble who knows how to speak, and is able to serve his prince as well at the seigniorial council as in rival courts or the interviews of overlords. " Do not speak lightly !—do not say ' Bah ! what does it matter ! '—Thou alone canst hold thy tongue— let no word escape thee !—Every word exacts its answer— and every virtue its price ! " [2] To say is to do, and it is even to have done, for he who speaks " so that he cannot be answered again " [3] is certainly innocent, but, on the other hand, he is guilty who has neither talent to speak well nor an advocate who can speak for him. The prince of Wei (631 B.C.) is accused of fratricide, a most astonishing charge in view of the feudal customs : but the lords of Chin (who have designs on Wei) put on the airs of leaders, and aspire to have justice done in the name of the sovereign. Chin seizes the accused man and judges him. They do not make him appear in person : the loyalty or the disloyalty of vassals suffices to prove the innocence or guilt of their master. A follower supported by an advocate (*fu*) and an attorney (*t'ai she*) take the place of the overlord who is accused (*tsuo*). This trio not having succeeded in bringing the cause of the prince of Wei to a successful issue, the prince is immediately imprisoned as guilty, but first (as a just reward) his defenders are condemned to death : two are executed on the spot, the advocate profiting by a delay of execution, for it was his duty to plead in the appeal before the sovereign.[4] It is just that the vassals should pay for the acts of the overlord, and the master for the words of his followers. The feudal group is an undivided whole. The acts of a chief involve the honour of the vassals, his virtues give them an eloquent soul—his misdeeds rob them of all verbal authority. His followers transmit the words of the overlord and represent him. Each of them is called upon to play the part of a herald, with all its perils, or rather he in whom the virtue of the chief is most truly reflected is fitted to be the herald of the chieftainship. Ch'i conquered Lu and robbed him of certain domains : the two princes (499 B.C.) [5] meet to swear renewed friendship,

---

[1] SMC, I, 150 ff.   [2] *She king*, C, 381.   [3] *Tso chuan*, C, II, 438.
[4] *Tso chuan*, C, I, 409.   [5] For this interview, see LV, p. 171 ff.

but Ch'i wishes to reduce Lu to a sort of vassalage. The camp of the princes is set up in the country : a mound of earth is raised which is reached by three steps : there the treaty will be sworn. Ch'i (who is the more powerful and the victor) must swear the first : it is his place to draw up the form of oath. If this does not satisfy the people of Lu, they must on the spot improvise a counter-clause. It is important for them to preserve all their self-possession : their prince must be seconded by a herald of imperturbable loyalty. The prince of Lu asks Confucius to assist him. The prince of Ch'i brings a famous personage with him, Yen-tsih, who is clever in discourse, but much more crafty than loyal : Yen-tsih in fact is celebrated for his cunning and his stratagems. [He succeeded at one blow in ridding the prince of Ch'i of three bravoes who might have become turbulent, and this simply by proposing to give a peach to the bravest among them. There were only two fruits to be given as prizes. Naturally, care was taken to invite those to speak first whose exploits were the least renowned, and immediately to let them take the peaches. The bravest committed suicide when he saw himself frustrated of the honour of the tourney. The others imitated him, on a point of honour.] Each of the princes has the helper he deserves. The duke of Ch'i is immoderate to the core. He loves pageantry : his court is filled with musicians, dancing women, and jesters. Yen-tsih his favourite, who is expert at inventing tragic buffooneries, is a dwarf. This elf has a contempt for rites : he has not learnt the art of ascending the steps of a staircase with dignity and of walking with elbows outstretched, flying to his master's service. He is an upholder of positive politics and not of religious forms. Lu has only a humble court, but it is the land of ritual traditions. Also it is a sage, a giant, the apostle of sincerity, Confucius himself, who assists the prince of Lu. The two princes ascend the mound of the treaty and sit down face to face, isolated and unarmed : naked authorities. The vassals are at a little distance, the assistants at the foot of the steps. Formerly, at such a meeting, and at a time when Ch'i also wished to impose a disastrous treaty upon Lu, there was a hero in Lu's camp who, climbing all the steps of the mound, threatened the duke of Ch'i with his dagger and extorted from him an unpremeditated promise. Ch'i had at

that time a wise prince and consequently, a wise minister :
they carried out the oath imposed by force with scrupulous
loyalty : it was a piece of good fortune for Ch'i. But the
times have changed : victory is still on the side of Ch'i : but
loyalty and the loyal counsellor are on the side of Lu. It is
therefore Ch'i which, seeking to confirm by violence a victory
which has not been deserved by wisdom, will try to intimidate
the prince of Lu, isolated upon the mound. An officer proposes to send for the dancers : " Yes " says the prince of Ch'i.
Straightway in a tumult of drums and shouting, advances
a forest of standards, pikes and halberds. But nothing shakes
the loyal soul of Confucius. " With a quick step, he climbs
the (first) steps of the mound, but not the last, and lifts his
sleeves in the air." Etiquette does not sanction more violent
gestures in a vassal. But, when the vassal has the sense of
deportment, he possesses the art of speaking. Raised on the
second step, Confucius spoke. Yen-tsih had no reply to make.
Thanks to the talents of his herald, Lu won the day against
Ch'i : a counter-clause was inserted in the treaty promising
the return of the stolen domains : and (every match between
princely prestige implying a chastisement of the vanquished—
who are guilty) Confucius, to mark the triumph of right,
ordered an execution. The tradition of the hagiographers
maintains that he had the jesters and the dwarfs cut in
pieces : was it not the best means of proclaiming the defeat
of a prince who was disloyal and an enemy to the rites, who
could only have a dwarf and a jester for his minister ? The
princely mind is spoken by the voice of the herald, and in
the oratorical tourneys which are the interviews of chiefs
this it is which wins glory or shame for the overlordship.
The eloquent counsellor, in times when half victories only
are sought for in battle, is the great winner of prestige and
the real second of the overlord, rather than the general.

The solidarity of the feudal group is established in court
assemblies rather than at war. In meetings for counsel the
vassals give themselves to the prince. They hold in possession
from the prince whatever wisdom they have : they give back
this wisdom to him in the form of advice. An overlordship
is lost if the same virtue does not animate all the vassals
and all the counsellors. " To appear to be in agreement
and to disparage each other—ah ! that is the greatest of

evils ! " " To fill with words the court of audience " [1] is of no use if hearts are not unanimous : on the contrary, each must be able to accept the responsibility (*kiu :* the effect, whether harmful or glorious) of the advice which he gave or that others have extolled, but which has been accepted by the overlord, in the name of all, when he said " yes." When advice is adopted all the counsellors are obliged to carry it out, unless they have been careful to free themselves from responsibility. But to repudiate a decision which in principle can only be unanimous, is to cut oneself off from the feudal group, to put one under a ban, to curse oneself and run the risk of bringing a curse upon one's fellows and upon the overlord. The reproof (*kien*)—contrary advice—is an act which is inconceivable in an overlordship which is possessed of happy fortune. It is a duty, a fatal duty, in the counsel of an overlordship which is declining. The vassal who pleads against the others condemns himself to expiate the harmful effect of the decisions which he repudiates. The similar advice of three counsellors constitutes unanimity of counsel. A protest, three times repeated, attacks the decision with a sort of opposition in suspension : provisionally it loosens the bonds of fate, but it pledges the destiny of the protester. It is his duty to retire, to lay down his office, to leave the country : he must expiate what he imputes to others as a fault. To give way would only be " to stay to hate " and to bring ill luck upon the act which has been determined.[2] The objector must, except in extreme cases, avoid cursing the others and excommunicating himself. When the vassal whose advice has been rejected quits his country, he breaks with his fatherland and with his ancestors : he cannot carry away the utensils which were employed by him in his patrimonial acts of worship. He loses his gods. " When he has crossed the frontier, he levels a piece of ground and builds a mound of earth. He turns his face towards his country and utters lamentations. He clothes himself in a tunic, an under-garment, a white head-covering without ornaments, and stripped of its coloured borders [mourning attire]. He wears shoes of undressed leather, the back of his carriage is covered with the skin of a white dog, the horses harnessed to it have not been cropped. He himself ceases to cut his

---

[1] *She king,* C, 244.   [2] *Li ki,* C, I, 96, and II, 10.

nails, his beard and his hair. When he eats, he abstains
from making any libation [he is debarred from communion
with the gods]. He refrains from saying that he is not guilty
[he also refrains from saying that he is guilty : only a chief
has enough spirit and authority to be able to make such
a formal confession]. His wives (or at the least, his chief
wife) are no longer admitted to his presence [his sexual life
and his relations with home are interrupted]. Not till three
months are past does he resume his ordinary clothes." [1] The
expatriated vassal mourns his lost fatherland, but it is also
his own mourning that he bears. He breaks off former
attachments, and makes an end of the personality which has
been his up till then. When, at the end of three months, he
lays aside the signs of woe, he is no longer the man of such
an overlord and such a country. In order to cease being an
opponent, he ought to die for his fatherland. All the time
that he is wearing mourning raiment and enduring abstinence,
he holds over his lord the threat of an act of suicide. This
threat has a horrible potency, and suffices, even when it is
aimed at a stranger, to put constraint upon his will. A vassal
of Ch'u succeeded in obtaining the help of the armies of
Ch'in for his conquered master by mourning for seven days,
leaning against a wall of the princely palace, while the sound
of his voice never ceased except when a spoonful of broth
was entering his mouth.[2] When the protesting vassal
expatriates himself and fasts, he is seeking to put constraint
upon his overlord, to make him repudiate the projects in
which he himself refuses to take part. In urgent cases, he
can employ a more brutal method. The prince of Chin,
circumvented by his wife, a daughter of Ch'in, sets free
some generals of Ch'in, whom he has conquered and taken
prisoner. One vassal presents himself, *reprimands* the prince,
then " spits on the ground, without turning aside." [3] Thus
he throws the most real of maledictions upon the princely
decision : henceforth a terrible alternative is imposed upon
the overlord : he must either renounce the accursed decision
(this was done by the prince of Chin) or else he must put his
vassal to death, thus incurring all the responsibility of an
execution deliberately provoked by the latter. But, without
incurring the penalty, a faithful vassal can deliver his overlord

[1] *Li ki*, C, I, 78.   [2] *Tso chuan*, C, III, 519.   [3] *Tso chuan*, C, I, 432.

from the ill fortune resulting from an ill-timed decision : it will suffice if the protester exclaims, while he points to the counsellors of the other side : " It is they who have desired it ! " [1] If the overlord follows their advice, but is prudent enough to suggest that he accepts it with limitations, it will be possible, in case of ill success, to wipe out the inauspicious act by getting rid of the evil counsellors. The calamity is transferred to their shoulders.[2] Doubtless it is nobler on the part of the overlord to claim the whole responsibility for himself and to say : " My generals and my ministers are only my arms and legs," but if in theory, the overlordship has one soul only, that of the chief, and if in principle, counsel must be unanimous, in practice, the principal use of the court reunion is to fix the responsibility for each counsel upon one individual : afterwards, the words which are uttered no longer commit one's fortune irremediably to a single path. Repentance becomes possible, and already victims are designated for the expiations which may be imposed. In council as in battle the aim is to dilute responsibility, for there is hesitation in pledging oneself irrevocably. Precisely because one's word pledges one's fate and shows the naked soul, it is the aim of every counsellor, not to speak in order to say nothing, but at least to express himself only with the help of proverbial formulas. These command respect by their traditional character, but while tradition has consecrated them, they have, on the other hand, a neutral value only, and above all they are capable of varied interpretations. The ideal is for the counsel to assume the guise of a tourney of proverbs and for the decision to have the appearance of a rebus. Duke Hien of Chin (659 B.C.) is deliberating to find out whether he shall entrust the command of the army to his eldest son. He is the designated heir. He has his party at court. Another party is grouped round a favourite of duke Hien who has a step-mother's hatred for the eldest son. This party proposes to nominate the young prince as general : it is the best way to destroy him. If he commits the crime of being conquered, he is guilty. He will be guilty, he is guilty already, if being victorious he lays himself open to the suspicion of wishing to employ the prestige given by victory, against his father. The friends of the young prince

---

[1] *Tso chuan*, C, II, 253.   [2] SMC, IV, 379.

try to make him escape the test. The duke of Chin makes his decision : he gives his eldest son the command of the troops, but when he invests him with the garments of a general, it is perceived that the young prince will have to wear a robe divided in half, and a half-circle of metal. Five excellent counsellors then exert themselves to discover the meaning of the rebus formed by this toilet. The result of the interpretation given by one of them is that the prince should go boldly forward, but the others conclude that he should avoid the battle. The subtlety of the discussions which then ensued give an exalted idea of the oratorical talents which must be required of a counsellor.[1] It is very curious to ascertain that the intrigue carried on under cover of these pompous deliberations in the Council of State was secretly led by a jester, who was a kind of intimate counsellor. Fools, singers, jesters [2] played a part in the feudal courts which gained in importance in proportion as the overlords, transformed into potentates, were decked with a more punctilious majesty : they ill brooked any but secret and disguised advice. The art of the apologue whose tradition was retained by the jesters, allowed them to give a strictly indirect turn to their remonstrances. And, for the rest, they did not speak in the name of a feudal group, and their discourse had not the terrible weight of that of a vassal bound by the brutal duty of sincerity. At court as at war, there was a tendency for specialists to supplant the nobles. Mean men, learned in the technique of songs, and apt at inventing tales, supplanted in the chiefs' favour the vassals who owed their ready tongue to their nobility alone and whose sincere soul was seen in their employment of nothing but proverbs in verse and ritual formulas wherein was recorded the wisdom of the ancestors.

One can neither dress well, bear oneself well, nor speak well, one is neither wise nor noble, unless one possesses, as one's own share, something of the soul of the overlord. The gentleman is he who eats much and knows how to eat. He it is who eats what is left over by the chief and should delight in it, an overlord alone having enough soul to be able to pretend to despise food and be content with the virtue of offerings. Those who boasted of belonging to a race which, for long

---

[1] *Tso chuan,* **C,** I, 222 ff.   [2] *Tso chuan,* **C,** III, 755.

generations, had enjoyed a fief and had the spending of a
noble salary, loved to repeat this old adage " Ssu êrh pu hiu."
This formula in former times seems to have signified : " Do
not allow the flesh of a dead man to rot ! " but while men
of refined feelings saw in it a straightforward piece of
advice : " [Leave good examples which] do not corrupt, even
after death ! " the great preferred the interpretation " [In
a noble race] death itself does not bring corruption [the
family remaining alive and strong]," and there is no doubt
that they would have liked it to be literally true, and to have
been able to say : " After his death [the body of a great
man] is not subject to corruption " [1]—so true is it that
the same ideas which drive men to invent rites by whose
help the dead may escape the horrors of a slow decomposition,
may also lead them to desire an indefinite preservation of the
corpse and (after gradual transpositions) its final transformation into simple precepts of morality. The nobles of
the feudal period were beautiful and pure in mind and body
because their food was pure and rich : because they ate
decently of well-cooked meats and ate them in presence of
the prince. They forbade themselves many varieties of food ; [2]
wolf's tripe, dog's kidney, brains of the sucking pig, entrails
of fish, rump of domestic goose, breast of stag, gizzard of
bustard, liver of chicken. In spring they mixed onions with
their minced meat, and in autumn mustard. They added
knot-grass to quail and chicken broth and to the flesh of
partridge : they added sweet-scented herbs, but never knot-
grass, to chicken and pheasant (when they were roasted) and
to bream and perch when they were steamed. When they
ate beef-steak, they seasoned it with ginger. The flesh of
the elk, the stag, the boar and the fallow-deer, was served
either cut in steaks, pounded and dried, or else raw, in which
case it was cut in very thin slices. For dainty dishes they
had snail's flesh, minced and preserved in vinegar, rice soup
mixed with pheasant broth, soup from glutinous rice which
has been coarsely ground mixed with broth of hare and of
dog, fish stuffed with knot-grass and fish's roe preserved in
salt. In addition to fermented drinks, they drank vinegar
water and the juice of plums. The skin of peaches was
rubbed to make it greenish and shining like gall (gall is the

[1] *Tso chuan*, C.   [2] *Li ki*, C, I, 640 ff.

seat of courage). At the most distinguished feasts there figured grilled tortoises, shoots of bamboo and rush, minced carp—these viands were specially suitable for the entertainment of a soldier, to whom was offered, in addition, a lump of salt shaped like a tiger.[1] Viands must be served and eaten in a fixed order. The meat dishes, for instance, were arranged in five rows : the venison came last, preceding the fish. The table utensils were placed in accordance with strict rules. The boiled fish was served with the tail turned towards the guest, but in such a way that in summer the back was turned to the right, and in winter the belly. At the princely table the lip of the amphora was turned towards the prince, and at every other table, towards the chief guest. All sauces and drinks made of more than one substance were taken with the right hand and were placed at the left. It was forbidden to eat millet otherwise than with a spoon, to drink broth without chewing the herbs, to drink pickle as though it were deficient in salt, to toss rice in the air (with the chop-sticks) to cool it, or to roll it into little balls to swallow it more quickly. Pieces were not snatched like prey, and the bones were not thrown to the dogs.[2] When melon was eaten, it was divided in two and covered with a cloth, if it was for a prince : if it was for a great officer, care was also taken to divide it, but the cloth was dispensed with. For a simple noble, it was sufficient to cut off the lower portion. As to the common people, they tore the melon with their teeth.[3] One must take care not to have perspiring hands, nor to make a noise or grimaces with one's mouth. Boiled meat was torn with the teeth and dried meat with the fingers. The bits of fish which were removed from the mouth were not returned to the dishes.[4] The mouth was never rinsed before the master of the house had tasted all the dishes : one should begin to eat with him and not cease till he had finished : at a chief's table (where one must be on one's best behaviour) a greedy air must be eschewed, and care taken to lean a little backwards when seating oneself on one's mat.[5] But as soon as the host had wiped the corners of his mouth with his fingers, they all brought their repast to an end with a drink, and,

---

[1] *She king*, **C**, 203 and 404 : *Tso chuan*, **C**, I, 419.
[2] *Li ki*, **C**, I, 639 ; I, 36 ff. ; II, 21 ff.
[3] *Li ki*, **C**, I, 40.
[4] *Li ki*, **C**, I, 35 ff. ; II, 20 ff.
[5] *Li ki*, **C**, I, 686 ff.

having offered to clear the table, they thanked him with the words : " We are full ! " Yet it was not correct for them to withdraw " dancing and cutting capers." Those who could not carry their drink were threatened with the " ram without a horn " : an overseer and a controller called them back to the proprieties. " We guests, when we are drunk—one roars and the other shouts—overturning our vessels and our pots— they dance and their body stumbles ! " [1] If no guest " must allow himself not to (say) that he is satisfied," all, on the other hand, must pretend that they are only tasting the viands. In the repasts offered by great chiefs, the meat is sliced and not cut up into small pieces. The gift of food, which ennobles, but enslaves and infeudates, is only accepted cautiously, with a mixture of respect and distrust, of pride and humility. With the vassal by birth, respect is the ruling emotion, and he cannot omit to eat abundantly of the food which the master offers him : but he ought while he eats to observe a perfect decorum : " If the prince gives you to eat what he has left, eat it off his own plate (that is, if it can be washed after you have eaten) " for the bond which will result from this communion will be the closer if you have shared both food and dish. " If the prince commands a stone-fruit to be given you, keep the stone in your bosom " : it is a mark of favour. If the prince gives you food, eat some of it, but above all, keep some of it for your parents : you will comfort them, you will enrich their life, and you will refer your titles of nobility to an older generation.[2]

The overlord feeds the vassal. The latter owns exactly as much nobility as he receives food, and he is faithful in the precise measure with which he is fed. A traitor is fomenting a rebellion. He has the palace cooks and the footmen in his pay. Instead of preparing each day for the great officers the chickens which are theirs by right, the cooks cook nothing but ducks, and the footmen, emphasizing the outrage, remove the ducks and serve up nothing but the gravy. It is enough to arouse a vendetta and to lead to the explosion of savage fury : " Would I could make me a couch of their skins ! " [3] The prince has received a magnificent present from a friendly overlord : a great marine tortoise.

[1] *She king*, C, 297 and 197.   [2] *Li ki*, C, I, 38 : SMC, IV, 314.
[3] *T'so chuan*, C, II, 508.

A vassal who appears at Court feels his index finger (the finger with which one eats) twitching. " Whenever that has happened to me," he says, " I have always eaten some marvellous food." But the prince, informed of the fact, and vexed that the vassal should think himself in advance sure of having his share in the feast, abstains from inviting him to table. The vassal, offended, dips his finger in the caldron, sucks it and goes out. From that moment the prince has in mind to kill his follower, and the follower to kill the prince. The communion has been broken between them.[1] When Confucius saw that his overlord preferred the pernicious songs of musicians sent by a cunning enemy of the land of Lu, to his own counsels, he refused at first to despair : he wished to wait for the time of a great sacrifice, saying : " If the prince sends the meat of the sacrifice to the great officers, I shall be able to remain." When the time came, Confucius received nothing to nourish his fidelity : he then departed, like one that had been excommunicated, condemning himself " to wander for ever hither and thither." [2] That which constitutes the bond of vassalship, is the right of eating daily at the overlord's table, but with the nobility, that which properly gives a place in the hierarchy, is participation in the seigniorial sacrifices, sacrifices to the soil, and above all, sacrifices to the princely ancestors. Beautiful hymns sing the praise of the overlord, whose happy virtue makes the fields prosper : he may offer rich sacrifices, at which, figured by a representative chosen from the family, the ancestors come to eat and take their portion of the harvests : after them feast the prince and his vassals : " Tend the fire with respect,—set up supports which shall be vast :— roast ! broil !—And you, princess of the serious air—set very many vessels in place !—Here are the hosts and the guests—cups which are offered and passed round !—Rites and actions quite perfect !—Laughter and talk quite correct !— The holy representative of the Spirits—is going to dispense great happiness to me :—ten thousand years, as a reward !— I have given my whole self :—I was lacking in nothing at the rite !—The invocator speaks his oracle,—the reward of the pious descendant :—' Fragrant was the pious offering !— The Spirits have eaten and drunk !—They prophesy every

[1] *Tso chuan*, **C**, I, 582.   [2] SMC, V, 329.

joy for thee—according to thy vows, according to the rules !—
Thou wast serious, thou wast active,—thou wast careful,
thou wast correct.—Therefore receive their gifts for ever—
by the myriad and the hundred thousand ! ' Rites and deeds
are ended—bells, drums, sound the end !—Pious descendant,
I take my seat :—the invocator speaks his oracle :—' The
Spirits have drunk their belly-full ! '—The representative of
the ancestors—departs at the sound of the drums and the
bells !—' Depart, representative of the Spirits !—And you,
servants, and you, princess,—clear the tables swiftly and
with no delay !—With my uncles and my cousins—in our
full number we will feast.'—The musicians enter and play !—
Thus our happiness is confirmed !—There are the victuals :—
Nothing displeases and all is magnificent !—Filled with wine,
gorged with meat,—say great and small prostrate on their
faces': ' The Spirits have eaten and drunk,—giving long life
to the overlord !—Very largely, exactly on the right day—
you gave good measure in everything !—Sons, and again
sons, grandsons—a continuous line, will follow you.' " [1]
The vassals contribute to the overlord's sacrifices. The
offerings which they present to the prince, he presents to
his ancestors : this supreme consecration enriches the food
and drink of the sacrifice with an august sanctity. In communion with the princely ancestors the vassals are nourished,
after the overlord, according to their rank, in sanctity and
nobility. " After the offering the remains were eaten. . . .
(First) the representative of the ancestors eats what remains
(of the sacrifice). When he is satisfied and rises, the overlord
and his ministers, *four* persons (all told) eat what he has
left. When the prince (is satisfied and) rises, the great officers
to the number of *six* eat the remains (in their turn) : the
vassals eat what is left over by the overlord. When (being
satisfied), the great officers rise, the officers (simple nobles)
to the number of *eight* eat the remains (in their turn) : the
lesser nobles eat what is left by the greater nobles (*kuei*).
When the officers rise (being satisfied) they carry away the
dishes and set them in order at the foot of the steps in the
hall : all the servants draw near the dessert : the humble
[*hsia* (low) : those who ought to remain at the foot of the
steps] eat what is left by their superiors [*shang* (high) : those

[1] *She king*, C, 276.

who are admitted into the hall of receptions]. The principle which governs the consumption of the remains is each time to increase the number of persons admitted to eat them : thus are marked the degrees of nobility : it is a symbol of the wide range of the princely generosity." " The most noble (those who eat not the most, but the best) receive the (meat adhering to) the most noble bones [these are said to have been the shoulders in the days of the Chou dynasty] : the less noble (those who can eat much, but less well) receive the (meat adhering to the) less noble bones." [1] The vassals pay tribute according to the dignity of their fief : the overlord distributes to them the offerings which are enriched by their dedication to the Spirits : he gorges them all with the holy substance, but he rewards them each in a registered proportion and order. Each in his rank obtains a strictly defined share of sacred force and of nobility, with a piece of meat which is more or less distinguished. But while it varies in quality as in quantity, this sacred force remains identical in essence for them all. They form all together a corps of nobles : they are the upper ranks, those who are admitted to eat, *after the chief, but on the chief's level*, the food by which the soul of defunct overlords is nourished. Like the chief, they have a soul which will not go, at the moment of death, to lose itself in the lowest parts of the earth : it will dwell, highly exalted, in the celestial regions where the dead chiefs still hold their court, and to which the burnt fat of victims ascends in smoke. And, during their life-time, they will enjoy in their families the sanctity of a chief, all the prestige by which a human group is enabled to rule, all the virtue which puts it in their power to make a domain fruitful, and which gives them the right to be possessors of land. When the chief leads the way at the first ploughing, he traces a small number of furrows by himself : immediately all the earth is fruitful and all the first fruits are due to the holy author of the removal of the ban upon the soil.[2] Meanwhile, the vassals, in the order of their dignity, plough after their overlord, all animated by the sacred force which is concentrated in their master and diffused in them, but working in greater numbers and each ploughing more numerous furrows according as they are poorer in nobility and in efficacious virtue : in his train

[1] *Li ki*, C, II, 329. [2] *Li ki*, C, I, 325.

they acquire an eminent right (subordinate, however, to that of the prince) over the fields, with which the peasants, boors as they are, have no connexion but that of labour—for the labour of mean men can confer none but mean rights.

Every noble is a chief with his virtue diluted. The same soul dwells in the overlord and in the bodyguard of gentlemen who make up his court. Moreover, the bond of vassaldom implies an entire concurrence of wills. It does not differ at all from the bond of parenthood, existing at the same epoch between father and son. The vassal wears mourning for the overlord with the same strictness with which he wears mourning for his own father. The feudal group is a species of family, just as we shall see that the family is a species of feudal group. Like the domestic group, the feudal group is a communal unity. The members of the group are possessed by the same genius, all sharing in it, but all sharing unequally, for the group is in the nature of a hierarchy. The brother who seeks to supplant his brother, the vassal who wishes to dethrone his overlord (such practices are of daily occurrence) do not put themselves outside the law of the group : they are only attacking its order. They do not break a communion : they are not guilty of a crime against the fatherland or the family, but simply of lèse-majesté, and this only in case they are unsuccessful. For their success would reveal a majesty in them superior to that of their victim, and he would be the true criminal. Thus, while the effort of a homogeneous group may tend only to uphold and strengthen a communal union, the effort of the feudal group is exercised more apparently to maintain the hierarchic rule which they have set over themselves : for this reason the ceremonies which periodically renew the communion of the faithful are regulated in such a way as to mark, in registered proportions, the share of prestige which is due to each one. All social symbolism has for its object the strengthening of the sense of discipline. Discipline is the ideal, because insubordination is the fact. No one thinks life to be possible outside a protected circle, but as soon as he forms a part of that circle, he possesses for himself a share of that contagious virtue which makes the sanctity of a recognized chief. The chief has no other occupation than to concentrate prestige in himself.

To remain an august prince, he must be a prince who does nothing. But when action is indispensable, it can be performed by a vassal alone, and he can only act with the help of a delegation of the princely virtue. Now, whether by a defeat he compromises the sanctity of the overlord, or by succeeding too well he sanctifies himself disproportionately, he must always be a menace to his overlord's dignity. Herald or general, the vassal dooms himself to expiation if he decides upon real action [for there is no distinction between absolute devotion and factious ambition]. He who would show himself to be emphatically a loyal servant, must be, not perhaps altogether a do-nothing minister, but without deviation a minister who acts only according to form and for form. Sincerity (ch'eng) which is the first duty of the vassal, is defined as conduct which is entirely conformable to the laws of etiquette. He who prides himself on his fidelity, must show clearly that he only acts, thinks and feels in accordance with registered rules. Parade, a regulated parade, is the whole of public life. So it remained up to the moment when the technicians ousted the old nobility from the prince's favour. But when private counsel, or worse still, the court of lawyers, replaces the court of vassals with its tourneys and its palavers, the days of the feudal nobility are ended. It is true that the honest man will take the place of the gentleman : the latter was apt at every service : the other will pride himself on knowing everything.—During the long centuries of its ascendancy, the Chinese acquired precious virtues through their feudal discipline. They recognized the merits of formalism, of regulated actions, of ready-made formulas. They understood the moral value of conformity. As an essential duty they laid down the practice of the most entire and genuine loyalty : they had the wisdom to define it by a formal adhesion to a whole collection of consecrated conventions, of established hierarchies, of good traditions. They made sincerity and honour the fundamental principles of their conduct and their thought. They codified with strictness the practice of these virtues, and when they decided to devote their lives to the worship of etiquette, they succeeded in avoiding the uneasiness of mind which may result from an anarchical pursuit of the just and the true.

Chapter IV

PRIVATE LIFE

If the Chinese may be believed, filial piety has been from all antiquity the foundation of domestic and even of civic morality. The respect due to paternal authority is considered to be the greatest of duties, a primary duty from which all social obligations are derived. If the prince deserves to be obeyed, it is because the people recognize a father in him. The authority of a government, of whatever kind, seems to be always patriarchal in essence, for duties toward the State are imagined only as an extension of family duties. The loyal subject results from the pious son. When the father instructed the son in piety (*hiao*) he taught him loyalty (*chong*). The father is then the first magistrate, and according to the classical theory the magistrature which he exercises is not held by delegation : it belongs to him by a right which is founded on nature.

These ideas correspond to sentiments which today are so completely consolidated that the Chinese feel justified in declaring them innate. But these sentiments have a history. They were inculcated into the nation through the propagandist effort of a school of ritualists and of masters of ceremonies. They liberated the principles of national morality when they set themselves to analyse the customs which were in force among the feudal nobles. Two rituals result from this work of analysis : the *Yi li* and the *Li ki*, which numerous collections of anecdotes may be used to illustrate. These collections are presented as historical narratives, while the rituals are placed under the distant patronage of Confucius. Nevertheless, their definite compilation only dates from the time of the Han, but from that time they acquire a sort of canonical value. They are read with the object of discovering in them the code of morality : no one would dare to imagine that this morality was not that of the ancients.

On the other hand, when historic data are taken into account, it is obvious that, far from issuing from a simple codification of natural sentiments, the rules of filial piety are derived from ancient rites by which in primitive times agnatic affiliation could be obtained. It was only at the end of a long evolution that father and son looked upon each other as relatives. The first bond which united them was a bond of infeudation, a juridical and not a natural bond, and moreover, a bond of extra-familial nature. The son saw a relative in his father only after he had recognized him as his overlord.

It is well then to invert the historic postulate which is at the foundation of Chinese theories. Civic morality is not a projection of domestic morality : it is, on the contrary, the law of the feudal citadel which has impregnated domestic life. When, under the influence of the rituals, the agnatic principle alone governed family organization, the piety of the son toward the father, a special aspect of the loyalty shown to an overlord, appeared, when it extended to all family relations, to lie at the root even of the bond of relationship. Hence arises a characteristic trait in the private life of the Chinese, which is so important that we must dwell upon it at length. While the domestic order seems to rest entirely upon paternal authority, the idea of respect takes absolute precedence of the idea of affection in family relationships. Regulated on the model of court assemblies, domestic life forbids all familiarity. Etiquette rules there and not intimacy.

I

The Noble Family

In addition to the historical interest which it yields by reason of its influence upon the development of Chinese customs, the organization of the noble family in feudal China is of great sociological interest. This family is of a rather rare and most curious type, for it is a type of transition. In fact, it holds the mean between the undivided agnatic family and the family which is truly patriarchal.[1]

Larger than the patriarchal family, it yet does not include the whole number of agnates. It is not undivided. Beyond

[1] I employ these two expressions in the strict sense given to them by Durkheim.

a certain number of degrees the relationship grows weaker. Certain obligations do not extend beyond a fixed circle of relatives. Others are limited to a circle which is still smaller. But the smallest of these circles always includes the collaterals and not a father with his descendants only. It is not enough for the father to die, for all his sons to acquire the paternal authority. The eldest alone can at once be invested with it. Thus the family, which is not undivided, is also not patriarchal in the strict sense of the word. Paternal authority is recognized, but it is limited and subordinated to other authorities. The rights of the eldest uncle compete with those of the father. The duties of children vary according to whether they are first-born or cadets. Authority, in short, is not exercised, in every field at once, by a single person. The parents as a whole are divided into distinct groups with varying functions. As an extended body of agnates, distributed in hierarchized groups of dependents, the noble family forms an articulated body, a complex unity, in which nevertheless no authority arises which can wield a truly monarchical power.

(1). *Domestic Organization*

Community of name (*t'ong sing*) is the essential element of relationship. Community of worship (*t'ong tsong*) is the principle of domestic organization.[1] All who bear the same name are related and, being committed to definite duties, they form one family (*sing*). On the other hand, relatives are distributed in a certain number of religious colleges (*tsong*). The *tsong* are more or less huge. They never include more than those relatives who are bound by definite ties to a common ancestor, him whose worship is celebrated by the college. Thus, while relationship does not rest upon the affinities of natural proximity, the religious communities whose union forms the one great family, are constituted through the consideration of individual ties.

It will be remembered that in the peasant family, which is undivided, the name is the sign of relationship : a sign charged with reality, a symbol rich in sentiments, it implies

---

[1] All the following analysis is taken from the chapter of the *Yi li* which deals with mourning according to degrees of relationship.

a virtue (*tö*) and characterizes a species (*lei*). In the noble family (and this is the first reason for thinking that it is derived by evolution from the undivided family) relationship is also defined by identity of name (*sing*). Two noble family groups are related if the same name is borne in them, and this even in the case where they trace no common ancestor. The name does not depend in any way upon ties of blood : no sort of remoteness, no complication of alliances can deprive the name of its power to create relationship. When a Chinese family name is given to a barbarian group, all the Barbarians of the group become related to the Chinese family groups which bear that name.[1] The name possesses the individual rather than that the individual possesses the name. It is inalienable. The married woman ceases to depend entirely upon the head of her family, and by the fact of her marriage her duties of filial piety are, if not suppressed, at least diminished ; yet she keeps her name. The orphan who follows his mother to the house of a second husband, contracts bonds of dependence towards the latter, which impose upon him the piety of a son. A prolonged residence under the same roof may result in making him the one to carry on the religious cult of his stepfather. Nevertheless he cannot acquire his name.[2] This rule clearly shows that the principles of relationship and those upon which the domestic organization of the nobility are founded, belong to two different categories. One parallel fact proves the priority of relationship : under normal conditions, only he can be adopted as successor who already bears the name of the adopter.[3]

Community of name (*t'ong sing*) implies a certain number of characteristic duties : between relatives there can be neither marriage nor vendetta. The jousts of revenge, like the sexual jousts, are the means by which those who are not united by identity of name and of nature, compare and ally themselves, approach and oppose each other. This identity, on the other hand, brings an obligation to take part in the same struggles and the same alliances. All the relatives must support the principal avenger of a slain relative.[4] When a matrimonial alliance is concluded, all the groups of

---

[1] The giving of a name to a group of Barbarians has the object of regulating the marriages between it and the Chinese family groups.
[2] *Yi li*, **C**, 395 and 401.   [3] *Yi li*, **C**, 398.   [4] *Li ki*, **C**, I, 148.

the same name take part in it : girl attendants accompany
the bride to her husband's house, sent by two different
groups. Thus three groups take part in the nuptial vows.
Three is a total number, and a triple vow attests that
the entire family connexion is taking part in it. It is a
significant fact that the participation of the attendants must
be spontaneous : it is as much a right as a duty.[1] The bonds
of relationship imply equality and indivisibility.

It is quite otherwise with the ties which result from
membership of a religious community (*t'ong tsong*). These
are susceptible of graduation and imply a hierarchy. The
members of a particular family (*shu sing*) bear a name
(cognomen : *she*) which properly belongs to them : in theory,
relatives who are not descended from the same great-great-
grandfather may distinguish themselves by adopting a
secondary name (*she*). These names are in no respect family
names. Family names (*sing*) are an obstacle to marriage
even when there is no evidence of a common ancestry. Those
who bear the same *cognomen* (*she*) may be united in marriage,
if they are of different *sing*, but, in that case, they cannot
participate in those family love-feasts in which people of the
same *sing* take part, and where rank is determined by age
(literally, by the teeth).[2] These equalizing communions are
significant of relationship, which is by nature undivided and
founded upon the idea of consubstantiality. People of the
same *cognomen* are " bound by food," but in quite another
way. Belonging to the same religious organization, they
unite to take part in the banquets of Ancestor Worship :
these banquets, which have the function of communion, in
no way resemble the equalizing love-feasts. Each one brings
his quota to them, but instead of merging it in the common
stock, he gives it to the religious chief. Each one receives
his allotted portion of food, but the portions, which are
allotted, like the contributions, by registered rules, are
divided by the chief and when they are distributed by him,
they are received as a gift : there is communion, but it is
hierarchized.

A particular family (*shu sing*) is divided into religious
colleges which are unequal in rank. The lowest are the
colleges formed by a band of brothers, who grouped with

[1] **LII**, 9, 14, 68 ff.   [2] *Li ki*, **C**, I, 779.

their descendants around the eldest, worship a deceased father. These fraternal communities, which form the smallest domestic unit, already have an hierarchical organization : they recognize the privilege of primogeniture. A son who is not his father's principal heir cannot himself make offerings to him : he merely takes part in the offerings made by the eldest.[1] A superior community, directed by the eldest uncle, groups together the descendants of the same grandfather : the fraternal communities are united within it, each having its rank determined by that of its chief. Above this is the group formed by all the descendants of the same great-grandfather, and higher again that which celebrates the worship of a common great-great-grandfather. These four species of religious colleges can unite with similar colleges to celebrate the worship of a more distant ancestor, the eldest-known ancestor of all the groups which still bear the same *cognomen* and have not broken away from each other to form a separate family (*shu sing*). The chief of this great college (*ta tsong*) is the chief of the highest college in the direct line. This domestic organization, in contrast to the conception of relationship founded upon indivisibility, is closely connected with Ancestor Worship. The latter is a privilege of the nobles who alone have the right to possess an ancestral temple. Now, the ordinance of this temple preserves the mark of an ancient indivisible organization upon which the organization into hierarchized groups appears to have been superimposed. Numerous reasons have already been pointed out which justify the idea that the uterine principle, which originally took precedence of the agnatic principle, gained strength from the time that a legal conception of filiation itself acquired a certain importance in the undivided organization. An adage of the Chinese rituals is worth quoting here. " The beasts know their mother and not their father. The country people say : ' Why should we discriminate between father and mother ? ' But the town nobles know how to honour their deceased father." [2] If the women, mothers of the village where their husbands were only annexed consorts, were in the beginning the mothers of all the children of the village, we can understand why the term which expressed the affection of children for their mothers (*tsin*) was used to

---

[1] *Li ki*, C, I, 784.　　　　　[2] *Yi li*, C, 399.

denote the parents and has remained descriptive of the sentiments which are implied by the ties of relationship, but on the other hand could never be used to denote the sentiments which actuate the father. The father cannot be *tsin*, near : he is *tsun*, worthy of respect, and this latter term (which exactly expresses the relationship between father and son in China) calls up the idea of the respect which requires a distance to be kept—the respect which is paid by the inferior to the superior (*tsun*).[1] But it is a significant fact, that while the grandfather, even more than the father, deserves to be honoured as a superior, he is said to be *tsin*, a near relative, a parent, and as a matter of fact, familiarities may be taken with the grandfather which would be considered unseemly with the father. This privileged situation is explained by the fact that before being reckoned in the agnatic line, the grandfather, as we saw before, by right of being maternal uncle to the mother, first occupied a place among the uterine relatives. It is the same with the great-great-grandfather, while the great-grandfather (like the father) could only be considered as a relation when the agnatic principle in its turn superseded the uterine principle. Now, the idea that the members of two consecutive agnatic generations are distant relatives, while the representatives of alternate generations are near, exactly explains, and can alone explain, the ordinance of the ancestral temple reserved solely for agnates and their wives. This ordinance (called the order *chao-mu*) requires the tablets of father and son, of great-grandfather and great-grandson to be placed opposite each other in two lines, while the tablets of grandson and grandfather appear in the same row. ·

In ·the same way, when the living unite to celebrate worship, they must place themselves in two opposite bands, the members of two consecutive generations facing each other, while the members of alternate generations mingle in one group.[2] Finally, when a child is qualified to preside at a religious ceremony and has to be carried, being too young to walk, no one may undertake this office if he belongs to the same generation as the father of the child. He must be carried by a representative of his grandfather's generation,

[1] LII, 10 and 46.
[2] *Li ki*, C, I, 777 ; I, 287 ; II, 336 and 446 ; LII, 61 ; LV, 14, note 1.

and it is as a result of this rule, wrested from its ritual meaning and taken in a purely moral sense, that the permission of familiarities between grandfathers and grandsons which are forbidden between fathers and sons, may be justified.[1] From the organization into religious colleges sprang a new conception of the idea of relationship. When the family was undivided, relationship was confounded with the idea of consubstantiality. But amongst the nobles, who are qualified to celebrate ancestral worship, the feasts which they hold in the temple of the Ancestors are more frequent and more honoured than the love-feasts where those who bear the same name meet together. Relationship, resulting from the sacrificial meal at the king's table, seems to be closest amongst those who feast together most frequently. And, as a matter of fact, amongst the nobles there are four degrees of mourning which serve to measure collateral relationship, as there are four religious colleges (beside the great *tsong*). The relationship is by so much the weaker (and the observances of mourning so much the lighter) as the collaterals, who make part of a vaster religious college, meet less frequently at the communions of the ancestral temple. The ties of relationship, while they are still the result of membership of a group, appear to be derived from proximity, since they vary in function from the latter. But the sacrificial communions of the ancestral temple are distinguished by another characteristic from the equalizing banquets of the undivided family. The chief of each religious college plays a part of the first importance by virtue of his duty as celebrant. It is by his mediation that the members of the college commune with the ancestors and with each other. The sacrifice which precedes the communion appears to serve to concentrate a virtue in the religious chief, which he exerts himself afterwards to put in circulation amongst the faithful. This virtue is not distinct from the family essence, but, in the case of the chief, the centre of the worship where it is extolled, it seems to assume an august character with a tincture of the sublime. When it is passed on from the chief to the faithful, it brings them more than a mere principle of consubstantiality : the happiness (*fu*) which he distributes with the meat of the sacrifice, is given to the beneficiaries as a part of prestige,

[1] *Li ki*, C, I, 47 ; LV, 274.

a share of authority and power. No one imagines that the virtue by which he feels himself enriched can only proceed from himself, and spring up in him as in each member of his family : in it he recognizes, as it were, the overflowing of a high fountain of authority which can be made to rise only by the officiator of the act of worship. It is this latter who seems to be the author of the principle of relationship which binds the members of the family college to each other. The ties of the family, if they continue to postulate an immanent essence amongst relatives, imply in a more obvious way the idea of a principle of prestige which is taken for granted. The religious chief is thus recognized to occupy, as it were, an eminent position, which makes it obligatory to wear mourning of a superior quality for him (mourning of the first class). Influential men, and first-born, separated from the rest of their kindred, appear to be the creators of parenthood. The joint ideas of domestic authority and of filiation, as conceptions which are more varied and capable of analysis, supersede the more obscure sentiment of identity of substance. Nevertheless, as long as the feudal order lasts, the notions of domestic authority and of filiation do not arrive at a combination sufficiently close to produce the idea of paternal authority. The right of presiding over a religious college constitutes a sort of sacrificial authority which, being delegated by the overlord when he confers nobility, is inherited without partition and by right of primogeniture together with the seigniorial power. A younger son cannot possess such authority, at least in his lifetime. If it be the right of every father, though he be a younger son, that his sons should wear the highest class of mourning for him, it is because death will make him an ancestor whose worship will be celebrated by a fraternal community. But a younger son, whose eldest son dies before him, has not the right to mourn him with the honours which would be accorded to his apparent successor if he were himself a religious chief. A younger son, in fact, cannot make a distinction between his nephews and any of his sons, even the eldest. These rules show that the hierarchy which characterizes the noble family has for its principle the establishment of the Worship of Ancestors, and not a natural authority resulting from the fact of paternity. They also show the power of resistance inherent in the old undivided organization. Although the religious colleges have a chief, although kinship seems to be the result of common subjection to this chief, the principle of indivisibility preserves its force. Thus in the fraternal community (the group *t'ong ts'ai*) all resources (*ts'ai*) are in principle held in common (*t'ong*). The rule is that, if a younger brother has a superabundance, the surplus shall be handed to the eldest. On the other hand, the eldest must provide for the needs of those younger brothers whose resources would be insufficient.[1] In the same way, the duty and right of guardianship belong indivisibly to the group of cousins : no one, as long as he still has cousins, can undertake the guardianship of a stranger.[2] The authority of the religious chief is limited by the superior rights of the community : if the chief of a *tsong* has no child, he can and should adopt a successor ; but, while he is obliged to adopt, he has not the liberty of adoption. The choice of his successor, far from being left to his discretion, is dictated to him by imperative rules.[3] He must take him from the nearest religious group.

Like feudal public law, the domestic law of feudal times is a transitional law, unsettled and movable. The rules of succession are changeable, even in seigniorial families. The principle of majority is often challenged. It does not always carry the day against the principle of paternal succession. Often the choice of the heir is determined by the intervention of parents or vassals : the latter base their preference upon rival regulations.[4] It happens, for example, that the inheritance does not come to the son, the representative of the eldest branch, until after it has been retained by the whole series of younger brothers of the father, or by the minor of them.[5] Again it happens that, amongst the sons, the heir is not he who is qualified to bear the title of eldest : the choice falls upon him whose mother enjoys the most honour. At every step we meet in the chronicles with the mention of facts which imply the vitality of the rights belonging to undivided communities, and even the vitality of the rules inspired by the old uterine principle. The family organization described by the rituals seems to be rather an ideal of equity than an actual reality. The patriarchal institutions found a

---

[1] *Yi li*, **C**, 396.   [2] *Yi li*, **C**, 401.   [3] *Yi li*, **C**, 388.
[4] SMC, IV, 112, 349, 78.   [5] SMC, IV, 233 and 380.

favourable soil in the feudal order. Though they were there only half realized, it was sufficient for the juridical conception, working upon rules proper to the religious organization, to draw from them the principles of domestic law. After the disappearance of the feudal nobility these principles were to impose themselves, if not upon the nation as a whole, at least upon all the upper classes of society. From the beginning of the feudal period, however, the idea appears to be definitely established that kinship, as a result of the religious community, implies a bond of dependence upon the religious chief. This idea is the principle of the authority which was the prerogative of the father of the family.

(2). *Paternal Authority*

The authority of the father of the family is derived, not from a right to command which is inherent in his paternity, but from the fact that the son, and more correctly, the eldest son, sees in him a future ancestor. As he is destined to preside over the paternal worship, and to retain authority by this position over his younger brothers, the son strives during the life of his father to nourish the holiness in him which will qualify him to pursue an ancestral career. He makes him live nobly. He treats him as a chief. He offers him the homage which confers the title of overlord. He prepares himself, so to speak, to be his priest, by first being his disciple. The life of the son (of the eldest son, for truth to tell, the father has only one son—who has brothers) is entirely spent in one long effort to affiliate himself with his father. To establish this affiliation is the more difficult because, by reason of the survival of the uterine right, son and father are gifted with different geniuses.[1] Intimacy between them is a thing impossible : their tablets will never be united : on the contrary, they will always be opposed to each other in the ancestral temple. But it is precisely this absence of kinship which permits the son to infeudate himself, and the father to arrogate to himself seigniorial authority. To define the authority of the father, the Chinese say of him, as they say of the overlord, that he is *tsun*, worthy of respect : that he ought to be severe, distant (*yen*) : that he

[1] LV, 273 ff.

is " Heaven " : that he commands the son as the *yang* commands the *yin*. The son behaves in the father's presence
like the vassal in the presence of the overlord, and—nothing
shows more clearly the feudal origins of the paternal authority
—all the rites by which the son draws near to the father, all
the rites which create agnatic affiliation are indistinguishable
from those by which the act of vassalage is performed.

The fact of paternity is not in itself the creator of any
bond. A man may treat his wife's child as his son, even
when he has not begotten him, or when, for example, he has
brought about his birth by throwing open his harem to his
dependents.[1] On the other hand, the fact of being the wife's
child never implies the right of being taken by the husband
for his son. There is, at the beginning, so great a distance
between the child and the father, that pregnancy, far from
drawing husband and wife together, separates them. As
soon as the embryo is perfectly formed (*ch'eng*), three months
before the delivery, the husband and wife are separated :
they live apart up to the time (the third month after the
birth) when the child may be presented to his father.[2] This
crowning ceremony of the third month is preceded by
numerous rites of approach. The father shares the mother's
pains, and if he is forbidden to go and see her, he sends to
ask news of her, the more frequently as she draws nearer
her time. During the last days, he subjects himself to fasting.
He cannot be present at the birth, but he is represented, at
the door of the woman confined, by vassals, the master of
music and the head cook. They are charged to watch over
the mother who is subject to numerous prohibitions relating
to her food,[3] her attitudes, and the tunes which she has
played for her. These vassals observe the first movements
of the new-born child, and in particular, the master of music
determines, by the help of a sort of octave, the note upon
which the child utters its first cries.[4] This inspection of the
voice is an important thing. In company with the father's
vassals, the whole family is on the watch. Tsih-wen of Cheng
(604 B.C.) has a son whose voice is like that of a wolf. Therefore Tsih-wen's eldest brother demands that this child be
put to death.[5] Only a free-thinker would fail to have a child

---

[1] SMC, V, 235, and *Sin louen*, 46.   [2] *Li ki*, **C**, I, 662, 671.
[3] *Sin shu*, 10.   [4] *Sin shu*, 10 ; **LV**, 155, note 2.   [5] *Tso chuan*, **C**, I, 584.

killed who was born unluckily, on the first of the fifth month
of the year, the month of solstice, or, more vexatiously still,
on the fifth of the fifth month, the day sacred to the owl,
and on which the principle *yang* reaches its apogee. A son
born at the period of the most important days must grow
up in a strange way : he is destined, as soon as his stature
attains the height of a door, to kill his father, for he shares
the parricide nature of the owls, which, as is well known,
are cannibals.[1] Ill-omened children were exposed in the
bush : it might happen to them to be rescued and suckled
by a wild beast, so evident was the animal virtue which the
inspection of the first days had revealed in them.[2] The
mothers were the first to demand the exposure of new-born
children marked with an unlucky sign : the father sometimes had difficulty in overcoming their desire. No doubt
the exposure of the child in ancient times depended upon
the mother alone. It corresponded rather to an ordeal than
to a sentence of death. The new-born child, abandoned on
the ground, sometimes by crying in the correct manner
extorted the sympathy of human beings as well as that of
the beasts. ("How far away one can hear him ! how well he
can be heard !—His cries fill the highway ! ")[3] The mother
then took him and gave him a name : such was the lot of
Hou-tsi, ancestor of the Chou kings. Even in the case of a
normal birth, the child must spend his three first days without
food, likewise upon the soil, for " the vital spirit and breath
of the child are without strength " [4] and it is only by contact
with Mother Earth that life can be confirmed in him. For
girls (who never completely escape from maternal dependence)
exposure on the soil appears to be a sufficient ordeal. For
boys there is the first rite of approach, the first habilitation
as successor, after which they must still be exposed upon the
paternal bed.[5] They are on this occasion lifted from the
ground by one of the father's vassals, and by his order.[6]
This procedure should be compared with the rites of etiquette
which are imposed when one wishes to recommend oneself
to a stranger by making him a gift. The gift is not transmitted from hand to hand ; it is deposited on the ground and

---

[1] **LV**, 532. *Lu she ch'un ch'iu*, 25, par. 4.   [2] *Tso chuan*, **C**, I, 586.
[3] *She king*, **C**, 350 ; **LIX**, 27 ff.   [4] **LIX**, 8.
[5] *She king*, **C**, 223 ; **LIX**, 3.   [6] *Li ki*, **C**, I, 663.

then lifted. It is remarkable that in the case when, by an analogous rite, the wife proposes to the husband to give him his child, it is not the father who directly receives the gift. He must employ an intermediary : between the father and the new-born child, as between the husband and the mother, communal contacts are difficult to make or to resume. As soon as the son is lifted from the ground, the vassal entrusted with this office shoots arrows in all directions. The defilements of birth are by this means scattered to a distance, for this rite seems to be connected with the purifying bath which is given to the child.[1] A connexion must also be established between the new-born child and the paternal earth which will supply him with nourishing grains : as soon as the arrows are shot, the child may at last be fed.[2] This shooting is only done for boys : the arrows are an emblem of virility. The warlike aspect of this ceremony is to be observed. This feature is the more remarkable because the third day after the birth, when the arrows must be shot, appears to have been in olden times the day when the name was given which was later deferred to the third month.[3] Now the father does not actually accept the son who is offered to him until the moment when he gives this son a name. On the other hand, it is known that a man might acquire a name for his child if he killed an enemy whose severed head was then buried beneath a gate.[4] The name of the victim thereupon descended to the new-born child : the father bound him to himself as a son, when he conferred upon him, with the name of a man whom he had conquered, a soul which was his property, having been vanquished by him : and from that time the paternal rights over the child which were thus purchased took precedence of the maternal rights. According to the Chinese theory, children when they are brought into the world by the mother, have as yet only an inferior soul, the soul *p'o*, the soul of the blood : then it is also naked, hairless and red (the word *red* denotes both new-born children and creatures without hair). Again it is said, when one wishes to define the manner in which children are bound to their father and to their mother, that they hold to the latter by the belly and to the former by the hair [5] and

---

[1] **LIX**, 9. [2] *Li ki*, II, 678. [3] **LIX**, 39, note 1.
[4] *Tso chuan*, **C**, I, 502. [5] *She king*, **C**, 250.

it is held that, physiologically, the hair partakes of the
nature of the breath (*k'i*). The higher soul (*hun*), which is a
soul-breath, only makes its appearance after the lower soul.
It is revealed first by the outcry of the new-born child, which
is proving its vitality by greeting life with resounding lamentations : thus it was originally possible to give it a name on
the third day. But the child is not really in a position to
possess a superior soul until it is capable of laughter. It is
the father who teaches it to laugh and straightway gives it
that personal name (*ming*) which the Chinese rites show to
be identical with the superior soul, with destiny, and with
life itself. At the third month [1] the child, which up till then
has been kept in seclusion, is at last presented to the father
who greets it with a smile. This solemn ceremony coincides
with the first arrangement of the child's hair and with the
mother's resumption of her place in the family, purified by
three months of abstinence, from the bloody stains of child-
birth.[2] The father and mother prepare themselves by ablutions
for the ceremony and must clothe themselves in new garments.
They sit down facing each other, the mother holding the
child in her arms. They do not speak. A duenna acts as
go-between, and says : " Such an one, mother of the child,
takes upon her today to present him to his father." The
husband, saying " Take care of him " seizes his son's right
hand, and laughing as the child laughs, he gives him a name.
The wife then breaks silence, to agree to her husband's commands. Afterwards she may resume her marital relations
with him. But before that, she receives from him a feast
identical with the marriage feast, exactly as if they had been
separated by a divorce. Thus the delivery of the child is
accomplished. It will be remarked that father and son are
bound by the palm of the hand : this is the rite employed to
bring two strangers together and is characteristic both of the
covenant of military brotherhood and of the matrimonial
contract (where it may be completed by a rite of bloody
alliance, the blood being taken from the arm). The relationship between father and son is not a relationship in the
original meaning of the word : it belongs rather to the type
of artificial relationship.[3]

---

[1] *Li ki*, **C**, I, 665 ff.   [2] **LIX**, 10.
[3] **LII**, 207, and *Tso chuan*, **C**, III, 319.

Bound to his father as a friend is bound to a friend, the son must pass his whole childhood outside the paternal influence. In the ceremony of the third month, a simple ceremony of approach, everything happens as though the father, being invited by the mother to take delivery of the child, were deferring this delivery, while he agreed to accept it. When the ceremony is over, the child is carried back to the women's apartments and no intimacy is set up between him and his father. The latter, however, must have the child presented to him once every ten days, to renew the gesture of the palm of the hand, so difficult is it to create the artificial relationship between them which must bind them in the end. The father confines himself to touching the head of those of his sons who are only secondary sons : it is with the eldest son alone, the only son in the strict sense of the word, that he binds himself by touching his right hand.[1] Up to their seventh year, the boys do not leave the women's apartments. They live the life of the women, although they are already instructed in masculine manners, and to say " yes " in a decided tone.[2] At ten years of age, they must leave the home of their birth, and live by day and night with a master who teaches them the art of the rites of politeness and of the words of sincerity. In theory, they ought to remain at school till they are twenty years of age, being trained in dancing, drawing the bow and driving a chariot. Tradition has it that in feudal times noble youths were gathered into a sort of school for pages, in company with the prince. The chronicles, on the contrary, seem to show that adolescence was spent with maternal relatives. There is little doubt that the practice of *foster-parentage* was the general rule. An author explaining that the father cannot undertake the education of his son, gives a curious and doubtless a profound reason for this.[3] Father and son may not hang up their garments on the same nail, just as two persons of different sex are prohibited from doing so by sexual tabus. Neither may father and son talk together about sexual matters. Education can only be carried on away from the father, in surroundings where it will not be improper to raise such questions. If one calls to mind that the custom of marrying the sons into their mother's family

---

[1] *Li ki*, C, I, 672.　　　[2] *Li ki*, C, I, 673.　　　[3] *Po hu t'ong*, 10.

is one of the fundamental customs of domestic life, it will easily be understood why the duty of educating the boys belonged to their maternal uncles. Their nephews were going to live with them on the footing of guests, or, we might say, of hostages, and underwent with them a sort of pre-nuptial test, before they could take their cousin-brides, who in their turn were becoming guests or hostages, to the paternal house. Another characteristic trait of Chinese manners (it may pass for a survival of the undivided family) testifies to the sexual rivalry, which, amongst other rivalries, is implied by the relationship between father and son : it frequently happens that the father attempts to ravish his son's betrothed, and in cases where he is successful, the son is usually dispossessed of the paternal succession.[1] Education in a school of pages is no doubt a development of foster-parentage : the overlord appropriates to himself the hostages (and perhaps, one may suppose, the various sexual services) which every family which was associated with another family group by a tradition of intermarriages had originally the right to exact from that allied group. For the rest, we must start from the custom of foster-parentage to explain the rites of majority.[2] These rites, known as the taking of the virile head-dress, bring adolescence to an end. The recipient takes the head-dress and distinctive garments of grown men and is initiated into public life. This ceremony completes the effects of the rites of the third month after birth : the young man then receives the name of a grown man, the name of a major (*tsih*) which is a public name, while the *ming*, the personal name given at the third month, is used as a private and secret appellation. The son being declared major is capable of rendering to his father the homage which is due to an overlord. He presents himself to his agnatic parents. He takes leave of his mother, in a significant fashion. Their interview takes place on either side of a half-open door : the major is no longer dependent upon his mother and is shut out from the women's apartments. But it is a remarkable fact that the rite of majority, which bestows virility and gives unquestioned entrance into the agnatic group, is only one rite detached from a more complex ceremony. The parallel rite for girls, the assuming of the hairpin, has remained connected with

---

[1] **LV,** 13 ; *Tso chuan,* III, 409.   [2] *Yi li,* chap. 1 ; *Li ki,* **C,** II, 636.

the ceremonies of betrothal.[1] Now, in the peasant customs, initiations and betrothals were performed for the two sexes at the same time, in the course of the spring festivals where drinking-bouts played an important part. The levy of a cup of drink is one of the most important rites in the ceremony of majority practised by the nobles : but amongst them the son cannot perform the rites of marriage until he has received a cup of drink from his father. The initiation of the peasants took place in the local Holy Place in the course of a collective festival. That of the nobles was performed in the paternal house : this gives proof of the new dignity and independence which the feudal order bestowed upon institutions which were properly domestic. Nevertheless, if the father (or the chief of *tsong*) occupies the place of honour during the ceremony of majority, he takes no active part in it. All the ritual acts are accomplished on the initiative of a personage called a host, who must not belong to the paternal family. We have the right to suppose that in principle the host belonged to the family from which the agnatic group of the recipient must take their wives, the family from which his mother came and from which his betrothed must come. All, at the time of the initiation, happens therefore as though the son, quitting the maternal group (which after having brought him up, now hands him over), is coming to join himself to the agnatic group—and promising his father to bring him a daughter-in-law.

Once become major, the boy is fitted to carry out the innumerable duties of piety which affiliate him to his father. But although, among nobles, marriage must not be entered into before thirty years of age, while majority is granted at twenty, a married son alone can act as a pious son. A lord and a lady are required to govern the State. Their prestige is upheld by the‚homage of a court of vassals and a court of vassal women. In the same way, a double judicature exists in the family : that of the master and that of the mistress of the house, a couple invested with lordly authority which exacts the joint service of infeudated couples. The head of a family must have a wife, for he is in charge of an ancestral temple where the tablets of husbands and wives are kept together : thus, if he is bereaved of all his wives,

[1] *Li ki*, C, I, 676.

and is less than seventy years old, he must marry again, or
if he has passed seventy, he must retire, and hand over the
charge to the religious chief.[1] To perform the office of a chief,
one must have a wife : a wife is also required for the practice
of filial piety. Filial piety, by which one approaches the
chiefs of the family, is crowned by the gift of their virtue.
The eldest son, the first vassal of the father, and his wife,
the first vassal of the mother, as a ministerial pair govern
the court of men and women vassals formed by the sons
and the daughters-in-law.[2] Their duties are those of followers
at a court : homage, counsel and service. In the family as
at the seigniorial court, homage, which is renewed each day,
consists of the morning and evening salutation. From the
obligation of homage are derived the rules of deportment and
cleanliness : sons and daughters-in-law wash and adorn themselves to do honour to the parents. At cock-crow, sons and
daughters-in-law wash their hands, rinse their mouth, comb
their hair, envelop it in a strip of material, the men carefully
brushing the hair which is left free upon the temples and
settling their caps with hanging ribands firmly upon their
heads. They then arrange their garments and adorn their
girdles with the small objects which are used in their daily
tasks : napkins to dry articles and their own hands, a knife,
a stone for sharpening bodkins, etc. The women do not
forget to fasten on a sachet of perfume. They all arrange
their shoe-ties with care. Their fine toilet is in itself a homage.
Their good deportment will be accounted an offering of
respect. In the presence of parents, gravity is requisite :
one must therefore be careful not to belch, to sneeze, to
cough, to yawn, to blow one's nose nor to spit. Every
expectoration would run the risk of soiling the paternal
sanctity. It would be a crime to show the lining of one's
garments. To show the father that one is treating him as
a chief, one ought always to stand in his presence, the eyes
right, the body upright upon the two legs, never daring to
lean upon any object, nor to bend, nor to stand on one foot.
It is thus that with the low and humble voice which becomes
a follower, one comes night and morning to pay homage.
After which, one waits for orders. One cannot avoid executing

---

[1] *Li ki*, C, I, 651 and 478 ; SMC, V, 287 ; LVIII, 10.
[2] *Li ki*, C, I, 620 ff. and 627.

them, but one is expected to give one's opinion. The son,
like the vassal, should offer advice in all sincerity and not
hesitate to administer reproofs : only, come what may, he
must preserve a gentle tone of voice, a pleasant expression
and a modest air. If the parents persist in their decision,
the children must only redouble their gentleness, that they
may return to favour and so be able to renew their warnings.
When wounded to the quick, they feel neither indignation
nor resentment, and they obey, not hesitating, for instance,
if it is a matter of their own home life, to take into favour
the one among their wives who pleases the father rather
than the one whom they find agreeable.[1] Obedience is
imposed in small as in great things : and even the service of
the son consists chiefly in the rendering of inconsiderable
services : it is through them that respect is shown. The
sons ask leave to mend the parents' garments when they
perceive a hole in them. They ask leave to wash the stains
on the head-dress, the girdle, the tunic or the under-garment,
with ashes tempered with water. Every five days, they heat
water and invite the parents to take a bath : every three
days, they prepare water for the parents to wash their faces,
and if in the interval between these regular ablutions the
parents happen to have a dirty face, they hasten to fetch
the water in which rice has been washed, for this supplementary toilet. They wash their parents' feet and dry them
in great haste that no one may perceive upon them the
spittle or the mucus of the heads of the house.[2] But, if a
religious chief must be clean, a future ancestor must be well
nourished. The first duty of filial piety is to look after the
food by which the substance of his parents is enriched. A
good son, said Tseng tsih, " sees that nothing is wanting in
his parents' bed-chamber (it is particularly when one is old
and chilly that one cannot sleep alone) and provides them
with food and drink with sincere affection." [3] He prepares
for them the dishes, which, when they are duly seasoned,
are suitable to the different seasons and the different times
of life. The older the parents, the more choice should be the
food which is offered to them : at seventy years of age, one
has constant need of delicate viands, and at eighty of dainties.
Every son must understand how to prepare *the eight choice*

---

[1] *Li ki*, C, I, 632, 633, 96.   [2] *Li ki*, C, I, 626–629.   [3] *Li ki*, C, I, 653.

dishes and above all *the rich fried meat* and the aromatic wine which sustain the strength of old men and give them mucilage.[1] Good cookery is not enough : one must also serve the meal and have an eye to its disposition. There is no family meal, but in every house there are court repasts, the pretext for hierarchized communions. The eldest son and his wife (the eldest daughter-in-law) are present, morning and evening, at the parents' meals, but solely to encourage them to eat heartily. To balance this, they get what is left (as the leavings of the overlord are the perquisite of the vassals) with the exception, however, of the sweet, tender and succulent dishes, which they must reserve for their own children.[2] The latter themselves require choice nourishment : besides, as we have seen, there is a particular nearness in the relationship between grandparents and grandchildren. As more distant vassals, the secondary sons and daughters-in-law make an end by eating what is left by their elders. Thus, in everyday life, the solid hierarchy is established which lies at the root of domestic order.

Filial obligations are particularly heavy when the father is passing through the ordeal of death. From his seventieth year he must prepare himself for this ordeal. Seventy years is the age for retirement, and (so strong is the connexion between the civil and feudal organization) the noble, when he leaves the seigniorial court, must also lay down the direction of his domestic group. Set free from wearing effort, from the painful observances of mourning as well as from his marital obligations, drinking and eating more plentifully, the father, with the help of his son, begins at once to follow the régime which will turn him into a venerated ancestor. For his own glory, as well as for that of his family, it is important that his death should occur as late as possible, at 100 years of age if he is worthy.[3] Thirty years of preparation for the career of an ancestor are most to be desired. Nevertheless, striving to share the paternal life in every way,[4] happy when the father is well, sad when he is ill, eating when the father has a good appetite, but fasting when he is ill and taking medicine with him, the son spends himself that there may be nothing lacking in the event of death and

[1] *Li ki*, **C**, I, 641 ff., 649, 655. [2] *Li ki*, **C**, I, 627.
[3] *Li ki*, **C**, II, 175 ; **LIX**, 9 ff. ; **LV**, 287 ff. [4] *Li ki*, **C**, I, 40, 495, 314.

above all that a beautiful coffin may not be wanting : for, " if it is better to begin to decompose immediately after death than to waste money " in having a luxurious coffin made for oneself, in the case of the father no casket will appear splendid enough.[1] Above all, it is the son's duty to take careful heed that the father can make a good death. It would indeed be unlucky if he died unexpectedly and away from home : he must let death take him only in accordance with the rites and in the room reserved for the master of the house. It would be unbecoming if the mat on which he spent his last moments were not a mat which corresponded exactly to his rank of nobility.[2] It would be a misfortune if one let oneself be taken unawares, and had not time to lift the dying man from his bed and lay him on the soil where he must breathe his last sigh, as when, a new-born child, he uttered his first cries upon the earth. Wadding must be kept in readiness : it will be used to receive the dying breath. Above all, the whole family must be summoned and hold themselves in readiness for the outcry which salutes the soul's departure. As head of the family choir, the eldest son takes the responsibility for the rites which, while making sure that death has taken place, render it final. One must proceed to the summons of the soul-breath (*hun*), which is done by shaking the garments of the dead man from the top of the roof, and crying his personal name. If this soul does not come to take possession of these familiar clothes, if, when they are flung upon the body, life does not reappear, the son causes the mouth of the dead man, which up till then has been held open with a horn spoon, to be filled with rice mixed with cowries or jade.[3] It is also the prerogative of the chief responsible for the mourning to gain the dead man's consent to shut his eyes : sometimes he will consent only after having exacted an oath of obedience to his supreme wishes. Finally, the corpse, having been washed, is replaced upon the mortuary bed and the garments are heaped upon it, after, it appears, a piece of jade has been placed over all the apertures of the body. No soul will henceforth be able to force its way into this hermetically sealed body, to turn it into a vampire, and, on the other hand, the jade, thanks to the virtues inherent

---

[1] *Li ki*, **C**, I, 165.   [2] *Li ki*, **C**, I, 125.
[3] *Li ki*, **C**, II, 202, and I, 175 ; **LIX**, 13.

in it, will, together with the heaped-up clothes, prevent too rapid a putrefaction.   For the great concern is that decomposition should take place neither too slowly nor too quickly : one must arrange for it to be produced in accordance with the rules of the protocol.   The body, in a shallow grave, must be kept in the house for several months, three for ordinary nobles, longer if the dead man, holding a higher rank in the hierarchy, was composed of a more richly nourished substance.   It is a sin of presumption to delay for too long a time, or to attempt to hinder the decomposition of the flesh, but it would be the blacker crime if the guests who had come to bring their tribute of condolence were able to see the worms, which had issued from the ill-kept corpse, pass through the door, robbing the domestic soil of a substance which ought to accrue to it.[1]   As long as the bones are infected, and it is yet not possible to go to the family cemetery to unite them to the bones of the ancestors, the relatives, while they help the dead man to cross a formidable threshold, deliver themselves from a defilement whose contagion has attacked them.   They free themselves from it by yelling and stamping, but not, like savages, with unrestrained cries and gestures, or simply as the consequence of sorrow, " like a child who regrets a lost object." [2]   The relatives yell and stamp in order and by order, each time that the ritual hour comes round to express the family sorrow, and at the signal given by the head of the choir.   Everyone " then moves his limbs," all shout " to calm their sorrow and lessen their anguish." [3]   They jump and cry a settled number of times and with a rhythm which expresses their proximity to the dead man,—the men alone baring the right arm and frankly leaping,—the women without uncovering and without allowing the toes to leave the ground, but beating their breasts,—the sons wailing like new-born children, never allowing the sound of their voices to cease, while the more distant relatives are only authorized to adopt a plaintive tone, and after three modulations, must let the sound lengthen and die away.[4]   But while the leaps and yells serve to classify sorrow and express the hierarchy of the relationships, if they relieve the family affliction, they are also useful to the dead

---

[1] *Li ki*, **C**, II, 141.
[2] *Li ki*, **C**, II, 558, 573, 581, 238 and 241.
[3] *Li ki*, **C**, II, 553.
[4] *Li ki*, **C**, II, 206 and 570.

man, and should be the more numerous as the substance of
the latter was more noble. The number of bounds is identical
with the number of months of the provisional interment in
the house.[1] Jumping and yelling in concert, the relatives
can make a sound like subterranean thunder : when they
produce this kind of disconnected rumbling they terrify and
put to flight the maleficent monsters who are making ready
underground to come and devour the corpse. Thus the
relatives can actively assist the dead man to issue triumphant
from the trial which is imposed like a purgatory upon him.
But, in very different ways, they can still share in the state
of the dead. It is even thanks to this complete participation
that the pious son gains for himself the title of religious and
family chief, while he helps his father to acquire the ancestral
dignity which will fit him to be the object of worship. Inasmuch as the dead man cannot be reunited to his ancestors
for the space of the active period of the mourning (called
the time of continual tears), he remains master of the house
in which his body rests. The relatives, during this interregnum, are united in body, but outside the house : each
son dwells in an isolated cabin which is set up in an enclosed
and retired spot. For the principal son, a sort of pent-house
is erected, which must have its back against the wall surrounding the family dwelling.[2] Because the dead man, in
the first days of mourning, is put into a coffin rather than
deeply buried, the hut, which is made of boughs, must not be
rough-cast : the chinks will not be stopped with clay until
after the final interment, when the body itself will be deeply
hidden in the ground. In this cabin, the son must at first
sleep upon straw (it appears that in very ancient times the
dead were buried in straw), his head resting on a clod of
earth, " thus afflicting himself because his father is in the
ground." [3] In the same way that death shuts out the dead
man from communion with the living, so does mourning shut
out the pious son. He lives in quarantine, and his right to
speak is so much the less as the succession which he is about
to enjoy is the more considerable (a king is qualified for his
kingship by not opening his mouth during the three years of
paternal mourning).[4] The son eats reluctantly, and for the

[1] SMC, IV, 60.   [2] Li ki, C, I, 216, and LX, 109.
[3] Li ki, C, II, 556.   [4] Li ki, C, I, 120, and II, 705.

first few days nothing more than a handful of rice. Moreover, the intervention of stranger families is required to persuade him to take nourishment and it must be offered to him in the form of a present.[1] There is no cooking possible in the house of the dead so long as the dead man himself cannot be nourished in his capacity of ancestor. The pious son must fast and grow thin, only preserving enough strength to carry out the ceremonies. But, if he is to succeed to a rich inheritance of vassals (who will be able henceforth to come to his help) he is obliged to weaken himself to such a degree that, like a corpse, he is unable to move without the help of others.[2] To become the chief of a family group, one must deserve to be the religious chief. To this end as chief mourner one must first endure the hard observances, which release the dead man from his critical situation and the family from its quarantine by purging away the funereal infection. Thus a son who has not presided over the mourning for his father does not feel himself entitled to succeed him.[3]

At the end of the provisional interment and the time of continual tears, the principal son, as head mourner, leads the procession which will unite the bones of the dead man to the bones of the ancestors. A rite which he then fulfils is the starting-point of the new cult with which he is about to be charged. When the remains are given to the earth, the pious son, baring his shoulder and uttering lamentations, walks three times round the grave from left to right. Thus he encloses and finally seals the last perishable remains in the tomb, but he separates from them that which formed the noblest part of the personality of the deceased. Exclaiming —" Flesh and bones return again to the earth : such is Fate ! But the *hun* and the breath—they may go where they will ! " he returns along the road to his home, followed by the higher soul which henceforth will be fixed in a tablet, the centre of worship.[4] So long as the mortal remains had not left the house, a sort of provisional tablet had been kept there. A simple wooden pole, this tablet is as it were the skeleton of a rude effigy which covers pans of rice and is surmounted by the banner of the deceased. As soon as the period of major impurity is past, it is a wooden tablet pure

[1] *Li ki*, C, II, 126, 170, 552.   [2] *Li ki*, C, I, 135, and II, 763.
[3] *Li ki*, C, I, 196 ff.   [4] *Li ki*, C, I, 246.

and simple which will act as a support for the spiritualized soul of the deceased : it suffices to represent him, for his name is written upon it. This tablet does not at once become the centre of worship. Before acquiring ancestral personality, the dead man has to pass through another stage : he achieves it under the protection, not of his father, but of his grand-father. The neophyte, newly arrived in the ancestral group, receives the sacrificial food at first only through the mediation of an older member of that section (section *chao* or section *mu*) of the agnatic group to which he has the right to ally himself.[1] He must wait for the end of the mourning (the beginning of the third year) to receive personal worship and to possess a dwelling of his own in the ancestral temple. The installation of the new tablet in a special hall has the effect of relegating the tablet of the great-great-grandfather or the grandfather to a coffer of stone, where it mingles with those of the distant ancestors, for each family has the right to a certain number of ancestors only, who are singled out by worship from the ancestral stock. The tablets which may be kept without returning them to the common stock, indicate by their number the noble rank of the family. The dead man keeps his personality for the exact length of time only that his tablet receives individual sacrifices : as soon as this tablet is put in the stone coffer the name of the dead man may be taken again by the family.[2] It is evident that nobility does not result from the possession of a long line of ancestors, but that on the contrary, ancestral survival is a function of the nobility. We perceive also the reason why ancestors are interested in the fate of their descendants : when their immediate heirs are longer-lived they themselves will be fed by sacrifices during a longer stretch of years. Ancestral religion is an exchange of benefits carried on between two portions of the family, which are made up by the living on the one hand, and on the other by the ancestors whose soul survives. This exchange is effected between group and group, through the mediation of the heads of the group. Whilst the head of the family offers the sacrificial food in the name of his brothers and cousins, it is received by the dead father or grandfather who shares it with the dead uncles or great-uncles : as a matter of fact, the tablets of the secondary

[1] *Li ki*, C, I, 206, 758 ff. ; 767 ff.   [2] *Li ki*, C, I, 57 and 745.

sons are associated in the temple with that of the principal son. He who occupies a subordinate place in the family group during his lifetime, remains only a supernumerary during his ancestral career.[1] Only, the promotion of younger sons in the order of nobility may happen to complicate the register of sacrifices. If a younger son should acquire a higher rank than that of his eldest brother, he gains from his elevation the right to feed his parents more richly, and for example, to slay two victims for them instead of one, but it must always be the eldest who presides at the sacrifice.

When the principal son has conducted the mourning for the head of the family after having served him in his lifetime in the same capacity, he receives from him, as the leader of his worship, an authority extending to those who were dependent upon him, as well as to those who, by their intermediary, would have become so. This authority is confirmed on the occasion of the sacrifices. The whole family then communes with the ancestors, but only the religious chief presides at this communion. He it is who officiates. His post as officiating minister imposes duties upon him from which he extracts a principle of superiority.

Above all, the duty of being pure is incumbent upon him, which is equivalent to the obligation of living nobly and knowing the rites. Aided, as we have seen, by the services of his own sons, he must devote himself to being clean in his outward appearance and sincere in his conversation. He must know in his own sphere the ritual technique and language as perfectly as a statesman. He would be wanting in the entire sincerity demanded by his religion, if, following the seasons, he did not understand how to offer at the stated times to his Ancestor cress, water-lilies, ants' eggs or grasshoppers. He would be disqualified if, when he offered a leek, a fish or a hare, he pronounced " leek " " fish " or " hare," and not " abundant root " " stiffened offering " or " quicksighted one." [2] It is not only a question of forcing oneself to choose the right offering and the right word, one has still to be put into a state of grace.[3] Before the sacrifice the pious son endures a retreat of ten days, which becomes more severe during the last three. He neglects his wives and

---

[1] *Li ki*, C, I, 100, 784, 287, 451 and 760.
[2] *Li ki*, C, I, 101, and II, 321.   [3] *Li ki*, C, I, 324.

abstains from music. He avoids every ill-regulated movement of the feet and hands. He holds his impulses and
desires in check, he puts aside personal reflections and dis-
tractions. He concentrates his whole thought upon the
august being with whom he is about to commune. Finally
he succeeds in entering into communication with the deified
soul of his ancestor : immediately his purified soul is illuminated and his whole being is clothed with a sanctity which
will confirm the sacrificial sacrament. His wife, who, like
him, has prepared herself for the sacrifice, is his assistant :
she is fitted to celebrate the worship of an ancestress who,
like her, was annexed to the family in the capacity of a
daughter-in-law. At the summons of this pure couple, the
ancestral souls arrive, wakened by the sound made by the
little bells on the sacrificial knife, and attracted by the smell
of the first blood drawn from the victim near the ear. To
ensure their presence, they are offered the possibility of a
momentary reincarnation. In fact, during the whole ceremony,
the ancestor is called upon to let his soul take possession of
a person who is charged to represent him. It was not long
before this archaic custom was criticized by the ritualists.
When the sacrifices were offered simultaneously to several
ancestors each of whom was represented, the ceremony was
found indeed to assume a displeasing likeness to a picnic.[1]
For a still stronger reason, however, the custom must inspire
hostility in those who desired to consider paternal authority
as an institution of natural law. By virtue of the rules of
the order *chao mu*, which governed the religious organization,
the representative must belong to the section of the family
of which the ancestor also formed a part. Normally he
should be taken from the generation of the grandsons of
this latter, and was as a rule his grandson. This regulation,
which perfectly explains the history of the Chinese family,
throws light upon the meaning of ancestor worship. One of
the chief aims of the ceremonies was precisely to obtain the
reincarnation of the grandfather in the person of the grandson.
Moreover, the rules for mourning have kept the trace of this
mode of transmission of the *sacra :* a grandfather wears a
particularly deep mourning for the grandson who would have
been his successor. But in a family which might appear to

[1] *Li ki*, **C**, I, 557.

Y

be founded on agnatic filiation, and in a class like that of the nobles in which the worship of the dead father seemed to be the essential religion, custom implied a consequence which could not fail to appear revolting. When the religious chief sacrificed to his father, it was one of his sons who represented the Ancestor.[1] The father appeared before his son in a humble posture. He could only address him, as he would the gods, through the mediation of an invocator. When the sacrifice was ended, the son ate first, in the place of the grandfather. Only after him did the father taste the viands sanctified by this first tasting : only through his go-between did he appear to receive the family good fortune (*fu*) which was incorporated in the viands. This reversal of the hierarchic order took place at the very moment when the religious chief, the distributor of the sacred food, was founding his domestic authority. Indeed with the one exception of this privileged communion of the grandson which appeared to be an aberration and has its own significance, the family hierarchy was respected in all the communions of the relatives. They had the character of infeudating communions like those, which in the feudal religion bound the vassal to the overlord.

The authority which belongs to the religious chief comes to him from the overlord. The latter conferred upon him with a certain degree of nobility the right to sacrifice to the same number of ancestors. The overlord who bestows the ancestors may also take away the right of possessing an ancestral temple. He who no longer has ancestors, is no longer head of a family. As a delegation of the seigniorial authority, domestic power is of the seigniorial essence. It is exercised upon brothers and cousins. For the ritualists themselves, piety towards the eldest (*ti*) is an obligation no less essential than piety towards the father (*hiao*), but according to them fraternal piety is only a result of the duties imposed by filial piety. This is an inversion of the order of the facts.

From the time of the undivided organization, the eldest son exercised a certain authority, for in his capacity of eldest brother he represented all his brothers. Reacting on the domestic organization, the feudal order transformed this simple power of representation into an authority of a seigniorial

[1] *Li ki*, C, II, 335.

order. It was not without difficulty that it extended to the members of the generation beneath him. Confined in its action to brothers and cousins by the survivals of the undivided organization, domestic authority is still more limited, in the case of the sons, by the survivals of the uterine right and of an ancient organization in which the idea of generation was of more importance than that of filiation. Long rites of approach make the son into the father's vassal, while they qualify him to become his religious successor. But one bond continues to exceed in importance the bond artificially set up between father and son, and that is the bond which unites grandson and grandfather. The father must respect in his son the representative of his own father. The authority of the ritual means which are employed to bring together the representatives of two consecutive agnatic generations, breaks down their original independence and opposition. In the beginning, father and son form a college of rival powers. Significant traces survive of this fundamental rivalry, particularly in the customs of marriage. It will appear—and here, in part, is found the principle of maternal authority—that the sons, in opposition to their father, depend upon their mother's family. This family provides them with their wives, as it provided those of their father. But normally, father and son have the right to take wives out of one generation only of the allied family, that which appears to correspond to theirs (by virtue of the equivalents established by the whole series of matrimonial precedents). Now, in the nobility, and especially in the highest classes—those in which the principle of hierarchy is already most firmly established—a man does not confine himself to marrying a group of sisters. He takes with them one of their nieces, and she must be the daughter of their eldest brother, that is to say, precisely the one among the daughters of the succeeding generation who ought to be destined for the principal son who will be born of the marriage thus concluded. Thus the father binds himself beforehand (and by the best union possible) with the generation of the maternal family in which the son is to look for support and a wife. Often indeed, when the son is of an age to conclude an alliance, and a portion of wives has been granted to him, it happens that he is robbed of it by the father. In this case, usually, this son is sacrificed by the father and he takes as his heir the child born of the woman who, as the pre-destined wife of the son whose stepmother she becomes, ought to have presented her actual husband, not with children, but grand-children. Inversely, it happens that, the father having died, one of the sons of the first marriage, taking the place of the eldest who was sacrificed, marries the stepmother who has become a widow. Duke Süan of Wei (718–700 B.C.), for example, took to wife Yi Kiang, one of his father's wives (it is not known if this stepmother was originally his destined wife). He had a son by her, named Ki, for whom a wife was sought in the Kiang family from which his mother had been taken. Duke Süan deserting the wife in the paternal succession whom he had appropriated, took possession of the betrothed who was destined for his son Ki. Then, in order to leave the inheritance to the son born of her who should have been his daughter-in-law, Ki, the son whom he had had by Yi Kiang, his stepmother and first wife, was slain by his order. Ki's former betrothed, who had become his stepmother with the name of Süan Kiang, instigated the murder of this eldest son. But at the death of Duke Süan, while the stepmother's eldest son first seized the power to the detriment of his brothers of the first marriage, who should have succeeded, he could only escape death by voluntary exile, and after bloody conflicts in which the maternal family (Kiang) played the chief part. Süan Kiang, under pressure from the represent-atives of this same family, was obliged to unite herself to one of the younger brothers of her former betrothed who were still living. This one of Ki's brothers, named Chao-po, had not time to assume the power, but the inheritance went to a child whom Süan Kiang, his stepmother, bore to him (in the place of his eldest brother who had been dispossessed and sacrificed).[1] These complications of succession (in which the theme of the *levir* and the minority joined to that of the sacrifice of the eldest, is interwoven with the theme of incest with the stepmother and the daughter-in-law) witness the difficulty encountered by the agnatic system of filiation in establishing itself as a regular usage. The importance of the rôle played by the wives and their families remains para-mount. It is on account of the wives that fathers and sons are in opposition, but it is also through the wives that they

[1] SMC, IV, 195 and 199 ; *Tso chuan*, C, I, 120 and 220.

are able to unite : in order to come together, these representatives of two antagonistic generations attempt, if I may so
say, to fuse them in a kind of intermediate generation—the
child born of a woman, who, in her capacity of wife, passes
from one generation to another, sharing the opposing rights
of these rival groups. The origin of the paternal authority
is found in these singular relations between father and son,
relations born of a type of approach which must seem
monstrous : forbidden at first by the difference in the quality
of the nature proper to the representatives of two consecutive
agnatic generations, it appeared later to be forbidden by the
sentiment which was supposed to be the foundation of
parenthood—the respect of the son for the father. It is
evident that this respect, far from being characteristic of
purely family relations, has its origin in an order of relationships which are outside the family and are akin to the
relationships of the vendetta, like the relationships of the
feudal type. The eldest son being infeudated on the one hand
to the father, as he is to the grandfather, but, on the other,
the successor of the grandfather who was the father's overlord, is subject to a seigniorial authority, which, being made
up of excesses, is always inconsistent though unlimited in
principle. A little tale will show this.[1] One of the younger
sons of the honourable Chu, being accused of a crime, is
threatened with death : the father, hoping to save him and
sure of succeeding if he sends the judge a fine present, thinks
of entrusting this delicate mission to his cleverest child, who
is not the eldest. The eldest protests : " When there is an
eldest son in a family, he is called the director of the family.
Now that my brother, younger than myself, has committed
a crime, if Your Excellency does not send me and sends my
younger brother, I shall kill myself." Although it was evident
that the mission would be ill accomplished, the mother
supported the claim of the eldest son, and the father was
obliged to yield. We will not fail to note the threat of suicide,
characteristic of the relations between vassal and overlord,
and always included, if latent, in this act of disavowal which
is really a remonstrance and an essential duty of the son as
of the vassal. The fact, perceptible in this story, will be
particularly noted, that the rights of the eldest over the

[1] SMC, IV, 442.

younger are superior to the rights of the father over the sons. The former are the result of a regular development of the indivisible law, under the pressure of the feudal order. The latter, the result of the same pressure, revolutionized the indivisible organization. After the feudal epoch they did not rule without opposition.

As the overlord of an eldest son who, that he may inherit the paternal nobility and become the head of the ancestral religion, consents to infeudate himself, and with him to infeudate the whole group of his younger brothers, the father wields an authority of the military type over his children, and first of all on the eldest. As the overlord, he bestows nobility, but on condition of disposing of the life. The son is no more master of his own body than the vassal. He must spend his entire energy in nourishing the paternal honour. Bound by the homage of a liege, he has no right to bind himself again, no matter to whom. He cannot have friends. That would involve a promise to devote himself till death to another person. But he possesses nothing in his own right, and above all, he does not possess his life.[1] The first rule of filial piety is that the son must do nothing which could lead to the suspicion that he was imperilling the soundness of a body whose sole master is his father. He must not climb a rampart, walk on thin ice, go near a precipice. Like a soldier for his captain, the son must watch and keep himself for his father. It is in this fundamental duty that theorists will seek for the foundation of civic morality. Every man is constrained to good behaviour that he may avoid chastisement, which by reducing his body would rob the father of a portion of his property and honour. The pious son exposes himself to danger, and that with prudence, only when the father leads him to war or orders him to follow his own overlord. We have seen that the soldier then fights first for his father and his father's honour. This is diminished if the son violates the rites of valour. When the prisoner is released from captivity, he must, after obtaining mercy from the overlord, persuade his father to pardon him : he might put him to death in the ancestral temple.[2] Expulsion from the family is a penalty which seems to have been imposed

---

[1] *Li ki*, C, I, 14.   [2] *Tso chuan*, C, II, 24.

upon those who proved intractable and careless in the archery exercises.[1]

These two examples, the only examples of paternal jurisdiction vouched for in ancient times, indicate that it had in the beginning a military character : it has already been said that in the family as in the city, the feudal and the agnatic order correspond to the appearance of martial law, the first embodiment of the penal code. The son takes his father's place in the army as he takes it in the criminal court : this double example of a custom is seen throughout the course of Chinese history : it shows that the son is essentially, in the feudal sense of the word, his father's *man*. In the case of a vendetta he is also his avenger. His mourning only ceases with the death of the murderer. Formerly the son never laid down his arms, even in a peaceful place, market or princely palace. Every night he slept on a mourning mat, with his head upon a shield.[2] It is not enough to defend or restore the paternal honour. It must be augmented. All the rewards which the son obtains are brought to the father, especially if it be a case of that substantial reward—a gift of food. But the best reward is that which, passing over the deserving son, goes straight to his father : such is the principle constantly observed in China on the occasion of ennoblement. All these rules form a remarkable counterpart to the imperious regulation which forbids every kind of familiarity, every kind of tender intimacy, to father and son. Their relations do not belong to the realm of affection, but to that of etiquette and honour. It would be still more exact to say that the relations between father and son are relations of honour to honour. Now we are about to see that this type of relationship which first extended to the relations between brothers, ended by dominating private life as a whole.

II

Home Life and the Part played by Women

At an unspecified time in Chinese history custom was scarcely removed from the matriarchal system. Women transmitted their name to their children. The husbands

---

[1] *Li ki*, C, I, 300, 302, 691.   [2] *Li ki*, C, I, 147.

were only consorts annexed to a group of wives. An entirely contrary system of morals developed under the feudal nobility. Marriage seemed to place the wife in subjection to her husband. On the other hand, the mother developed a power which, while preserving some of its former characteristics, assumed more and more the attributes proper to paternal authority.

(1). *Home Life*

Noble girls are brought up to go and live in the capacity of daughters-in-law in a strange family. From their childhood they are instructed in the arts which will enable them to work for the prestige of their family, and in the modesty which will save their parents from entering into cruel vendettas, for while the birth of a boy was regarded as a principle of honour, a girl appeared like a principle of influence. Little girls were laid on the ground at birth, exactly like their brothers.[1] Instead of receiving a jade sceptre for a toy, they were given a spindle. The first garment in which they were clothed was a garment fit for night and not for public ceremonies. To signalize their coming into the world, a sort of cloth or towel was hung up at the door in place of a bow and arrows. Girls are not made for public life and for war, but for the labours and service of the women's apartments. They will be wives and spinners. A girl of ill-omened appearance, if for example she is red and hairy, will be abandoned in the open field.[2] When one augurs well of the little girl she is lifted from the ground where she is supposed to have learnt humility, and to save her from any temptation to pride, she is not exposed on the paternal bed. Moreover the father gives no order for any further ceremony. If one be held, as appears to have been the case, the women alone take part in it and the rituals do not condescend to mention it. Neither is it stated that the father has the little girl presented to him : between her and him no rite of approach seems to have been performed. The name, which was particularly secret, was no doubt given by the mother. A daughter has not to be incorporated in the agnatic group. As long as she lives, she will depend upon her mother alone. As soon as she can speak, she is inclined to a destiny of submission by

---

[1] *She king,* **C**, 350.   [2] *Tso chuan,* **C**, II, 457.

learning to say " yes " in the humble tone suitable to women.[1]
At the end of seven years she is separated from her brothers.
Seven years, the time when the new teeth appear, is the age
of a sort of new formation : there was in old times a girl
who was capable of conceiving from her seventh year. From
that time sexual bans begin to come into play : the little
girl cannot sit on the same mat with her brothers nor eat
with them. After the tenth year these taboos impose complete
seclusion, which coincides with instruction in the work,
language, deportment and virtue proper to women. This
instruction is given under the direction of a duenna. Authors
are careful not to write of it with any precision. It is only
known that the little girl learnt to obey with a gentle air, to
peel hemp, to weave stuffs, to plait ribands, to make garments.
She was also initiated into the art of preparing and serving
the ceremonial repasts which were offered to the ancestors.[2]
The marriageable age is fixed at fifteen years, although
according to theory, feminine life was regulated by the
number seven, and girls were supposed to arrive at puberty
at the age of fourteen. In contrast with the boys, the girl
is declared major as soon as she is marriageable, and a new
name is bestowed upon her in the course of a ceremony in
which she must alter the mode of doing her hair, for she is
then given a head-pin.[3] No information is granted us about
this feminine festival. It is most probable that it ushered in
a period of particularly severe seclusion, for it is acknowledged
to have coincided with the betrothal. Now the noble girl
who was betrothed must live in complete confinement : no
man may see her, except for the gravest reasons.[4] To signalize
this betrothed state, she is made to wear a sort of cord round
her neck. There are certain themes of miraculous conceptions
which indicate that the marriageable girl, during her period
of pre-nuptial claustration, was held between heaven and
earth, shut up, for example, in a high tower, and completely
sheltered from the rays of the sun.[5] The daughters of the
great nobility lived for three months like recluses in the
ancestral temple, or rather, it appears, the daughters of
princely families occupied the temple of the Great Ancestor,

---

[1] *Li ki,* C, I, 673.   [2] *Li ki,* C, I, 675 ff.
[3] *Yi li,* C, 45.   [4] *Li ki,* C, I, 30.
[5] *Lu she ch'un ch'iu,* 6, par. 3 ; *Hu han shu,* 115, and *Wei shu,* 100.

a place of profound seclusion.[1] Girls in retreat were called
" pure girls," and it was understood that they preserved their
chastity. Nevertheless these and other similar expressions
are found in the songs of rendezvous.[2] Moreover, the legends
of the Great Ancestors recall the themes of the peasant
initiations of spring, whilst their temple is sometimes called
the Temple of the Great Mediator, who, we are assured,
presided over these festivals. These indications lead one to
believe that the pre-nuptial retreat of noble virgins did not
at first entirely exclude the rites of pre-union which were
customary with the peasants. We have seen that the youths
were frequently sent to their mother's family, from which
they were to take wives, and where they were received in the
capacity of guests. Now it was the custom to offer a guest
one of the daughters of the family : it was hoped that,
" keeping close to him as a servant, she would fix his heart." [3]
This kind of marriage with the host or the hostage was always
of an unstable nature and had the air of a trial marriage.[4]
There was a period when, making their retreat under the
direction of an experienced duenna and of the mother of
the family, the young girls exerted themselves to attach the
hearts of their young cousins who were the predestined
bridegrooms preferred by their mother. But, through the
efforts of the ritualists, the pre-nuptial seclusion assumed a
more rigid interpretation and the taboo of the betrothed
was understood in a totally different way. " A boy and
girl, when there has been no action by a go-between, cannot
know each other's names. Until the marriage presents have
been given, they can have no intercourse and no proximity." [5]
According to the rituals, the rule is that the boy does not see
the face of his betrothed till after the nuptial celebrations.
This rule of modesty may be the occasion for charming
adventures. A prince of Ch'u, who was conquered in 505 B.C.,
and fled with the women of his household, went to lodge in
the midst of a marsh, and during the difficult crossing, Chong
Kien, a faithful vassal, was good enough to carry his lord's
daughter on his back. In the end the prince left the marsh
and having returned to his capital, he found a husband for
his daughter. But she declared, with all suitable humility,

[1] *She king*, 452.   [2] **LII**, 71 and 111.   [3] SMC, IV, 282.
[4] SMC, IV, 284 and 285.   [5] *Li ki*, C, I, 30.

" When one acts as a maiden one keeps men at a distance. . . .
Chong Kien carried me on his back ! " She had only to say
the word : her father married her to the man of the marsh.[1]

The marriage of a noble girl is a quasi-diplomatic affair.
It serves to maintain an old alliance or to procure a new
one, for, in the instability of the feudal world, it happens
more and more frequently that families, rejecting " the old
relationships " seek for " fortune (*li*) " by attaching themselves
to another system of alliances.[2] To enter into commerce, one
must have recourse to the good offices of a go-between.
The go-between, who was formerly charged with the over-
sight of the pre-nuptial lustrations, becomes a sort of ambassador. This obliging intermediary will become in the end
a veritable match-maker whose duty it is to provide the
partners and to assort the households. In feudal times, his
intervention seems to have been necessary, because the old
rule (which was still respected, in theory if not in fact) [3]
that a marriage is only fortunate between families traditionally
united by the obligation of intermarriages, survived in another
form, namely, the idea that marriage is not a free contract :
a girl who is asked in marriage cannot be refused without
her people exposing themselves to a vendetta.[4] This misfortune may be avoided if the two families come to an agreement through the go-between, before the formal demand.
The official rites do not come into play until the agreement
is concluded. The go-between then resigns his place to a
qualified ambassador whom the head of the family of the
would-be bridegroom sends to the family of the girl.[5] He
proceeds with the rites of betrothal, at which neither the
bridegroom nor his father may be present. At each of these
rites he exchanges a certain number of sacramental formulas
with the head of the girl's family. At the first rite, for
instance, when he presents the demand, he receives the
prescribed reply as follows : " Such-an-one's daughter is
stupid. It was impossible to bring her up properly. My
lord, you command me. (I), Such-an-one, will not have the
audacity to refuse." [6] These words of becoming modesty
have the object of declining in advance all responsibility

[1] *Tso chuan*, **C**, III, 512 and 525.   [2] *Kuo yu*, 2.
[3] *Tso chuan*, **C**, III, 752, and SMC, IV, 398 and 466.
    Tso chuan, **C**, II, 21.   [5] *Yi li*, 2.   [6] *Yi li*, **C**, 49.

should the marriage turn out badly. Again they witness to the old obligatory character of the taking of a wife. A second embassy is necessary to ask the personal name of the bride which must be known before casting lots,[1] a third to come and tell the result of the lots, a fourth to bring the ritual presents, two deer-skins and two pieces of silk (the betrothal then acquires a definite character), a fifth to fix the day of the wedding celebrations. So much red tape is not superfluous, for the honour of the contracting parties must be taken into consideration, and it is necessary to conceal the character of prescribed contract which belongs to the contract of matrimony. Their honour is particularly sensitive in the marriages of the ruling class, when the taking of wives is very often the equivalent of a composition which provisionally puts an end to a vendetta. Duke P'ing of Chin, after having made war against the country of Ch'i, had married a girl from Ch'i, Shao Kiang, and the vendetta had almost broken out again at the marriage, for Shao Kiang had not been accompanied to Chin with as many honours as had been paid in demanding her. A short time after her marriage, she died.[2] Ch'i was required to renew the contract of marriage which had failed (no one doubted that the prince would fulfil this duty). He himself offered to do so. " There are still girls in my house born of my father and his principal wife. . . . They are quite ordinary girls. . . . If you deign to choose one among them to make up the number in your harem, my hope will revive." [3] Elsewhere, a more complete formula exists, used as reply to a demand in marriage : " My wife has given me so many daughters : my secondary wives so many. . . . I still have so many aunts on the father's side, and sisters." [4] These formulas assume their whole significance when they are taken in connexion with the severe reproaches merited by Huan of Ch'i when he constantly refused to marry his sisters and aunts.[5] History insinuates that this leader had incestuous relations with them. Incest between brother and sister is by the way a crime frequently imputed to the princes of Ch'i (but not to them alone). Nevertheless these relations, whether they were begun before

---

[1] Tso chuan, C, I, 179.
[2] Tso chuan, C, III, 46 and 52.
[3] Tso chuan, C, III, 54.
[4] Tso chuan, C, II, 281.
[5] Huai-nan tsih, 10 ; Shuo yuan, 8.

marriage or not, were no impediment if they were continued after it.[1] Huan of Ch'i is particularly taxed with infamy because, in his pride as a Leader, he wished to deprive the rival families of the guarantee conferred by the possession of a married woman as a sort of hostage. There is present here a curious principle of endogamy, but the fact, while it may seem peculiar to the families of potentates, exhibits the value of the exogamic regulation. The girls must be married outside the family because the rival families have rights in them. If, normally, they are brought up with the view of becoming wives, it is thought preferable to hand them over as hostages, and not the sons : or, more correctly perhaps, because formerly the sons, having been entertained by foster-fathers, were only retrieved after compensation had been paid, by despatching their sisters in the capacity of brides. The boys, in a noble family, counted as depositaries of the family honour, but a daughter had, above all, the value of a substitute.

Girls are also a source of prestige. When, by the help of betrothal rites, one family has proved its right to exact the delivery of a bride from another family, the latter is put upon its honour to pay a large sum. The splendour of the nuptial ceremony is a contribution to the glory of the son-in-law, but it is a profitable contribution. This can be felt from the tone of the marriage hymns alone : " The prince of Han is taking to wife—the daughter of the King of the Fen !—the daughter of the overlord of Kuei !—The prince of Han is coming to her !—he comes to the village of Kuei !—One hundred chariots roll along with mighty noise !—Their eight bells make a great sound !—Can anything more brilliant be seen ?—The younger sisters form an escort—moving forward like clouds ! The prince of Han looks upon them !—their splendour fills the palace." [2] There is scanty information on the subject of the dowry brought by the bride, but the essential part of this dowry was surely the escort made up of attendants and particularly women attendants who composed her suite. We have seen that it sometimes happens that the overlords chose their counsellors from among the bride's attendants.[3] We learn from a nuptial hymn that

---

[1] *Tso chuan*, **C**, III, 587 ; SMC, IV, 109. [2] *She king*, **C**, 405.
[3] SMC, I, 178, and II, 26.

their eyes were dazzled by the women attendants. As a measure of the nobility of the bridegroom, the number of the women attendants is fixed by the register. In certain cases it is augmented to do honour to the husband, but it is augmented in the same way to do honour to the bride. " The great number of women attendants constitutes magnificence for a wife " and magnificence " bestows prestige." This number however must not be such as to exhaust, for a generation, the matrimonial capabilities of a family group. Not more than two sisters must come from each of the family groups which contribute to the marriage celebrations, for three is a total. This rule serves to justify the custom by which one of their nieces is given as companion to two sisters. It is understood that the niece is provided to bind the husband beforehand to the rising generation of the allied family. As a matter of fact, if this family does not hesitate to give its daughters magnificently, it is because the son-in-law is definitely attached to his wife's family when he is provided by a single marriage, with an ample share of wives. An overlord who receives nine wives at one time has no right to contract a second marriage. Polygyny implies monogamy, even for the simple noble who receives no more than two wives : on his part, a second marriage, possible in law and frequent in fact, is always condemned by opinion (but feudal instability also permits overlords to violate the monogamic rule). When he is bereft of his wives by repeated deaths, the son-in-law has the right to have them replaced, and there is no second marriage, strictly speaking, in such a case : the wives whom the family-in-law makes haste to send are simply substituted for those of the first batch, which was not durable enough. The function of polygynic monogamy is to limit the matrimonial future of the husband : the wife's family purchased, during his lifetime, his fidelity to the alliance which had been concluded. At the same time, it acquired certain rights over the children who would be born to him : all would be subject to a strong and unique influence, for every woman, during her whole career as wife and mother, takes pains to remain a good daughter to her own family.[1]

When the betrothed girl is handed over to her husband there is no true delivery or complete transfer of authority.

[1] LII, 14, 87 and 22 ; SMC, I, 265.

The husband is not completely substituted for the rights of the head of her own family. The woman passes from obedience (*tsong*) towards this chief to obedience towards her husband. Doubtless the authority of the husband (who was called lord) tended to assume a seigniorial character, after the pattern of the paternal authority. Nevertheless, by obedience (*tsong*) one must above all understand the idea that the wife, condemned to a sort of minority, has no place in society save in the capacity of daughter or wife. As a widow, she is placed under the obedience (*tsong*) of the son, which does not imply that he possesses the slightest power of commanding her. He is simply a sort of responsible guardian, after the father and husband. The transference of the guardianship to the husband does not in any way put an end to the father's rights nor even to his responsibility. For example, we may see paternal justice executed upon a married daughter, in order to avert responsibility : it is true that the ritualists declare that this is a case of infringement upon the rights and duties of the husband.[1] On the other hand, there is nothing decisive in the transference of the guardianship ; sometimes in case of widowhood, and always in case of repudiation, the daughter returns to the guardianship of her own family. A significant provision of the law forbids the repudiation of any woman who has no relations remaining to take her under their guardianship.[2] The dismissal of the wife is accomplished with the forms of the nuptial celebration. A procession accompanies the repudiated wife. Formulas of ritual modesty are exchanged between the husband's messenger and the head of the wife's family. Their object is to prevent the starting of a vendetta through the rupture of the marriage.[3] In the same way, the consecrated formulas which must be used by the father and mother of the bride, when the bridegroom comes to fetch her, imply neither abandonment nor transference of authority : they are in the nature of imperative advice given to the girl, so that in her new function as wife and daughter-in-law, she may avoid doing anything which would involve the responsibility and honour of her own family. As she was given to heal or prevent a vendetta, the wife belongs to the two contracting families like a pledge in which the two parties

---

[1] SMC, IV, 114.   [2] *Ta tai li ki*, 80.   [3] *Li ki*, C, II, 197 ff.

have conflicting rights. The situation which the wife occupies is that of a *Sabine*, but it is clear that her father's interests remain more dear to her than those of her husband. Daughters are known to give their fathers warning of an ambush laid by the husband.[1] They are known to ask their mother's advice : " Who is the nearest, father or husband, and who ought to be dearest ? "—" Anyone can make a husband but we can only have one father ! " replies the mother, who has no hesitation over the duty to be chosen : but the wife had already listened to her filial heart, for she confesses that by carefully seducing and " amusing " her husband she has succeeded in gaining information, which while it saved her father, would cost her husband his life.[2] While she is in her husband's service, the wife must think how she may serve her parents. Thus, after the marriage, which is a pacification, wife and husband live in a state of armed peace, each, in their games, trying to rob the other of prestige for the profit of their own family. The games are a delicate matter : one must understand how not to gain too great a victory. Ch'ai Ki and her husband make up a boating party, and following an old rite, amuse themselves in making the boat heel over. The wife plays boldly : the husband shows that he is frightened. He sends this too adventurous woman back to her family. They take offence, marry their daughter again, and a vendetta breaks out between the former allies.[3]

During the nuptial celebrations (well begun is half done) everything is regulated so that neither can take too decided a precedence of his partner. The bridegroom must come in person to fetch his bride. A provisional lodging was prepared for him near the house of his betrothed (a probable survival of the times when the aspirant must first take service with his father-in-law). Received as a guest, he lays a wild goose at the feet of his father-in-law and does homage by saluting him twice on his knees, with his forehead touching the ground. This salutation is not returned to him, and the father-in-law does not accompany him back, but, without a word, his betrothed follows him, guided by a duenna.[4] Though he is called henceforth by the name of son-in-law, the husband shows no less humility towards the wife than towards the

---

[1] *Tso chuan*, C, II, 251. [2] *Tso chuan*, C, I, 117.
[3] SMC, IV, 52. [4] *Yi li*, C, 32.

father-in-law. He conducts the nuptial chariot and invites
the bride to climb into it, holding out a cord to help her.
But the duenna immediately declines this homage (for the
bride does not speak). The son-in-law starts the chariot.
After three turns of the wheel, he stops it and his place is
taken by a vassal while he mounts another chariot. Having
first acted as charioteer, he now goes forward and shows the
way. He receives the bride, as one receives a guest, at the
threshold of his house, and bows himself to let her enter.
Before they take the communal meal together, both purify
themselves, with the help of their attendants, by washing
their hands.[1] When Ch'ong-êrh of Chin received as a present
from his host, the duke of Ch'in, a consignment of five wives
(instead of three)—too big a present, and too great an
obligation—he ascertained, in addition, that one of these
wives had acted as a temporary wife to one of his relatives
who was a hostage to Ch'in. She it was who helped Ch'ong-êrh
to perform the preliminary purification, holding the pitcher
of water in the capacity of attendant. Profiting by the
opportunity to draw attention to his action and to retrieve
his position, Ch'ong-êrh took care, when he made her the
sign to retire, to splash her with his wet hand. But she
broke out in a rage : " Ch'in and Chin are equals in rank!
Why do you humiliate me ? " Immediately Ch'ong-êrh,
dropping his (ceremonial) robe (from his shoulders) posed
before her as a captive. Having conquered in this first
conjugal duel, which might have set up a vendetta if it had
been pushed too far, she was straightway treated as the
principal wife, though she had only figured in the consignment of wives under the name of an attendant. The extent
of her credit could be seen later, when, after she had become
a dowager and sanguinary quarrels had broken out between
Ch'in and Chin, she was able to have the three brave chiefs
whom Chin had taken prisoner, restored to her father.[2]

The wife who is introduced to one's hearth keeps the soul
of a stranger, but, while she is separated from her husband
by the divergent interests of their families, she is still further
removed by the force of sexual tabus which the sacrament
of marriage diminishes but has not the power to suppress.
In consequence of the sly contests which take place between

---

[1] *Yi li*, C, 33. [2] *Tso chuan*, C, I, 348.

the partners, inflaming the sentiments of family and sexual honour, home life is lacking in intimacy. It is inaugurated by a communal repast at which husband and wife eat side by side, and not face to face, and where everything is ordered to the end that they shall henceforth be halves of the same body—but separated halves. Each seated upon a separate mat, they eat the same food without using the same dish. They make private libations to the spirits, and each tastes of the pair of lungs which are served to them, and of the rib which is his portion of the two cut from either side of a pig's back. They each have their dish of millet, and their seven fishes, and when they have tasted the food, each one three times, they drink, three times each one—the last time (which is the supreme rite) out of two cups each made from half of the same calabash. While they ate and drank, they saluted each other ceremoniously. They could then go and undress, each in his apartment, and when they met again for the night, each would have his own mat.[1] Near the nuptial chamber, men and women attendants stayed to keep guard. Torches were lighted. For three days torches burned also in the bride's house. It appears that the marriage was not consummated until the third day : the learned affirm that great officers waited for the third month (the importance of the sexual union increasing in the ratio of nobility).[2] This union indeed called for great precautions. The woman must be veiled during the nuptial celebrations. No rite of betrothal or of marriage took place in full daylight, but in the twilight hours, the first rites in the morning (when the *Yang* triumphs over the *Yin*) the celebration of marriage in the evening twilight (when the male principle is vanquished by the female). The word *hun* (twilight) also means to take a wife. The same word again designates the woman's parents. These different values of the word suggest the idea that in old times the marriage was consummated in the bride's house. If the wife of a simple noble presented herself before her parents-in-law, who treated her henceforth, after the third day, as a daughter-in-law (*fu*), the presentation before the husband's ancestors only took place in the third month

[1] Only after death, husband and wife might make use of a common crock, to eat the offerings. Cf. *Li ki*, C, II, 334.
[2] LVI, App.

(at least among the great officers, who are said to have waited till the third month to consummate the marriage). Moreover, it is only after this stage of three months that the woman has the right to bear the title of daughter-in-law (*fu*) which is used to designate the married woman. If she dies beforehand, she has not the right to be mourned in the husband's family with the mourning due to a wife. In the third month, according to the classic rite, the escort of the betrothed returns to her parents, but it is also in the third month that the son-in-law must make a call upon his wife's parents which has all the characteristics of a farewell ceremony.[1] The three months and the three days are, in the agnatic organization, a period of probation indispensable before the wife can be admitted into her husband's family. They correspond, it may be, with the trial period which had formerly to elapse before the wife and her husband could leave the home of her family. In both cases this time of trial is justified by the difficulties of conjugal assimilation. In old times the bride could do no work before the third month (in modern usage she does not begin to do the cooking till the third day).[2] Similarly the noble husband, who was on leave owing to the fact of his marriage, might not appear at court for a whole year.[3] The trial period, which is the introduction to married life, doubtless lasted until the third year. During this time the husband and wife, as though smitten with impurity, live in a quarantine, which is most strict at its beginning. It is still a ruling idea that repudiation only becomes a serious matter after three years of life in common.[4] Indeed, three years is not too long for a husband to arrive at seducing or winning his wife. There are anecdotes which disclose the difficulties of this long initial struggle. A woman (who had, it is true, been carried off by her husband) only consented to speak to him after she had borne him two children.[5] Another who was married quite regularly (but she is said to have been beautiful and her husband plain) remained also obstinately dumb.[6] The unwelcome husband succeeded at last in obtaining a first word and a first smile, by proving his prowess at the chase : they were then in their third year

---

[1] *Yi li*, C, 55 ff.
[2] *She king*, C, 42 and 113.
[3] *Li ki*, C, I, 510.
[4] *She king*, 69.
[5] *Tso chuan*, C, I, 162.
[6] *Tso chuan*, C, III, 443.

of married life. This life does not take on a more intimate character once the wife has been tamed.

The sentiments of sexual or domestic honour may perhaps be stifled, but etiquette maintains its rights. Out of mutual respect, husband and wife never allow themselves to call each other by their names.[1] Not only do they give each other nothing from hand to hand, but when one takes up the object which the other has placed before him, he is careful not to take hold of it where it has already been touched by his consort, avoiding even indirect contact.[2] When the wife presents the husband with a cup of drink, he drinks as is right, but out of another cup. In the same way there must be no contact between their personal effects. Marriage does not give the consorts permission to hang their garments from the same nail nor to keep them in the same basket. They have no right to the same towel or the same comb. It is the worst scandal of all for husband and wife to take a bath together.[3] The stateliness of their relations is increased when they are to be united (for their sexual intercourse is not free, but strictly regulated). Conjugal duty is imposed upon the husband towards each of his wives according to a settled register whose details are given by the ritualists.[4] They also give minute information about the toilet which is obligatory in such a case, for such a woman, given her husband's rank of nobility and her own rank in the harem. The secondary wife of a great officer [5] for example, before going into her master's presence, must purify herself by fasting, rinse her mouth, clothe herself in newly washed garments, arrange her hair in a certain way, bind a sachet of scent to her girdle, and above all, tie her shoe-strings securely. Frequency of sexual intercourse is a duty which husband and wife owe to their nobility, but, on a stated day, the husband owes himself to such or such of his wives, the chief duty of the first wife consisting in the maintenance of respect for the registered order which rules the life of the harem.[6] It is a fault, laden with consequences (for society as well as for nature) to neglect one of his wives, as it is a fault to leave one of the daughters of the family without a husband. But, as Chinese physiology teaches that the flow of sexual humours ceases with men at

---

[1] *Li ki,* C, I, 72.   [2] *Li ki,* C, I, 29, and II, 339.   [3] *Li ki,* C, I, 660.
[4] LIII, 39 ff.   [5] *Li ki,* C, I, 661.   [6] LII, 35, 111 ff.

seventy years, and with women at fifty, the husband is free from his conjugal obligations towards those of his wives who have reached fifty, every obligation ceasing for himself at his seventieth year.[1] At that time sexual embargoes also come to an end. A husband of seventy years, and a wife of fifty need no longer keep apart. They can pack their things in the same place without any separation. Intimacy is only established in conjugal life at the time when sexual differentiations are effaced and the husband and wife enter upon a period of retreat and begin in company to prepare for death. When their bodies are united in the same tomb and their tablets in the same hall, they will form a pair of ancestors in close union. Then, and then alone, will the wife definitely become one with the family group, in which her marriage gave her the rank of daughter-in-law, and then mother of a family.

(2). *The Mother of a Family*

When a girl who is placed at the head of a group of brides, takes the part of female protagonist in the nuptial rites, she fills the place of first wife in her husband's harem. A first wife whose husband is the principal son has the rank of principal wife in the generation of which he is a part. We have seen that the principal son, when he presides over the ceremonies of domestic piety and directs all his brothers, ought to be seconded by his wife : she directs all her sisters-in-law. The chief daughter-in-law, while she fulfils her pious duties, is preparing to play the part of mother-of-the-family to which she will succeed when her husband himself has assumed authority as head of the family. A Chinese adage expresses the facts when it remarks simply that the wife (the first wife), by the mere fact of her marriage, is given a status which corresponds to that of her husband in her husband's family. Strictly speaking, this formula is exact, in the degree that the ideal of morals elaborated in noble circles is realized. From the time that the woman, considered as a dependant upon the husband, acknowledged her lord in him, the authority of the mistress of the house seems to have become a delegation of the authority of the head of the family. This authority then takes on a seigniorial character.

[1] **LVIII,** 7 and 10 ; *Li ki,* C, I, 610.

In consequence, all the relations of the harem are modified. They were, in principle, governed by the fact that the rule of the first wife over her servants and that of the principal wife over her sisters-in-law were exercised in virtue of their own right and not by delegation.

The judicial status which is the prerogative of the first wife is derived from the rights which she possesses over her attendants previously to the marriage. She is a first-born. The attendants who are younger daughters (or nieces) have had from childhood to respect her authority. This authority, established from old time, is the foundation of the discipline of the harem, which from that time has had the value of a statutory order. Precisely from this value the ritualists draw their argument, when they are justifying polygyny with sisters as a wise institution; there can be no dissension amongst sisters who are accustomed from childhood to obey and to command. " Sexual conflicts and jealousy " [1] seem to be avoided from the one fact that the sisters (who have received the same education and represent the interests of a single family) form a united whole and are, in legal parlance, a collective personality. One marriage is enough to marry them all together. A man is not a complete widower till after the disappearance of the entire group. If there is not succession (there is no succession possible within the same generation) the younger sister is substituted for the elder, in the character of substitute, and everything goes on as though no death had taken place so long as one representative of the group survives. Thus a husband who has lost his first wife only, will meet with a refusal if he seeks to form a new union: this would be a case of bigamy, since a younger sister survives.[2] Inversely, repudiation acts automatically upon the entire group of brides. An anecdote which illustrates this principle exhibits at the same time the solidarity which exists between the rule of monogamy and the polygynic institution. It also shows the small account which was taken of sentiment in domestic life. A personage of Wei (485 B.C.) repudiated his wife in order to conclude a profitable alliance, although her younger sister and attendant was agreeable to him. Having married out of policy, but still remaining faithful to his sentiment, he succeeded in bringing back the younger sister,

---

[1] LIII, 13.   [2] *Tso chuan*, C, I, 485.

who had left the harem with the first wife, building a new home for her. " It was (then) as if he had two wives," and the father of the new bride, who had instigated the divorce to provide a position for his daughter, took her back immediately : in other ways, the bigamy came to a bad end.[1] The polygynic institution wears a different face when, under the influence of the agnatic law which sought to bind successive generations together, it ceased to be strictly sisterly. Solidarity in the group of brides was less close when the group included a niece. Between the niece, the daughter of an eldest brother, and the younger sister (if not between the niece and the eldest sister) a question of precedence arose which the ritualists hesitate to settle. Their discussions reveal the rivalry between the principle of indivisibility (which rules in plebeian families and favours the fraternal succession) and the hierarchical principle (which is triumphant among the nobility, and favours the patriarchal order of succession with the primogeniture).[2] As a matter of fact, even when it is disguised by incorporating the niece in the group of the first brides, it is a case of double marriage. In the same way, one may take the case of feudal overlords who marry three groups of wives at one time. It is a single marriage in theory, for the wives bear the same name, though they are sprung from distinct family groups. But in fact, the homogeneity of the harem is broken, for each of the three groups wishes to make its influence predominate. Rivalries become complicated when, contrary to the regulation, groups of wives of a different name insinuate themselves into the nuptial celebrations, or still worse, when the husband, increasing his harem to multiply his alliances, contracts several successive marriages. These offences against the customs are multiplied, because of the growing complications of the systems of alliance in the upper classes of feudal society, where an hierarchical order which has been set up for the profit of the males does precisely tend to predominate. The classification of wives within the harem is apt to depend upon the good will of the husband, who can be led astray by the cleverest—and then jealous quarrels break out which are expressed in the threatening incantations of which the *She*

---

[1] *Tso chuan*, C, III, 674 and 185.　　　　[2] **LIII**, 10.

King has preserved examples.[1] Or else his good will may be won over by the most powerful, in which case it will all end in cruel vendettas, in which the wives who represent a rejected alliance in the harem will have no mercy shown them. Husbands have been known to order their wives to *avenge themselves* on a first wife, who is held responsible for the treason of which her brother had been accused.[2] Other husbands are known, who intend by a simple decree of marital authority to degrade the wife who is entitled to be first, for the benefit of a favourite.[3] A master of ceremonies who is consulted in such a case, replies by recalling the old principle : the first wife is she who is provided as such, by the family with whom the husband's family is connected by an old tradition of intermarriage. He does not succeed in altering the husband's decision. It was necessary to admit another principle to maintain some stability in the life of the harem : the title of first wife is definitely acquired by the wife whom the husband authorized to take the chief part in the ceremony of the initial marriage. The first wife (and with her, her children, who are the chief consideration) is thus protected against the arbitrary will of her husband : only the judicial status of women seems to have been derived henceforth, no longer from the rights belonging to the eldest daughter, but from a title received by investiture from the marital authority.

In the same way, the principal wife seems to hold authority which is acknowledged by the group of her sisters-in-law, solely as the result of her participation in the authority of her husband, the principal son. Her authority however was originally of an independent character. As a matter of fact, the polygynic marriage practised among the nobility is derived from a group marriage, which united, by a single contract of alliance, a group of brothers to a group of sisters, so as to form a kind of great indivisible household, in which each member, beside the principal rights which he is admitted to hold over one of the members of the other sex, possessed secondary rights over all the members of that sex. The prohibitions which separate brothers and sisters-in-law, amongst the nobility, prohibitions from all contact, even oral, and above all a prohibition from wearing mourning for each

---

[1] *She king*, C, 39, 218, 219, 230.　　[2] *Tso chuan*, C, III, 761.
[3] *Tso chuan*, C, III, 752.

other, are more severe when they apply to a younger brother
and the eldest sister-in-law, and nevertheless significant survivals of the levirate are authenticated : at one time the
eldest son will pass on a woman who has been offered to him
to a younger brother : at another time the younger brother,
who wishes to substitute his authority for that of the elder
who has died, first tries to seduce and marry his eldest sister-
in-law.[1] One must therefore see in the prohibitions which
aim at separating brothers and sisters-in-law an inverted
consequence of the laws which originally drew them together.
As the representative of the entire group of his brothers,
the eldest has annexed the entire group of sisters. The
younger sisters, over whom he had at first only secondary
rights, become his second wives : the eldest, who is the
first wife, stays with him under this title, but the younger
brothers only keep the secondary rights which they had over
her in the form of eventual rights (rights of levirate, which
were shortly abolished). From this necessary hypothesis, it
results that the rights of the principal wife over her sisters-
in-law, the wives of younger brothers, are derived from
ancient rights held by the eldest bride over her younger
sisters. Moreover, these original rights of the eldest were,
as the result of collective marriage, extended to the brothers-
in-law, the husbands of the younger sisters. The power of
control possessed by the principal wife over all the households
of her husband's brothers resulted, in the first instance, from
the right of judicature which belonged to her as eldest sister,
and bestowed upon her the rôle of female protagonist in the
collective marriage. The ceremony of marriage among the
nobility can only be explained by the survival of this first
situation.[2] The bridegroom and the bride must have their
own attendants : but if those of the bride are still younger
sisters in principle, the husband's younger brothers are
removed and replaced simply by representatives. As marriage
served originally to unite two groups of consorts and not a
bride and bridegroom, the latter are still unable to come
together without the help of the joint effort of men and
women attendants. These " open the way " for them, by a
" cross action " which is significant. One of the bridegroom's
attendants offers the betrothed the ewer which is necessary

[1] *Tso chuan*, C, I, 196, and III, 551 ; LV, I, note 2. [2] LIII, 34 ff. ; 80 ff.

for her first purifying ablutions : one of the women attendants
renders the same service to the husband. He, when he
disrobes after the communal repast, must hand his garments
to a woman attendant : the bride, by a still more remarkable
rule, gives hers to one of the men. The banquet of the
polygynic marriage can no longer be a repast of equals, at
which all the consorts commune together. Nevertheless men
and women attendants commune on an equal footing, like
the chief bride and bridegroom, but after them ; the remains
of the husband's meal come to the women and of the bride's
meal to the men. This collection of rites has no meaning
unless the men and women attendants are to be united by
a bond analogous to the marriage tie which they are helping
to create between the protagonists of each group. We may
therefore suppose, that as the women attendants are younger
sisters, the men were originally younger brothers. We then
discover the origin of the powers of the principal bride :
they do not differ, in principle, from the powers belonging
to the first wife. Being bound to the eldest brother, for
whom she procured rights over her own younger sisters
which were confirmed by an infeudating communion, she
herself acquired rights over the bridegroom's younger brothers :
being attached to her by their union with her sisters, they
acknowledged this infeudation by themselves consenting to
share in the communion in the character of subject-slaves.
But, when the authority of the first-born, modelling itself
upon the paternal authority, assumed a seigniorial character
—when, for the advantage of the eldest son, sororal polygyny
was instituted, and when, out of respect for him, once the
rights of the eldest branch had been consolidated, the levirate
was forbidden—the eldest sister-in-law, instead of being
drawn to the younger brothers, her brothers-in-law, by a
common bond, was separated from them by prohibitions
She had no other rights than those which came to her as
a delegation of the authority belonging to her husband.
Here again, marital authority encroached upon female
judicature. The younger brothers were no longer bound to
the woman, who in their generation held the rank of principal
wife, by an infeudating communion which implied secondary
conjugal rights, but by the fact that, sharing now in the
ceremonies of domestic piety in the character of subjects,

they tended to be placed in a situation similar to that of the
sons in relation to their elder brother, and consequently to
his wife. A Chinese adage (invoked precisely in order to
justify the impossibility of all mourning between sisters and
brothers-in-law) reveals the novelty of this situation which
has even now a paradoxical appearance. Between agnates
and wives, mourning is possible only *if they cannot call each
other by the name of husband or wife* except in cases when as
members of different generations they can call each other,
father, mother, daughters-in-law, or sons (= nephews). If
there were mourning between agnates and wives of the
same generation, everything would happen as " *if the wife
of a younger brother were called* daughter-in-law (son's wife),
but then *would it not be necessary to call the wife of the eldest
brother* mother ? " [1] This formula shows the legal importance
of the appellations (*ming*) which signify domestic ties. In
the course of her life, the eldest sister-in-law, being judicially
unnameable, is simply given a title of honour (*sao* = *seu*, the
old woman, a term which does not evoke the idea of any
judicial tie). It is undesirable at present to call her mother,
and so clothe her with the authority of a mother of the
family which would extend to her husband's brothers, and
it is impossible to continue to give her a name which would
imply between her and them the relation of husband and
wife. Contrasted with this, and of so much the more significance, is the fact that the principal wife continues to call
the wives of her husband's younger brothers *younger sisters*
(= younger sisters-in-law) [2] although as a matter of fact the
latter frequently do, and in law always may, spring from
another family than the eldest son's wife. In company with
the latter they have necessarily the rank of younger sisters
and the position of *sister substitutes* (just as, in company with
the parents of a deceased wife, the wife of the second marriage,
even when she springs from another family, has the position
of a *daughter substitute*.[3] Thus the principle of female judicature is maintained, but only inside the woman's apartments
—with this result, however, that in every secondary household,
the wife is subject to two rival authorities : that of the
husband, chief in his own household, yet subject to his eldest

---

[1] *Yi li*, **CXXIII**, vol. I, 29, and *Li ki*, **C**, I, 780.
[2] *Êrh ya*, 4.   [3] **LIII**, 65.

brother, and that of the principal wife, who is always looked upon as being invested with the rights proper to eldest daughters. There is however a tendency to see in her a coadjutress (with future succession) of the mother-in-law, just as a coadjutor of the father of the family is seen in the eldest son.

The father of the family has only one son, the principal son, who has brothers. In the same way, the mother of the family has only one daughter-in-law, the first wife of the principal son, who has junior sisters (her sisters-in-law). The principal wife alone (though surrounded by her attendants) is received by the parents-in-law, and presented to the Ancestors, once the various stages of the matrimonial essay are passed. The husband does not figure in the ceremony at which his wife, when she has served the parents-in-law with food, accepts what they have left : but the attendants have a place in it. The bride eats the first portion of what is left by the mother-in-law : she refuses to consume that of the father-in-law : she is forbidden to communicate with him who, as a matter of fact, frequently attempts to exercise marital, or pre-marital, rights upon the bride destined for his son. Nevertheless, as a " crossed " arrangement is still the rule here, as in the rites which are properly nuptial, the remains of the father-in-law's meal are eaten by the female attendants, the younger sisters of the bride. And in the same way, if the son, being absent, is not called upon to eat what his mother has left, what is left of it by the bride belongs to the son's attendants, who are simply passive representatives, but representatives substituted for the younger brothers. Now, as has been seen, if the father often wishes to gain possession of the betrothed set apart for his son, the son frequently appropriates the widow left by the father (who is presented to us in that case as having contracted a second marriage). The communion of the women attendants with the father-in-law, the sign of ancient matrimonial rights, is evidently connected with the second of the two cycles of conjugal relations which are sought after by each individual in order to bind himself to two successive generations. We may therefore suppose that the communion of the attendants with the bridegroom's mother is a trace of the first cycle of these relations, those of the son and the stepmother, in

which it is known that the younger son may be called upon
to replace the elder. Whatever may be the value of these
ritual survivals, at the time when the ceremonies inspired by
the principle of indivisibility were ordained for the purpose
of establishing the patriarchal order, the son could no longer
be present nor the daughter-in-law hold communion with the
father-in-law, otherwise than by go-betweens or representatives. It is indeed astonishing that the order of the rites was
completely revolutionized in such a way as to make the son,
like his attendants, hold communion with his father, the
women attendants, like the bride, with the mother-in-law.
As a matter of fact, what alone mattered in the new spirit
of the ceremony, was to create a bond of dependence between
the mother-in-law and the bride, who is about to qualify
herself to bear the title of chief daughter-in-law by infeudating
herself to her through communion. When the communal
rites were ended, whilst the parents-in-law left the hall of
ceremonies by the western staircase, which is that of the
guests, the daughter-in-law on the contrary descended the
eastern stairs, usually reserved for the master of the house :
the rituals say that by these rites the apartment (*she*) was
handed over to her in which she was to live.[1]

After being thus welcomed by the parents, and after she
had presented a first sacrifice to the Ancestors, a sacrifice
before which it was thought impossible to have real conjugal
relations, or " to bring up children " [2] the wife acquired the
aptitude of being a mother, that is to say, of having a son,
who in his turn would practise the rites of piety, for, in the
patriarchal order, the mother derives her authority from her
character as a pious daughter-in-law, as the father holds his
through his character as a pious son. Thus, just as in a
family group one wife only is called the principal daughter-
in-law, so there can only be one mother (by which is understood, one mother of a principal son) that is, the woman
qualified to give her parents-in-law a grandson successor—
all the other children (secondary grandsons) forming, even
in the eyes of the women whom we should call their mothers,
an indistinct group of nephews. Inversely, among all the
children descended from the same grandfather, the eldest son
of the principal daughter-in-law is alone in possessing a real

[1] *Li ki*, **C**, I, 160. [2] *Tso chuan*, **C**, I, 45.

mother. The eldest sons of secondary daughters-in-law will become the leaders of the worship of the latter ; but as, during their lifetime, they were not able to preside over the pious rites, the future leaders of their worship could not at that time treat them as mothers of the family, or rather, they could only do so in private (*ssu*). This half-privilege, the result of the religious organization, is a step towards the recognition of the individual ties of relationship between mothers and sons : it is also strictly limited to the first-born who are favoured by the principle of single succession. The younger sons, on the other hand, though more duties are imposed upon them towards their father's first wife than towards any other woman of the mother's generation, have no mother of their own. If he be the son of the principal or the first wife, the younger son effaces himself before the eldest son and can only be a son by secondary title. If he be the son of a secondary wife, he can recognize nothing more than an aunt in her, and again he is only a secondary son for the first wife, although he must treat her as a mother, at any rate in private.

This last case throws light upon the meaning of the original relations of mother and son as well as upon their evolution under the influence of feudal customs. Maternal rights are those which, being held in indivisible title by a group of sisters who formed a body of co-wives, were originally exercised by the eldest of these sisters in her capacity of mother-dowager, before they were assigned to her in her own right as wife or rather as principal daughter-in-law. Maternal authority, which was founded originally upon the rights of nature, which were direct though they cannot be called natural, seemed later to be derived from a right of command held by the parents-in-law and the husband. It was then exercised secondarily upon a group of children, and by principal title, upon a son and successor. Thus, at the time when it began to assume the character of an individual tie, maternity became radically distinct from every tie of blood. Not only is it unnecessary to bring a child into the world, to have a son (it is enough to be first wife and for a second wife to have a child) but again (without reckoning that she is not the mother of her child, if she is not the first wife) when she brings forth a son and is the first wife, she may cease to be the mother of that child : it is enough for the husband to repudiate her—for example by order of the parents-in-law. It is enough also for him to degrade her and appoint another principal wife. This latter will become the mother and in her favour the son will have to show piety : it is true that as a rule the son of a degraded mother was killed, or else, himself being degraded, he was counted henceforth among the indivisible group of secondary sons. The ritualists seek to oppose these excesses of marital or paternal authority, which are harmful to the correct order of successions. On the other hand, the rupture of the ties between the child and the repudiated mother seemed to them to occur automatically. The grandson of Confucius, himself a great philosopher, is credited with this weighty saying : " She who was my wife was also my son's mother. When she ceased (by repudiation) to be my wife, she ceased to be the mother of my son." [1] The facts could not be stated with more force : all the ties of parentage seem to depend upon the bond between the father and the son which is conceived upon the model of the bond between the overlord and vassal, so that the relationship with the mother is only the result of a decree which can be revoked by the father. Thus the father of a family may be seen dividing his children by a decree (*ming*) amongst his various secondary wives (at least when these children have lost their natural mother and when the mother has by decree no child of her own).[2] The son who is thus attributed must treat this imposed mother as though she were his own ; in the same way, the son of the first marriage must not make any difference between his stepmother and his first mother.[3] Marital or paternal omnipotence is not enough to explain such indifference towards what we should call the ties of nature. These ties had already only a very secondary importance, at the time when maternal authority was the result of a direct right belonging to the female judicature as such. Significant survivals are preserved in the Chinese customs on this point. In justification of sororal polygyny, it is stated that its object is to prevent both female and maternal jealousy : when one of the wives of a polygynic group has a son, the others rejoice, and it is thus that one can " multiply descendants." [4] When the institution is respected, the first wife's

[1] *Li ki*, C, I, 112. [2] *Yi li*, C, 392. [3] *Yi li*, C, 391. [4] **LIII**, 15.

prestige is increased if, by regulating the order of the harem and favouring the approaches of the husband and the secondary wives, she is fortunate, thanks to their labours, in becoming the mother of many children : thus, the wife of King Wen gained one hundred sons and immortal glory.[1] When by a deviation of custom, the harem admits women who come from different families, maternal jealousy is added to conjugal jealousy, but this jealousy, like the maternal sentiment itself, is of a collective order and does not spring from a sentiment of personal affection. The mother who struggles and endangers herself for her child does not do so out of love to him : she works for the prestige of the group of brides under her command, she acts in the interests of her own family which made her the head of its delegates in her husband's house. In her maternal ardour she may, disengaging herself from the duty which in our eyes is imposed by nature upon a mother, confide her child to an attendant who is in greater favour. A prince of Ch'i (558 B.C.) married at Lu (into the family of *Ki*) had no child by his principal wife. They sent him one of her nieces, who had a son : as a gift from the principal wife's group, this child took rank as principal son. But the prince had also a group of wives who came from Song and represented the interests of the *Tsih* family. A fierce struggle arose between the wives of the name Ki and the name Tsih. The eldest wife among the Tsih had a son, while the younger succeeded in pleasing the prince. The natural mother did not hesitate to confide her child to the attendant who was in greater favour : she, on her part, did not hesitate to do her utmost to secure that this child of another mother, but of her own group, should be preferred to the child of the rival group. Less prudent than the natural mother, she ended by being put to death, and the rival group, in the flush of its victory, had her body exposed on the public square, contrary to the rules of modesty and right. The child was killed, but its mother escaped.[2] It is evident that at bottom, maternity remains collective in essence, but that a son is no more than a principle of prestige for his mothers, or even for his own mother. This trait of Chinese manners explains one of the facts which have most contributed to maintain female judicature. As a principle

[1] *She king*, Preface, and **XV**, 183.   [2] *Tso chuan*, **C**, II, 348, and SMC, IV, 68.

of influence, the child, girl or boy, is destined to procure an alliance for his father's family. Now it is quite evident that the mothers (and the maternal relatives) have always played a decisive part in the education and marriage of the children. At all times, the mothers have striven that their sons should take wives in their own family. They have no doubt succeeded in preserving this ancient custom which is favourable to female authority, because, even at the time when the fathers had succeeded in infeudating the sons, the daughters, brought up in the women's apartments, remained in dependence upon their mother. Now, as a rule, a youth only acquires his portion of wives for a consideration, and when he has sisters to bestow on the brothers of his future wife. As they ordered their daughters' marriages, the mothers were enabled to order the marriages of their sons, and to direct the choice of their daughters-in-law. They aimed at introducing to their sons the daughters of their own brothers who already called them aunts $(Ku=$mothers-in-law.) [1] This custom, which was rigorously forbidden, accounts for the omnipotence of the mother-in-law over her daughter-in-law. It is otherwise evident that when daughters and mothers-in-law formed a sort of female dynasty attached to the same outside interests, the group of wives existed as a compact body in each family, fully armed to defend the traditional rights of female judicature. Faced by the group of wives, the agnates, who were divided by the rivalry existing between two successive generations, had only one means of gaining their point : they must break up the homogeneity of the female group. They were striving to this end when, violating the rule of the single marriage, they brought into the harem successive groups of wives sprung from different families. The success of these masculine tactics could not be decisive. A son would sometimes ally himself with his mother and his maternal relatives, against his father : against his mother the son can only find hurtful allies once his father is dead, for he has no prestige unless his mother's prestige remains intact.[2] Overshadowed during the life of the husband by the marital authority, the maternal authority becomes entire, unlimited, unconditioned, when the wife has the good fortune to survive into widowhood and to take rank as a dowager. The independence of the agnatic

---

[1] *Êrh ya*, 4 ; *Tso chuan*, **C**, III, 437.   [2] *Tso chuan*, **C**, I, 106.

2 A

family and the patriarchal right could only have been fully established if the custom of sacrificing the first wives had itself been accepted.   But on this very question widows are known to have exerted themselves to divert the responsibilities of their mourning upon others : and it is usually the second wives who are employed as victim substitutes.[1]   Again and again in their history the Chinese will attempt to save the agnatic order from the crisis brought about by the passing of domestic authority into the hands of a dowager : for example, by devising a sacrifice of the mother in advance, as soon as the son takes rank as heir.[2]   But during the feudal epoch, husbands were reduced to using stratagems with their wives, who were rival powers, to extort from them the oath that they would follow them to the tomb.   It even happened that, not content with having survived and ruled, the dowager would publish her intention of having an independent tomb, and be followed to it by her favourite lover.[3]   The debauches of the dowagers are one of the great themes of the Chinese chronicles. If it be taken together with another theme, equal in importance, that of the exactions and rapine of the favourites, one discovers the secret of the stability of the female judicature which endured even at the time of the feudal order, which was so favourable to males.[4]   Enriched by the presents made by the husband to the women, whom as mistress of the harem she admits to his presence, a first wife, if she stays on and understands how to govern her followers, ends by acquiring a financial power which counterbalances the husband's power of command.   The latter is supported by the possession of an estate and of palladiums kept in the ancestral temple.   Ill-informed as we are upon the economic aspect of the family organization, it appears that the women also retained a considerable fortune in the shape of ornaments, jade, pearls, and jewels, which movable property was better suited to be fruitfully employed in the course of the struggle for influence.   When, at Ch'i, the princely house was threatened by a vassal family of increasing wealth, it was the intervention

[1] *Li ki*, **C**, I, 209 and 226.

[2] The Wei dynasty systematically employed this method.   The emperor Wu seems to have considered it. Cf. above, p. 124.

[3] *Chan kuo ch'e*, 4.

[4] *Tso chuan*, **C**, I, 79, 120, 220, 295, 536.   *Lu she ch'un ch'iu*, 9, par. 2.   *Mei ti*, 4. *Sun cheu*, 19.

of a dowager which alone could restore the rival fortunes
to their former footing.[1] The dowagers directed their son's
harem, after having directed that of their husband. They
procure the favourites (who are sometimes recruited by the
exertions of their own women attendants,[2] so great is the
solidarity of the female groups). Woe to the son, if they
set up a favourite in his place! Pao the brother of Duke
Chao of Song (610 B.C.) was well made and had a fine com-
plexion. He was besides full of amiable domestic sentiments.
His grandmother, having singled him out, wished to take
him for her lover. He is said to have refused, but he must
have done so with tact, for the dowager decided to have her
other grandson, Duke Chao, who was less pleasant and " did
not conduct himself well," killed for her favourite's advancement. Duke Chao had a following among whom he distributed all his wealth, but without success : the dowager
had helped her favourite " to be generous." The mother of
the family treats her husband as a " lord " : she must be
submissive and adept at women's work : but she is the
" lady " of the harem. She is the equal of her husband,
placed in the same rank at Court receptions or the ceremonies
of the Ancestral Temple.[3] Her power depends upon the
prestige of her parents and the authority which she is able
to acquire over her husband and over his sons when she
wisely organizes their sexual life. A slave for the time that
she is a daughter-in-law, once death has freed her from her
husband she is a queen-mother, whom there is no power in
the family capable of opposing. But all her prestige and all
her authority is acquired and augmented by a woman, while
she spends her life confined in the women's apartments.
This seclusion actually appears to have been the principle of
female judicature. The women's abode should be as far as
possible from the street. Its door must be " carefully shut."
A door-keeper, one of the chief eunuchs, has charge of it. The
women cannot come out of it : men must not penetrate into
it,[4] at any rate, in men's clothes : for it happens that gallants
sometimes succeed in being received in disguise. For the
rest, it is in the shelter of the women's apartments that
intrigues and conspiracies are usually concocted.[5] It happens

[1] *Tso chuan*, C, II, 457.   [2] *Tso chuan*, C, I, 536 ff.
[3] *Li ki*, C, I, 609.   [4] *Li ki*, C, I, 259.   [5] *Tso chuan*, C, II, 80.

too, friendships may be there formed between men; for example, when they chance to have the same mistress : such was the case of the prince of Ch'en (599 B.C.) and his two ministers—so closely united in affection that each of them when they were together, far from their lady love, delighted to wear one of the garments of their common friend.[1] The sport of these debauchees (they came to a bad end) shows the premium set upon the severe seclusion of women and all that belonged to them. A wife who was mindful of her prestige took care not to go abroad except veiled and accompanied by a duenna. She kept to the left side of the road (the right side was reserved for men) so that no man could jostle her. At night, she was careful to have a light.[2] Even when she was old, if the house caught fire she waited to leave it till she had received orders from the housekeeper who directed her steps.[3] Everything could be forgiven her, while she preserved decorum. Princess Nan-tsih, to whom the peasants gave the title of Sow, because she was her own brother's lover (the husband, " to please her," had summoned this brother to his court) [4] wished to receive a visit from Confucius. The sage did not hesitate and had no reason to be dissatisfied with the interview. In fact, Nan-tsih received him " concealed behind the hangings." When he had crossed the threshold, he prostrated himself, with his face to the north, as a subject should. Nan-tsih, behind the curtains, responded, according to the rites, by saluting twice, for one could hear the twice-repeated jingle of jade upon her bracelets and eardrops. A few ill-wishers only accused the philosopher of having visited a woman of bad life. He himself never admitted that he had done wrong. It is true that in addressing him Nan-tsih had designated herself by a personal pronoun which is suitable for a princess speaking to an overlord whom she holds in fee.[5] Woman's virtue is made up of ritual modesty and of fine deportment. Thence her empire is derived. The most fascinating portrait of a lady of high nobility which has come down to us, is that of Chuang Kiang. It is composed of themes, which if they give little information upon the physical type of the ancient Chinese, at least show that since old times the metaphors of the poets have scarcely changed, nor the kind of emotion

---

[1] *Tso chuan*, **C**, I, 599. [2] *Li ki*, **C**, I, 630 ff.
[3] *Tso chuan*, **C**, II, 547. [4] *Tso chuan*, **C**, III, 586. [5] SMC, V, 334 ff.

aroused by beauty. When Chuang Kiang appears, with her
fingers as delicate as young twigs, her skin as white as paint,
her neck slender as a worm, her teeth like the seeds of a
pumpkin, her forehead as broad as that of the grasshopper,
her eyebrows like the antennæ of silkworms, the poet cries
to the people to make haste to withdraw, and not to weary
by their company the happy lord of this lovely lady of commanding presence.[1] Another lady, Süan Kiang, merited
equal admiration and respect when she came, she who had
no need of a wig, wearing a rich head-dress adorned with
borrowed hair. Her forehead looked broad and white beneath
beautiful pins of ivory, and precious stones hung at her ears.
In her sumptuous robe of ceremony, she advanced with the
majesty of a river, and (although they might have accused
her of bad morals) all present were mastered by a sentiment
of religious veneration before this richly adorned woman, and
exclaimed : " Oh, is she not Heaven itself ! is she not the
Sovereign ! " [2]

---

[1] *She king*, **C**, 65.   [2] *She king*, **C**, 53.

BOOK FOUR

SOCIETY AT THE BEGINNING OF THE IMPERIAL ERA

A VERY important but little-known transformation of society corresponds with the foundation of the Empire. I propose to limit myself to indicating the chief starting-point of this movement. Nothing has more interest, perhaps, than the new conception of the Sovereign which then arose. It combines in itself elements varied both in origin and fortune. Furthermore, a regrouping of the classes of society, which seems long foreshadowed, but which from that time is hastened, is accompanied by a reform of manners and morals, for which both the propaganda of certain teachers of morals and the action of the government have a share of responsibility.

CHAPTER I

THE EMPEROR

THE first Emperor, Ch'in Shih Huang-ti, belonged to a great seigniorial house, that of Ch'in. On the other hand, Kao-chu, who established again for the benefit of the Han the imperial unity, which was in danger after the death of its founder, was a man of the people.—In the overlordship of Ch'in, with the regulations (359 B.C.) attributed to Wei-yang, the legal adviser of Duke Hiao, a new conception of the Prince and his rights had appeared. Ch'in Shih Huang-ti, like Duke Hiao and some potentates of the same period, was regarded as a tyrant. He is reproached with having governed by the help of punishments, that is to say by the abuse of prosecutions for treason. In fact, at the base of the new order which he wished to establish, was the idea of the Majesty peculiar to the imperial person.—The Han presented themselves as the restorers of an ancient order. They claimed to put an end to the age of tyranny. A new dynasty, rediscovering the old sources of privilege, they wished people to see in them the continuers of the three royal dynasties, and the true successors of the Chou. They founded their power on the Prestige peculiar to the Sons of Heaven. But if they pretend to preserve for the Chief of State the outward signs which mark a simple suzerain, they bear the imperial title which Shih Huang-ti created. Like him, they sustain, with the help of more or less new practices, the majesty of the Emperor. Anxious, however, to appear as restorers and not as innovators, they endeavour to incorporate into the notion of the Son of Heaven the constituent elements of the idea of majesty. They mean to profit by a double heritage, and do not despise the principles of authority designed in the age of tyranny. Helped by the learned effort of the mandarins, who, in their reign and for their benefit, reconstructed the antiquities of China, they succeed in getting acceptance of the new idea of the imperial majesty, by presenting it as an ancient attribute of the Sons of Heaven, the wise authors of the national civilization.

I

The Suzerain, Son of Heaven

The most learned Chinese recognize in the *Chou-li* (Ritual of the Chou)—and in some productions of the same type—the achievements of Utopian administrators, working in the service of the Han.[1] Leaving to scholars, sure of their criticism, the care of reconstructing, even in detail, the Constitution of the Chou (and even that of the Yin), I shall try only to disentangle the idea which, under the Han, could be conceived of a Son of Heaven. If, by chance, the Chou kings (at an undefined epoch) were sovereigns such as the Han represented them to be, it is early enough to speak of it here. These kings, in fact, from the epoch at which Chinese history opens (the period *Ch'un Ch'iu*), played no political part. They are envisaged at times under the aspect of great masters of a sort of national religion. To assign to them this chief function at the outset, is simply to let oneself be circumvented by the pious forgers who reconstructed the dynastic history of antiquity. A critical analysis can, at the most, disentangle some antecedents of the traditional notion of Son of Heaven, as it became fixed under the Han.

The dated chronicles do not, at any moment, show us a Chou king exercising a religious authority peculiar to him. The king like all the nobles, possesses Ancestors and gods of the Soil. Like them, he honours, as the founder of his race, a Hero who won fame by setting the World in order. The ancestor of the Chou bears the title of *Hou-tsi* (Prince Millet), Lord of the Harvests. His descendants, bearing the same title, continue his work. Each year they refertilize the ground by a first tillage ; each year they preside at the harvest feast. The chiefs of the smallest overlordships have the same duties.—The chronicles, on the other hand, make apparent certain traits of a moral authority which seems

---

[1] See in BEFEO, 1924, p. 496, the formula of Hu Shih : " The dynasty of the Han is an epoch in which apocryphal books were fabricated, in which it was sought to reform institutions by invoking antiquity."

peculiar to the suzerain. The Son of Heaven appears as the war-lord of the Chinese Confederation. He commands (in principle) the expeditions which alone are true wars, being directed against the Barbarians. To be exact, every noble is a hunter of Barbarians, but each one operates only in the bounds of his overlordship. The Son of Heaven alone conducts the war or presides over it when the Chinese Confederation is opposed to a Barbarian confederation. Prior to the dated chronicles, three Chou kings perhaps played a historical rôle. Now lyric or epic tradition presents these Sons of Heaven, the Chao kings, Mu and Süan, as leaders of great expeditions against the Barbarians of the remote frontiers.[1] In the epoch *Ch'un Ch'iu* it is only nobles who command these levies of the Confederation. Ritual tradition has it that they always acted on behalf of the king. When they were victors, the suzerain triumphed.[2] The most famous of these chiefs invested with the *imperium* for the conduct of war against the Barbarians is Huan of Ch'i, the first of the Leaders. To him is attributed the glory of having broken a violent onset of the Ti. We shall notice that the term, which, after the Leaders, was used to designate the Tyrants, is identical with the title which, it is said, was conferred by the investiture granting military *imperium*.[3] War-lord of the Confederation, the king is withdrawn from the feudal vendettas. So his town is a headquarters of peace. A noble setting out to meet a rival in battle, may not pass in arms in sight of the ramparts of the Capital. It is not enough for the warriors to remove their helmets and descend from their chariots ; their arms, hidden in their sheaths, must also remain invisible.[4] The suzerain, in fact, presides over Chinese peace. He seems to act as judge of appeal in the feudal lawsuits.[5] In theory, at least, he presides over the treaties (*meng*) which close the vendettas ; the effective president, a simple noble, is supposed to replace him by virtue of Leadership : that is to say, to preside, he must possess a delegation of the *imperium* of the sovereign.[6]

It is in his function as war-leader that the suzerain seems to hold a special religious qualification. This qualification

---

[1] *She-king*, **L**, 281, 284, 555. Mu t'ien ssu chuan. SMC, I, 251, 277.
[2] **LV**, 109 ff. ; *Chou li*, **VII**, vol. II, 182.
[3] SMC, IV, 56 ff.
[4] *Tso chuan*, **C**, I, 427.
[5] *Tso chuan*, **C**, I, 409
[6] SMC, IV, 303, 305.

which (in consequence of magnifying due to the work of historical reconstruction) appeared to be the source of a prestige of a superior order, passed as the attribute peculiar to the Son of Heaven. He, whether he is celebrating a triumph, or presiding over feudal peace celebrations, is master of a sacrifice of exceptional splendour. The Ancestors and the Soil are associated in the triumph, but Heaven is so also, and more than any other divinity (agrarian or ancestral), for Heaven is the God of oaths. He is the god of treaties, the god of interfeudal gatherings ; he is the only divinity who is common to all and national. He is also the only god to whom human characteristics are attributed. It is to be presumed that he owes this anthropomorphic nature to the sacrifices which, as a justiciary god, nourish him with human flesh.[1] We have seen that, according to tradition, the first penal laws were promulgated in the course of those hunting expeditions, which are not distinguishable from levies against the Barbarians.[2] Thus also, the most significant cases of human sacrifice, the memory of which has been preserved for us, are connected with military parades made on the confines of the Barbarian lands.[3] Further, the legends relating to the first forms of the worship of Heaven reveal to us the mythical sovereigns sacrificing, at the required season, on the mountains of the four cardinal points.[4] Now, it is just one of the poems which gives us the best information about the prestige of the suzerain,—showing him in his rôle of pacifier, drawing on himself the protection of the divinities of the great Rivers and the great Mountains (*Yo*, the principal mountains)—that explains also (and in characteristic fashion) the title of *Son of Heaven*. " At the required time, I go into the principalities !—the August Heaven, behold how he treats me as *son*." Tradition declares that the poem relates to the parades of the four great seasonal hunts, thanks to which, " by circulating throughout the Empire," the King " both cultivates and spreads his Virtue." [5] The dated chronicles do not show any Chou king circulating throughout the Empire and sacrificing in the High Places. They relate, on the other hand, how the first of the Leaders, Huan of Ch'i (Shan-tung), after having achieved victories on behalf of

---

[1] **LV,** 111 ff.   [2] See p. 219 ff.   [3] **LV,** 149, 345 ff.
[4] **LV,** 338.   [5] *She-king*, **C,** 424.

the Son of Heaven, wished to celebrate, for his own benefit, a sacrifice on *T'ai Shan* (Shantung), the cardinal mountain of the East.[1] Further the nobles of Ch'in (who gradually established a number of sacred High Places, where they sacrificed to regional hypostases of Heaven) attributed the title of Leader to one of their ancestors, Duke Mu. He claimed to sacrifice to Heaven a conquered prisoner, whom he placed first, for the period of preliminary purifications, in the tower *Ling*, the tower of happy Influences.[2] In the royal capital (and there only after certain ritual) there was supposed to be a tower *Ling*, which was never spoken of without connecting it with a temple named *Ming t'ang*. While the tower *Ling* is named on the occasion of triumphs and of offerings of captives, it is also the place where manifestations of the heavenly Will take place. Correspondingly, *Ming t'ang* (where tradition says that the Chou celebrated the defeat of the Yin by a triumphal sacrifice) is both the place where the interfeudal gatherings are held, at which the Son of Heaven presides, and the place where it is customary to promulgate the monthly ordinances (*yue ling*) which apply to the whole kingdom.[3] These ordinances have as their aim to make the occupations of men agree with the happenings of nature, controlled by Heaven. Heaven orders the seasons, the *Ming t'ang* is a House of the Calendar. The king acts as Son of Heaven when he promulgates the monthly ordinances. To do that he has to go round the House of the Calendar which is square (like the Earth) and oriented to the points of the compass, but which must be covered by a roof of thatch, circular (like Heaven). The circulation of the Son of Heaven about the *Ming t'ang* is assimilated by tradition to the circulation of the mythical sovereigns of the Empire. Both ought to be carried out in such a way that the king, placed at the east, promulgates the times and ordinances of spring ; at the south, the times and ordinances of summer, etc. Thus, there is established (by virtue of the Chinese belief, which postulates an exact coincidence of Spaces and Times) the twin order of the Orients and the Seasons.[4] The Son of Heaven extends to the entire Empire his regulating Virtue, because in the House of the Calendar

---

[1] SMC, IV, 56 ; **LV,** 101 ff.　　　[2] SMC, II, 33 ; **LV,** 147.
[3] **LV,** 116 ff.　　　[4] **LV,** 116, note 2, and **LIV,** 52 ff.

he rules, in the name of Heaven, the course of Time,—after
having, in the seasonal parades of the hunts, presided over
the sacrifices which the whole of the confederated nobles
offered to the divinity guaranteeing good order and rational
peace.

Sole master of the Calendar, and by virtue of this, prime
mover of the whole Chinese territory, such appears, in the
tradition of the Han, the Son of Heaven. It is far from
certain that this was his rôle from remote antiquity. In the
epoch *Ch'un Ch'iu*, in any case, the different overlordships
did not use one single calendar system. If the dates in the
chronicles are indicated for us according to the royal calendar,
it is thanks to the pious intervention of the historians of the
imperial era. They have, in this way, taken a good deal
of the value from the data of the ancient chronology.[1] On
the other hand, they furnish us with testimony as to the
extreme but late importance, among the functions of the
Son of Heaven, of the idea that he is alone to rule the whole
of China and dictate the Time for all. No document allows
of the deduction that the suzerain lived, under the thatched
roof of Ming t'ang, subjected, alone among the nobles, to
particular observances. He had apparently, as had every
chief, to submit himself at regulated times to a life of exposure
in the bush, or of confinement in an obscure retreat. Thus
he achieved intimate association of his person with the life
of nature. But the expiations which he took upon himself,
and whence he drew an animating virtue, do not differ in
any respect from those which the overlord of the humblest
chieftainship imposed on himself. It is significant that the
devotions of Yü and of T'ang, founders of the first two royal
dynasties of Chinese tradition, are of identical nature with
the devotion of the plain nobles of the historical period.[2]
The suzerain, however, has sole right to the qualification of
Unique Man. He alone is related to Heaven, in taking upon
himself the hardest and most glorious task of expiation, that
exacted by a victory won by the united forces of the Confederation. He leads the triumphal dance of the sacrifice
to Heaven and communicates first with a divinity venerated
by all the federated nobles. Related intimately to this
divinity, he can call himself its son, in the proper meaning

<hr>

[1] SMC, V, 472 ff.   [2] See pp. 191 and 252.

of the term. Historical tradition places at the beginning
of a dynasty of the Sons of Heaven, a Hero born by celestial
operation.[1] Although, amongst the ancestors of seigniorial
houses, only one may be expressly qualified as Mediator, it
appears that all the feudal chiefs had a mission to preside at
the spring feasts of fertility. According to the authors of
rituals, however, only the wives of the family of the suzerain
had the right to fête in spring the supreme Mediator, that
unique husband of the Great Ancestors who, by the grace
of Heaven, gave birth to the different founders of the royal
dynasties.[2] The mythical or ritual theme of the union of
the Queen-Mothers with a heavenly divinity inspires some
beautiful dynastic hymns. They no doubt aided much in
adorning the house of the suzerain with outstanding nobility.
This subject recalls in exact fashion the power of the mothers,
and the dualism which is at the base of the power of the
chief, the father and mother of the people. The queen has
as her emblem the Moon, in which scholars seek to recognize
only a mirror, but which is, *par excellence*, the reservoir of
all terrestrial fertility. The *Chou-li* itself admits that the
queen alone is capable of preserving life in the seeds. As
compared with the king, who possesses the emblem of the
Sun, and who is Son of Heaven, the Queen retains a part
of the respect which she deserved in the time when the sum
of the energies peculiar to the Earth-Mother was assigned
to her.

The Han Emperors represented themselves to the Chinese
as perfect Sons of Heaven. They lent credit to the idea
that Kao-Chu, their founder, had been conceived in a
miraculous way by his mother.[3] In the course of the year
113 B.C., during which the Emperor Wu thought to inaugurate
a new era, he made (in yellow garments) a sacrifice to the
Sovereign Earth, in its character of " opulent mother," by
way of marking the express intention that this sacrifice was
the pendant of the sacrifice to the sovereign Heaven.[4] The
Emperor Ch'êng (31 B.C.) had erected in the northern outskirts of the capital, the altar of the Earth, first erected at
Fen-yin (Shan-si) ; sacrifices were made to heaven in the
south suburbs. From an undetermined epoch, but certainly

[1] See p. 14.   [2] *Li ki*, C, I, 341 ; LII, 164 ff.
[3] SMC, II, 325.   [4] SMC, III, 474, 475, 614.

before the seventh century of our era, the Earth was represented by the statue of a woman.[1] There is a possibility that this anthropomorphic conception of the Chinese divinity of the soil is ancient, just as the anthropomorphic conception of Heaven is certainly ancient. In the old texts of prayers or oaths, the Sovereign Earth is already opposed to the August Heaven.[2] These texts belong to works revised under the Han. They prove, at least, that the Han accepted the principle of a religious dualism. It is difficult to believe (as the Chinese savants and, following them, the Western scholars would have it), that they invented it in its entirety. The Emperor Wu, presented as the Creator of the worship of the Sovereign Earth, is one of the Chinese monarchs who felt most the dangers with which political dualism, depending on religious dualism, threatened the State, by giving too much prestige to the Empresses and too much authority to the dowagers.[3] It is reasonable to admit that, if he made an innovation in sacrificing to the Earth, the innovation consisted in the fact that the Emperor presided, in person and publicly, at a sacrifice at which the Empress (perhaps in the privacy of the women's apartments), ought to have officiated. The tactics of the ambitious Empresses, such as the Empress Wu Tso-T'ien of the T'ang (684–704 A.D.) was to claim first the privilege of presiding at the sacrifices to the Earth before claiming the right to sacrifice to Heaven.[4] The most likely interpretation of the sacrifice to the Earth inaugurated by the Emperor Wu is that it was made with the intention of benefiting the Son of Heaven alone, by the religious prestige which belonged without doubt to the queens as officiators in a feminine worship of the Earth, the importance of which the rituals have veiled.

This interpretation accords perfectly with that which can be given to the sacrifices *fong* and *shan*, inaugurated by the same emperor Wu. The history of these sacrifices appears to be much more complex than is ordinarily supposed. For these again, it is impossible to believe in a complete innovation. The traditional data made use of by the Han to confer on this ceremony the value of a supreme religious act, clearly reveal that they refer to ancient rites in connexion with triumphal feasts. In the mythical antecedents of the sacrifice

---

[1] **XVI**, 524.　　[2] **XVI**, 521.　　[3] See p. 126.　　[4] **XVI**, 184, 185.

PLATE IX

TOMB OF HO K' U-P'ING
(Photo by the Lartigue Expedition)

[face p. 384

fong, it is a case at one and the same time, of celebrating a taking possession, and of expiating the consequences of a victory. Now the sacrifice *fong* of the Emperor Wu was performed on *T'ai shan*, the cardinal mountain of the East, at the very time when that sovereign wanted to ensure the Empire of the Han over all the eastern provinces of China. The first Emperor, who was also the first conqueror of Eastern China, had made the ascent of *T'ai shan* (219 B.C.) but the Han historians take care to tell us (and their stories show some embarrassment) that Shih Huang-ti did not achieve the sacrifice.[1] The penalty of a sacrifice that fails falls on the head of the presumptuous officiator ; the premature death (210 B.C.) of the first Emperor took place in the course of a new inspection of the eastern territories. The Emperor Wu succeeded, after much hesitation, in performing the sacrifice *fong* on *T'ai shan* (110 B.C.) but, a little before (in 119 B.C.) his favourite general, Ho K'ü-p'ing, after having captured eighty Barbarian chiefs, had, in order to take possession of their country with triumph, celebrated on the Lang-kü-sü and Hu-yen mountains, the sacrifices *fong* and *shan*.[2] Ho K'ü-p'ing was the nephew of the Empress Wei, whose brother was Commander-in-chief of the Chinese forces, and who was the mother of the heir-designate of the Emperor Wu. It turns out that precisely the one person allowed to accompany the Emperor Wu in the ascent of the *T'ai shan*, in 110 B.C., was the son of Ho K'ü-p'ing. He (whom his sovereign made mount his own chariot, and whom he loved as much as he had loved his father) died mysteriously from the consequences of the sacrifice ; the expressions used by the historians show clearly that he was the victim of it.[3] These facts are so much the more significant because (in spite of the disgrace which later on befell the Empress Wei and her son) the principal regent designated by the Emperor Wu to protect his new heir was Ho Kuang, brother of Ho K'ü-p'ing. Now, the grand-daughter of Ho Kuang, married to the Emperor Chao, possessed from the death of this successor of the Emperor Wu (74 B.C.) all the authority of a dowager. She exercised it to the advantage of the Ho family, one of whose members had assured the triumph of

---

[1] SMC, III, 431, and II, 219. [2] SMC, Introd., CXVIII. *Ch'ien Han Shu*, 55.
[3] SMC, III, 504 ; *Ch'ien Han Shu*, 55.

2 B

the Han over the Barbarians while the other had expiated the victory.

If delving into the underlying political significance of the sacrifice *fong* reveals the persistence of dualism in the organization of the State and of the family, dualism is again to be found in the religious aspect of the ceremony. A double ceremony is involved in which the sacrifice to Heaven (*fong*) performed on the summit of a peak by the Emperor in person (but accompanied by a second), is preceded by the sacrifice *shan*. The word *shan* is, according to Chinese tradition, equivalent to the word *jang* (= to *drive out* and hand over) the ancient significance of which has already been explained. This last term designates the act by which a sovereign, before assuming power to himself alone, begins by *handing it over* to a dynastic herald—taken, it appears, from his wife's group and sometimes *guardian* to the son and heir, but sometimes also, *sacrificed*.[1] The sacrifice *shan*, a preliminary condition to the sacrifice *fong*, is a sacrifice to the Earth. It is performed on a low hillock, in the midst of a lake surrounding a small mound. We know that for the ceremonies performed at Fen-yin in honour of the Sovereign Earth, the place chosen had the form of a human rump. The hillock in the form of a rump (*shuei*) is designated *jang*, a word (which the written form as well as the pronunciation relates to *jang, to sacrifice, to hand over*, but) which conjures up one of the inaugural games of the year as well as a well-worked earth.[2] On the other hand, the word *fong* conveys the double idea of a cairn of broken pebbles and of a high stone set up as a sign of victory.[3] In celebrating his great sacrifice, the Emperor Wu made a prayer destined to assure him immortality or at least to exalt in his person the Majesty befitting an Emperor ; but, besides this, the symbolism of the ceremonies *fong* and *shan* is clear enough to show that, appropriating to himself the benefit of these connected rites, the Emperor sought also to complete, by annexing the virtues gained by officiating in honour of the Earth, the prestige peculiar to the Son of Heaven. Here again, the Empress Wu Tso-t'ien of the T'ang understood very exactly the religious tradition, when she made use of it by reversing the rôle, to the great scandal of the learned men, and arranged

[1] See p. 208 ff.   [2] SMC, III, 475, 476 (note 3).   [3] *Ch'ien Han Shu*, 55.

to preside alone at the double ceremony (695 B.C.) taking the place of the Emperor. She had first succeeded (666 B.C.) in getting control of the ceremony of the single sacrifice *shan*, which she performed, putting herself at the head of the whole harem, whilst her husband restricted himself to accomplishing the rite *fong*.[1]

We have seen further back that the whole history of the celebration of the sacrifice *fong* by the Emperor Wu of the Han is connected with that of the preparation of a calendar which fitted in with the new dynasty. It is in 113 B.C. (the year of the sacrifice to the Sovereign Earth) that the Emperor actually took, in the name of the Han, possession of the Empire as Son of Heaven. In that year, indeed, he gave a fief to a descendant of the Chou, so that, in the interior of this territory, the religious traditions of the dynasty henceforth fallen might be continued. (If the same was not done in favour of dynasties which had perished even further back, it is because nothing remained of them).[2] This year again, " the Son of Heaven, for the first time, made the inspection " of the Empire, beginning with the East and the T'ai-shan : a census of the holy places seems to have accompanied this inspection, both equivalent to an actual taking possession. At the end of this same year, the winter solstice falling on the morning of the first day, it was intended to institute the new era and to make the course of time begin again.[3] But the sacrifice *fong* had to be put off to 110 B.C., because of the war undertaken against the Nan-yue (South-East). It took place after a new tour of inspection and, when the ceremony was ended, the Emperor went to hold an assembly in a *Ming t'ang* (House of the Calendar) or rather on the supposed site of an ancient *Ming t'ang*. But a House of the Calendar was built and inaugurated in 106 B.C. on the occasion of the second *fong* ceremony celebrated by the Emperor Wu.[4] On the day *kia tsih* (the first day of the sixty years' cycle) which coincided with the first day of the eleventh month, and on which fell the winter solstice, the Emperor sacrificed in the *Ming t'ang* and the formula was pronounced : " The period has revolved ! It begins again ! " Thus, " those who calculated the calendar made of this date (25th Nov. 105 B.C.)

[1] **XVI**, 184, 200, 207.   [2] SMC, III, 477.
[3] SMC, III, 486–491.   [4] SMC, III, 502, 510.

the first starting-point." [1]   As a matter of fact, it was only in the fifth month (the summer solstice) of the year 104 B.C. that the calendar was changed. From that time the colour yellow and the number five were raised to honour, as dynastic emblems. This reform of the calendar involved a total recasting of the system of measures, and particularly of the musical pipes which determined the scale. "The divisions of the year were (from that time) correct ; the note *yu* was again pure, . . . *the principles* Yin *and* Yang *were separated and united in a regular fashion.*" [2]   It is highly probable that all the work of monetary reform, which was the great business of the reign, may have been in connexion with this dynastic recasting of the measures. In any case, it is in 110 B.C., the year of the first *fong* sacrifice, that the system of regulation of prices advocated by San Hong-yang was put in force. It was designed, in the mind of its author, to assure the economic equilibrium of the Empire of the Han.[3] All these facts lead us to think that the authority of the Son of Heaven is derived from a religious qualification, obtained by the consecration of the victory of the dynasty. It is significant that this was celebrated in the East and after a fortunate war against the Barbarians of the East. The prestige of the Son of Heaven has as principle a triumph which conditions and realizes the unity of China, conceived as a unity of civilization.

"Under the Heaven," that is to say in the Chinese world, the Son of Heaven, alone benefiting from the triumphal expiation which makes victory consecrated by Heaven,— takes rank as the Unique Man. To benefit by all and expiate for all, such was already the function fulfilled, for a limited territory, by every noble. It is clear that a prestige which was nourished by expiations performed on behalf of others corresponds to a power held by delegation and not to an autonomous and properly sovereign authority. This power, besides, by virtue of its very nature, brings with it, for the suzerain as for the feudatory, a life regulated by etiquette and tradition. The Chief, from that time, can only act by delegating his authority and distributing a part of his prestige. He only reigns on condition of not governing. It is, especially, very dangerous for him to act in a military capacity, for, in

[1] SMC, III, 515.   [2] SMC, III, 331.   [3] SMC, III, 596.

this case, he must invest his general with an entire *imperium* the use of which it is not always easy to limit solely to the Barbarian marches. Tradition claimed that the Chou kings had seen their authority eclipsed by that of their leaders. The Emperors had to beware lest the power of their generals-in-chief came in any degree to rival theirs. The history of the Han dynasty in fact shows the power of the Marshals continually increasing. The Marshal is most often the (father or the) brother of the Empress. She serves as a hostage to the Emperor, her husband, but when he is dead she becomes dowager, and the Marshal, guardian of the sovereign if a minor and of the dynasty, then assumes all the powers of a Mayor of the Palace. The dynasty only maintains itself by sacrificing periodically the great military chiefs to whom the Emperor has to pass on the *imperium*. But, against them, it can depend on supporters of its own. The Han Emperor, like a simple suzerain, had to distribute fiefs and consider his own relations as protectors, as " barrier vassals." The Empire is the prey of a family group and it is only by artifice and trickery that it is possible to introduce into it a State administration. The Emperor, who affects to be a simple Son of Heaven and proclaims that " the principle of all faults has its origin in himself," is reduced to inactivity. Such was the case with the Emperor Wen of the first Han (180–157 B.C.) who owes to his ritual modesty the glory which the learned men have heaped upon him. But in his reign, feudalism was re-established and the Barbarians became threatening. His successor nearly lost his power. It was then that the great man of the dynasty, the Emperor Wu, returning in part to the tradition of Ch'in Shih Huang-ti, undertook to add to the prestige of the Son of Heaven all the principles of force on which, at the end of the age of tyrants, the first Emperor had nourished his majesty.

II

The Autocratic Sovereign

Towards the end of the feudal period (the *Combatant Kingdoms*) there were formed powerful overlordships animated by a new spirit. Their chiefs are warriors, indifferent to the glory to be won by care for matters of etiquette and by moderation, but greedy of conquests, of effective power, of real riches. They draw their treasures from the mines and the salt-pans, the marshes and the woods, from borderlands which they take from the Barbarians and from uncultivated lands which they know how to keep in order. They encourage traders and make wealth circulate. They have granaries and treasuries. They accumulate provisions for armies, metals and precious stones which serve to form alliances. It is the epoch of competitive sumptuousness, of measureless ambitions and annexations. We have already seen that there is then formulated the notion of a power of a superior order, which belongs to the Prince as head of the State. But, as against the lawyers whom they revile, the learned men who write the history, consider all the growth of the State as so much usurpation. The great potentates, stigmatized for their folly of pride, are painted with the features that tradition begins to lend to the ancient kings of perdition. In the sumptuous capitals of the Kingdoms, the vassals belonging to the country are lost amid the crowd of adventurers from afar, sorcerers, doctors, astrologers, philosophers, hired ruffians, dialecticians, actors, jurists, each one bearing a recipe for power and becoming the favourite of a day.

The life of the Court resembles a perpetual quarrel in which professional groups and bands of supporters oppose one another fiercely. The noble takes on the air of a tyrant. More than ever, he is a creator of a hierarchy, but of a hierarchy changing to such a degree that nothing seems acquired in it by hereditary title and the authority of the Chief himself seems attached to his person more than to his race. The prestige he seeks appears no longer to result from the observance of customary interdicts or the regular acquisition of the traditional sacraments. To these magnificent princes, the endowments of magic seem better suited than those of religion. They despise the poor knowledge bequeathed by their ancestors and preserved by those masters of ceremony, the hereditary vassals. They place their trust in upstarts, full of new learning, who promise them limitless success. They confide their fortune, now to one, now to another of these experts in the knowledge of magic. They make them second to themselves in power, offering them the half of their fortune, then turning on them the calamity of a set-back, or the danger which lies at the heart of a too great success. As long as the favourites are fortunate, and not too much so, they are allowed to work for the glory of their master. Their banishment or their death will compensate for reverses and purify successes. The splendour of their ascent and of their fall combine to give to the glory of the potentate a new brilliance and to reclothe his person with majesty.

If it appears true that the last period of feudal times was marked by furious competitions wherein, struggling by means of piled-up wealth and new magic, some princes gained the rank of potentates and the name of tyrants, the facts show also that at the beginning of the feudal age the prestige necessary for the chief was acquired in contests, in which were employed knowledge and worth which were not solely of a traditional nature, although they were all of a mystical order. The principles of majesty sought after by the tyrants and, after them, by the Emperors, are not, whatever Chinese tradition may say, novelties imagined in an era of decadence and anarchy. In fact, to create as to destroy the feudal order, efforts of the same nature were necessary. The sources of majesty are closely related to the sources of prestige. Neither were they more slow to be discovered. For orthodox criticism, the prestige of the Son of Heaven rises out of the observance of Confucian etiquette, identified with the wisdom of the happy times when civilization was inaugurated. The glory sought by the potentates is derived, on the contrary, from illusory ambitions born of the decadent speculations of the Taoists. These declarations are not bare of truth, but only on condition of eliminating from them all that constitutes a judgment of values and all that prejudices them from the historic standpoint. The practices and the theories from which the sovereigns drew the elements which go to make up the imperial majesty, are not recent superstitions, and it was only after the establishment of an orthodox School that they could pass as specifically Taoist. Shih Huang-ti is held to be an enemy of the learned men, but it is impossible to extend the same judgment to the Emperor Wu, who was in all things eclectic and a patron of religious syncretism. Kao-Chu in any case, a national and popular hero, did not in any way seek to be a Son of Heaven according to the orthodox definition. If this fortunate adventurer succeeded in making a figure as Emperor, it is because he knew how to use a mystic current, which was both large and profound. A suggestive indication of this is furnished by the fact that he was marked on the left thigh with 72 black spots ; 72 is the characteristic number of the brotherhoods.[1] A more remarkable fact still, history elicits from Kao-Chu that he owed the greater part of his success to his intimate counsellor Chang Leang [2] (who was afterwards to be considered one of the first patrons of the Taoist sects).[3] After having directed the policy of Kao-Chu and that of the Empress Lu, by depending at need on the authority of the. divine ancients,[4] Chang Leang was clever enough to escape from the disgrace which was the lot of too fortunate favourites. He went in time into retirement, and he employed himself in training in the art of *the long life*. Ssu-ma Ch'ien states that he belonged to the ascetic school of the Immortal Ch'e-song-ssu.[5] Chang Leang knew, according to the saying of Kao-Chu, '' how to make plans in the fastness of a tent and to gain the victory from a distance of a thousand *li*." [6] Such is, in fact, the principle and sign of majesty and of omnipotence. The Emperor came to be an autocratic sovereign, when (in the manner of an ascetic) he lived in a glorious retreat— exalting the power of life which is in him in such a way as to acquire the immortality, which is proper to spirits and the sign of unlimited power—and exercising this power, without ever delegating it, by a simple effect of influence, which directs as a whole the acts of all men and the entire universe.

Shih Huang-ti had first adopted, to designate himself, a term (*chen*), meaning, say the glosses, that he acted without being seen and without making his voice heard.[7] Later, on the advice of the master, Lu, a magician whom he employed to make spirits come to him, he decided to live in a place unknown to all his subjects, in order that nothing impure might soil him.[8] He moved about in a palace which,—a more adequate representation of the world than the Ming T'ang itself,—contained, undoubtedly, as many rooms as the year

[1] SMC, II, 325.　　　　　　　　　[2] SMC, II, 383, 378.
[3] **LXXX** and **CXLV**, 917 and 1658.　[4] SMC, 55, and *Ch'ien Han Shu*, 40.
[5] SMC, 55.　　　　　　　　　　　[6] SMC, II, 383.
[7] SMC, II, 127, 206.　　　　　　　[8] SMC, 164,

has days. Those who divulged his retreat were punished with death ; as were those suspected of having divulged his words. Within a radius of 200 *li* round his palace, all the roadways were bordered by walls and covered in. The sovereign, no longer putting matters forward for discussion, made decisions all alone in his walled palace. Thenceforth, having done what was necessary to enter into direct communication with those " *True Men*," the spirits, he designated himself no longer by the word *chen*, but by the expression " *the True Man*." [1] In the same way, Êrh-shih Huang-ti his son, to avoid hearing " evil discourse " and not to " show his imperfections," resolved to stay confined in his private apartments. He never came out.[2] His father did not hesitate to go on inspections, but incognito, when he went round his capital in the night,[3] or in a closed carriage, when he went about the Empire—an incognito so well preserved, that he might die without anyone in his train knowing.[4]

Protected by his sealed retreat from the contagions which might soil him, and from all fear of the dispersal of his energy, the autocratic sovereign is, so to speak, a microcosm, for the Universe envelops, in its great bosom, a series of Universes, one within the other. These are the more concentrated the more close they are to the universal controller. His palace is a microcosm, in which the art of the architects, by representing on a magnificent scale the Milky Way and the triumphal bridge which crosses it, has put within reach of the Master of the World the celestial energy with which he ought to be impregnated.[5] The imperial chariot, the imperial dress, are themselves also made of the essence of the world. The square body of the chariot is the earth itself, its circular throne is equivalent to Heaven, the most important constellations are represented in the emblems of the flags, and thanks to the choice of insignia (sun, moon, constellation, lightning, etc.) which figure on his clothes, the Unique Man finds himself in direct contact with the most efficacious of beneficent forces.

The Emperor Wu did not submit to confinement with the determination of the Ch'in sovereigns, but spent liberally to make his palace a splendid concentration of the Universe.[6]

---

[1] SMC, II, 178–180.   [2] SMC, II, 207.   [3] SMC, II, 163.   [4] SMC, II, 192.
[5] SMC, II, 175, 243.   [6] Pan Ku, *Fu des deux capitales*, Part I.

All the beasts of the air, of the water, of the earth, thronged in his fish-ponds and his parks. No species was wanting in his botanic garden; the waves of his lakes could be seen breaking against the distant lands in which could be recognized the mysterious Isles of the Immortals; perched on high columns above the dust of the world, bronze genii gathered for him the purest dew. He could, by means of a twofold spiral path, mount to the summit of a tower, whence his gaze lost itself in the immensity beyond Heaven, and he dominated the entire Universe. By the prestige of his arms he had gained the privilege of owning the scarlet-foamed Celestial Horse; [1] six red geese, drawn by his power of attraction, had come in a flock.[2] Everything awaited the arrival of the Dragon, who would bear away the Emperor beyond K'un-lun, into Heaven.[3] That the lost sacred tripods of the Sons of Heaven could not be withdrawn from the river, where they had become invisible, mattered little; already, manifesting the glory of the Emperor Wu, a magic tripod had come for him out of the depths of the earth, whilst above, in the sky, a yellow cloud formed a throne.[4] Like Huang-ti, the Yellow Sovereign, who after having " found the stalks of magic millfoil which went with the precious tripod " saw a dragon with a long beard come to him, on which, with his wives and his faithful followers (70 in number), he was snatched away to the heavens,—the Emperor was ready for apotheosis, and even thought of it with the calmness becoming to an autocrat. " Ah! if I can become like Huang-ti, to leave my wives and children will be, in my eyes, easier than to leave my slippers." [5]

No renunciation is too much for one who desires pure power. The Emperor exhausted his treasures so that the magician Shao-wong, whom he treated not as subject but as guest, could construct chariots in which were incorporated the victorious emanations, which dispel evil spirits, and terraces where he could live in the midst of all the divine powers, figured in paintings as well as on Earth and in Heaven.[6] He abstained from eating and drinking; he lived in a state of purity, so that he might present himself, as a guest, in the palace of Longevity. Thither the sorceress of the Princess

---

[1] SMC, III, 620.
[4] SMC, III, 483, 482.
[2] SMC, III, 628.
[5] SMC, III, 489.
[3] SMC, II, 621.
[6] SMC, III, 470.

of Spirits attracted the gods, whose arrival aroused a terrifying
wind and whose words were recorded to form the collection
of " Written Laws." [1] To the Mage Luan-ta, who was a
eunuch, he married his eldest daughter, providing her with
a dowry of 10,000 gold pounds. He had a seal of jade, brought
him by a messenger clothed in feathers which the Mage,
himself clothed in feathers, received, in the posture of a
master, standing on a litter of purifying herbs. This seal
bore the title " Master of the heavenly Way," for the Emperor
hoped that the eunuch would introduce him to the Gods
of Heaven.[2] Shih Huang-ti had sent hundreds of pairs of
virgin girls and boys into the Eastern Sea as tribute to the
Immortals. In the same way, the Emperor Wu, who also
strove to attain to the Happy Isles and the Sacred Mountains,[3]
" gazing on them from afar," made young couples dance on
the summit of a high terrace " communicating with Heaven,"
with the object of attracting the gods, while torches reared
in the air symbolized a rain of stars.[4] It is by these actions
that he was able to make brilliant comets appear, and great
stars like pumpkins.[5] His invokers, also, when he sacrificed
to T'ai yi (the supreme Unity), were able to proclaim : " The
star of Virtue sheds its brilliance afar ! . . . The star of
Long Life . . . lights us with its penetrating clearness." [6]
And while the first Emperor had never succeeded in obtaining
the branched agaric (the plant che) from which the marvellous
Drug is procured,[7] and although he himself had had it sought
for by 10,000 magicians,[8] so far in vain, yet in the very walls
of the palace of the Emperor Wu, and even in the hall where
he was performing his purifications—while in the nine-
storeyed tower communicating with Heaven, a divine brightness appeared—this agaric, the concentration of immortal
omnipotence, was produced spontaneously and in full
perfection, for it had exactly nine stalks.[9] But since happiness
must be paid for, as soon as the Emperor had progressed
in the way of Spirits, thanks to the art of his professors of
immortality, he sacrificed them, delivering successively to
death Shao-wong, whom he had formerly named Marshal

---

[1] SMC, III, 472 ff.   [2] SMC, III, 478 ff.   [3] SMC, III, 504.
[4] San fu huang t'u, 5, and SMC, III, 458.   [5] SMC, III, 505.
[6] SMC, III, 505–506.   [7] SMC, II, 180.
[8] SMC, III, 506.   [9] SMC, III, 508 ; **XII**, 418.

of Learned Perfection, and Luan-ta, his son-in-law, promoted formerly to be Marshal of the Five Privileges.[1]

The lot of the favourite Mage differs from that of the nearest vassal only in that his changes of fortune depend, not on ritual dates, but on the pleasure of the Master. Only, before he becomes the emissary on whom all the ill chances of fortune descend, a creator of immortality is able to bring down upon the imperial person other splendid favours, far greater than those which a chief can acquire by presiding at the head of his vassals over the traditional worship. As a result of the recipes of his Mage, the Emperor assumes the form of a spirit—that is to say he realizes in himself the greatest possibilities open to a living being. He becomes the great Man, the *ta jen*, he whose life, at every moment, is an apotheosis.[2] His substance, refined by training in the practices of the long life, is so etherealized that, using all the resources of levitation, he can move about, not only on the paths of men and the ways of the Holy Places, but in the actual world of the Spirits ; there he wanders (*yuan yu*) at length, calling to him the Count of the Wind, the Master of the Rain, the Lord of Thunder, the God of the River, all the beatified ascetics with whom he consorts at the very sources of life, in that River, the Milky Way, conversing with Si-wang-mu (the Ogress of Death and Patron of Immortality) and all the sinless Fairies (*yu-nü*), and knocking, when he pleases, at the door of the Sovereign of the Realm On-High. It would be indiscreet to ask if the Emperors, like the ascetics, tasted the intoxication of magic diversions apart from having them sung by the poets who composed the official odes, seeing them represented in the apotheoses of the opera, in which a whole crowd of jugglers and ballet-dancers took part. The essential thing is to note that, nourished by mystic dreams and magnified by art, the power assigned to the autocratic Emperor is identical with the powers which the ascetic aims at obtaining. Shih Huang-ti wished to equal the True Men who " enter water without becoming wet, fire without being burnt, and raise themselves on clouds and vapours." [3] Such is in general the initial programme, such are the first proofs of power which the Taoist ascetic, heir

---

[1] SMC, III, 471, and Introd., xcv.
[2] *Ta jen*, a poem by Ssu-ma Siang-ju in SMC, 117.   [3] SMC, II, 177.

PLATE X

DANCES AND JUGGLERY

(Bas-relief from Shan-tung. Rubbing by the Chavannes Expedition)

of an ancient Shamanism, proposes. The great aim is " to become eternal, like Heaven and Earth." [1] It is achieved when the ascetic feels that he has identified his will with the order of the Universe. The ascetic then is in possession of complete, unconditional power, which has no other principle than his own will, and would enable him, if he wished, to invert the order of the seasons according to his fancy.[2] But the Sovereign, as ascetic, is master of the Universe only while he remains master of himself. He must not be capricious, if he wishes to remain a pure power. He reigns, then, without arbitrary intervention ; he governs without administrative interference, by allowing events to happen—which is not to say that he does not command. He commands everything to the smallest detail, but without ever using his power for any particular act. In so far as his will accords with the universal order, the actions of all living beings, by the immediate effect of his irresistible ascendancy, are themselves in accord, like the caprices of a dream, with the smallest motions of his desire.

He does not secure obedience by the mediation of subordinates, or as a result of regulations. It suffices that he is a Great Man, a True Man ; the power within him, concentrated in the pure state, causes, as by a subtle current of induction, a unanimous convergence of desires and actions. The imperial will sustains the whole Empire, and the Empire and the world only exist to add to the glory of the autocrat.

III

THE CONSTITUTIONAL DOCTRINE

Being a Son of Heaven, the Emperor is vested with a Prestige which, when his power is exercised, carries with it an element of weakness. The traditional worship makes him appear a human delegate of Heaven, but, in all the ceremonies in which he is supposed to revive this Prestige, he is also supposed, by communicating with his faithful followers, to share it with them. A Suzerain placed at the

[1] SMC, II, 177.
[2] LIV, 143 ff. I limit myself to indicating here the results of an inquiry into the idea of Majesty, for which I hope to give justification in a forthcoming work (*Le Roi boit*).

head of a hierarchy, he can cause his authority to spread, but on the dangerous condition of delegating the very principle of his power, for all *imperium*, even when delegated, remains whole. There can henceforth be a hierarchy (more or less variable), but not an administration or a State. On the other hand, the Autocrat really appears as Sovereign, for, by magic and mystic power, he is identified with, or rather substituted for, the Celestial Sovereign, until the latter is nothing more than a projection into the ideal world of the real master of the Universe. The authority with which the Sovereign is thus endued, though not subject to the smallest diminution, becomes, on the other hand, non-transmissible, for it is wholly personal and at the same time all-embracing. Nothing ties the Emperor any longer either to his subjects or to his domain. All is dust before his Majesty, but if thenceforth no feudatory can possess an authority which can possibly equal his, any fortunate chief of a mystic sect can become his equal. Above the Empire is the Autocrat. There is no place for a State administration. There is no State.

In the age of the Tyrannies, the lawyers, using the notion of Majesty, but falsifying the mystic doctrine, attempted to establish a certain idea of the State. Among the attributes of the Suzerain, the leader in war and peace, was included a vague power of executing justice. Further, in the new lands acquired by conquest of the Barbarians and of Nature, lands which escaped the feudal customs and formed a private domain, the Tyrants, by imposing regulations as they chose, assumed the rôle of legislators. The jurists whom they employed, justifying the delight of conquest by the claims of civilization, worked out a theory of the Prince, conceived no longer as the preserver of customary laws, whose observance maintains peace, but as the free author of Laws which create civilization as a complete whole.[1] In the world in which the lawyers lived, and in which, together with the military spirit, there reigned the taste for novelties, princely authority seemed to express itself, above all, by the promulgation of a penal code, the idea of law being stringently opposed to that of custom, and allied to the belief that civilization is imposed by force. The code was considered to be the foundation of an administrative organization whose first object was to

---

[1] The chief of these theorizers is Han Fei-tsih (died 233 B.C.).

reform manners and customs by the aid of punishments. The lawyers, when, to fix tasks, they assigned penalties, thought they were repressing an attempt against that civilizing function which, as they believed, formed the Majesty of the Prince.

Such was also the spirit in which the first Emperor administered the Empire. He was regarded as a tyrant both because he wished " to oppress the people " by the aid of magic, and because he applied the principles of the lawyers, the first servants of the rights of the State. In the greater part of his inscriptions, Shih Huang-ti boasts of having reformed morals by the aid of the Laws ; " . . . exercising his authority with vigilance,—he made and decided upon clear laws ;— his subjects under him became more perfect and better (219 B.C.)." " He corrected and improved foreign customs . . . he removed error ; he fixed what must be done (219)." " The sage of Ch'in having taken the government in hand— was the first to determine punishments and names.—Each thing has the name suited to it.—His great government purified morals.—All conform to his rules and principles.— Men are pleased with a uniform rule ;—they are happy to preserve universal peace.—Posterity will receive his laws with respect (211 B.C.)." [1]

The Han, after the ruin of the Ch'in, made as much use of jurists, as did the latter, but took care to repudiate their theories. " When the Han were triumphant they suppressed the cruel government of the Ch'in. They kept a check on laws and ordinances. They spread abroad their beneficence and their compassion." [2] One of the first decrees of the Emperor Wen (179 B.C.) admits the usefulness of the laws but assigns to them a double object : they no doubt have as their aim to " repress the wicked," but they ought also " to encourage the good." A little later (178 B.C.), omitting mention of negative sanctions, the Emperor declares that Heaven establishes Princes " in the favour of the people " and " in order that they may nourish and govern them." [3] This inversion of governmental doctrine confirms the check on the theory of the lawyers and reveals the causes of this check. Confounding administrative practice with a straightforward inquiry into the circumstances of Majesty, they

---

[1] SMC, II, 185–188.   [2] SMC, II, 445.   [3] SMC, II, 461.

made the law rest on the arbitrary will of the despot. Now neither the prestige of the Son of Heaven, which assumes the observance of customary practices, nor the Majesty of the Autocrat, which excludes all possibility of caprice, could be fitted into a theory of " good pleasure." The Han, then, had to seek, outside an idea of the State identified with the all-powerful will of a despot, a justification for the intervention which the most limited of administrative techniques presupposes.

A syncretic theory (which was principally the work of scholars) got them out of the difficulty. It admitted as a fundamental principle that the action of Heaven and that of the Emperor on the people were exercised on parallel lines, and both in a beneficent way,—the first in maintaining the order of the world, the second in maintaining the order of society. In this conception the idea of Majesty proper to the Sovereign is not absent, but it is transposed ; it passes from the mystic to the moral plane. The reservoir of all the moral (and no longer the mystic) energies, the Emperor determines (always by means of an immediate effect, due to an irresistible ascendancy) a satisfactory conduct of the universe, whose good physical order is " one and indivisible." [1] In this kind of governmental college formed by the Emperor and Heaven, Heaven has only a subordinate rôle. The imperial Majesty remains the first power. In order to save the religious dignity of Heaven, it was admitted, at last, in the constitutional rhetoric, that a natural calamity was a sort of " reproach " expressed by the supreme divinity. But, in fact, the order of the Universe cannot be in any way troubled, and Heaven remains passive while the Sovereign is in a position to make the moral order prevail ; that covers all that remains of the mystical element in a conception which is presented under the guise of a theory of pure morality.

The Emperor, occupying " a position of trust above the masses and above princes and kings," must be virtuous ; otherwise his administration is neither equitable nor beneficent. He is responsible for the happiness of his subjects and, in

---

[1] This theory served as a guiding thread to the authors under the Han, who were charged with reconstructing ancient history. (See Book I of the first part.) It inspires in particular a celebrated chapter of the *Shu-king*, the " Hong fan " (SMC, IV, 218 ff.). Some Chinese scholars make these ideas go back to the time of the Chou dynasty. (**XCIII**, 437.)

principle, he is solely responsible. The Majesty of the
Emperor is limited from the moment when we cease to consider it in the light of a Majesty, mystic in essence and
consequently unconditioned, and identify it with a centre of
moral radiation. It does not, of course, justify a despotic
domination or even the use of power for personal ends. The
Emperor Wu did not cease to be dominated by a mystical
ambition, when he made use of the sacrifice *fong* to formulate
a prayer for omnipotence. This prayer was secret. That is
to say it was essentially personal (*ssu*). It was believed that
the Emperor asked of the Immortals absolute power, and
that, if his companion died soon after the sacrifice, it was
because the Sovereign had been able to make the calamities
which threatened his own person pass over to him. But the
T'ang (725 A.D.) no longer wished to maintain secrecy concerning the prayer of the sacrifice *fong* ; the ceremony was
accomplished " entirely with the object of imploring happiness
for the multitude of the people." [1] And already the Emperor
Wen (167 B.C.) had laid down the principle : " According
to what I know of the Heavenly Way (*T'ien tao*) calamities
come from bad actions and happiness comes as a result of
virtue. The faults of all the officials must have their origin
in me. Now the officers charged with secret prayers transfer
calamities to their inferiors ; to act so is to make manifest
that I have no Virtue." [2] So he abolished the office of secret
intercessor. We should, however, notice that in 178 B.C.,
he had used a more elastic formula : " When the order of
the Empire is troubled, (that concerns) me only, the Unique
Man, and *perhaps two or three persons who hold in their hands
the administration and are like my legs and my arms.*" [3] In
the practice of feudal times, it is because the ministers are
the arms and legs of the prince and because, as a group of
brothers, they form a single body with their master, that
they can be substituted for him to remove calamities. The
Emperor Wen, then, reserved the possibility of an expiatory
transfer, but he understood how to limit the application of
penalties to the great chiefs of the imperial Administration
alone. Even for the great officials, however, the admitted
principle was that penal condemnations, after having been
the occasion for the Emperor to confess his lack of Virtue,

---

[1] **XVI**, 19, 224. [2] SMC, II, 473, 478. [3] SMC, II, 462.

2 C

ought to be wiped out by a pardon in which the imperial beneficence shone out in all its majesty.[1] A system of promotions and periodical amnesties, then, replaced the repressive system adopted by the Ch'in. The amnesties were accompanied by grants made to the heads of families of a certain stage of advancement in the hierarchy, the mothers of families for their part receiving a substantial present of wine and beef.[2] In the theory, which became constitutional, of government by beneficence, the Emperor exercises power by representing it as a universal source of strength and ennoblement.

The administrative organization depends on the same principle. In the decree of 178 B.C., immediately after he had turned aside the misfortune of an eclipse of the sun by humiliating himself and confessing his lack of Virtue, the Emperor Wen orders everyone to " reflect on the faults which he might have committed, on the imperfections in his knowledge, his views, and his thoughts," and to " declare them to him clearly." [3] The same year, proclaiming afresh the value of the right of criticism, he abrogates a law punishing " unconsidered words." To authorize free criticism is to avoid " the pronunciation of imprecations against the Emperor by the common people, and the forming of bonds among them by oaths." Besides this essential but negative result, the sovereign, " by allowing each one to unveil the depths of his feelings," can attract to him, from the farthest parts of the Empire, " people of great virtue," i.e. officials practising a sincere morality. " Commend to me (men) wise and good, upright and correct in behaviour, capable of speaking with integrity, and of carrying remonstrances to their conclusions." [4] Like the vassal, the official is a counsellor rather than an executive agent. The chief function of the Emperor, and below him, of all his helpers, is to bring out the vocations of upright counsellors. We have seen that lawyers and fiscal experts carried on their profession, receiving the honourable appellation of upright guides.[5] The body of officials is conceived of as representing the conscience of the Empire. It is, to be exact, the projected conscience of the Emperor. It is worth, morally, just what the Unique Man

---

[1] SMC, II, 471.
[2] SMC, II, 458. The amnesties are completed by remission of taxes (*ibid.*, 477) and distribution of grain, from the imperial granaries (*ibid.*, 485).
[3] SMC, II, 462. [4] SMC, II, 465. [5] SMC, III, 558.

is worth, the mass of sincerity that is to be found in the country giving the measure of the imperial sincerity. The efficacy which the sovereign holds from his Majesty, presented under the aspect of a moralizing energy, permeates the people, after having rendered more virtuous a body of administrators, whom it recruits by a simple effect of attraction.

Thereafter, both the administrative and the sovereign function itself seem reduced to a task of instruction. The imperial Virtue preserves in its essence the value of a power of edification, and it sometimes appears as if the sovereign proceeds to the work of edification after the manner of an ascetic. We hear, for example, the Emperor Wen (162 B.C.) cry:—" I rise with the dawn! I lie down after nightfall! I consecrate all my strength to the Empire! I afflict myself, I suffer, for the mass of the people! " [1] But these expiatory cries are uttered in the Council Chamber, and published by decree, while the imperial penitence, if it were to continue to resemble that of a great ascetic, ought, in order to be fully efficacious, to remain silent. In fact, under the influence of learned men, heirs of the feudal tradition (even when they employ the mystic tradition), the task of edification is transformed into a simply educative task. The Emperor is no longer a master who transmutes things and beings, without divulging anything of his marvellous recipe. Like the counsellors of State, who seek to turn out from the imperial court the favourites of the secret counsels, he takes the rôle of a preaching professor. [2] The imperial sermon relays, with the same efficacy, the mystic recipe. It is no longer a question of endowing the State with a rôle of command, or of conceiving the princely power as a power of coercion. The Emperor, as far as possible, refrains from legislating. He applies himself, by decrees of benevolence, to abolishing the legal prescriptions, or to annulling the effects of the laws by frequent amnesties. In the place of regulating, he educates, and his officials exhort instead of commanding. The entire administration disguises itself as a sort of teaching college. It guards itself against the least semblance of constraint. It affects to expect everything from the results of an ennobling discipline alone. It

[1] SMC, II, 482.
[2] The institution of the body of " Learned men with vast knowledge of the Five Canonical Books " in 136 B.C. (SMC, Introd., XCIII).

sets before itself as its sole object to promote all the Emperor's subjects to the dignity of honest men (*kün tsih*), which was formerly the privilege of the nobles only. An overlord or a sovereign taught to his immediate followers the art of noble living. The Son of Heaven assumes the part of Sovereign from the time when he takes as his aim the ennobling of his entire people with the help of a moralizing propaganda,— that is to say, as soon as he assimilates the task of administration to the spread of an old ideal of culture, and assigns to the State as its first function the accomplishment of a civilizing task, understood in an entirely moral sense.

CHAPTER II

SOCIAL CHANGES

ABOUT the time of the Christian era, Chinese society underwent a complete remoulding. The distinction between nobles
and commoners, people of property and people without it,
loses all importance. The opposition between rich and poor
becomes the great principle of classification. The epoch of
the Tyrannies is considered as the age of luxury ; at any rate
it was the great epoch of declarations against luxury. It is
these last and the bitterness of their tone, which reveal the
gravity of the crisis passed through by Chinese Society. To
this crisis we have little remaining witness ; they do not make
clear either its causes or its results. But the fullness of these
results is evident from the time of the Emperor Wu, and it
seems that from his reign onwards the crisis is precipitated.
The main lines of the movement can be distinguished from
the more or less skilful measures which sought to stem it.
Its effects and its starting-point can be surmised. It appears
that the crisis had as origin :—first, the ruin of the old nobility
decimated by the wars of the Combatant Kingdoms ; then
(and above all) the work of colonization and taming the soil,
begun by the Tyrants, and followed, with added resources,
by the Emperors. The setting of the land in order allowed
of the appearance, together with new sources of wealth and
a new taste for it, of new men, whose influence at court and
in the towns removed all authority from the last representatives of the old nobility. Thus was created a back-
ground favourable to a reform of manners and customs.

I

THE COURT AND THE IMPERIAL NOBILITY

Tyrants and Emperors live in the midst of a numerous
Court, which could not have existed in the humble villages,

where the great nobles and the early suzerains placed their capitals. The feudal villages were confined and sparsely populated. They were held to be very large if the circle of their fortifications reached 3000 feet.[1] The Chou kings who, in 256 B.C., ruled over a population of 30,000 subjects, had to plant them in 36 towns,[2] a fact which does not prevent the *Shu li* from attributing to them an administration composed of six ministerial services,—of which one only (the first—including only the people of the palace, but not all of them), comprised more than 3000 offices. The total number of these services could only have been easily maintained in a very large capital such as that of Ch'in Shih Huang-ti. Indeed, the First Emperor was able to transfer to his town of Hien-yang, to the number of 120,000 families, all the powerful and rich people of the Empire.[3] It is thus that he was able to furnish it with inhabitants. Further, each time he destroyed an overlordship, he took plans of the noble's palace, and had it rebuilt in his capital, in order to place there the women and the trophies taken from the conquered. It is evident that the imperial Town is, in other than a mystical sense, a concentration of the Empire. It contains hostages taken from the whole of China, and elements of influence valuable for each of the provinces. The Han adopted the customs of the Ch'in, scarcely lightened by a measure of the Emperor Wen (179 B.C.) who authorized some of the nobles with grants of estates, or their heirs, to go and live in their own territory. He was afraid that the Capital might perish from congestion. " To-day the nobles live for the greater part at Ch'ang-ngan ; their lands are distant, their officers and their soldiers are only provisioned at the price of much expense and effort." [4] The capital is enriched by the spoils of the whole Empire, while the territorial nobility, supervised and domesticated, is transformed into a court nobility.

The nobles retained at the court received only honorary offices. All the active posts were entrusted to the newcomers. In the reign of the Emperor Wu, this was a principle strictly followed. Kong-sun Hong, who became a great counsellor, started as a gaoler and was actually a swineherd. Chu-fu Yen began his life as a vagabond and Ni K'uan as a porter ;

---

[1] *Tso chuan*, C, I, 5 ; Mencius, L, 85. [2] SMC, II, 55.
[3] SMC, II, 137. [4] SMC, II, 461.

they both formed part of the immediate entourage of the Emperor. Kin Mi-ti also, who was to become regent of the Empire, was a captive who served first as a groom.[1] More serious still : " the bravery of a warrior " was sufficient to " open the door to office " and " took an exaggerated place." [2] A good soldier could become a marquis : such was the case of Ho K'ü-p'ing. As for his uncle, Wei Ch'ing, who was raised to the rank of general-in-chief, he was a bastard who, during his youth, had been treated as a slave by his half-brothers and set to guard the sheep.[3] It was then possible to attain to the highest positions after starting from nothing and having carried on any trade. The success " of the people whose means of existence were uncertain, and whose trades were only provisional," scandalized those who admired old times, the advocates of stable hierarchies, where all was hereditary : noble duties as well as low trades.[4] In those happy times, " those who filled an office kept it till their sons or grandsons were adults ; those who exercised a public function took from it their family name and their surname. All men were content with their lot," which they knew to be fixed in advance.[5] In the régime adopted by the Empire, on the contrary " the principles of promotion to offices were perverted." [6] " The people (those of low birth) could escape from their incapacity to achieve public office " by acquiring " titles in the hierarchy of nobility," created by the Ch'in and preserved by the Han. " As the ways of seeking office were various, and as there were many methods of attaining it, the positions of officials lost their value." [7] Such are the complaints of the embittered conservative Ssu-ma Ch'ien. He boasted of descent from an ancient family, possessing by heredity the office of *ssu-ma* (general) ; he had succeeded his father in the employment of Grand Annalist, which was one of the chief duties attached to a feudal court ; but, under the Emperor Wu, his father was considered " as a plaything." The sovereign " amused himself with him " and treated him only " as a singer or a comedian." [8]

Decayed nobles and new men jostled each other at the Court. Everything there depended, not on birth, but on

---

[1] SMC, Introd., xci. [2] SMC, III, 550. [3] SMC, Introd., xci.
[4] SMC, III, 570. [5] SMC, III, 546. [6] SMC, III, 555.
[7] SMC, III, 557. [8] SMC, Introd., x.

merit; and a man was distinguished for his merit when he had proved it by making a fortune, whatever was the trade pursued. Already " the Empress Lu had relaxed the regulations regarding traders . . . but, as in the past, descendants of the market folk could not become officials." [1] In the reign of the Emperor Wu, it is clear that riches became the outstanding sign of merit. " From this moment men appeared, clever in successful profit-making." [2] In fact, as soon as the Empire is established, it has great budgetary needs, and the finances become the chief preoccupation of the government. In 120 B.C. the public treasury was organized ; immediately, three persons become high officials. " Tong-kuo Hien-yang was a great (salt) boiler from the country of Ch'i. K'ong Kin was a great smelter of Nan Yang. Both were upstarts with fortunes of several thousands of gold pounds. For this reason Cheng Tang-she (who was Minister in charge of the national economy, *ta-nong*) recommended them to the Emperor. Sang Hong-yang was the son of a shopkeeper of Lo-yang. As he made calculations in his head, he became *che-chong* at the age of 13 years. These three men, when they discussed financial questions, cut hairs into four pieces." [3] " Those who were previously the richest salt-merchants and ironmasters were named officials. The official career was thus endowed with new, strange elements. Merit (of birth) was no longer the principle of choice, and merchants were numerous.[4] Ssu-ma Ch'ien refers back to Duke Huan of Ch'i, the first Leader, this new power attached to wealth which, according to him, explains the appearance of tyrannical rule. " From this moment, . . . riches and possessions are put in the first rank, and modesty and humility in the last." [5] " The reverse of the feudal courts, the imperial Court is no longer the theatre for those tourneys of politeness where the sense of moderation was formed. Display and ostentation reign there. All the women of the capital may be compared with the princesses of the noblest houses, all the men with dukes, marquises, the famous knights of legend. In the utmost congestion, the high officials, the celebrated provincials, the rich merchants, mix with the ambassadors sent by the subject Barbarians.[6] This sumptuous crowd is invited to

---

[1] SMC, III, 541.　　[2] SMC, III, 550.　　[3] SMC, III, 567.　　[4] SMC, III, 571.
[5] SMC, III, 602　　[6] Pan Ku, *Fu des deux capitales*, Part I.

the feasts which the Emperor gives in the vast museum of his palace. His eunuchs command companies of jugglers and musicians. His harem contains a crowd of singers and dancers; the cleverest become empresses or favourites. Such, under the Emperor Wu, were the Empress Wei and the *fu-jen* Li, the one a clever singer and the other expert in dancing. A vast building, the palace Kia-yi, is completely furnished for opera. There the great jousts take place, whence arise the Chinese theatre.[1] Mechanicians are able to show snow falling and clouds rising there, while the tumult of storms, the rolling of thunder, and flashes of lightning make the majestic power of Heaven appear quite close. Processions of the Immortals or of strange Beasts pass, alternating with mountebanks, who climb poles or lift weights. Jugglers swallow swords, spit fire, make water spurt from the earth by tracing drawings on it, play with serpents, while women with long sleeves, clothed in gauze and painted dance the most lascivious of their dances, and whilst at the top of a mast, perched on a carriage, acrobats hang by their feet, or wheel round indefinitely, shooting arrows in all directions, towards the land of the Tibetans, as towards the land of the Sien-pi,—everywhere where the Majesty of the Emperor should triumph. Hunts and fishing excursions are also the occasion of triumphal galas. This great succession of feasts and of sumptuary expenses is not reserved for the sovereign alone. Princes with small estates possess splendid palaces, where from ceilings ornamented with square panels and with a round boss at the centre there hang downwards carved flowers, lotuses and poppies. The beams are ornamented with clouds, while the plinths are surmounted with carved dragons; the Red Bird opens its wings on the topmost beam; the Dragon holds up on its coils the lintel of the door; Barbarians with large heads, and deeply sunk orbits, open large eyes, like vultures, crouched on all the cross-beams. On the walls, the gods of the mountains and the seas are painted in the colour proper to them, and beside them the whole history of the world is depicted, from the separation of Heaven and Earth.[2] " Those members of the imperial family who had estates granted to them, the dukes of the palace, the high dignitaries, the great officials, and those who

[1] Chang Heng, *Tong king fu.*   [2] **XVII**, 32.

were below them, rivalled in display and prodigality in their dwellings. Their country seats, their equipages, their clothes, encroached on the imperial privileges ; there was no longer any moderation." [1]

Poets and moralists in no wise exaggerate when they show that the taste for luxury was at the time of the Han spread throughout the whole of Chinese society. This taste corresponds to a development of the artistic industries which recent Japanese excavations allow us to appreciate. These excavations, made in the north of Korea, on the site of a prefectoral town, dating from the conquest of the country by the Emperor Wu, have resulted in the exhumation of abundant funeral material.[2] Several objects are dated from the years just before the Christian era. Their execution is of an extreme refinement. The pieces of lacquer and gold and silver work bear witness in particular to a remarkable technique. The objects in lacquer, sometimes executed in lacquered wood, sometimes made of cloth covered with lacquer, are often decorated with silver, or gilded copper, and frequently painted with brush-work or finely engraved. In some pieces, above a thin sheet of gold, there appear, traced in brilliant lacquer, animals and birds. The inscriptions give an idea of the care brought to their execution ; they name the workmen who took part in it ; one prepared the lacquer, another gave the form, another executed the borders, another the designs, another put on the red lacquer and, after them two artists added the finishing touches and completed the work. A large box, discovered in one of these' tombs, contained a mirror with a silken cord and below it hairpins, a comb in a case, and some small boxes containing white and red powder. The most beautiful find was a belt buckle ; it is in massive gold with turquoises inset, and represents two intertwining dragons. Its filigree shows the mastery over gold and silversmith's work. Bears of gilded copper, which served as table legs, various statues of beasts and birds in baked enamelled clay, also bear witness to the perfection attained by industrial art under the Han. The fact that the artisans were specialists in the highest degree,

---

[1] SMC, III, 548.

[2] **CXXXV,** M. Umehara insists with good reason on the technical perfection of the exhumed objects.

PLATE XI

LACQUERED ORNAMENT AND GOLDEN BELT-BUCKLE
(Japanese excavations in Korea. Photo Umehara)

[face p. 410

and worked under the direction of officials in the State workshops is not less worthy of remark, and still more significant is the abundance of art treasures accumulated in a town on the extreme frontier. It is no longer the period of straggling villages, half peasant in population, isolated from one another by the barriers of the feudal tolls. Riches and luxury circulate throughout the whole Empire. All the town administrations set themselves to follow the tastes of the Court. The fortunate people engaged in trade or industry who dwell in them aspire to take rank in the imperial nobility.

In feudal times, artisans and merchants lived in the suburbs on the border of the seigniorial town. Some traces of their growing importance can however be discovered. An old tradition declares that a hawker gained the confidence of the Leader, Huan of Ch'i, and became his minister.[1] Harshly exploited by the nobles, the artisans did not let themselves be always used as beasts of burden. In 471 B.C. at Wei, they are seen in revolt against the prince.[2] It does not seem, however, that the industrial classes counted in the State, before the unification of the Empire. The measures and works which accompanied this, and, more still perhaps, the military policy followed by the great Emperors, seem to have favoured a sudden increase of industry and commerce.

The reason for the Empire's existence was the struggle against the Barbarians. To lead it to success, it was necessary to have control of a mobile and well-supplied army. The day of feudal levies, when a few chariots went out for a few days, is over. The strength of the imperial army is in its light cavalry, capable of carrying out extensive raids in the steppes. These horsemen need provisioning with mounts, arms, forage, meat and grain. The first need of the Empire is to facilitate the mobilization of its army. Such is the principle which inspired the measures and labours whence emerged the unification of the country. The ordering of the lands which had been uncultivated served to bring nearer together centres of social life which till then had remained isolated. The adoption of a single system of writing, and of weights and measures, tended to the same end. The great work was the construction of roads and canals. Ch'in Shih

[1] *Huai nan tsih*, 10.   [2] *Tso chuan*, **C,** III, 755.

Huang-ti and the Emperor Wu set their capital at the centre of a great network of cross-roads. They could in this way supply their Court and their Guard. They were able also to establish a central granary, and workshops and arsenals capable of furnishing the needs of the armies operating on the different frontiers. Their chief object was first, it seems, to mobilize grain. Thus are explained, no doubt, the legislative measures of Ch'in, suppressing the ancient system of tenure. In making the peasants proprietors of the soil, it was hoped to increase its produce, and in granting liberty to trade in grain it was thought to end the old feudal idea that the harvest ought not to go outside the frontiers; thus the power of the imperial granaries could be increased.

All these measures seem to have been taken in favour of agriculture, which is, it is constantly declared, the only honourable profession. " The lowest of the professions," that of the artisans and shopkeepers, was the first to profit by it. " The country within the seas was unified; passes and bridges were opened; prohibitions which closed the mountains and the lakes were removed. That is why the rich merchants ran to and fro about the Empire; there was no object of exchange which did not go everywhere." [1] The Emperors were led to favour the transport industry and all the army contractors. Willy-nilly, they had to come to an arrangement with the big fortunes, created in great enterprises, without which their military projects could not have succeeded. When in the reign of the Emperor Wu, the Hiong-nu attacked the frontier in the north, local stocks were found insufficient to keep alive the military colonies, which had to be reinforced. It was, then, necessary " to make an appeal to the common people; ranks were distinguished in the hierarchy of those who could carry on transport and get grain to the frontier. It was possible for them to attain to the grade of *ta chou chang*." [2] This grade was one of the highest (the 18th); it gave the highest rank in the category of the high dignitaries; above were only the various titles of marquis.[3] There was need, further, of transport-contractors, when enormous crowds were sent into the lands opened up for colonization. Some of them, says Ssu-ma Ch'ien, were capable of forming " convoys of several

---

[1] SMC, Introd., CI.   [2] SMC, III, 543.   [3] SMC, II, 529.

hundreds of vehicles." [1] The historian notes this significant fact, that the contractors were at the same time rich merchants. He speaks in the same passage of the immense fortunes made by the˙ salt-merchants and the ironmasters. Transport enterprise and military contractors brought in their train the formation of capital, which was employed in commerce and industry, but which helped also in the establishment of great territorial domains.

Salt-pans and forges are the principal industries; we have seen that smelters and salt-merchants attained to the highest positions in the State. The smelters, in particular the iron smelters, worked for the army. There were also reasons of a military order which made breeding on a grand scale, both of sheep and of horses, prosper. The raids of the light horse, in which it happened that, in one campaign, more than 100,000 horses were lost, demanded a quantity of mounts which the imperial studs themselves could not furnish. [2] These State studs were indeed very important. In 119 B.C. the horses collected in the neighbourhood of the capital " were to the number of several myriads." [3] But they did not all come from the imperial studs and care had been taken to encourage private breeding. [4] While at the beginning of the Han period the high officials had themselves carried about in ox-drawn vehicles, [5] under the Emperor Wu, horses were seen " even in the alleys where the common people lived," and it was considered a dishonour to mount a mare. [6] Sheep-breeding underwent a comparable expansion, for the army had to be provided with meat. Ssu-ma Ch'ien notes with indignation that, by giving sheep to the State, the title *lang* is obtainable. In this connexion, the career of a great sheep-breeder, Pu-she is significant. After offering half his fortune to the Emperor Wu, he received with the title of *lang* the charge of making the imperial sheep-farms prosper. After that he became prefect, then *yu-she-ta-fu* which was one of the highest dignities in the State. [7] It is clear that breeding on a large scale, like industry and trade on a large scale, led to honours.

For large scale breeding, large domains are necessary, as

[1] SMC, III, 562.   [2] SMC, III, 569.
[3] SMC, III, 561.   [4] SMC, III, 594.
[5] SMC, III, 539; *ibid.*, 541 : " A horse is worth 100 gold pounds."
[6] SMC, III, 545.   [7] SMC, III, 575 ff., 594 ff.

well as abundant labour for manufactures and transport. Now, the measures at first destined to increase the produce of the land and the mobility of grain had the unforeseen consequence of favouring the allied development of *latifundia* and slavery. At the time when the peasants were simply tenants, they could not sell either their land or their persons. As soon as the Ch'in had broken the ties which bound the cultivators to the soil, they found that, to carry through the labour of the great works and that of distant colonization, frequent recourse was made to forced labour, which detached the peasants from the place of their birth.[1] Landless or hard hit by want—there were (for example in 113 B.C.) great famines when men devoured their fellows,—the poor were often reduced to selling their patrimony, themselves, and above all their children. Then one sees " the fields of the rich laid out in hundreds and thousands, while the poor have not enough land to plant a needle." [2] The State itself had need of slaves for convoys or army attendants. It acquired plenty of them, designated as penal slaves, by making use of the monetary laws, and entrusting their application to brutal lawyers. Ssu-ma Ch'ien declares that " almost everyone in the Empire was melting down money." It was easy for the imperial inquisitors to get more than a million persons condemned on this pretext alone (in 115 B.C.).[3] These unhappy people, after having been amnestied, were employed as colonists or army attendants. But it was necessary continually to renew the crowd of slaves employed in transport on the River.[4] The Empire then had recourse to private individuals and sanctioned private slavery. In 128 B.C. rank was offered to persons who agreed to give up their slaves to the State.[5] This was a recognition of the ennobling worth of a new element in movable fortunes.

The Empire, in tolerating slavery, anticipated the agrarian crisis which was to sweep away the two Han dynasties, and culminate in the epoch of the Three Kingdoms in a revival of feudalism. From the reign of the Emperor Wu, complaints were made in the imperial councils, " of the rich people who, by creating monopolies enslave the poor." Questions were frequently raised concerning " illegal associations," " con-

---

[1] SMC, III, 561, 562.   [2] BEFEO, 1924, 497.   [3] SMC, III, 580.
[4] SMC, III, 588.   [5] SMC, III, 582.

cerning dictators," " concerning audacious people who form
themselves into bands and force their will by violence on the
small towns and hamlets." [1] Various expedients were tried
to fight against the monopolizers : lawsuits, confiscation of
fields and of slaves for the benefit of the State ; the setting
up of monopolies designed to compete with the private
industries and trades. A step taken in 119 B.C. shows that
the imperial counsellors had felt the gravity of the crisis and
its deep-seated causes. Merchants were forbidden to invest
their fortunes in landed property either directly or through
an intermediary.[2] Nothing, however, put a stop to the
movement which had begun, just as nothing had been able
to stop the development of movable property. Ch'in Shih
Huang-ti, no doubt in order to impede it, issued a heavy
coinage, so that its use was inconvenient.[3] The Han adopted
the system of light coinage ; they had the type varied
frequently ; they started a new standard ; they allowed
free mintage, then forbade it ; they seem to have tried
everything to discredit transferable securities and their
hoarding. They merely succeeded in encouraging the stocking
of goods and the spirit of speculation.[4] After having tried to
mortify the merchants " by vexing and humiliating them,"
" by forbidding them to ride in a chariot or to wear silk
clothing," " by heaping on them taxes and duties," [5] they
found themselves obliged to recognize the importance of
money. One after another the different forms of personal
wealth were accepted by them as contributions, giving (like
the old agricultural tribute of grain and silk) the right of
entry into an official career. They succeeded in reabsorbing
into the treasury part of the wealth in process of formation.
To this end, they proceeded to issue titles of nobility which
each one was bound to acquire if he wished to clear himself
of the dishonour attached to those who had newly-acquired
fortunes. Thus was authorized the regrouping which placed
highest in society the rich inhabitants of the cities. They
kept in the towns those even who had succeeded, by inter-
mediaries, in acquiring great domains. The great landed
proprietors remained attached to the urban districts, where
fortunes were created and honours distributed. All the

[1] SMC, III, 503, 562, 581, 563, 547.   [2] SMC, III, 575.
[3] SMC, III, 559.   [4] SMC, III, 571   [5] SMC, III, 541.

members of the new imperial nobility were people of the town, living close to officials, from whom they could learn the rules of conduct which were becoming in official classes.

II

THE REFORM OF MORALS

The old nobility, decimated, lost all prestige ; the various populations of China were intermixed and stirred up as a result of the long wars and transplantations, ordered by the great Emperors ; towns were built, centres of administration and commerce, rich with a new activity ; they were populated with men, soldiers of fortune, fortunate leaders of industry, wholly detached from feudal traditions ; yet what appears to come out of this new setting is an archaic morality. The imperial nobility sets itself to imitate the rules of conduct of the feudal nobility which it has come to replace. The ruin of this latter class ends in the spread of an ideal of life which takes inspiration from its traditions.

The spread of this ideal is due for the most part to official pressure. This, however, was exercised in very varied ways. Ch'in Shih Huang-ti, in his inscriptions, boasts of having " purified morals," " corrected and improved foreign morals." This refers principally to sexual morals. The first Emperor boasts of having re-established in its ancient strength the principle of the separation of the sexes instituted in the beginning of time by the sovereigns Fu-hsi and Nü-kua. His monoliths proclaim that " he separated conclusively the interior from the exterior " and that thenceforth " man and woman conform to certain rites." " The men devote themselves with joy to the cultivation of the fields—The women devote themselves to their tasks with care—Everything has its station," for the Emperor " has set up barriers between the exterior and the interior—He has forbidden and suppressed debauchery—Men and women obey the rules and are upright." [1] The first Emperor desired to gain for himself a similar glory to that of the founder of the Chou dynasty. King Wen—by a direct effect of his virtue (it first enabled him to discipline his own wife) had secured, even in the

[1] SMC, II, 142, 146, 167, 180, 188.

countries of the South, the practice of perfect chastity.[1]
Chinese scholars believe that Shih Huang-ti prided himself
on having re-established good morals in the southern country
of Yue, which he attached again to China ; they had forgotten
there the morality of King Wen, since the time of Kou-chien,
for this potentate, it seems, had adopted a policy of birth-
control little in conformity with healthy traditions.[2] But
what we are told only proves that the people of Yue kept the
morals characteristic of an undivided organization of the
family ; old women married young men and old men took
young wives. Like customs, we have seen, subsisted even
among the nobles in feudal society. Kou-chien, in forbidding
them, with the intention of securing, through better-assorted
couples, more prolific families, did nothing to prevent the
ritual separation of the sexes. He helped the movement
which made the patriarchal family emerge from the undivided
family. Ch'in Shih Huang-ti worked in the same direction.
He gave to the rule of the separation of the sexes a significance
favourable to the development of marital and paternal
authority. He wished to oppose conjugal instability : " If
a wife flees to marry (another husband) the children no
longer have a mother ! " He condemned adultery severely.
" If a man goes into a house which is not his to behave there
unseemly—whoever kills him is not guilty." He forbids the
marriage of widows (at least widows with children) as an
infidelity to the duty of conjugal obedience. " If a woman
has children and marries again—she disobeys the dead and
is not chaste ! " [3] Finally—and this last fact shows clearly
the tendency of the reform of morals attempted by the first
Emperor,—he incorporated in the great bands employed in
conquering Kuang-tong (214 B.C.) equally with ruffians and
shopkeepers all the husband sons-in-law.[4]

He did not succeed in destroying the custom, and there
were always in peasant circles, sons who left their paternal
houses to go and earn their living by working for their wives'
parents. Ch'in Shih Huang-ti, however, as his brutal decision
proves, aimed at making the authority of the father the sole
basis of domestic order in all classes of society.

Scion of a noble line, it was natural for the first Emperor

[1] **LII,** 84, 98.
[2] SMC, II, 188, note 1. See above, p. 32.
[3] SMC, II, 188–189.
[4] SMC, II, 168 ; **LV,** 17, note 2.

2 D

to try to impose on his whole people the rules of the patriarchal morals peculiar to the nobility. The Han, having come from the people, show less decision. They were, moreover, reluctant to legislate or to punish. They interfered little to fix domestic law, except perhaps to lessen the rigour of the passive solidarity which united the members of one family. By a famous decree (which however remained a gesture without result), the Emperor Wen (179 B.C.) abolished the regulation regarding the " seizing of relations." [1] He forbade the incrimination, simply because of their relationship, of the father, mother, wife, children and brothers of a guilty person. The collective responsibility of relatives of three consecutive generations (*san tsu*) had been carefully maintained by the lawyers of the Ch'in ; it was the counterpart to this " solidarity of heart " which made the strength of the fraternal community. We must no doubt see in the edict of the Emperor Wen a sign that the family is narrowing and tends to rest on the relations of father and son rather than on collateral connexions. This evolution is perhaps one of the consequences of the conditions of life peculiar to urban settings. The fraternal community had formerly as its basis work in common on the paternal lands. The *Yi li* already admits, for brothers, not the personal property of private possessions, but at least a certain right to use them privately.[2] It is not possible to decide to what date the custom goes back, of dividing goods between brothers when mourning for the father is ended, and when an end was put thereby to a provisional community ; but it is possible that this custom crept in, as soon as transferable securities gained an ascendancy over landed property. The independence of collateral relatives seems to be an ancient product of urban law and trading customs. Further, it seems legitimate to deduce that the paternal authority and marital power could not make effective progress till the most serious survivals of the ancient insistence on an undivided family were effaced. Now from the time of the Han, the rights of the husband and the father appear absolute, or rather, they are only limited by wholly moral rules of equity.

The part played by the Han in the reform of morals was, in conformity with constitutional doctrine, a part of moral propaganda. Face to face with the progress of luxury, they

---

[1] SMC, II, 454 ; cf. *ibid.*, 474. [2] *Yi li*, C, 396.

preached return to the ancient simplicity. One of the most significant documents is a passage written by Pan Ku to the glory of the Emperor Kuang-Wu, founder of the eastern Han. This wise sovereign knew how to purify and transform the people by his benefits. He feared the spirit of prodigality, and the disdain which it brings for agricultural labour. He ordered trial to be made of moderation and of economy, and the observance of the extremest simplicity. Following the example of the mythical sovereigns, he buried gold in the mountains and pearls in the gulfs. He counselled his subjects to despise the rare and the precious and to use pitchers of clay or gourds, and to wear the simplest clothing. It is thus that man can free himself from desire and from vices, and live in purity, preserving the calm and composed bearing which becomes those freed from vulgar passions.[1] As early as 122 B.C., the Emperor Wu had thought of giving the same teaching, but through an intermediary. The great counsellor, Kong-sun Hong, was charged to set " a good example to the Empire." " He wore (then) linen garments and ate of one dish only at his meals." Ssu-ma Ch'ien notes maliciously that " none of this improved morals ; little by little men threw themselves into the search for honours and profits." [2] Example not proving sufficient, recourse was had to propaganda by tract and picture to discipline the appetites. The master in this was Liu Hiang (end of the first century B.C.), a much suspected librarian, to whom are owed, apparently, many fraudulent alterations in rare, ancient documents, but, on the other hand, an excellent writer of works on morals. They are collections of illustrated anecdotes. These little histories were very popular, copied in indefinite numbers, like the pictures to which they served as texts. A considerable number of them are found engraved on the walls of funeral chambers (dating from the second Han) which have been studied by Chavannes. The greater part are borrowed from antiquity, from which comes their authority. Here are some examples offered for the meditation of wives. A very beautiful and very virtuous woman, of the country of Leang, was left a widow with a son of tender years. Several men of noble family proposed marriage to her, but she refused them. Now the king of Leang himself fell in love with her.

[1] Pan Ku, *Fu des deux capitales*, Part II.   [2] SMC, III, 557–559.

He sent a messenger to offer her betrothal presents. After a declaration that a woman ought to remain faithful to her first husband, she took in one hand a mirror, in the other a knife, and cut off her nose, adding that if she did not kill herself it was because of the orphan whom she had to look after. Now that she had inflicted on herself a mutilation similar to that with which certain crimes were punished, the king would no doubt renounce her. Moved by such conjugal fidelity, the king awarded her the title of " she who acts nobly." [1] " A man from the country of Lu named Ch'iu Hu, left his wife five days after her marriage and went to a foreign kingdom where he stayed five years. When he came home, a little before arriving at his house he saw his wife picking mulberry leaves ; they did not recognize each other. Ch'iu Hu, seduced by the charm of the young woman, made dishonest proposals to her, which she rejected indignantly. Going on his road, he entered his home and asked for his wife to be brought to him. When she appeared, he was stunned to recognize the person with whom he had just spoken by the roadside. As for her, she reproached her husband violently and then went out, to go and throw herself into the river." [2] " At Ch'ang-ngan . . . lived a man who had a mortal enemy. As his wife was wholly possessed with filial piety, the enemy profited by this to threaten her that he would cause her father to perish, if she did not give him the opportunity to kill her husband. Torn between her duty as wife and her duty as daughter . . . she indicated the place where her husband would be sleeping the next night, but she went and lay there alone and the enemy cut off her head." [3] Then come models of pious sons. " Min Ssu-k'ien and his younger brother lost their mother. Their father married again and had two other sons. One day when Ssu-k'ien was driving his father's chariot he let the reins fall. His father seized his hand and noticed that his clothes were very thin. The father went home, called the sons of the second wife, took them by the hand and realized that their garments were very thick. He then said to his wife : ' If I married you, it was for the good of my sons. You have deceived me. Go, and stay here no longer.' Ssu-k'ien then said : ' As long as the mother was here, it was only

[1] **XIX**, 135.   [2] **XIX**, 136.   [3] **XIX**, 139.

I who had thin clothing ; but if she goes all four will be cold.' " The father kept silence.[1] " Lao Lai-tsu was a man of the country of Ch'u. When he was 70 years old, his parents were still alive. His filial piety was very strong. Constantly clothed in a medley of garments (like children), when he carried drink to his parents, he pretended to stumble on arriving at the hall, then remained lying on the ground, uttering cries after the manner of little children." Or else, with the object of rejuvenating his old parents, he remained before them playing with his long sleeves, or amusing himself with chickens.[2]

This moral imagery seeks dramatic effect. It passes easily from the comic to the horrible, from the ingenious son who masticates the food for his toothless father, to the heroic son, who, too poor to nourish both his old mother and his little child, keeps the child as long as his wife can suckle it but as soon as it is weaned prepares to bury it,—which leads him to the discovery of a pot of gold, for Heaven knows how to reward virtue.[3] All these laboured and puerile anecdotes savour of the schoolmaster. It is, indeed, by establishing schools in the chief centres and villages that the sovereign ought to teach the people humanity (*jen*), equity (*yi*) and ceremonial (*li*), for education produces excellent manners. Such was the opinion that Tong Chong-chu developed at length before the Emperor Wu. He did not hesitate to declare that such was the practice of the ancient sovereigns, and we in fact find, in the ritual brought into fashion under the Han, signs of the academic programme of the most remote ages.[4] After the instruments of music had been consecrated, by a bloody anointing, the academic year was inaugurated by a concert and a feast given to the old men ; on this occasion too a little cress was offered to the souls of former professors. The pupils began by singing some verses of the *She-king*, then " to the accompaniment of a rolling of drums, drew from their boxes books and instruments. They set to work submissively, (for) the baton of catalpa wood, and the rods of thorny wood, were there, all ready, to inspire them with respect." [5] " The instruction varied according to the seasons." " In Spring and in Summer, they

[1] **XIX**, 141, 182.   [2] **XIX**, 142, 183.   [3] **XIX**, 65.
[4] See especially, *Li ki*, **C**, I, 468 ff.   [5] *Li ki*, **C**, II, 31–32.

learnt to handle the lance and buckler (*i.e.* to dance military steps) ; in Autumn and in Winter, to hold the pheasant's feather and the flute (*i.e.* to dance civil dances)." [1] In Spring, they sang ; in Autumn, they played on stringed instruments. In Autumn, also, under the direction of the masters of ceremonies, the rites (*li*) were taught in the Blind Schools, and the winter was spent in learning history in the High School. That lasted for nine years. The pupils each year passed an examination. In the first, they had to prove " that they knew how to dissect the phrases of authors according to the meaning, and to discern the tendencies, good and bad, of their hearts." In the leaving examination they showed that " they understood the reasons of things and that they could classify things in categories." " Their character was then formed " and " they walked with a firm step in the path of duty." They knew, in fact, the Six Sciences (knowing : 1st, the five kinds of rites ; 2nd, the six kinds of music ; 3rd, the five ways of shooting arrows ; 4th, the five ways to drive chariots ; 5th, the six types of writing ; 6th, the nine methods of calculating) ; the Six Etiquettes : [knowing : 1st, the manner of sacrificing ; (circumspection) ; 2nd, the bearing of the guest (respectful attention) ; 3rd, the bearing of the courtier (marked attention) ; 4th, the bearing of the mourner (seriousness) ; 5th, the bearing of the soldier (that of the protector) ; 6th, the bearing in a chariot (vigilance) ; the Three Virtues (Sincerity, Vigilance, Filial Piety) ; and the Three Practices (Filial Piety, Friendship, Deference towards the master)]. In actual fact, we know nothing in detail about the feudal schools, and next to nothing about those of the Han, except that in the former, fine deportment was taught, with the help of practical exercises, as befitted the schools for pages : and that in the latter, exercises in rhetoric on the subjects of good bearing and etiquette were above all practised. The essential fact is that the instruction was purely bookish. " The masters who teach at present content themselves with reading in sing-song the books which are under their eyes." [2]

" At thirteen years of age I could weave,—at 14 I could make garments,—at 15 I played the lute,—at 16 I read

---

[1] *Li ki*, **C**, I, 468, and *Chou li*, **VII**, vol. I, 297 and 292.   [2] *Li ki*, **C**, II, 34.

Verses and History,—at 17 I became thy wife." [1] This idyllic
beginning shows that, even for the education of girls, a literary
culture was prescribed. It was even more rigorously prescribed for any man who wished to enter on an official career.
Nothing is more significant on this point than some inscriptions
where the praise of official personages of the second Han
dynasty were engraved. We read for example, on the memorial
plinth raised in honour of Wu Jong, (died 167 A.D.): "This
honoured man had as personal name Jong, and as title
Han-ho. He devoted himself to the study of the Book of
Verses as revised by Lu, divided into paragraphs and sentences by the Master Wei. Before having even attained
manhood, he taught and explained it. The *Hiao king* (The
Book of Filial Piety), the *Luen yu* (Discourses of Confucius),
the Book of the Han, the Historical Memoirs (of Ssu-ma
Ch'ien), the Book of Tso (the *Tso chuan*), the *Kuo yu* (The
Discourse of the Kingdoms),—he had fully studied all of
them and had discerned their subtleties. There was nothing
in the writings which he had not penetrated and absorbed.
For a long time he attended the High School. In an un-
fathomable way he was dignified and serious. There are
few men who could be compared with him. In the time left
over from his studies, he filled public offices. He was successively. . . . When he had reached the age of 36 years,
the governor Ts'ai . . . noticed him, and commended him
for his filial piety and integrity. . . . He was promoted to
the rank of deputy chief of the guards of the interior of
the imperial palace. . . . Looking towards that which was
sublime and seeking to penetrate what stood in the path—
he truly had civil talents! He truly had military talents!
. . . His standards gave a red light to the Heavens! It was
like a crash of thunder, like a flash of lightning!—The clearness which he spread was terrifying. His roaring, like a tiger,
was most impressive!" [2]

From the epoch of the Emperor Wu, wrote Chavannes,
" the tendency of the Chinese spirit to seek in classic books
the principle of all wisdom begins to show itself." [2] We
must add, " and of all the social virtues," including bravery,

---

[1] Opening of an old anonymous poem of the third century A.D., **XXXIII**, and
Chang Fong, *Le Paon*, Paris, 1924.
[2] **XIX**, 106–109.

as the eulogy of Wu Jong has shown. It is very possible that this exclusive importance accorded to a strictly literary culture, is considerably more ancient. There are even reasons to believe that bold spirits had considered it dangerous. It is known that Ch'in Shih Huang-ti had taken great care to preserve the technical and scientific treatises (medicine, pharmacy, agriculture, arboriculture), but had specially proscribed Verse and History. He no doubt felt that the services of the definitely specialized technicians were necessary to the newly-formed State, but that, as much in council as in battle, speeches fed by literary ballads and historical precedents were a feeble source of help. The pamphleteers from the beginning of the Han accused the first Emperor of " having burnt the Books of Instruction of a hundred schools, in order *to make* the Blackheads (= the people) *stupid.*" [1] The Han, in fact, affected to consider the right of remonstrance to be the sole principle of agreement which ought to reign between a prince and his subjects, under the supervision of Heaven. In the reign of the Emperor Wu, the great Counsellor K'ong-sun Hong " governed the Ministers and the people in the name of the interpretation of the Annals of Confucius (*Ch'un Ch'iu*)." [2] Strong in a very minute knowledge of the ancient facts of History, and of the corresponding tokens put forth by Nature, classed in symmetrical categories,[3] he felt himself in possession of a complete science, both physical and political, which allowed him to foresee and to govern. It is the same Kong-suen Hong, who, preaching by example, aimed at teaching the crowd of arrogant rich people, the simplicity of manners and customs which is the mark of an honest man. Princes and subjects ought to regulate their lives by comparing them with those of their ancestors. To the rich, whose factions were to be dreaded, the Han ordered the apprenticeship of modesty and of external ritual. This etiquette had proved its use. It had served to discipline the passions of the feudal nobles, whom it had transformed into gentlemen. When, reversing the Ch'in policy, the Han induced their people to set their steps in the footprints of the ancients and to live in an atmosphere of meditative respect for the past, they did not aim at " making

---

[1] SMC, Introd., cvi.   [2] SMC, III, 557.
[3] *Ch'un Ch'iu fan lu* and *Ch'ien Han Shu*, 27.

them stupid." They wished to make them wise. Condemning the technical teaching, whence only could come the taste for riches and belief in force, among the new men who peopled the enriched cities, the Han put forward, as a condition of ennoblement, a life entirely occupied by the teaching of the classics.

PLATE XII

LAO LUI-TSU PLAYING WITH HIS LONG SLEEVES
(Bas-relief from Shan-tung taken from the Kin she suo)

CONCLUSION

In concluding this book, I ought to attempt to define the essence of Chinese manners and customs. But is that possible, before having presented a sketch of the history of ideas? This definition will not find a suitable place until the volume which will complete this one is concluded. In the present volume, however, in which social history holds the largest place, it has been necessary to insist on that which is specially characteristic in the discipline of life peculiar to the Chinese. Its isolated presentation runs the risk of giving an impression which it is no doubt best to correct at once.

The absence of intimacy is the dominant feature of family organization. This was a significant feature at first in the relations between husbands and wives, and between fathers and sons. It appears to have become the rule for all family relations. Dominated by ideas of respect, domestic morality seems in the end to become mixed up with a ceremonial of family life. On the other hand, the relations of society, animated first by the spirit of contest, or the passion for prestige, end, it seems, by being governed by an exclusive taste for decorum. Civic morality, having gravitated towards an ideal of strained politeness, seems to tend solely to organizing among men, a regulated system of relations, in which the actions befitting each age are fixed by edict, as are also those for each sex, each social condition and each actual situation. Finally, in political life, where the stage is reached of advocating the principle of government by history, it appears that it is claimed as sufficient for everything to follow solely the virtues of a traditionalist conformity. So, at the moment when, towards the beginning of the imperial era, Chinese civilization seems to arrive at a point of maturity, everything co-operates to bring to light the reign of formalism.

But what is the real bearing of this system of conventions, tending to re-establish the archaic, by the aid of which it was claimed to direct the entire life of the nation? Is it true, as it may be tempting to think, that it contributed to the impoverishment and drying up of the whole moral life of the Chinese ? Is it even certain that its effects were such for the official class, deliberately devoted to the cult of conformity as to the only discipline capable of forming the *honest man* ? Ought we, on this point, to fix our opinion after reading only propagandist works and the biographies of famous men ? In spite of the knowledge that these are derived from the funeral eulogies, and that it would be an excess of confidence to take the tone of a sermon for a just verdict, it is difficult to escape from the feeling that the evolution of morals in China went on by way of progressive drying up, and that, in the moral life, under the increasing weight of a conventional etiquette, spontaneity saw its part reduced to nothing. The history of thought alone may lead to the conviction that, on the contrary, the acceptance by the *honest people* of an attitude of conformity has, in part, as its reason the hope of preserving for the life of the spirit, a sort of sheltered independence and a deep-seated plasticity.

But we can now indicate some facts which will suffice to mark the limits of the formalist ideal. We have already pointed out the part played by mysticism in court circles. Its part among the masses of the people is no less important. If this is scarcely apparent, it is because the dynastic Annals only interest themselves in the life of the court and in persons of high station. The great mystical crisis of the year 3 B.C. (noted by accident on the occasion of an episode of court life) was certainly not an isolated crisis ; we only have a few details of it, but they all show that, in peasant circles, certain mystical ideals, going far back in the ages, were preserved with perfect freshness. On the other hand, during the troubled period of the Three Kingdoms, the old feudal spirit seems suddenly to recover all its strength ; we may assume that, in the great rural domains created under the Han, habits of life and a discipline of morals were maintained that were less remote, no doubt, from the ancient feudal morality, which was the archaic ideal brought into favour by the orthodox teaching. History, however, refused to register the facts, and we know nothing of the permanence of the feudal elements of the social life. History, in short, hardly gives any information on the evolution of morals and manners in the new urban atmosphere (except among the official classes) ; in this atmosphere, however, there was created a morality peculiar to traders, characterized, it seems, by the spirit of association and the liking for equitable agreements. We may assume that its influence on the whole of Chinese life was not negligible ; yet, for the ancient period, we know hardly anything of the real life of the industrial classes, of the part played by the villages in the general economy, of the juridical and moral evolution of the urban areas. It would be extraordinary if they did not elaborate active ideals, and if their activity was reduced to the practice of the orthodox etiquette. The action of the official classes must not be underestimated ; but it is fitting, in closing this book, to emphasize that history, in consequence of an aristocratic tradition, neglected to register the movements among the masses. With the imperial era, which closes the history of ancient China, Chinese civilization certainly arrives at maturity, but although, by defining with increasing strictness its traditional ideals, the believers in orthodoxy wished to adorn it with a static dignity, it remains rich in youthful forces.

BIBLIOGRAPHY

N.B.—The references to Chinese works are made by the aid of a reference giving the usual title of the work, followed by an indication of the chapter.—When reference to a translation has been possible, the usual name of the work is followed by a number in Roman figures, relating to the following table. The arabic figures indicate the page in the translation. The references to the translations of the classics by LEGGE or by COUVREUR are indicated by the usual name of the classic followed by the letter L or C. The references to the "Historical Memoirs" of Ssu-ma Ch'ien are indicated by the abbreviation SMC, followed, in the case of parts not translated, by the indication of the chapter ; and in the case of translated parts, by the indication of the volume and of the page in the Chavannes translation.

The list of works given below does not claim to be a critical bibliography. In it, there are mentioned articles judged important, side by side with books considered of less use for consultation.

PERIODICALS

Asia Major	As. Maj.
Bulletin de l'École française d'Extrême Orient	BEFEO.
China Review	ChR.
Journal Asiatique	JA.
Journal of the Peking Oriental Society	JPOS.
Journal of the Royal Asiatic Society	JRAS.
Mémoires concernant l'Asie orientale	MAO.
Mitteilungen des Seminars für orientalische Sprachen	MSOS.
New China Review	NChR.
Ostasiatische Zeitschrift	OZ.
Ostasiatische Studien	OS.
Shinagaku	Sh.
T'oung pao	TP.
Variétés sinologiques	VS.

VARIOUS WORKS

J. G. ANDERSSON, *An Early Chinese Culture*, Pekin, 1923   **I**

—— *Preliminary Report on Archæological Research in Kansu*, Pekin, 1925   **II**

H. D'ARDENNE DE TIZAC, *L'art chinois classique*, Paris, 1928   **III**

ARNE, *Painted Stone Age Pottery from the Province of Honan, China*, Pekin, 1925   **IV**

L. ASHTON, *An Introduction to the Study of Chinese Sculpture*, London, 1924   **V**

L. AUROUSSEAU, *La première conquête chinoise des pays annamites*, BEFEO, 1923   **VI**

E. BIOT, *Le Tcheou li ou les rites des Tcheou*, Paris, 1851   **VII**

—— *Recherches sur les mœurs des anciens Chinois d'après le Che king* (JA, 1843)   **VIII**

BLACK, *The Human Skeleton Remains from Sha kuo t'un*, Pekin, 1925   **IX**

—— *A Note on Physical Characters of the Prehistoric Kansu Race*, Pekin, 1925   **X**

E. BOERSCHAN, *Chinesische Architektur*, Berlin, 1926   **XI**

432 BIBLIOGRAPHY

BRETSCHNEIDER, *Botanicon Sinicum* (Journal of the China Branch of the R.A.S., XXV) — XII

S. W. BUSSHEL, *Chinese Art*, London, 1914 — XIII

CHALFANT, *Early Chinese Writing*, Chicago, 1906 — XIV

ED. CHAVANNES, *Les mémoires historiques de Se-ma Ts'ien*, 5 vols., Paris, 1895–1905 [Ssu-ma Ch'ien] — SMC

—— *La sculpture sur pierre au temps des deux dynasties Han*, Paris, 1893 — XV

—— *Le T'ai chan*, Paris, 1910 — XVI

—— *Mission archéologique dans la Chine septentrionale*, Paris, 1913 — XVII

—— *Le jet des Dragons* (MAO, III), Paris, 1919 — XVIII

—— *Confucius* (Revue de Paris, 1903) — XIX

—— *La divination par l'écaille de tortue dans la haute antiquité chinoise d'après un livre de M. Lo Tchen-yu* (JA, 1911) — XX

—— *Trois généraux chinois de la dynastie Han* (TP, 1906) — XXI

—— *Les documents chinois découverts par Aurel Stein dans les sables de Turkestan*, Oxford, 1913 — XXII

—— *De l'expression des vœux dans l'art populaire chinois*, Paris, 1922 — XXIII

CONRADY, *China*, Berlin, 1902 — XXIV

H. CORDIER, *Histoire générale de la Chine et de ses relations avec les pays étrangers*, Paris, 1920 — XXV

TCHANG HONG-TCHAO DEMIÉVILLE, Che ya, *Lapidarium sinicum* (BEFEO, 1924) — XXVI

—— *La méthode d'architecture de* LI MING-TCHONG *des Song* (BEFEO, 1925) — XXVII

HOU-CHE DEMIÉVILLE, *Tchang che tsi* (BEFEO, 1924) — XXVIII

R. DVORAK, *China's Religionen*, Munster, 1903 — XXIX

EDKINS, *The Evolution of Chinese Language* (JPOS, 1887) — XXX

ERKES, *Das Weltbild des Huai-nan-tze* (OZ, 1917) — XXXI

—— *Das älteste Dokument z. chines. u. Kunstgeschichte : T'ien-wen ; die " Himmelsfragen " des K'üh Yuan*, Leipzig, 1928 — XXXII

ESCARRA and GERMAIN, *La conception de la loi et les théories des légistes à la veille des Ts'in*, Pekin, 1925 — XXXIII

Études asiatiques, publiées à l'occasion du XXVe anniversaire de l'École française d'Extrême Orient, Paris, 1925 — XXXIV

A. FORKE, *Lun-Heng. Selected Essays of the Philosopher Wang Ch'ung* (MSOS, 1911) — XXXV

—— *Mo Ti, des Socialethikers und seiner Schüler philosophische Werke* (MSOS, 1923) — XXXVI

—— *The World Conception of the Chinese*, London, 1925 — XXXVII

—— *Yang Chu, the Epicurean in his Relation to Lieh-tse the Pantheist* (JPOS, III) — XXXVIII

—— *Geschichte der alten chinesischen Philosophie*, Hamburg, 1927 — XXXIX

—— *Der Ursprung der Chinesen* — XL

A. FRANKE, *Das Confuzianische Dogma und die chinesische Staatsreligion*, 1920 — XLI

FUJITA, *The River Huang in the Reign of Yu* (Sh., 1921) — XLII

Q. v. d. GABELENTZ, *Beiträge z. chines. Grammatik* (Abhandl. d. Sachsischen Gesells. f. Wissens., 1888) — XLIII

—— *Confucius und seine Lehre*, Leipzig, 1888 — XLIV

GIESLER, *La tablette* Tsong *du* Tcheou li (Rev. Arch., 1915) — XLV

H. A. GILES, *History of Chinese Literature*, London, 1901 — XLVI

—— *Chuang Tsu, Mystic Moralist and Social Reformer*, London, 1889 — XLVII

—— *Lao Tzu and the* Tao te king (Adversaria sinica, III) — XLVIII

H. A. GILES, *The Remains of Lao Tzu* (ChR, 1886–1889)   **XLIX**

—— *Religion of Ancient China*, London, 1905   **L**

—— *Confucianism and its Rivals*, London, 1915   **LI**

M. GRANET, *Fêtes et chansons anciennes de la Chine*, Paris, 1919   **LII**

—— *La Polygynie sororale et le Sororat dans la Chine féodale*, Paris, 1920   **LIII**

—— *La religion des Chinois*, Paris, 1922   **LIV**

—— *Danses et légendes de la Chine ancienne*, Paris, 1926   **LV**

—— *Coutumes matrimoniales de la Chine antique* (TP, 1912)   **LVI**

—— *Quelques particularités de la langue et de la pensée chinoises* (Rev. philos., 1920)   **LVII**

—— *La vie et la mort, croyances et doctrines de l'antiquité chinoise* (Ann. de l'Ec. des Hautes Études, 1920)   **LVIII**

—— *Le dépôt de l'enfant sur le sol* (Rev. arch., 1922)   **LIX**

—— *Le langage de la douleur d'après le rituel funéraire de la Chine classique* (Rev. de Psychologie, 1922)   **LX**

R. GROUSSET, *Histoire de l'Asie*, Paris, 1922   **LXI**

J. J. M. DE GROOT, *The Religious System of China*, Leyden, 1892–1921   **LXII**

—— *The Religion of the Chinese*, New York, 1910   **LXIII**

—— *Universismus*, Berlin, 1918   **LXIV**

—— *Sectarianism and Religious Persecution in China*, Amsterdam, 1903   **LXV**

—— *Chinesische Urkunden z. Gesch. Asiens*, 1921   **LXVI**

GRUBE, *Geschichte der chinesischen Literatur*, Leipzig, 1902   **LXVII**

—— *Die Religion der alten Chinesen*, Tübingen, 1908   **LXVIII**

—— *Religion und Cultus der Chinesen*, Leipzig, 1908   **LXIX**

G. HALOUN, *Contribution to the History of the Clan Settlement in Ancient China* (As. Maj., 1926)   **LXX**

—— *Seit wann kannten die Chinesen die Tocharer* (As. Maj., 1926)   **LXXI**

HAUER, *Die Chinesische Dichtung*, Berlin, 1909   **LXXII**

HAVRET and CHAMBEAU, *Notes concernant la chronologie chinoise* (VS, 1920)   **LXXIII**

HIRTH, *The Ancient History of China to the End of the Chou Dynasty*, New York, 1909   **LXXIV**

—— *Chinese Metallic Mirrors*, New York, 1906   **LXXV**

HONDA, *On the Date of Compilation of the Yi king* (Sh., 1921)   **LXXVI**

HOPKINS, *Chinese Writings in the Chou Dynasty in the Light of Recent Discoveries* (JRAS, 1911)   **LXXVII**

—— *Metamorphic Stylization and the Sabotage of Signification, a Study in Ancient and Modern Chinese Writing* (JRAS, 1925)   **LXXVIII**

HU SHIH, *The Development of Logical Method in Ancient China*, Shanghai, 1922   **LXXIX**

IMBAULT-HUART, *La légende des premiers papes taoïstes* (JA, 1884)   **LXXX**

B. KARLGREN, *Études sur la phonologie chinoise*, Leyden and Stockholm, 1913   **LXXXI**

—— *Sound and Symbol in China*, London, 1923   **LXXXII**

—— *Analytic Dictionary*, Paris, 1923   **LXXXIII**

—— *On the Authenticity and Nature of the Tso chuan*, Göteborg, 1926   **LXXXIV**

—— *Philology and Ancient China*, Oslo, 1926   **LXXXV**

—— *Le protochinois, langue flexionnelle* (JA, 1920)   **LXXXVI**

L. LALOY, *La musique chinoise*, Paris   **LXXXVII**

B. LAUFER, *Jade, a Study in Chinese Archæology and Religion*, Chicago, 1912   **LXXXVIII**

—— *Chinese Pottery of the Han Dynasty*, Leyden, 1909   **LXXXIX**

—— *Ethnographische Sagen der Chinesen* (*in* Festsch. f. Kuhn)   **XC**

2 E

Père de Mailla, *Histoire Générale de la Chine*, translated from the Tong-kien-kang-mou, Paris, 1777–1789   XCI

Martin, *Diplomacy in Ancient China* (JPOS, 1889)   XCII

H. Maspero, *La Chine antique*, Paris, 1927   XCIII

—— *Les origines de la civilisation chinoise* (Ann. de géographie, 1926)   XCIV

—— *Les légendes mythologiques dans le* Chou king (JA, 1924)   XCV

—— *Notes sur la logique de Mo tseu* (TP, 1927)   XCVI

—— *Le mot* ming (JA, 1927)   XCVII

—— *Le saint et la vie mystique chez Lao-tseu et Tchouang-tseu* (Bull. de l'Assoc. franç. des amis de l'Orient, 1922)   XCVIII

—— *Le songe et l'ambassade de l'empereur Ming* (BEFEO, 1910).   XCIX

P. Masson-Oursel, *La philosophie comparée*, Paris, 1923   C

—— *Études de logique comparée* (Rev. Philos., 1927)   CI

—— *La demonstration confucienne* (Rev. d'hist. des relig., 1916)   CII

Masson-Oursel and Kia Kien-tchou, Yin Wen-tsen (TP, 1914)   CIII

Mayers, *Chinese Reader's Manual*   CIV

Mémoires concernant les Chinois, par les missionnaires de Pekin, Paris, 1776–1814   CV

E. Mestre, *Quelques resultats d'une comparaison entre les caractères chinois modernes et les siao-tchouan*, Paris, 1925   CVI

Naito, *On the Compilation of the* Shoo King (Sh., 1923)   CVII

Parker, *Kwan-tze* (NChR, 1921)   CVIII

—— *Hwai-nan-tze* (NChR, 1919)   CIX

P. Pelliot, *Le Chou king en caractères anciens et le Chang chou che wen* (MAO), Paris, 1919   CX

—— *Jades archaïques de la collection C. T. Loo*, Paris, 1921   CXI

—— *Notes sur les anciens itinéraires chinois dans l'Orient romain* (JA, 1921)   CXII

—— *Meou tseu ou les Doutes levés* (TP, 1818–1819)   CXIII

Plath, *Fremde barbarische Stämme in alten China*, Munich, 1874   ·CXIV

Przyluski, *Le sino-tibétain* (*in* Langues du monde, Paris, 1924)   CXV

Richthofen, *China*, Berlin, 1877–1912   CXVI

Rosthorn, *Geschichte China*, Stuttgart, 1923   CXVII

L. de Saussure, *Le système astronomique des Chinois*, Geneva, 1919   CXVIII

B. Schindler, *On the Travel, Wayside and Wing Offerings in Ancient China* (As. Maj., I)   CXIX

—— *The Development of Chinese Conception of Supreme Beings* (As. Maj., 1923)   CXX

—— *Das Priestertum im alten China*, Leipzig, 1919   CXXI

E. Schmitt, *Die Grundlagen der chinesischen Che*, 1927   CXXII

J. Steele, *I Li, or the Book of Etiquette and Ceremonial*, London, 1917   CXXIII

Suzuki, *A Brief History of Early Chinese Philosophy*, London, 1914   CXXIV

Tchang Fong, *Recherches sur les os du Ho-nan et quelques caractères de l'écriture ancienne*, Paris, 1925   CXXV

Père M. Tchang, *Synchronismes chinois* (VS, 1905)   CXXVI

Terrien de Lacouperie, *Western Origin of Chinese Civilization*, London, 1894   CXXVII

—— *Language of China before the Chinese*, London, 1887   CXXVIII

Père Tscheppe, *Histoire du Royaume de Wou* (VS, 1896)   CXXIX

—— *Histoire du royaume de Tch'ou* (VS, 1903)   CXXX

—— *Histoire du royaume de Ts'in* (VS, 1909)   CXXXI

—— *Histoire du royaume de Tsin* (VS, 1910)   CXXXII

—— *Histoire des trois royaumes de Han, Wei et Tchao* (VS, 1910)   CXXXIII

G. TUCCI, *Storia della filosofia cinese antica*, Bologna, 1922   **CXXXIV**

UMEHARA, *Deux grandes découvertes archéologiques en Corée* (Rev. des arts asiatiques, 1926)   **CXXXV**

M. W. DE VISSER, *The Dragon, in China and Japan*, Amsterdam, 1913   **CXXXVI**

E. A. VORETZCH, *Altchinesische Bronzen*, Berlin, 1924   **CXXXVII**

A. WALEY, *The Temple and Other Poems*, London, 1923   **CXXXVIII**

WEDEMAYER, *Schauplätze und Vorgänge der alten chinesischen Geschichte* (As. Maj., Prel. V)   **CXL**

E. T. C. WERNER, *Myths and Legends of China*, London, 1924   **CXLI**

PÈRE L. WIEGER, *Histoire des croyances religieuses et des opinions philosophiques en Chine, depuis l'origine jusqu'à nos jours*, Hien-hien, 1917   **CXLII**

—— *Les Pères du système taoïste*, Hien-hien, 1913   **CXLIII**

—— *La Chine à travers les âges*, Hien-hien, 1920   **CXLIV**

—— *Textes historiques*, Ho-kien-fu, 1902   **CXLV**

—— *Caractères* (Rudiments, V, 12), Ho-kien-fu, 1903   **CXLVI**

R. WILHELM, *Dchuang dsi, das wahre Buch vom südlischen Blutenland*, Jena, 1920   **CXLVII**

—— *Lia dsi, das wahre Buch vom quellenden Urgrund*, Jena, 1921   **CXLVIII**

—— *Lü Puh-wei, Frühling und Herbst*, Jena, 1927   **CXLIX**

WYLIE, *Notes on Chinese Literature*, Shanghai, 1902   **CL**

CHAUCER YUAN, *La philosophie politique de Mencius*, Paris, 1927   **CLI**

E. VON ZACH, *Lexicographische Beiträge*, Pekin, 1902   **CLII**

PÈRE ZOTTOLI, *Cursus litteraturœ sinicœ*, Shanghai, 1879–1882   **CLIII**

INDEX

437